THE
BUREAUCRATIC
EXPERIENCE

A Critique of Life in
the Modern Organization

Fourth Edition

THE BUREAUCRATIC EXPERIENCE

A Critique of Life in the Modern Organization

Fourth Edition

Ralph P. Hummel

University of Oklahoma

St. Martin's Press
New York

Executive Editor: Don Reisman
Manager, publishing services: Emily Berleth
Publishing services associate: Kalea Chapman
Project management: Till & Till
Art director: Sheree Goodman
Cover design: Douglas Thompson
Cover photo: Joel Gordon

For information, write:
St. Martin's Press, Inc.
175 Fifth Avenue
New York, NY 10010

ISBN: 0-312-09554-6

ACKNOWLEDGMENTS

James R. Killingsworth, "Idle Talk in Modern Organizations" from
Administration and Society, vol 16, no. 3 (November 1984), pp. 346–84;
chart from p. 352, originally produced as a satire by Polish students.
Reprinted by permission of Sage Publications, Inc.

"Haigledygook and Secretaryspeak," Copyright 1981 Time Inc.
All rights reserved. Reprinted by permission from TIME.

John F. Forester. *Planning in the Face of Power,* table titled "Correcting
Communicative Disorders" page 151. Copyright © 1988 John Forester.
Reprinted by permission of the University of California Press.

"Batboy Is Called Out; U.S. Is Reviewing Law." Copyright © 1993
by The New York Times Company. Reprinted by permission.

In Memory
of
Pat Boughton

Preface

This new and totally revised edition of *The Bureaucratic Experience* appears during one of modernity's recurrent periods of paroxysm and promise. Bureaucracy and factory, government and corporation twist and turn to reform and reinvent—if not revolutionize—themselves. The attention of almost all analysts is on the promise that modern institutions, created to produce control and quantity, can be retooled to produce care and quality.*

Everything that previous editions said about bureaucracy is now freely admitted.

Everyone has trouble with bureaucracy. Citizens and politicians have trouble controlling the runaway bureaucratic machine. Managers have trouble managing it. Employees dislike working in it. Clients can't get the goods from it. Teachers have trouble getting an overall grip on it. Students are mystified by the complexity of it.†

But, optimists argue, soon all this will be fixed.‡ From Japanese management through quality circles to excellence management, total quality management, and corporate reengineering, systems that claim revolutionary innovation promise to lead us beyond bureaucracy into the post-industrial, the postbureaucratic, the postmodern era. There, presumably, the human spirit will be renewed in humane and effective work, and human beings will rejoice in products, services, and even controls that are tailored to human needs.

Meanwhile, it is only necessary to ignore some pesty facts: Economically, the world is still a world of scarcity and the values that this implies. Growth and physical survival depend on capital reinvestment. Capital reinvestment as an economic strategy, far from retreating, spreads into the last corners of the globe, including the vast territories where socialism has collapsed. What emerges from under the ruined facades of evil em-

---

*The exception is made up of forthright bureaucracy advocates who sense its permanence but find themselves in the backwaters of public opinion. For an example, see Charles Goodsell's *The Case for Bureaucracy: A Public Administration Polemic*, 3rd ed. (Chatham, NJ: Chatham House, 1994).

†This paragraph is from the preceding three editions.

‡See, for example, Warren Bennis, *Beyond Bureaucracy: Essays on the Development and Evolution of Human Organization* (San Francisco: Jossey-Bass, 1993).

pires is nothing else but bureaucracies. These sustained those empires for decades and are relied on now to order the playing field for new investment. In Japan, where quality management originated, economic strain and political bankruptcy led to a reassertion of the traditional means of bureaucratic control: the iron fist always was in the gloved hand. In America, quality management has been quickly translated through management information systems into a familiar Tayloristic tightening of the tolerances; its totalitarian culture of smiling acquiescence blatantly accompanies cutback management and downsizing. In the words of a constant companion and critic: "The rhetoric has evolved, but it masks a permanent reality."*

Against the forces of rhetoric, *The Bureaucratic Experience,* Fourth Edition, returns to the attack with renewed vigor. Earlier editions could strike a responsive chord by the telling of bureaucratic experiences. Their impact could be analyzed and understood in social–scientific terms— socially, culturally, psychologically, linguistically, cognitively, and politically. These analyses continue.

But this new edition seeks to dig deeper into the human condition in modernity. The new edition shifts the focus from an attack on bureaucratic institutions to an examination of ourselves. We must ask ourselves: Can we work our way out of bureaucracy? To this, the book gives a resounding "No!"

A critical school has, over the last two decades, rejuvenated and deepened the study of modern organizations. Where others engage in paeans of praise and sing hymns of liberation, it is our motto to be optimists by obligation yet pessimists by profession.

Are bureaucratic *society*'s hierarchies flattened? Our task is to shine a harsh light on the authoritarian and elitist spirit that congeals even in such "revolutionary" redesign, as in Chapter 1.

Are new values touted for the bureaucratic culture? Our task is to ferret out and critique the living ghost of efficiency, quantity, and uncaring instrumental reason in any organizational culture movement, as in Chapter 2.

Does *psychology* promise a therapy to soothe the pain of work inhumanly organized? Our task is to follow the pain to its origin and see what this tells us about the modern psyche's fundamental constriction of human potential, as in Chapter 3.

Is *speech* made to flow more easily and openly in ever-multiplying conferences, committees, training groups, quality circles, strategic planning, and other "facilitative" exercises? Our task is to expose the babble of such talk and its reduction of human discourse to triviality, as in Chapter 4.

Are computers extolled as the *thinking* machines that supersede all human thinking? Our task is to give evidence of the existence of practical

*Thanks to Jay White.

domains of thinking in and about work that can never be captured in either managerial or computer concept processing, as in Chapter 5.

Is *politics* declared ineffective and political deliberation inefficient? Our task is to show how bureaucratic standards are not only inappropriate but dangerous to the only means human beings have developed for formulating where they are in contrast to where they could yet be—and thus designing ways of living together, as in Chapter 6.

Finally, on the subject of *escape* from the modern way of organizing life in general: Are we dissatisfied with "mere" critique? Are we called to rush into action? Our task is to cut through the increasing subtleties of rhetoric and the easy response to "lend a hand, let's *do* something." We need to see the seriousness of the rethinking task that is at hand. Nothing less than the state of mind of an entire civilization is at stake. A new chapter, Conclusions, attempts to engage you in this task.

More clearly than ever, in its new stories and in the explicit theories newly developed in each chapter, this edition values *work* as the basis for a socially sound and humanly productive civilization: a civilization *for* human beings. The experience of *workers* is valued not because it is nice and ethical to be humane but because the civilization stands before a widening and undeniable gap between knowledge that enframes us top-down and knowledge that constructs life bottom-up. This division of knowledge portends the division between what today is openly recognized as virtual reality imposed by technical and administrative forces and actuality enacted and lived by human beings.

Work also becomes the touchstone for recognizing human potential. In previous editions, bureaucracy was contrasted sociologically against society as the stage of human organization that preceded it. Now bureaucracy is contrasted against its inmates' sense that it denies them their authentic future: the possibility toward living lives full of human potential.

Newly and appropriately subtitled "A Critique of Life in the Modern Organization," the new edition draws on fresh critical incidents that disclose bureaucracy's specific ways of foreclosing human potential. Stories, anecdotes, and situations are updated to reflect how the bureaucracy/humanity conflict works itself out in current developments.

A move toward synthesis is reflected in two innovations. Each central chapter now includes an explicit statement of the theory underlying that chapter's approach. And, more than one chapter shows how, in the treatment of actual events, help is needed from approaches other than the one used in that chapter's analysis.

The Conclusions, an entirely new chapter, is atypical for a critique written in the American context. That context always, persistently, and peremptorily demands solutions. This chapter resists quick and easy solutions. It shows how mere critique can lead to quietism and the constant call for action to repeatism. The chapter challenges anyone who suggests a quick fix to the problem of bureaucratic civilization. There are here no new managerial systems, tactics, or ploys. What is required is to go beyond modernity by beginning to understand the assumptions present at the laying of its foundations; to go with modernity against modernity. For this kind of thinking the Conclusions becomes an introduction.

What began as a critical social–scientific critique ends as critique of the modern human being.

* * *

Over the course of four editions, I owe debts for intellectual and physical survival to Guy Adams, Howell Baum, Peter Berger, Renee Berger, Morton Berkowitz, Paul Bernstein, David Carnevale, Bayard Catron, Raymond Cox, Fred Dallmayr, Robert Denhardt, Stephen Dracopoulos, John Everett, Karl Everett, Michael Diamond, Glenn Cowley, John Forester, Sandra Fish, Frank Fischer, Claudette Ford, James M. Glass, Charles Goodsell, Mary Hale, Michael Harmon, Charles Hayes, Hans Held, Larry Hill, Marc Holzer, Patricia Ingraham, Robert Isaak, Hwa Yol Jung, Jong S. Jun, Louis Koenig, Douglas LaBier, the late Charles Levine, Donna Lavins, Bert Lummus, Tommie Sue Montgomery, Dail Neugarten, the late Max Mark, Bruce Marquand, Edward Mazze, Roger Mazze, Brinton Milward, Kirsten Moy, Carl Nelson, J. Steven Ott, H. Mark Roelofs, David Rosenbloom, Barry Rossinoff, Conrad Rutkowski, Mary Schmidt, David Schuman, Howard Schwartz, Jay Shafritz, Eli Silverman, the late Kalman Silvert, Michael P. Smith, Patricia Snow, the late Kathryn Speicher, Harry Steinberg, Clarence Stone, Peter Vaill, Richard VrMeer, Dwight Waldo, Stephen Wasby, Richard Wells, constantly Jay White, and ever the memory of Patricia Boughton.

My thanks to the editors at St. Martin's Press: from Barry Rossinoff, the original and courageous acquisitions editor who never published a book he didn't like; through Glen Cowley, who gave this book its title; to Don Reisman, who gave it its subtitle, and Gabriela Jasin, Mary Hugh Lester, and Brendan P. McFeely, who professionally labored on the present edition.

The publisher and the author wish to thank the following reviewers for their helpful comments: Ronald Brecke, Park College; Larry Cobb, Slippery Rock University; Dee Harper, Loyola University; and Yung-Mei Tsai, Texas Tech University.

Special thanks are owed to the citizens of Oklahoma who, through the University of Oklahoma, contributed the half-pay of a year's sabbatical to the completion of this work, and the citizens of Maine who, through the University of Maine at Orono, provided space, outstanding colleagues, and challenging students.

Ralph P. Hummel
Spruce Head Island,
Maine

Contents

Introduction: Understanding Bureaucracy

This book is a practical guide to bureaucracy. It is practical because a group of twenty-five student interns in the New York City Urban Corps challenged an academician to be practical.

THE CHALLENGE

The challenge came in the form of an invitation. Would I, asked a voice at the other end of the telephone, come down to New York's City Hall and tell interns about to enter the city bureaucracy what to expect? No matter how down-to-earth an academician is in the classroom, there is only one reaction to such a request: stark, naked panic. After years of work in generalizations and abstractions, I was asked to give practical advice *that would be tested*. Not only was my own reputation at stake with the interns, who would soon enough encounter the realities of bureaucracy, but the interns themselves would be tested by seasoned bureaucrats.

The credibility of the academic world and its relevance to society had been very much on my mind. I had just become director of a small consulting firm on urban educational and administrative problems. Half the reason for the existence of that firm was my own experience that academicians had created around themselves their own little world of unreality. The other half was the remnant of an earlier faith that academicians still *did* have something to tell practitioners. Here was my first personal test.

What was bureaucracy all about? What could an individual expect the first day he or she walked into an office? What *should* he or she expect in order to survive?

What could I tell newcomers about modern bureaucracy?

THE CHALLENGE REVISITED

In the intervening twenty years, a critical school of the study of modern organization* has taken up the challenge. Generations of newcomers to organizations have subscribed to our advice: Think critically about work.

The beginning had been made by a great founder of sociology, Max Weber. Since the recovery of his critique in the 1970s, the critical school has shown that the modern organization of work is questionable in all its aspects.†

We can now question *structure*. Is top-down command really necessary? Is it effective? Can hierarchy be flattened? Can division of labor be eased? Both scholars and reality itself have given answers to these.

We can question *culture*. Are efficiency and control the only values to be pursued by bureaucracies, public and private? What about human purposes beyond these? Some now say that quality of products and services should be the ultimate value, the consumer or client the final judge.

We can question *psychology*. Do we need to accept the destruction of our self when we enter employment? Is it necessary for organizations to take away our sense of mastery over how we do work and our sense of conscience over whom we are responsible to? Throughout organizations, critical consultants pry inmates loose from their bureaucratic personalities and ease the structures that formed them.

We can question bureaucracy's devaluation of *speech*. Surely top-down commands shouted at us in an atmosphere of fear are not the only tools for getting us to do the work. What about being able to communicate back to managers what we ourselves have learned on the job? This question even suggests that low-level employees may come to know things at work that management will never know. As a result, a new chapter is added in this edition: one on thinking.

Must we even *think* in a special way in bureaucracy? The answer seems to be, yes. But as far back as the turn of the century, experts have warned that such thinking disconnects us from reality. What can workers, especially clients and consumers as well as citizens and legislators, do about this?

Finally, there is *the political question*. For a while it seemed there was no alternative to the bureaucratic transformation of politics. Efficiency

---

*With Max Weber, we use the term "bureaucracy" as a shorthand for all *modern* organization, public or private, including business and industrial corporations as well as public service and voluntary agencies organized according to the rationalized principles of modernity.
†The critical school does not attack everything that is popularly known as government bureaucracy. Its critique applies only to those institutions of producing and delivering goods and services that follow the strict principles of *modern* organization. For a statement of that agenda, see Ralph P. Hummel, "The Case for Public Servants," *The Bureaucrat*, vol. 17, no. 2 (Summer 1988), pp. 24–28.

and control had become the standards to measure success even there. Lost was any sense of political imagination. Lost was the belief that all and any of us are the source for political ideas. Now there are ideas and processes that advance new, nonbureaucratic forms of politics.

How does the critical school respond to the challenge issued by those about to enter bureaucracy and the salute of those already at work? Can it bring organizations back in the service of citizens and legislators, clients and consumers?

THE KEY

Half a century ago, sociologist Max Weber recoiled from the bureaucratic future in horror. Like George Orwell and Aldous Huxley he saw a strange new world in which not the brave but the dehumanized would survive. What if we started taking seriously Weber's classic characterization of bureaucracy and his condemnation of its inmates? After all, he did foresee a future populated by nonentities—"Specialists without spirit, sensualists without heart; this nullity imagines that it has attained a level of civilization never before achieved."[1]

Planted like time bombs through his famous essay on bureaucracy, temporarily defused by the neutral language of his "constructive" insights, lay the fragments of Weber's vision of a terrifying reality.

Bureaucracy gives birth to a new species of inhuman beings. People's social relations are being converted into control relations.[2] Their norms and beliefs concerning human ends are torn from them and replaced with skills affirming the ascendancy of technical means, whether of administration or production.[3] Psychologically, the new personality type is that of the rationalistic expert, incapable of emotion and devoid of will.[4] Language, once the means of bringing people into communication, becomes the secretive tool of one-way commands.[5] Politics, especially democratic politics, fades away as the method of publicly determining society-wide goals based on human needs; it is replaced by administration.[6]

Daily experience with bureaucracy showed this picture matched reality. The time had come, I decided, to set off the time bombs. And—as bureaucrats themselves reacted to the resulting explosions[7]—it has become increasingly necessary to show what goes into the building of bureaucracy as the bomb that threatens humanity.

Newcomers deserve to be told they are not facing minor adjustments when they enter or deal with bureaucracy but a challenge to alter all their orientations and behaviors. Old-timers in bureaucracy deserve to be told what lurks behind the pressures that threaten to turn them not only into one of the most severely criticized category of jobholders anywhere in the world[8] but into the most suspect of human beings.[9]

A president may say this of bureaucrats:

You may have been told that government workers are clockwatchers; you will soon find that the vast majority of them are dedicated not to their pay checks but to the job to be done. You may have heard that government positions involve nothing but plodding routine tasks; you will see some of the most exciting, interesting work in the world being done here. You may have read that public servants are unimaginative, security-seeking, uncreative, skilled only at the techniques of empire building; you will quickly discover that we have far more than our share of lively minds, endowed with vigor and courage.[10]

But bureaucrats themselves find it useful to draw radical distinctions between what it takes to survive in bureaucracy and what it takes to live social life on the outside.[11] Especially those who survive and are successful know that:

1. Life in bureaucracy is radically different from life in society.
2. Unique pressures—social, cultural, psychological, linguistic, cognitive, and political—shape the bureaucrat's life and determine what he or she will become.

One way of achieving an overview of the distinctions is to visualize them in terms of misunderstandings and understandings of bureaucracy:

Misunderstandings	*Understandings*
Socially—	
Bureaucrats deal with people.	Bureaucrats deal with cases.
Culturally—	
Bureaucrats care about the same things we do: justice, freedom, violence, oppression, illness, death, victory, defeat, love, hate, salvation, and damnation.	Bureaucrats aim at control and efficiency.
Psychologically—	
Bureaucrats are people like us.	Bureaucrats are a new personality type, headless and soulless.*
Linguistically—	
Communication with bureaucrats is possible: We all speak the same language, we think the same way.	Bureaucrats shape and inform rather than communicate.
Cognitively—	
Bureaucrats think the way we do: logically *and* sensibly.	Bureaucrats use logic only: They are trained to think the way computers think.
Politically—	
Bureaucracies are service institutions accountable to society and ruled by politics and government.	Bureaucracies are control institutions increasingly ruling society, politics, and government.

*The terms "headless" and "soulless" here evoked strong protests from some employees of modern organizations. It may be worthwhile to point out that these terms reflect a tendency that bureaucratic life forces on bureaucrats, rather than the actual characteristics of specific individuals.

The issue is not whether there are among bureaucrats those dedicated to getting the job done, those doing exciting and interesting work, and those of lively mind and hearts endowed with vigor and courage. Such dedication, excitement, and interest, such hearts and minds do exist. The question is whether they exist because of or despite bureaucracy. If bureaucracy enables, what are the kind of social life, the kind of values, the kind of psyche, the kind of speaking and thinking, the kind of politics that are enabled? And what qualities of human life are disabled or destroyed? No one denies the monumental accomplishments of modern civilization, with bureaucracy—public and private—at its spearhead. But the question human beings will inevitably ask is: Who or what is being speared?

Newcomers or outsiders, in order to deal with bureaucracy, need to understand just how the bureaucratic experience differs from ordinary social life. If bureaucrats are to understand just what sacrifices this most powerful of human organizations requires of them as human beings, they themselves need to learn just what it is that bureaucratic structures around them require of them.

In sum, the bureaucratic experience that awaits us differs from the social experience behind us in six ways: socially, culturally, psychologically, linguistically, cognitively, and politically. Each of these differences deserves exploration in depth. The rest of this introduction provides a survey; it is based on the lecture I delivered to those twenty-five interns. Chapters 1 through 6 provide the details.

BUREAUCRACY AS A STRANGE NEW WORLD

Anyone who has set out from familiar daily life to tangle with bureaucracy knows that bureaucracy and society are worlds apart. The distance can seem as far as that from the earth to the moon. It is not impossible to get there and back, but surviving the journey requires learning not only a new set of behaviors but a new mode of life. We must be attuned to both the home world and the new world.

The Bureaucratic Experience

People have difficulties with bureaucracy. This is true for the administrator who suddenly finds himself or herself in charge of and held responsible for an instrument of purported power and control that eternally squirms and wriggles to escape the grasp. It is true for newly hired workers in a bureaucracy who have to learn a new set of behaviors, norms, and speech patterns to get along and keep their jobs. And it is true for the outsider who wants to do business with a bureaucracy—get a tax refund, register a birth or death, secure a passport, license an enterprise, obtain police protection, or enter a child in school. Quite similar problems exist for the manager trying to control a corporation's sales force; the employee learning to talk, act, and think the way employees typically talk, act, and think at IBM, GM, or ITT; and the customer attempting to get Macy's credit department to correct a mistake the computer made.

If we have experienced bureaucracy in any of these roles, and none of us can long avoid such contact, we have to admit to ourselves that we have great difficulty with bureaucracy—attuning to it, communicating our needs to it, and obtaining satisfactions from it. No matter how astute we are, these difficulties exist, and we may feel that if only we could explain the reasons for such tensions we might be able to do better for ourselves in future contacts.

BUREAUCRATIC SOCIETY

The fundamental reasons for our difficulties were spelled out by Max Weber in warnings to which we seem not to have paid much attention. Perhaps to do so would result in too painful a recognition of the vastness of the chasm between social life and bureaucratic existence. Bureaucracy in its modern form, Weber concluded, constitutes the creation of a new world of human interaction. A transformation of normal human life began specifically with the development of modern organization. (See Chapter 1.)

In this new world of organized human interaction, it is entirely possible that a baby entrusted to welfare agencies may die of neglect even though, in the words of a welfare administrator, "everyone concerned did his or her job conscientiously."[12]

In normal human life, Weber points out, people relate to one another through the meaning each attaches to his or her actions—a meaning to which the other responds.[13] Responsibility means acting in keeping with mutually defined meanings. The bureaucrat, on the other hand, is restricted to those actions permitted by the job rules and program requirements. These are defined systemically and from the top down. As a welfare administrator said in the case of the baby cited above—an eight-month-old who died weighing only seven (7) pounds: "There was never a complaint filed with the state's Central Registry charging neglect or abuse."[14]

In the organized system, the bureaucrat is not officially allowed to tune in to the subjective meanings and needs that a client may be trying to convey. The bureaucrat must tune in only to those meanings and needs that have official standing. The result: It is possible for a baby to die even though advocates for the homeless may charge that the baby "spent repeated nights without shelter sleeping on the floor" of a welfare office and that "he was constantly seen dying by Human Resource Administration workers, but none intervened to protect him."[15]

When social interaction becomes organized, those actions become rational that are logically in line with the goals of the organization. This is what Weber meant when he said, "Bureaucracy is *the* means of transforming social action into rationally organized action."[16] Personal responsibility becomes systemic accountability. The system may have faults, but this does not mean we can assign blame to persons operating the system according to rules defined by those faults.

Thus the press may roast the Pentagon bureaucracy for being unable to find an officer who would shoulder responsibility for a crash that, in 1985, killed 248 soldiers aboard a chartered plane at Gander, Newfoundland, but such criticism is simply inappropriate.[17] Accountability, like the military's transport system as a whole, is systemic: The system might be maldesigned but, at best, the dutiful officer is accountable to that system and not responsible to outsiders with their separate social values.

That generals act like bureaucrats rather than warriors may be frustrating, but it is surprising only to the uninitiated.

In the case of the dying baby, the government charged with his care could honestly report that while the system had weaknesses—which could be corrected after the fact by introducing nurses and physicians to welfare offices—all the system's workers did their jobs properly.[18]

The goals of the bureaucratic social system may in themselves be human or humane. It is just that other human and humane goals not encompassed in the system's objectives cannot be considered by those functionaries who carry out its objectives—at least not in their official capacity. Such goals or needs stand logically outside the goals and needs of the bureaucratic system. They are, in the system's terms, "illogical" and therefore "irrational." It is one of the great ironies of bureaucratic interference in social life that those most in need of whatever help bureaucracy might be able to offer also feel least effective in dealing with it. A study for the U.S. Congress showed that only 46 percent of people with an income below $5,000 felt themselves to be highly effective when dealing with bureaucracy; the figure was 69 percent for those with an income over $15,000.[19]

Great care must therefore be taken, it would seem, in the design of the objectives of bureaucratic systems so as to give a chance to human interaction at the functionary/client level. But this may not be enough. Bureaucracy's need for control may impose a form of social interaction incompatible with situations in which people need to care for each other. It may be true, as defenders of public bureaucracy have argued, that "Government gets the messy jobs, and government agencies have many goals imposed on them,"[20] goals that private bureaucracy—business—

can't handle. But the problem may be that *any* type of organization that insists on rationally organizing social interaction may be systemically unfit to take *care* of goals and policies that require caring human interaction.

In summary, bureaucracy changes the way human beings relate to one another as social beings:

1. Bureaucracy replaces ordinary *social interaction,* in which individuals act by mutually orienting themselves to each other, by *rationally organized action,* in which individuals orient themselves to goals and meanings defined from the top down.
2. Bureaucracy replaces mutually defined *meaning* of social action by orientation toward systems *functions.*

The extent to which the bureaucratic world is not the normal human world can also be understood psychologically. Weber himself pointed out that bureaucratization favors the development of "the [new] personality type of the professional expert."[21] Because Weber did not develop this theme further in psychological terms, we may have missed that he was speaking about the creation of a new, truncated type of human being.

THE BUREAUCRATIC PERSONALITY

Clients find bureaucrats cold and impersonal. But clients have an escape. They can sacrifice what bureaucracy has to offer. They can cut down on dealing with bureaucratic personalities. Most clients, except the most dependent, can turn to other aspects of life—like economic enterprise, social life, and politics. Their own personality is shaped by other than bureaucratic demands.

Bureaucrats are not so lucky. Their job contract with bureaucracy soon becomes a psychological contract. This they cannot escape. Pulled on a daily basis between the human demands of social life and the organizational demands of work life, they live in the tension between two personalities. One is integrated and in charge of itself. The other is fragmented by division of labor and hierarchy and under the control of others. (See Chapter 3.)

Two forces originating in organizations' structure shape the bureaucratic personality. First, there is always someone else who is in charge of what you do (hierarchy): deciding whether what you do is socially right or wrong. Hierarchy relieves you of personal conscience and guilt. In psychological terms, hierarchy acts as the individual's superego. Second, what you do is predefined by job description, rules, and the division of labor. This relieves you of having to decide for yourself what work activity is most appropriate for the task at hand. In psychological terms, job definition replaces ego function, the function of mastering the world out of one's own sense of what works.[22]

Individuals respond quite differently to modern organization's demand that, when push comes to shove, members must check their conscience and sense of mastery at the plant gate or office door. One consultant reports this response from bureaucrats to whom the institution's demand for ego and superego control was pointed out[23]:

Now, clearly, they would make this argument: Yeah, there are those people who work there whose ego may be questioned in terms of the fact that they are conformist or that they are terribly compliant civil servants, and therefore will do whatever their superiors tell them to do.

But this total collapse in front of bureaucracy's demands is not the experience of most:

Their experience was more often that political appointees in leadership positions, for example, would make things difficult for them, but that they could make things difficult for those political appointees, given their position in bureaucracy over time and the history they have in their organization, and so forth. So in that sense what they were describing was this tension: Given the constraints how can they maintain ego integrity or self integrity?

Psychologically, then, the bureaucrat lives a daily life suspended in the tension between organization structure and self. Psychology itself, however, cannot tell us anything about the ultimate degree to which bureaucracy is the enemy of self. Human beings, it could be argued, have always had to adapt themselves to their environment. Yet, in the bureaucratic environment, which human beings themselves constructed, they may have overemphasized essentials of human nature that so finally challenge other essentials as to nearly destroy human nature. There is something fundamentally wrong with bureaucracy and not with the individual bureaucrat. The individual always retains his or her human potential. This becomes apparent only when the psycho-logic of bureaucracy is pushed to its logical conclusions. The result becomes clear in two ways: when bureaucracy pushes a human being to the ultimate extreme by "terminating" him or her, and when bureaucracy's basic values themselves are changed as has happened in recent attempts to humanize bureaucracy.

Douglas LaBier, a Washington psychoanalyst dealing with government employees, describes the pain of a perfectly well-adapted federal bureaucrat when the environment became less bureaucratic:

A federal bureaucrat went along for years perfectly happy in his role of giving pain to other bureaucrats on behalf of his boss. This individual's sado-masochistic personality fitted his official role of "hatchet man." The hatchet man's boss upheld a strictly top-down chain of command by a reign of terror. Finally the boss was replaced by a new boss who believed in letting employees help in deciding policy as part of a participative management style.

No longer afforded a legitimate channel for expression the hatchet man's previously "well adjusted pathology" now "erupted as the work environment changed to become healthier."

The hatchet man now began to actively interfere in the work of the division, badmouthing people behind their backs, sabotaging projects that were being worked on, trying to disrupt communications by impeding the flow of memos, and the like. Finally, in pain, he went to see the psychoanalyst, who asked not the usual questions about childhood, but: "Has anything changed in your work lately?"[24]

The symptoms and the pathology are specific to the hatchet man and his situation, but the pain is universal. An entire new movement of psychoanalytically oriented analysis beginning in the 1970s has found that bureaucracy produces pain. (See Chapter 3.) The efforts of psychoanalysts focusing on work is to alleviate such pain. But there is something that psychoanalysts are specifically prevented from doing by their own competence in dealing with the psyche. This is to undertake the social and cultural analysis that shows *why* bureaucracy is an ultimate challenge to all human beings. Psychoanalysis must become organization analysis.

The origin of emotional tension at work, of pain, of an ultimate challenge to the humanity of people lies in the structure of modern organizations itself. It is not to be sought in the individual weaknesses of inmates. This becomes most clear when the bureaucracy "terminates" a bureaucrat. A former contract administrator for a private bureaucracy—the office of a mining company:[25]

I didn't really mind getting fired. The company had been in trouble for a long time. What I did mind was passing my boss every day in the hallway and his being unable to look me in the eye, say hello, much less smile. I still had two weeks to go before I'd actually have to leave. He'd see me coming down the hall and he'd turn away.

How did that feel?

Why, it makes you feel like you're nobody—a *nonentity!*

The challenge of bureaucracy to all humankind is not essentially a psychological one. Bureaucracy is not satisfied with disordering the psyche by breaking away large chunks of it and reordering the psyche by distributing it over organizational structures. Bureaucracy also challenges an individual's entire being. The Greeks had a word for it: being = *ontos*. The fundamental challenge of bureaucracy is not merely a psychological one, it is an ontological challenge. The individual submits to it in agreeing to the initial work contract. Once major functions of the self are placed outside the self—conscience in hierarchy and mastery in job definition—the individual has identified his or her being with the organization. This also explains how the organization retains its hold over the individual. An individual trained in letting the organization make decisions of conscience and mastery for her or him over many years loses the ability to refer to her or his own standards for what is right or wrong and whether work is done well. Without the functions originally surrendered to the organization and now lodged there, she or he is—nobody. Not accidentally do we speak of "incorporation." The driving force for all social relations, political power, and administrative control in bureaucracy therefore is the experience of a nameless fear that without one's job one will cease to exist. The driving force of bureaucracy, its hold over humankind, is existential anxiety.[26]

In summary, bureaucracy radically alters the psyche of human beings:

1. Bureaucracy replaces autonomous *personality* with organizational *identity*.
2. Bureaucracy takes the functions of *conscience* (superego) and *mastery* (ego) out of the individual's psyche and distributes them across organizational structures: *hierarchy* and the *division of labor*.
3. Bureaucracy, in creating *dependency* of the individual self on structures of the organization (in identification, mingling self and organization), controls its functionaries by manipulating the *existential anxiety* over loss of being that a separation from the job threatens.

BUREAUCRATIC CULTURE: PARADOX OF NEEDS

Modern organization was designed to take care of human needs; yet everywhere in modern organization human needs lie in chains. This paradox of bureaucracy is already evident in the new type of action and the new type of personality required. Each person involved with bureaucracy—administrator, employee, client—experiences this paradox in his or her own way. Each stands in a different location in relation to the bureaucracy and therefore has his or her own perspective.[27]

The daughter of an eighty-five-year-old woman admitted to a Bakersfield, California, hospital with a heart attack is told three weeks later that her mother is being moved to a nursing home:[28]

I said what she needs is acute-level care and they said, Well, they can give her the same care over there. And I said, Well, I *know* they can't because they're not equipped for that, you know. So—uh—she said, I'm sorry—this is one of the sisters at the hospital. She said, we're losing money on her and Medicare won't allow her to be here any longer. So, she said, she has got to go. [Two days after the phone call, the woman was moved out.] . . . And they strapped her down, and put her in the ambulance, and took her over to the convalescent hospital. Well, I stayed with her all day, and I came home about 9/9:30 that night, and in three hours they called me and said she was dead.

A hospital spokesman, denying that the woman was moved for economic rather than medical reasons:

We have the responsibility, too, to remind the physician of his responsibility to let the patient and the patient's family know where they stand in terms of the benefits of an insurance plan, or Medicare plan, versus the economic resources that have been expended toward the patient's care.

The physician who approved the woman's discharge:

Question: Was that based on medical reasons or what you call pressure from the hospital to get her out of here?
Physician: I think I can honestly say I just felt pressure to release her. I'll never be coerced into doing something like that again.

The case, an entirely predictable result if we understand the bureaucratization of human needs, is not unique. These instances are the result of a government-mandated program in which physicians are asked to place patients in standard categories—diagnostic-related groups or DRGs—for which typical length of stay in hospital has been established. If length of stay exceeds the norm, the hospital is no longer reimbursed by Medicare.

The origins of the cultural paradox lie in this: The client approaches the bureaucracy with a full set of human needs. These are interrelated. But a policy or program is designed to satisfy only one or a few of them. More important, there is the essential difference of how needs are defined by a living human being and an organization, constructed by humans but not human itself. (See Chapter 2.)

You and I as human beings define our needs according to *projects*— something we as yet hope to accomplish in our lives. Literally: project = a plan that throws us ahead of ourselves on behalf of ourselves. We are not what we have just finished being yesterday but what we intend to be tomorrow and are becoming today. In short: Life goes on. (Or, it will, if bureaucracy lets us.)

In contrast, bureaucracy defines needs not by projects for the future but by standards of policies and programs defined in the past. The legislation, the policies, and the programs that bureaucracy administers set standards of yesterday for what it takes for a human being to become a "case" today—to be served or controlled. The evidence for becoming a case, including assessment of need, is determined by rational, scientific, and legal standards; these look to the past: to what already is. The artificial construct that is the organization cannot encompass the ongoing fullness of human life, which looks not only backward, but lives on-goingly in the present and looks in anticipation toward the future. This is so simply because organization is not life. Bureaucracy in its administrative function must, to follow the policy standards that authorize it to act, look at human needs not as if they were part of an ongoing *project* of a living subject but as if they were *finished characteristics* of a dead object.

This backward-looking orientation of bureaucracy is often obscured by the actual experience of bureaucrats. In actually applying the standards of the past—for example, those of the lawbooks or of the precinct captain's orders of the day—the cop on the beat must hurl himself or herself into the future and its not-yet-defined possibilities. In short, the officer must make contact with reality. That reality creates itself ongoingly before the officer; to survive on the job he or she must deal with it. The cultural tension within which the bureaucrat lives is defined by being torn between past enactments of a *model* of reality and present encounters with reality itself. No work at all can be done if the bureaucrat clings strictly to the enacted model of reality without hurling himself or herself into reality itself. Yet in even touching what is real—the objects and people in front of us, with whom we must deal—we desert the previously enacted model of that reality. That is why it is in the interests of managers and administrators —the police captain, for example—to have their subordinates do *nothing* rather than be accused of corrupting the pure model of mandated actions and values that is inevitably tainted by contact with reality.

Thus the City of New York saw to it that all work of two "supercops" was halted when they succeeded in stopping the heroin flow in one precinct by permitting heroin to be available for their informers; the story is told in *The Supercops*. All work of bureaucrats is measured by past standards, not by current exigencies that rise out of reality. Examples abound; they may not be as extreme as the above, but their very subtlety testifies to their omnipresence.

All too often, studies have found that confidence and potential efficacy are reduced as future opportunities are increasingly defined by standards determined by the past. In the case of those who have allowed themselves to be defined as "the poor," the experience of the past—"the culture of poverty"—closes in on them.[29]

But the middle class does not escape unscathed. It cannot fail to strike an ironic eye that the often praised ability of the middle class to adapt to and even manipulate bureaucratic rules may merely subject members voluntarily to the past orientation of the bureaucratic environment, whereas their lower-class fellow citizens are forced into it.[30]

A past orientation, in fact, also characterizes top-level bureaucrats. When Robert S. McNamara, and his generation of computer geniuses, took over the Department of Defense in 1961, they also assumed that the defense needs of the nation could be satisfied by designing programs that would efficiently adhere to previously established and well-defined measurable goals. Following the advice of economists[31] instead of soldiers, McNamara then went ahead to conduct a war by past standards and by the numbers—the Vietnam War. He lost it to those who treated war not as a means to achieve past ends but as a way of shaping a future whose exact character could not be known.

The Bureaucratic War

Since Max Weber, we have recognized two cultures at war with each other in modern civilization. One still clings to what we hold worthwhile in ordinary social life. The other, rising culture defines what the bureaucratized believe worthwhile in the all-encompassing world of modern organizations.

The traditional values of human life, as the contemporary philosopher and sociologist Jürgen Habermas has said, focus on "justice and freedom, violence and oppression, happiness and gratification, poverty, illness and death, . . . victory and defeat, love and hate, salvation and damnation."[32] They are ultimate values: They define what Life is all about.

In contrast Weber summarized the norms of bureaucratic life as "precision . . . stability . . . stringency of discipline . . . reliability . . . calculability of results . . . formal rationality . . . formalistic impersonality . . . formal equality of treatment."[33] These are instrumental values: They promise to serve as instruments by which human beings can achieve some ultimate values. By design bureaucrats are intended to be instruments. They are expected to fulfill their tasks without anger or predisposition.[34] Or as Weber says elsewhere:

Sine ira ac studio, without hatred or passion, and hence without affection or enthusiasm. The dominant norms are concepts of straightforward duty without regard to personal considerations. Everyone is subject to formal equality of treatment; that is, everyone in the same empirical situation. This is the spirit in which the ideal official conducts his office.[35]

But from the beginning there is this question: Can neutral—in a specific sense: heartless—administration take care of basic human needs that are never experienced in a neutral way? If I am wrongly accused of a crime, I want justice. Procedural correctness may protect the interests of the investigating organization, not mine. It does not satisfy me one bit, once my accuser recants, to hear the prosecutor who jailed me defend the investigators, saying, "Everybody, I think, did their job, and did their job fully."[36]

It is not with formal rationality or even with the demand for formal equality of treatment that I, as the average client, approach bureaucracy. I want *my* needs taken care of, ill-defined and even contradictory as they are. I experience myself in my own unique way, through my own personality, with my own unique set of problems. I do not easily present myself as a "case" to the bureaucrat, to be processed following universal rules. The quality of my life, my problems, my needs do not lend themselves easily to definition, measurement, and decision.

In contrast the bureaucrat's experience of me is quite different. Viewing the world through a perspective shaped by bureaucratic values, the bureaucrat sees me not as a distinct individual with qualitatively unique problems and needs but as number 98 of a class of cases whose claim to service or control can be logically determined and quantitatively measured.

To the registrar of births and the county clerk, the addition of a new family member is just "another birth," the addition of a simple mark in a book of accounts. To me the birth of my daughter is an event full of affection, enthusiasm, anxiety, joy, emotion, passion, and import. She is *my* daughter. She has my eyes. My feelings about her, awakened by her from within me, make me laugh and cry. She is my future, my burden, my redemption—the transcending testimony of enduring love, my wife's and mine.

To the Social Security official, a man's death is just another form filled out; to his wife it is the death of her beloved or hated husband and all he meant and all the things they ever did together and were to each other.

To the welfare case worker, you and I are "cases" or we are not "cases." If we are not "cases," the "case worker" is not allowed, on eventual pain of losing his or her job, to recognize us or our troubles. Even if we are cases, our troubles are troubles only if they fall within the bureaucracy's predefined cases of trouble. Bureaucracy encases us. We obtain its services or we are subjected to its controls if we fit its frame-work. To the extent that none of us ever fits perfectly into frames pre-constructed to us by the reason of others, we can say, with the wrongly accused: We wuz framed! Originally designed as the tool of humankind, bureaucracy has turned humankind into a tool for its own ends.

Two basic critiques have been launched against bureaucracy as the result of the observed culture conflict:

1. We *value* life differently from bureaucracy.
2. We *know* life differently from bureaucracy.

The first is a simple cultural critique. Its tradition goes from Max Weber to Jürgen Habermas. Cultural critique juxtaposes patterns of val-ues. It simply points out that bureaucracy finds different things worth-while than do the rest of us who are outside it. These values—such as efficiency—were at one time considered tools for achieving human ends. Today, critics not only question whether a modern organization's internal values are compatible with human beings' values but point to instances in which bureaucratic values have distorted human values. For example, the closest the Pentagon has come to satisfying the human longing for peace has been to offer something sold as the bureaucratic equivalent: "perma-nent prehostility." This literally means always being ready for war, which is not everyone's idea of peace.

The second critique is more basic. If human beings outside bureauc-racy *know* life in ways radically different from the way bureaucrats can know life, then the adequacy of all modern civilization for knowing what human life is can be put into question. For bureaucracy is the vanguard of modern civilization; it is *the* modernizer wherever it goes because it hones modern ways of valuing and knowing to a sharp cutting edge. Critics such as Edmund Husserl and Martin Heidegger point out that ways of knowing define reality. If we accept modernity's method of knowledge—knowing the world by reference to laws of nature and human nature outside of ourselves[37]—we can no longer legitimately know those experiences of what it means to live life and be human that stand apart from such laws. On the practical level this means that I, as a client, am permitted to know myself only in bureaucratic terms. If I cannot accept the bureaucratic way of knowing me—taking cognizance of me—then I will simply not receive its goods. Or, in the extreme, if I don't know enough to get out of bureaucracy's way, it will simply steamroller over me. This critique is the more basic one because it puts once again in the forefront of our thinking the question: *How* do we know *what* we are as human beings? The suggestion is that modern knowing leaves us largely unknown to ourselves. Bureaucracy stands in the way of knowing our humanity.

BUREAUCRATIC LANGUAGE

Bureaucracy's values and bureaucrats' way of knowing cut straight to the heart of how we speak and think in the modern world. As outsiders, as clients, we hear ourselves addressed from the top down in language that rings strange in our ears. Our very way of thinking about ourselves is questioned by the way we are challenged to think if we want to make contact with a corporation or government agency. The ordinary human being recoils from that encounter with bureaucratic language and thought in essentially the same way as this man trying to track down his delayed Social Security checks in Washington, D.C.:

Well, I'll tell you something about this town. They got a secret language here. You know that? Bureaucratese. Same thing we used to call doubletalk. These government people, they don't hear you. They don't listen. You start to say something and they shut you out mentally, figuring they know right away what you're going to say before you say it. . . .*

Here a client puts his finger on central experiences of all those dealing with bureaucratic language:

1. That bureaucratic language is *different* from ordinary language. It is, in fact, encoded in terms all its own. To the outsider these are secret terms, the language is a *secret language.*
2. That bureaucratic language is a *power language.* Bureaucrats address clients as if they had the right not to listen to them, assuming, rather, that clients must listen to them. This implies the presumption of power, that the bureaucrat has the means to enforce a speech situation in which he or she speaks (predefines) and others listen (are predefined).

*For the full text of these observations, see the report of Pasquale Plescia in Chapter 4.

BUREAUCRATIC THOUGHT

Later we discover that the secret of bureaucratic language lies *behind* its technical terms, its jargon, and its affinity for acronyms in the way bureaucrats are taught to *think*. Reasoning deductively from general rules and by analogy from previously established case norms, bureaucrats speak a language that differs from ordinary speech exactly because it is created on a knowledge base that is top down and prior to experience: derived from the universal laws and rules that constitute modern knowledge of reality.[38] We will conclude that:

1. In bureaucracy a new form of speech arises that is top-down instead of reciprocal in defining reality; *information* replaces *communication*.
2. In bureaucracy a new form of thinking comes to predominate: *analogous thinking* in which bureaucrats are trained to recognize reality only to the extent that aspects of it match a previously conceived model of reality; *analogous thinking* replaces *thinking* with its original commitment to the exploration and discovery of new realities and possibilities.

In a classic example of dependence both on top-down speech as definition erectof reality and on analogous thinking, employees of an airline simply denied as unreal the repeated reports by two passengers of a crashed plane that they had seen two fellow passengers fall out of the broken fuselage into Boston Harbor. A computer printout had not contained the names of the extra passengers. If they were not on the printout, they were not real.

As long as people trust that kind of knowledge and distrust their own experience that things in reality work quite differently from the way the rules say they should, bureaucracy retains the power to define reality through top-down speech. However, as we enter postmodernity, we find problems in industrial production and the provision of human services that cannot be defined top-down.[39] Then new forms of speech, new ways of speaking to each other, new words arise from the bottom up and do battle with top-down words and thoughts that seem increasingly detached from reality. This also calls for a new focus on politics.

Politics: The Revolt against Control

Politics is the enemy of administration. This is why wherever possible, bureaucracy attempts to transform politics into administration. As early as 1917, Max Weber asked questions such as these about the fate of politics:

Given the basic fact of the irresistible advance of bureaucratization, the question about the future forms of political organization can only be asked in the following way:

1. How can one possibly save *any remnants* of "individualist" freedom in any sense? . . .

2. How will democracy even in this limited sense [of a check and control on bureaucracy] be *at all possible?*
3. A third question, and the most important of all, is raised by a consideration of what bureaucracy as such *cannot* achieve. [How are politics and political leadership still possible in the sense of] battle for personal power and what follows from that power: personal *responsibility for his own cause* [which] is the lifeblood of the politician as well as of the entrepreneur[?].[40]

By the end of our century, the replacement of politics by administration and the resulting loss of political vision have become epidemic. While political theorist Sheldon Wolin could write of the nineteenth century, "At bottom the century desperately longed to transcend the political,"[41] twentieth-century organization theorists and political scientists could report solid and growing fulfillment of that longing. Wherever organization became dominant, democracy had to be, as Weber anticipated, redefined. While Wolin points to Lenin's redefinition of democracy as " 'bureaucratic' in the sense that the Party is built from the top downwards,"[42] we can point to the rationalist redefinition of democracy by American political scientist Robert Dahl and others who empirically observed that democracy actually works as rule by shifting minorities—later called the plurality of elites.[43] Politicians, political scientists, and other students of modern organization today observe not only the bureaucratization of democracy but of citizens, of politics through campaign management and technology, of interest groups, of courts, of Congress and other legislatures, even of the president.[44] The same president who praised bureaucrats also complained of the bureaucratization of everything that came before him:

Sooner or later it seems that every problem mankind is faced with gets dumped into the lap of the president right here in the center of it all. But by the time it reaches here, the problem has been dissected, sanitized, and cast into a series of options—almost as though they were engraved in stone. What is missing is the heart behind them, what they mean in human terms.[45]

In fact a number of presidents have limited their political potential by checking off alternatives presented on "option papers." This is a bureaucratic approach to politics that assumes that choices are already present in the environment when, in reality, not even problems emerge fully shaped from the environment.

As a leading consultant and scholar on bureaucracy has noted, "Underlying every public debate and every formal conflict over policy there is a barely visible process through which issues come to the awareness and ideas about them become powerful."[46] Political scientists have only of late issued warnings about keeping this process alive. Examining the increased use of staff by members of Congress, Michael Malbin warned that members of Congress were increasingly denying themselves the opportunity to get a sense for what was going on in other people's districts by personal contact with other members of Congress.

A representative system would require elected members from one district with one set of needs and interests, to talk to members from districts with different needs and interests, if the members hoped to achieve anything. Indirect communication, such as we see today, was not what was envisioned: direct communication among elected members was considered essential to informed deliberation.[47]

Similarly, organization theorist Raymond Cox, a longtime staffer in the Massachusetts legislature, cautioned against applying bureaucratic standards to legislative performance: "A legislature may be entirely functional without being either efficient or productive."[48]

Ironically, it has been in business that a politics of focusing on how problems are shaping up received its most potent recognition in recent years. After decades of making policy from alternatives presented them by middle managers, engineers, and executive staff, the American automotive industry suddenly was confronted in the 1970s with the fact that its huge bureaucratic machinery had lost touch with reality. American car buyers were turning to Japanese products that actually functioned as cars. That is, Japanese cars had the ability to get you from one place to another with greater reliability than American cars. After defending itself like any bureaucracy against any input from reality that would endanger internal values, the industry finally turned to input from workers for knowledge as to *what* was actually going on in the production line. Quality management systems institutionalized such consultation. A politics of what is good for the entire organization was implicit, though management did not seem to realize until the late days of this movement that the power implications put their own rule at risk.[49] By 1992, similar consultative, quality-oriented management systems had been installed in all United States military branches, large parts of the federal government, thirty-six states, and local governments, while by late 1993 the president and vice president of the United States launched a program for all of the federal government bureaucracy to "reinvent" itself.

The problem with the bureaucratization of politics is simply this: Bureaucracy, both private and public, is infested with the modern bias toward believing that what is real is measurable. As early as the turn of the century, the philosopher Edmund Husserl, himself a mathematician, predicted that an increasingly mathematized civilization would eventually lose touch with the physical things it was measuring. The civilization had come to believe that all human activities could be predesigned according to universal laws. The model was physics. But an increase in mathematical knowledge *about* physics ultimately led to a neglect of the knowledge *of* the physical that comes to the worker when he or she lays hands on a wheel and an axle and tries to fit the two together.[50] Similarly, in official politics and public service, faith grew in policy clearly predefined and programs with measurable performance standards. These would produce intended results all by themselves. This faith now is challenged by the bureaucratic experience of those who actually lay their hand on things or on clients.

The collision between bureaucracy and politics can be summarized in terms of two opposing tendencies observable in modern civilization today:

1. There is a tendency to "rationalize" politics, to conduct it as if it were a rational process of making decisions among clear choices already formed in people's minds. This leads to the evaluation of politics and politicians according to bureaucratic standards. The central standard is measurability.
2. There is a countertendency to "derationalize" politics: to give renewed care to those processes by which human beings define who they are, what their problems might be, and what possibilities arise out of conflict between what is already here and what is still possible. This leads to a conduct of politics according to a concern for how problems are framed *before* decisions are made about alternatives. The mode is one of discovery. New possibilities are evoked; the body politic is convoked. The central standard in politics as much as in economics, private production, or public service is quality: from *qua* = *what* things are.

Six Foundations of Conflict

Bureaucracy continues its victory march around the globe. It changes human life socially, culturally, psychologically, linguistically, cognitively, and politically. It takes human needs and promises to erect a huge storehouse of goods and services that satisfies these needs. Only the most advanced modernized countries, and others modernizing but with a strong culture of their own, begin to suspect the cost: that, in order to satisfy human needs, bureaucracy must change them. The mentality is best expressed in the words of an American commander in Vietnam:

> We had to destroy the town in order to save it.

Bureaucracy, as one psychoanalytic organization theorist has pointed out, is an externalized self system. It promises to construct an outer world of total security for a species of beings whose psyche is destined to struggle between both love and war. In its most grandiose worldwide structure, the military bureaucracy has produced permanent worldwide readiness for war as its answer to human longing for peace. Even at this early a stage of examining the bureaucratic experience, we can see that both its solutions to human problems and its methods are shot through with paradoxes like this.

Socially, bureaucracy brings people in a sense closer to each other than ever, by making them more interdependent; yet it does this by pushing them farther apart through replacing *mutually oriented social action* by *rationally organized action*. Strangers fill positions next to each other without ever looking at each other, each looking upward and outward for hierarchy or the system to tell him or her what to do. Ironically, this system of getting work done is the most powerful yet devised in human history—for that kind of work that can be conceived of and organized from the top down. Only the extent of informal organizations and actual work behavior that falls outside of the formal structure indicates just how much this top-down social structuring of work relies for its success on the voluntary associations of its workers as social beings and on the bottom-up knowledge of reality that only hands-on workers can have.

Psychologically, bureaucracy rips control over conscience and mastery out of the psyche of the individual bureaucrat and deposits these functions in organizational structures: hierarchy and division of labor. What sense of self is left to the individual comes in terms of organizational *identity*—what the organization says he or she is—not *personality*—who a person becomes when left to grow and utilize all of individual psychic potential. In the absence of the inner strength of knowing who we are that comes from an autonomous personality, we suffer recurrent attacks of existential anxiety whenever separation from the bureaucratic home is threatened. This anxiety also explains why we stay with bureaucracy even when it destroys us, and it is the basis for managers' manipulation of employees.

Culturally, bureaucracy replaces ordinary human cultural values with values of its own: values compatible with the inner needs of the bureaucratic machine. Permanent prehostility as a quantitatively measurable but qualitatively inadequate substitute for peace is only the most blatant and globe-spanning example. Ultimately, bureaucracy, like modern science and technology, places a faith in *quantitative* measurement as a standard for what is real where there used to be a faith of human beings in the inner *qualitative* experience of human life. However, this triumph of quantity is today being challenged, beginning with the decline in quality when control over quantitative aspects of time and space is exaggerated beyond human tolerances and below the utility of products in the mass production and delivery of goods.

Linguistically, bureaucracy commands through the top-down definition of language: defining what things are. Top-down speech and analogous thinking, however, preclude the discovery of new problems and the shaping of solutions continuously adapted to a changing reality.

Cognitively, by instilling the practice of *analagous thinking*, bureaucrats are trained to act only when they recognize aspects of *reality* matching predefined *models* for action. Thinking in terms of the *logic* of *technique* replaces *sensibility* to human needs.

Power-politically, bureaucracy reaches its peak. Max Weber called it *a control instrument* without compare. Created as the tool and servant of politics, bureaucracy today redefines politics by imposing on it bureaucratic standards. But especially in its encounter with politics, bureaucracy's limits become intolerably obvious. The more bureaucracy relies on the rationalization of everything—which ultimately means placing its faith in the most rational of all mental constructs: the world of numbers—the more it becomes detached from physical, social, and psychological reality. Politics, itself seduced into the process of rationalization and bureaucratization, shows its potential for being the single most important human tool for getting in touch with new realities exactly when rationalization and bureaucracy achieve their triumph. There is potential for both release and tragedy here.

The Nonbureaucratic Promise

In both politics and economics today there is again the promise of a nonbureaucratic future. Both governments and corporations are "reinventing" themselves.

On the international scale, there is, in the dissolution (read: fragmentation) of the global balance of terror, an opportunity for less-than-global tools for the "administration" of peace.

The dissolution of the bureaucratic governments of Eastern Europe and the Soviet Union—the latter at once identified by Max Weber as bureaucratic at the moment of its creation—should show the limits of rationalistic planning that sells short the human needs of the planned.

Corporations, government institutions, and voluntary institutions talk a good game of bringing worker know-how and customer needs into their calculations.

Surely this is a good time to abandon a project such as the present one. Where bureaucracy is everywhere dissolving, a critique is unnecessary. But is it dissolving?

Against Critique

When the chaos of nonbureaucratic government and business befalls us, who of us is willing to give up his or her false security even temporarily to make a new beginning?

After all, the old international administration, though terrorizing billions with its end-of-the-world scenarios, did provide some sort of security. Now any small country with a bomb can terrorize its neighbors.

The fallen governments and shattered systems, though having killed tens of millions, did provide some sense of stability. Now millions go hungry as they attempt to design new ways of living together.

Our own bureaucratized economy provided a predictable playing field for corporate enterprise. Now the government safety net is removed and enterprises call for reregulation.

Corporations themselves, when they could control our needs instead of having to become agile in responding to them, proved profitable and provided employment. Now profits are again dictated by markets, and markets by perceptions of quality, and as quality goes up the employment rolls go down. Life and work become less assured in their predictable course.

FOR CRITIQUE

No doubt security, stability, predictability, and control were endangered by critique in all these fields of human endeavor. But then these are precisely the values of modernity itself. Critique, the child of modernity, is also the enemy not only of modern organizations but of modernity.

Yes, for all of us used to nothing but the false security of bureaucratic government, it is difficult to face up to being self-responsible in the world.

But then who said being human is easy? Shortly after this book was written, the author discovered, too late to stop publication, research showing that almost every citizen who was studied but no one in academe was criticizing bureaucracy. Obviously there was no need for a critical book as seen by those in academe. Even today there are those in Washington who would not have a critical author or critical student newcomers in their midst.*

The attempt to repress critique is the final corruption. Not only does it wave us off from what we might come to know, it denies citizens access to what we already know. As such, repression of critique—need this be said?!—is no more appropriate or ethical than we ourselves would be if as human beings we should fail to face the hard questions: how to design a human life *for* human beings. Or, as Edmund Husserl put it, how to stop being functionaries of technical systems and become "functionaries of mankind."[51]

SOME BENEFITS OF THINKING CRITICALLY

The book began with a claim to be practical. But overall, thinking critically gives us no practical benefits in the sense of making life easier. It tends to make the thinker unhappy. Things as they are lose their appeal. The critical thinker finds no satisfaction in even the most insightful of results.

*The director of the Volcker Commission, at the Region VII meeting of the American Society for Public Administration in 1989, suggested that academicians could have a major impact on toning up the image of the public service by toning down their criticisms in front of their students. A former president of the society, present at these remarks, expressed no objection to this.

Once the results are in, he or she is called to do something about it. In short, critical thinking in bureaucracy is a managerial talent. It calls us to take on the human fate of constructing that part of the world that is in our care and being responsible for it.

This recalls the author's meeting a Washington civil servant who had just come back from Portland, Maine, where he was asked for tens of thousands of dollars for the blueprints of a ship the government had already paid for.

"I told them, 'I'm a citizen and a taxpayer, too!'" he said. "'And I'm not going to pay your price.'"

"What will your manager do to you when you get back?" I asked.

"Oh, he'll send someone else."

As future bureaucrats—and most of us will have jobs making bureaucratic demands—we can be that "someone else." We can be the thoughtless and anonymous one of whom managers can say, "I call and he cometh." Or we can be the civil servant in the most profound sense, who can say of himself or herself in the highest ethical sense, "I see through this, and I am doing my best."

This is what managers tell me as I try to evoke the bureaucratic experience in the classroom. Inevitably, there is one who will say:

"If things are as bad as you say, what can we do about it?"

Then I look that manager straight in the eyes, and try not to smile and be a wise guy, and I say as seriously as I can:

"You do your best."

Inevitably, a little surreptitious smile comes onto the manager's face, and he or she will say:

"Yeah, I'm already doing that."

NOTES

1. Max Weber, *The Protestant Ethic and the Spirit of Capitalism,* tr. Talcott Parsons (New York: Scribner's, 1958), p. 182.

2. Max Weber, *Economy and Society: An Outline of Interpretive Sociology,* 3 vols. Guenther Roth and Claus Wittich, eds. Ephraim Fischoff trans. (New York: Bedminster Press, 1968). All of the points made here are in the essay entitled "Bureaucracy," pp. 956–1005. On the transformation of social relations, Weber writes, p. 987: "Bureaucracy is *the* way of translating social action into rationally organized action."

3. Ibid., p. 975: "Bureaucracy develops the more perfectly, the more it is 'dehumanized,' the more completely it succeeds in eliminating from official business love, hatred, and all personal, irrational, and emotional elements which escape calculation."

4. Ibid., p. 998: Bureaucratization favors development of "the [new] personality type of the professional expert." P. 968: Bureaucracy develops "the official's readiness to subordinate himself to his superior without any will of his own."

5. Ibid., p. 992. This is my expansion on Weber's comment regarding bureaucracy's interest in secrecy, extending even to the use of a "secret script." See Chapter 4.

6. Ibid., pp. 987 and 991. See also p. 1403.

7. The book has now been used by all strata of civil servants at the federal, state, and local levels, in quasi-independent agencies, and in the private bureaucracy of corporations. This fourth edition is fundamentally a response to their input.

8. For example, a congressional survey showed that 65 percent of the public and 57 percent of elected officials agreed with the statement, "The trouble with government is that elected officials have lost control over the bureaucrats, who really run the country." Source: U.S. Congress, Committee on Government Operations, Subcommittee on Intergovernmental Relations, *Confidence and Concern: Citizens View American Government* (Washington, D.C.: U.S. Government Printing Office, 1974), part 2, p. 115, and part 3, p. 61. Similarly 73 percent of citizens and 80 percent of elected officials agreed that the federal government had become too bureaucratic. Ibid., part 2, p. 114, and part 3, p. 60.

9. Here bureaucrats are caught in a classic bureaucratic paradox: They may do their job well and yet the work itself may be criticized. A study that reports that 69 percent of a bureaucratic office's clients were "satisfied with the way the office handled your problem" says nothing about whether the clients wanted to be handled at all or whether the bureaucracy created the problem. Perhaps the office was the Internal Revenue Service, the local police station, or the county jail. See Charles T. Goodsell, *The Case for Bureaucracy—A Public Administration Polemic*, 2nd ed. (Chatham, N.J.: Chatham House, 1985), p. 23, reporting analysts' explanations for lower satisfaction in generalized attitudes toward bureaucracy in contrast to higher specific satisfactions. (Study cited: Daniel Katz, Barbara A. Gutek, Robert L. Kahn, and Eugenia Barton, *Bureaucratic Encounters* [Ann Arbor: Institute for Social Research, University of Michigan, 1975.]) Questions about human satisfaction with bureaucracy cannot be asked from within the bureaucratic framework, when what is suspect is the framework itself.

10. President John F. Kennedy quoted in Bernard Rosen, "Who Needs Bureaucrats?—In the National Interest," *The Bureaucrat—The Journal for Public Managers*, vol. 12, no. 1 (Spring 1983), pp. 41–43; citation from pp. 41–42.

11. Every civil servant I have ever taught has acknowledged the problem of attuning oneself to the realities inside the organization as distinguished from and often opposed to the realities outside the organization. People, situations, and things to be trusted are simply different in modern organizations than they are in ordinary social life. In fact, the issue of trust looms ever large for inmates of bureaucracies. For example, the 1979–80 Federal Employees Attitudes Survey asked bureaucrats to respond to the statement, "Employees here feel you can't trust this organization." Out of a survey of 13,799 bureaucrats, a total of 42.4 percent agreed, 16.2 percent were undecided, and 41.4 percent disagreed. Source: U.S. Office of Personnel Management, 1979–80 Federal Employees Attitudes Survey, "Measures of Trust, Efficacy, Participation, Authority and Communication and Their Distribution" reported in David Nachmias, "Determinants of Trust Within the Federal Bureaucracy," in David Nachmias, ed., *Public Personnel Policy: The Politics of Civil Service* (Port Washington, N.Y.: Associated Faculty Press, 1985), pp. 133–43; citation from p. 139. See also: David Carnevale, *Trust: Creating the High Performing Public Organization* (San Francisco: Jossey-Bass, 1994).

12. Barbara Basler, "A Blind and Deaf Infant's Short Life on the Rolls of New York's Homeless," *New York Times*, Dec. 20, 1985, pp. B1 and B5; citation from p. B1.

13. Weber, *Economy and Society*, p. 4.

14. Basler, p. B5.

15. Ibid., p. B1.

16. Weber, *Economy and Society*, p. 987.

17. "The Broken Chain of Command," editorial, *New York Times*, Dec. 21, 1985, p. 26.

18. Basler, p. B5.

19. U.S. Congress, Committee on Government Operations, Subcommittee on Intergovernmental Relations, *Confidence and Concern: Citizens View American Government* (Washington, D.C.: U.S. Government Printing Office, 1973), part 2, pp. 275–76.

20. H. Brinton Milward, and Hal G. Rainey, "Don't Blame the Bureaucracy!" *Journal of Public Policy*, vol. 3, pt. 2 (May 1983), pp. 149–68; citation from pp. 154–55.

21. Weber, *Economy and Society*, p. 998.

22. The technical terms "superego" and "ego" used here are Sigmund Freud's. But any modern psychology focuses on the conscience and mastery functions.

23. Personal communication with Prof. Michael A. Diamond of the University of Missouri, who has served as consultant for federal and state governments.

24. Case paraphrased from personal communication with Douglas LaBier, Jan. 2, 1986. The case is discussed in Douglas LaBier, *Modern Madness: The Emotional Fallout of Success* (Reading, Mass.: Addison-Wesley, 1986).

25. Personal communication with Cynthia Confer, Jan. 13, 1986.

26. The differentiation here between a psychological concept of anxiety and an ontological one is derived from a comparison of Sigmund Freud and Martin Heidegger on anxiety in R. P. Hummel, "Anxiety in Organizations: Heidegger and Freud," paper delivered at the annual scientific meeting of the International Society for Political Psychology, June 1983, Toronto, Canada.

27. The theory of how social place affects what we get to see of reality belongs to the sociology of knowledge. See especially Karl Mannheim, *Ideology and Utopia*, various editions, and Peter Berger and Thomas Luckmann, *The Social Construction of Reality* (Garden City, N.Y.: Doubleday, 1967).

28. This case is reported from a transcription of an ABC "Nightline" television broadcast, Feb. 4, 1986.

29. See Frank Riessman, Jerome Cohen, and Arthur Pearl, eds., *Mental Health of the Poor* (New York: Free Press, 1964).

30. As against the "culture of poverty" argument, it might be argued that some of the poor, because they tend to personalize human relations while middle-class people are better able to relate to one another impersonally, may actually escape bureaucratization. For the personal/impersonal difference between lower class and middle class, see Herbert Gans, *The Urban Villagers* (New York: Free Press, 1965).

31. McNamara was reported to have been strongly influenced by the work of economists Charles J. Hitch and Roland N. McKean, *The Economics of Defense in the Nuclear Age* (Cambridge, Mass.: Harvard University Press, 1960). My thanks to Gideon Sjoberg for pointing this out.

32. Jürgen Habermas, *Toward a Rational Society* (Boston: Beacon Press, 1971), p. 96.

33. Weber, *Economy and Society*, pp. 956–58; cf, pp. 224–25. Similar norms hold for bureaucracy in private enterprise. See ibid., "The Conditions of Maximum Formal Rationality of Capital Accounting," pp. 161–64.

34. Max Weber, *Staatssoziologie—Soziologie der rationalen Staatsanstalt und der modernen politischen Parteien und Parlamente*, 2nd ed., ed. Johannes Winckelmann (Berlin: Duncker & Humblot, 1966), p. 45.

35. Max Weber, *Economy and Society*, p. 225. Here *sine ira ac studio* is rendered differently. The German terms Weber used in the *Staatssoziologie* compilation are *ohne Zorn und Eingenommenheit*.

36. "Boy Who Accused Jersey City Man of Rape Recants His Story," *The New York Times*, May 28, 1993, p. B6.

37. Edmund Husserl, *The Crisis of European Sciences and Transcendental Phenomenology*, tr. David Carr (Evanston, Ill.: Northwestern University Press, 1970), p. 32, and Martin Heidegger, *What Is a Thing?* trs. W. B. Barton, Jr., and Vera Deutsch (South Bend, Ind.: Regnery/Gateway, 1967). This refers to Husserl and Heidegger's point that with the advent of modern physics, what constitutes knowledge for the entire civilization is not based on qualities *inside* of things, as ancient Greek physics (valid up to Galileo) used to assume. Instead, knowledge is based on *external laws*, which measure quantities of things and their relations. Scientific knowledge of this sort denies the validity of the inner experience of life.

38. See Husserl and Heidegger, above, footnote 37, as well as the discussions of culture and cognition in Chapters 2 and 5 based on Heidegger.

39. This theme is further developed in R. P. Hummel, "The Two Traditions of Knowledge: Quality Management and the Crisis of Quantity," in Don Calista, ed., *Bureaucratic and Governmental Reform*, vol. 9 of *Public Policy Studies Series: A Multivolume Treatise* (New York: JAI Press, 1986).

40. From Max Weber's essay "Parliament and Government in a Reconstructed Germany," Appendix II of *Economy and Society*, pp. 1381–1469; citation from pp. 1403 and 1404. The last paragraph has been retranslated by the present author from the German "Parlament und Regierung im Neugeordneten Deutschland: Zur politischen Kritik des Beamtentums

und Parteiwesens," in Max Weber, *Gesammelte Politische Schriften*, 2nd ed., ed. Johannes Winckelmann (Tübingen [West Germany]: J. C. B. Mohr [Paul Siebeck], 1958), pp. 294–431, from pp. 322–23, because of omissions in the original translation. The material in brackets represents a synthesis of Weber's third point, which he himself neglected to put in question form.

41. Sheldon Wolin, *Politics and Vision: Continuity and Innovation in Western Political Thought* (Boston: Little, Brown, 1960), p. 416.

42. Wolin, op. cit., p. 425, citing Lenin, *Selected Works*, Vol. II, pp. 447–48, 456 (Footnote 1).

43. Ralph P. Hummel and Robert A. Isaak, *The Real American Politics* (Englewood Cliffs, N.J.: Prentice-Hall, 1986), pp. 88–89, 104–105, and 109.

44. For a thorough survey, see David Nachmias and David H. Rosenbloom, *Bureaucratic Government U.S.A.* (New York: St. Martin's Press, 1980).

45. John F. Kennedy, quoted by Lou Harris in *The Anguish of Change* (New York: Norton, 1973), p. 15.

46. Donald Schön, *Beyond the Stable State* (New York: Norton, 1971), p. 123.

47. Michael Malbin, *Unelected Representatives: Congressional Staff and the Future of Representative Government* (New York: Basic Books, 1980), p. 247.

48. Personal communication with Prof. Raymond Cox, then of Northern Arizona State University. See also Raymond Cox and Michael R. King, "American State Legislatures: Models of Organization and Reform," paper presented at the annual meeting of the Midwest Political Science Association, Chicago, April 17–20, 1985.

49. The issue is explored in Shoshana Zuboff, *In the Age of the Smart Machine: The Future of Work and Power* (New York: Basic Books, 1988). For an application to the public service: David Carnevale and Ralph Hummel, "The Soul in the Machine: Quality, Power, and the Future of Work," forthcoming.

50. See Ralph P. Hummel, "Behind Quality Management: What Workers and a Few Philosophers Have Always Known and How It Adds Up to Excellence in Production," vol. 16, no. 1 (Summer 1987), pp. 71–78.

51. Husserl, *The Crisis of European Sciences*, p. 17: "In our philosophizing, then—how can we avoid it?—we are *functionaries of mankind*." His emphasis.

1

Bureaucracy as the New Society

Bureaucracy is the means of transforming social action into rationally organized action.

—Max Weber[1]

Imagine you are in a box. Operating instructions tell you how to use various levers to operate tools attached to the box to work on objects outside the box. You can see the objects through a glass bottom and you can also see there are tools protruding from other boxes; these work on the same objects you work on. In these other boxes, you assume, there are people like yourself. Occasionally, you would like to speak to them to get one of their tools out of your way or to work with you in jointly grasping an object. However, this is prevented by the fact that each of you is in a box.

The good news is that you can relate to people in other boxes if you first ask permission from a person in a box above you. You can see this person because there is a glass ceiling in your box. You are linked to him through a speaking tube. The bad news is that the up-valve is open only when he or she decides to open a down-valve, through which come orders. In short the system of boxes is set up so you can do the job assigned to you—but without much questioning of the orders or the job description and without contact with your co-workers.

Congratulations! You are working in a bureaucracy. You will recognize the division of labor so characteristic of bureaucracy: your box and the working boxes next to you. And you will recognize hierarchy: the box just a little higher up that has a one-way channel of ordering you around and that controls whether and how you relate to the working of others.

This is what the founding sociologist of the study of bureaucracy meant when he said: "Bureaucracy is *the* means of transforming social action into rationally organized action." Its guiding image is the organization chart. It places people into the boxes of jobs, all of which are so designed as to be perfectly logical means to the goal of the totality of boxes: the organization. This organization looks like this:

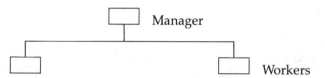

Its advantages and frustrations are cut from the same blueprint. Workers in their assigned jobs soon work out more sensible ways of relating to their work than can be contained in the instructions.* Since workers in related jobs focus on the same work, they soon respond to the possibility of using their tools in a coordinated way that makes sense from observation of how the object responds. In short, their natural contact with the work and others jointly working on the work inspires them to turn the shape of hierarchy upside down:

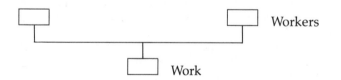

This conflict represents the core tension in the social relations of bureaucracy. The conflict is that between bureaucracy and society. To the extent this rebellion succeeds, the organization falls apart or is destroyed. But to the extent that the organization can keep people from relating to work and others in their own way, it becomes, in Weber's words, *the* control instrument without compare. It takes the place of society. Society, as the system of social relations built by people engaged in a common project, is replaced when bureaucracy assigns a project from the top down and takes all our relating to each other out of our hands.

All the pathologies of social relationships associated with bureaucracy —between clients and bureaucracy, between citizens and bureaucracy, between managers and functionaries of bureaucracy, and most important between workers and their work—result from this original seizure of the society-building impulse of human beings.

---

*The special problems this creates for modern organizations are discussed in the chapters on language and thought.

HOW PEOPLE ACT

The Citizen versus Bureaucracy

The man and woman in the street experience the upside-down nature of bureaucratic society every day.* They feel the coldness and impersonality with which they are typically treated by the street-level functionaries of a bureaucracy. They, of course, mistake these for fellow citizens, not realizing that these are functionaries imprisoned in the box of their jobs. Citizens expect to be treated as citizens, but the job instructs functionaries to treat them as objects on which to perform work. Before he walked into the doors of, say, the New York Motor Vehicles Department, our man in the street was a proud car owner, a man of substance because he could own a car, a man with some degree of self-esteem because he just steered that car through difficult traffic—in other words, a human being with class, status, and unique personality. Once inside the door, he is told to stand in line, fill out forms just so, accept the rejection of the way he filled out his forms, told to stand in the same line again to wait another hour or so, required to answer the questions of the man or woman behind the desk, directed to another line, and so on.

> They made me feel like a kid, like I didn't have a brain in my head. The whole thing didn't make sense. First one line, then another. Then they sent me back to my insurance agent for my F-1 form I didn't know I was supposed to have. I told them I just took off the day to get my license plates and couldn't take off another. Couldn't they just give me my plates and I would mail in my form? No! The rules say . . . blah, blah . . . another day shot.
> —*Man interviewed outside a Motor Vehicles Department office*[2]

"They made me feel like a kid. . . ." The client here commits his first and almost universal error in misunderstanding bureaucracy. Actually, he is turned into less than a child in the eyes of the bureaucrat. He is turned into a "case." The bureaucrat has no time and no permission to become involved in the personal problems of clients. From the bureaucrats' point of view, the more they can depersonalize the client into a thing devoid of unique features, the more easily and smoothly they will be able to handle cases before them.

Here is where the client commits a second mistake of misunderstanding. In the world from which the client has just come, the world outside the bureaucracy's door, there are many areas of life in which it is absolutely necessary to take into account the unique personality of the person

---

*As throughout the book, each difference between society and bureaucracy is here first treated experientially. A theory of the bureaucratic society is offered at the end of this first section. The insights of experts, whose work serves as a foundation for the theory, are presented in a later section.

with whom you are dealing. Friendship and salesmanship are two of these areas. When you go to a friend for help, he or she helps you in a personal and intimate way precisely because you are unique—because you are you, a friend. If you are trying to sell door-to-door, whether it is cosmetics or life insurance, you had better take into account the unique state of mind of the individual you are selling to. It may make a difference to know that a housewife's husband has just put her on a strict budget or that the person you are trying to sell life insurance to has just that day lost a relative.

Yet when the Avon representative and the sales people from Prudential walk into the Motor Vehicles Department, they see themselves treated in exactly the opposite way from how they would treat their clients, their customers. The normal assumption, the second misunderstanding engaged in, runs along the following lines:

> Those goddamn bureaucrats behind the counter got it soft. They got Civil Service, can't get fired. I knock myself out with every customer; they can just kiss me off. They should have my job for a while, they'd try harder.
> —*The same man interviewed outside the Motor Vehicles Department*[3]

The misunderstanding is typical. What the client here fails to understand is that the pressures on the bureaucrat behind the counter are such that the very same behaviors that a client finds objectionable guarantee the bureaucrat "success" within the rules of his or her bureaucracy—not just this bureaucracy, any organization running on the modern bureaucratic model. In Weber's words, "Bureaucracy develops the more perfectly, the more it is 'dehumanized'."[4]

This kind of statement seems to fly in the face of all common sense. Is not a public service bureaucracy, especially, set up to provide public service? The answer has to be yes. By definition it is set up to provide service. But it is also set up to be a bureaucracy!

The Bureaucrat and the Client

There are many ways of giving public service. The Salvation Army gives public service. Parishioners in your local church collect money to give to the poor at Christmas. Society women hold a charity ball. You give to a poorly dressed man holding out his hand on a street corner. Whether any of these ways of giving are bureaucratic remains to be examined. The last two examples are likely to be unbureaucratic.

SERVICE WITHOUT A SMILE

Bureaucracy is a particular strategy, chosen from among others, through which public service can be given. Weber indicated the chief characteristic of bureaucracy as a specific organizational strategy for giving service: It is characterized by "rationally organized action" not by "social action." In fact, it transforms social action into rationally organized action.

In brief, the way bureaucrats relate to clients is analogous to the way people in one country relate to people from an entirely different country. Bureaucrats can't help the way they act—if they want to remain employed members of bureaucracy. There is something innate in bureaucracy that turns bureaucrats into people who provide service coldly, impersonally, without a frown or a smile. Even when there are smiles, to the extent that a bureaucracy is to remain a control instrument, these smiles must be authorized.

The newcomer to a bureaucracy, intending to keep the job, and the client approaching a bureaucracy, wanting to get service and still remain sane, had better understand the difference in the codes of behavior built into society and bureaucracy; that is, the conflict of "social action" versus "rationally organized action."

The alternative, even for the experienced bureaucrat, can be eternal puzzlement. A social worker for Catholic Charities talks about her attempts to get humane, personal attention for her clients from welfare case workers:

In dealing with clients we would eventually have to take certain clients down to welfare, Social Security, the board of education and they would see a caseworker.

Still, no one is interested in what your problem is. The caseworker screens you like you have applied for a Banker's Trust loan.

Eventually you get pretty tired of all the bullshit questions and ask, Are you so inhuman that you can't deal with the client as a person? Then, being the dedicated caseworkers that they are, they'll give you some crap about the manual not allowing for that.

If you still continue along this line of questioning the caseworker—or, as they call it, harassment of the caseworker—they will read you the rules and regulations of the welfare department.

All of this keeps you in line and keeps them uninvolved. . . .

Bureaucracy, as you say, is *the* means of transforming social action into rationally organized action. Which is what any well-organized agency will do, in that they cut through the bull and get to *their* main objectives, not *yours*.[5]

Ultimately, functionaries who cannot accept the restrictions of bureaucratic service leave, or are forced to leave, the bureaucracy. A former social worker tells of the frustrations that led to her being fired:

For two and a half years, I was a social worker for a private child caring agency which cared for dependent and neglected children. Since these children were all from New York City, our agency was funded by the City of New York and thus we were bound by the rules of the Bureau of Child Welfare of the city's Social Service Department.

My job was to provide casework services to the children and their families. The goal was to come up with some long-range plans for the child—hopefully to reunite him with his family or to place him in a long-range foster home. I had a regular caseload and visited the families every two weeks.

I had a difficult time adjusting to some of the rules set up by both New York City and the agency that employed me. We always had to become somewhat detached from our clients. It was not my job to get involved in determining how much welfare money my clients received. Almost all of them were receiving public assistance and it was easy to see that it wasn't enough.

I recall using my own money to buy Christmas gifts so that the parents would give them to the children when they spent the holidays with them. I occasionally brought food with me to my clients because it was easy to see that their public assistance allotment wasn't enough.

I never told this to my employer.

Our agency had a rule that the parents could come and visit the children every other Sunday. I remember feeling frustrated over this, as I felt that it was hardly enough contact. I remember asking how this decision was arrived at and being told by my supervisor that he didn't know: It had always been that way.

I always felt that the bureaucratic process placed a great gap between the social worker and the client. This created much frustration because I guess I felt some human feelings toward these people and couldn't give them what I wanted to. There were too many regulations and forms that got in the way of what I considered to be a good relationship based on needs and feelings.

Thus, I didn't last long.

> —*Elaine G., currently personnel director*
> *for a detention shelter for juveniles*[6]

Despite puzzlement, resentment, and an overpowering sense of frustration, both the Catholic Charities social worker and the child care agency social worker put their finger on essential characteristics of bureaucracy. Their only problem is that they perceive these essentials as pathology.* In their own words, these essentials are:

1. Bureaucracies "get to *their* main objectives, not *yours*."
2. "Regulations and forms" get in the way of "a good [social] relationship based on needs and feelings."

Why is this so? Why should this be so?

WHAT PRICE EFFICIENCY?

Bureaucracy is an efficient means for handling large numbers of people— "efficient" in its own terms. It would be impossible to handle large numbers of people in their full depth and complexity. Bureaucracy is a tool for ferreting out what is relevant to the task for which the bureaucracy was

---

*The citizen of the social world typically has this difficulty of being unable to believe that the dehumanizing characteristics of bureaucracy are the result of design rather than the result of a systems breakdown. This is exactly equivalent to the story of an old Italian immigrant to the United States who remembers: "When I first came to New York, off the boat, I thought the people were crazy. They couldn't even speak Italian." This observation neglected the fact that Americans were all crazy the same way: They all spoke English.

established. As a result, only those facts in the complex lives of individuals that are relevant to that task need be communicated between the individual and the bureaucracy.

To achieve this simplification, the modern bureaucrat has invented the "case." At the intake level, individual personalities are converted into cases. Only if a person can qualify as a case is he or she allowed treatment. More accurately, a bureaucracy is never set up to treat or deal with persons: It "processes" only "cases."

Once this is understood, the uncanny fact is explained that within a bureaucracy you will never find clients in the form of human beings. They can have existence for the bureaucracy only as truncated paper ghosts of their former selves—as cases.

This simple fact of bureaucratic life is seldom communicated to prospective clients in any explanatory way. Clients continue to assume they are addressing the bureaucracy for help as they define it in all their complex individuality. The intake section of a bureaucracy usually resembles a theater of war. In fact it *is* a theater of war. The war is one between two cultures. It is conducted by two totally different personality types, according to two totally different rules of war. The opposing armies cannot even shout threats or imprecations at one another very well; their languages are too different.

The Client as "Case" and the Policymaker

What is a case? A case is never a real person. A case is a series of characteristics abstracted from persons; it is a model of those characteristics that a potential client must display in order to qualify for the attention of a bureaucracy, whether for service or control. Definitions of what constitutes a case have far-flung impact not only directly on clients—who are accepted or rejected by comparison to those definitions—but on policy formation.

For example, case definition was crucial when one of the watchdog organizations appointed to keep an eye on New York City's finances noted a strange phenomenon in 1984: The city's public assistance "caseload" was continuing to rise at a time of high economic growth at both the national and local level.[7] In its attempts to explain such public assistance growth and to forecast future trends, the state's Office of the Special Deputy Comptroller for the City of New York needed to do two things: define what constituted "public assistance" and define under what conditions people could be expected to become "cases" that would add to the city's financial burden: that is, its caseload.

The Deputy Comptroller's Office defined public assistance as including benefits to indigent people under two major programs: Aid to Families with Dependent Children (AFDC) and Home Relief (HR).

AFDC was defined as providing "assistance to families with dependent children that are deprived of support due to the death, prolonged absence, incapacity or unemployment of a parent."

HR was defined as providing "financial assistance to indigent persons who do not meet Federal eligibility requirements for the AFDC program, including persons with substantial physical or mental impairments, unemployed young adults with limited training or work experience, and families with very low incomes." It also was defined as providing "temporary assistance to persons who are awaiting eligibility determination for the Supplemental Security Income (SSI) program, a Federally administered program which provides assistance to certain aged, blind or disabled individuals." These, of course, are summary definitions based on operational case definitions authorized for case "intake."

USING THE CASE IN POLICY ANALYSIS

Without definitions of who is likely to come onto the city's "case rolls," it would be impossible to explain or predict the financial load on the city's coffers. Using such definitions, the Deputy Comptroller's Office was able

Figure 1.1: Gross City Product (Lagged 1 Year) vs. Number of AFDC Recipients in New York City

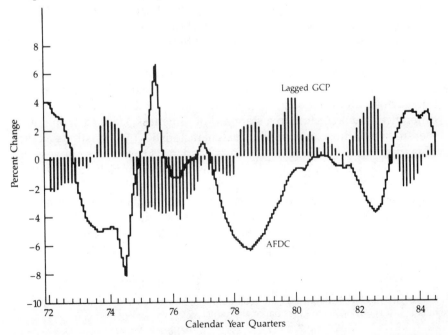

to construct an econometric model to explain the relationship between caseload and fluctuations in the city's economy as measured by gross city product, an indicator of the city's economic strength.*

By lagging gross city product one year behind the number of cases of AFDC, technical staff concluded that any trickledown effect of prosperity on the poor was delayed. Based on the past pattern of such delay, staff was able to predict that the growth in the city's AFDC caseload would level off or possibly decline over the near term, a trend already evident in a recipient decline of ten thousand between May and October of 1984—a drop of about 1 percent.

Even for those less than interested in whether the City of New York can survive carrying its public assistance caseload there is a lesson here. The "case" is not only the basic definition of whether a person in need officially can come to exist to the eyes and ears of bureaucracy; it is also the basis for all calculation of future needs of a bureaucracy and of the entire political system as it engages in providing government services and controls. By the time a human being is allowed to enter a bureaucracy as a case, that human being already no longer exists as a human being. That human being becomes a list of specific characteristics that the bureaucracy has been authorized by law to recognize as a case. Given our bias today toward measurement and numbers, such characteristics are believed to be more real if they can be defined in terms of calculations. For example, imposing an age range on who is meant by unemployed "young" adults makes it possible for all future calculations of an agency's needs and operations to be based on the *same* unit of calculation.

Herein lies not only a fundamental difference between people's self-perception when they stand in society and the client's official status as perceived by bureaucrats as the clients enter bureaucracy. In ordinary social life, each of us considers ourself to be a unique human being. In bureaucratic life, each of us is examined not according to our individual differences but according to a standard of sameness: Does each one of us measure up to those universally *same* characteristics that constitute a case? This trust in being able to create units of analysis based on sameness out of a population defining itself in terms of differences has, of course, fundamental and ultimate impact on this ultimate policy question: Can a policy and an administrative system based on calculations of *sameness* be designed to satisfy the needs of a population defining itself on the basis of *differentness*? To the extent that this is not possible, the calculations may be exact and even aesthetically pleasing, but they will have little or nothing to do with reality.

---

*Gross city product is defined as the total output of city goods and services adjusted for inflation. It is analogous to gross national product.

The Functionary and the Manager

The dehumanization of the functionary–client relationship is hard to understand, especially in public service agencies. After all, such agencies were set up to serve clients, or so clients keep saying. The classic remonstrance from a client with taxpayer consciousness is and always has been: "You're *my* employee. My taxes pay your salary. Now let's get some service around here!"

Bureaucracy as Organization

Yet this attitude ignores the nature of bureaucracy. After all, why do we have bureaucracy? If we stop thinking of it for a moment in its negative, dehumanizing role and compare bureaucracy to previous forms of organizing administration, we are left with one answer only. Bureaucracy, as a form of organization, is the most powerful instrument yet developed for getting people to work together on monumentally large common tasks. Modern bureaucracy harnesses more power than any, and possibly all, of the great projects of antiquity. As a form of organization, it makes possible the control of literally millions of people. And all these millions can be directed to one big project—bigger than building the pyramids, larger than the Roman Empire.

We live, as Weber pointed out, in an age of "universal bureaucratization."[8] "In a modern state," he wrote, essaying the impact of World War I on the process of bureaucratization, "the actual ruler is necessarily and unavoidably the bureaucracy. . . ."[9] Similarly, in a more recent work, Henry Jacoby explores, as the book's title indicates, "the bureaucratization of the world."[10]

What underlies this triumph of bureaucracy is its ability to amass and direct power.* It does so better than any competing organization. And it does so whether in the private sector, as in the organization of modern business and industry, or in the public or political sectors, as in public service or the management of campaigns. The world over, those countries that have resisted "modernization"—that is, the introduction of bureaucratic organization and its norms—have been pushed aside and into the backwaters of history by modern, bureaucratized countries. In this sense the organization of China's Communist party was as much a triumph of bureaucracy as *the* form of modern organization as was the conquest of countries and continents by Western European nations in the nineteenth century.[11] Similarly, the state apparatus of one of the world's largest polit-

---

*Its weakness, of course, comes from hierarchy's increasing detachment from the practical imperative emanating from work itself.

ical organizations, the Soviet Union, up to the point of its final petrification became one of the most successful control mechanisms in the world for exactly the reason that Weber predicted when socialism was first introduced in Russia: "Increasing 'socialization' today unavoidably means increasing bureaucratization."[12]

BUREAUCRACY AS CONTROL

What does the victory of bureaucracy as a control instrument of unparalleled power mean to people in everyday life? Listen to the complaint of a functionary in the personnel department of the Cleveland, Ohio, Board of Education.

For a long time, I felt my role within the bureaucracy was to deal with human needs. In recent years, accountability has become so important, however, that I now must spend more and more time completing forms and compiling records. In many instances this work is duplicated by others and there is less time devoted to rendering service.

My program director is caught up in this control situation and is constantly seeking new control methods and reactivating dormant rules. We had the sign-in and the sign-out procedure, the daily log, weekly, bi-weekly, monthly and yearly reports; now, we have a management information retrieval system.

When similar information about all workers in the program is placed in the system, management can then analyze this data and attempt to control the daily work schedule and work distribution. Before all this paperwork there was more productivity. It seems that accountability and productivity are not compatible.
—*Richard W., curriculum specialist*[13]

Here a functionary has put his finger on two countervailing pressures of bureaucracy that express themselves in the meaning of "rationally organized action."

VISIBLE VERSUS INVISIBLE ACTION

In bureaucracy, action is rational on two grounds: first, if an action is a *logical* means to a clearly defined end; second, if and only if action is performed in such a manner that its means–ends logic is *visible*. Action within bureaucracy must not only be action; it must also be subject to control. If it is not subject to control, it is not action. Or, rather, it may be action, but bureaucracy itself cannot take official notice of it.

This double aspect of action as defined in the modern era stems from our concept of science and pervades all the kinds of technology that institutionalize action. Science recommends this definition; technology, including modern bureaucracy as the technology of management, enforces it.

A social scientist like sociologist Talcott Parsons will include the double demand for both logic and visibility in a definition:

Action is rational in so far as it pursues ends possible within the conditions of the situation, and by the means which, among those available to the actor, are intrinsically best adapted to the end *for reasons understandable and verifiable by positive empirical science.* [14]

And a bureaucracy will enforce the double aspect by insisting both that work be done in a manner suitable to an overall purpose and that it be done in a visible manner so it can be checked and controlled from above.

Functionaries have a hard time accepting the double aspect. "Why," they typically ask, "do I have to spend hours filling out reports when anybody can see that I've got my work done?" The demand for visibility is especially irritating to civil service personnel whose work is already highly visible to them. A battalion chief in the New York City Fire Department complains:

When the fire's out, the fire's out. Anybody can see that. We've done our job. There's a lot of satisfaction in that.

I don't even mind going over what happened at a big fire with the captains involved. I think it's necessary to debrief. You learn from that. Other people can see things that happened that you missed.

But then there are the reports. And the second guessing from upstairs. And the insisting on regs [regulations]: Does your watch guy have his shirt buttoned, are shoes shined, are buttons on?

If I've got a good team that turns out a topnotch performance at a fire, I'm going to hassle them about a missing button? [15]

Yet bureaucracy is a control instrument and a control instrument without compare. Control is the source of power for this type of organization, and it is natural that those charged with control will emphasize the visible portions of what their subordinates do. As a result, instituting standard operating procedures and basing assessment of performance on observed compliance with these is a natural and normal solution to the problem of control experienced by an organization that grows larger and larger.

The results of such emphasis on the visible are also inevitable. Eventually control comes to mean largely checking that procedures are followed—instead of looking at impact. [16]

What can be controlled are jobs; these are not necessarily the same as work. Jobs are defined top down according to goals as understood rationalistically by management; work is what functionaries actually do to carry out actions that mesh with reality. These then must be made to resemble job descriptions in official reports. A weakness of bureaucracy is that, when jobs and work diverge, managers tend to mistake official reports for work actually done. In other words, for the sake of visible procedures that can be easily supervised by control personnel (management), the first condition of modern rational action—that action be logically connected to some substantive end or purpose—is finally abandoned. Formality conquers substance.

The Organization and the Training of Citizens

A classic example of the loss of substance is the way teachers are forced to organize their teaching in most public schools. In an essay on alienation and bureaucracy, Michael P. Smith puts his finger on exactly that point at which the demand for controllable, visible work, with no other reason for being than its visibility, actually destroys work that is purposeful.

In many urban school systems excessive bureaucratization also has resulted in the routinization of teaching practices, which, in turn, has added to the deindividualization of the learning process. Even those teachers and principals who are person-oriented rather than task-oriented can be constrained by the weight of procedural strictures and paper work emanating from the central headquarters staff. In the St. Louis public school system, for example, teachers at the elementary level are required to organize their entire work week according to a printed form. Such behavior leaves little room for spontaneity or that leap of imagination we call creativity.[17]

The bias in favor of the visible, which can be recorded on paper and preferably in numbers, inevitably leads to results contrary to human intentions simply because less visible and qualitative aspects of human relations are left out of account. The following summary of a qualitative study of four high schools in the San Francisco Bay area is not atypical:

We have inadvertently designed a system in which being good at what you do as a teacher is not formally rewarded, while being poor at what you do is seldom corrected or penalized.[18]

"Every 50 minutes," the principal investigator said, "1,500 people play musical chairs. Like clockwork, people are moving from one place to another and, in the course of four to five minutes, must switch from thinking about the industrial revolution to the solution of a quadratic equation."[19]

How does this feel from a student's perspective? A star pupil, Charlotte Krepismann:

What it all comes down to is that the average student is remarkably unquestioning, accepting as normal that one moves from little box to little box [sometimes with the teacher in mid-sentence].[20]

This early training for service in bureaucracy—by inculcating an acceptance of hierarchy and division of labor—does ultimately have its comeuppance in adult reality. But by then the victim is safely removed from the school, and the school can continue to pride itself in its internal fragmentation not only of social relationships but of the meaning of the entire formal school experience. Political scientist and educational administration specialist David Schuman reports, for example, that his own in-depth study of college graduates showed these adults most critical of one thing: the fragmenting experience of their college life, disabling them from making coherent sense of real life, which after all is experienced in its totality.[21]

These examples contain two truths about the nature of bureaucratic action:

1. In bureaucracy, action can be recognized and rewarded even though it has become totally detached from people, as in the contrast between person-oriented and task-oriented school personnel.
2. In bureaucracy, action can be recognized and required even though it has become totally detached from an object—the teaching process from what is being learned, for example,

But where does bureaucratic action come from? How does bureaucratic society get its origins?

A THEORY OF BUREAUCRATIC SOCIETY

What It Means to Be Social

Being social has always meant establishing a sense that each of us is not alone. This is so basic to human existence that people who lose their sense of society engage in extreme behaviors such as suicide[22] and homicide.[23] Being social means establishing a sense that we live in the world secure in the company of others, sharing a meaningful life with fellow human beings. The word comes from the Latin *socius*, companion. The dictionary defines society as a group of persons living in a single community. But what makes such a life possible? I know myself; how can I know others? I could answer that it is impossible to think of myself without already assuming the existence of others.[24] Traditionally sociologists have thought that to know others I must discover some kind of bridge to them. Something must be held in common to which we all can refer and, in the sharing of which, we see each other as essentially the same: fellow human beings.

The Working Origins of Society

In the past, what was shared by people in a society was work.

Say they were working together on something. Perhaps something physical like emptying a boat of water. The physical serves as a corrective to mere idle thinking about what is going on. But in serving as a corrective to what otherwise would be the arbitrary idea of each, the physical serves also as a common point of reference.

As the hammer betrays me in trying to shovel water, so it betrays the body that I see hammering away at water next to me. Appropriate approaches to accomplishing work can be observed among myself and a body that also looks like me. Seeing that body discard the hammer and reach for a bailer, just as I do, raises in me the suspicion that he is a being affected by physical reality in the same way as I am.

As our acts are observed to shape the orientation of each one of us toward the physical, we are able to conclude that we are beings capable of sharing the same or similar experience.

In the words of the sociologist Alfred Schutz:

By my working acts I gear myself into the outer world, I change it; and these changes, although provoked by my working, can be experienced and tested both by myself and others, as occurrences within this world independently of my working acts in which they originated. I share this world and its objects with Others; with Others, I have ends and means in common; I work with them in manifold social acts and relationships, checking with Others and checked by them. And the world of working is the reality within which communication and the interplay of mutual motivation becomes effective.[25]

In short we know each other socially by reference to something we hold in common: each act of work.

This is how we used to approach society in a natural attitude toward work and fellow human beings. Modern organization does not totally destroy this basis of fellow being; it tries to totally control it. Above all, it attempts to control the natural growth of the sense of fellow being that arises from the natural relation of individuals with shared work. If shared working on objects, their "give" and their resistances, is the common reference point for a sense of fellow being, then the organization that wants to control the sense of fellow being must control the reference point. This hierarchy does by assigning to itself, and to itself alone, the right to design work. It encapsules work in prescriptions of how to approach it designed ahead of the approach: jobs.

The Origins of Bureaucratic Society in Jobs

In modern organization, the best I can do to establish a sense of fellow human being with someone else is to look to the assigned content of job roles. Descriptions of typical action and orientation are assigned to each job role; these can be printed, read, and in a formal sense understood. Since we are able to learn each other's job roles, we can orient ourselves to each other—have reasonable expectations of each other's behavior—based on these roles. The strength of the organization—the ability to rely on constant and entirely predictable job behavior—comes from our orienting ourselves to what each job directs the inmate to do. Set aside in organizational expectations are the entirely unpredictable emotionality and spontaneity of the inmate her- or himself.

In modern organization we know each other as fellow beings by reference to shared jobs; these are frozen patterns of expectations, *typifications*, of what we are to do and what we can expect others to do. Jobs seem to act independent of the holder of the job. But their patterns are constructed not by us but by management.[26]

The basis for a sense of social being is now at least once removed from my own ability to construct it; we have to trust that the social structure to which we are assigned by our jobs *does* have a basis somewhere in a reality of work. We must engage in an act of faith that the social structure represented as necessary is not just the arbitrary fantasy of those in the hierarchy. Much against our natural tendency, we ourselves are no longer permitted to reality-test our social relations on the basis of our contact with work. And, when our contact with work casts doubt on the validity of typifications of each other assigned by management, we are supposed to ignore such doubts. Does this reduce our ability to forecast the behavior of others? Can we find some sense of identity and stability in the social structure? Don't worry! Management can and will enforce the typifications that box in others as much as yourself.

The Basis of Sociality in Late Modern Organization

A further step of distancing our sense of social being from its direct ground in contact with the physical is taken in late modernity: when the computer puts another "interface" between us and reality. Listen to what one operator of a computer-controlled factory says of his sense of social being:

The new technology really brings people together. You need people who can understand electronics, programming, and the complexity of the information. It requires teamwork because you need to have different specialties and understanding to work together. This type of computer system will always bring people together because you have to discuss what you see, what you understand, what you know, and what should be done.[27]

Here what brings people together is not directly the knowledge of each other's job description—though this lurks in the background as "specialties"—but the images that are projected on the computer screen. What can be displayed on the screen, however, is more than ever controlled by someone other than the worker: namely, computer engineers and programmers hired by management.

The social structure of the late modern organization is built on reference to jointly experienced computer images. Social structure is not built on the reality of the machines or the skills needed to lay hands on the processes behind the computer, out there in the bleach plant. But the images do not always correspond to what is really happening. Operators frequently run out into the plant to see what really is going on. The result is a sense of disjointed reality.

The managed social structure is as shaky here, if not more so,[28] as it is in the early modern organization. Here is how one manager expressed both the challenge from work and the shakiness of the social power structure:

They [the workers] want to have access to real-time data from the mills. But as plant manager, I do not want to be second-guessed. I don't want them breathing down my neck or wasting their time on the nitty-gritty from the shop floor. Right now, I have some flexibility in terms of deciding what data they need to see, when they see it, and how it is presented. If I lose control over that, it is an important piece of my job over which I will have less control.[29]

As work-centered skills are replaced by job-centered and computer-mediated routines, the researcher from whom the above examples are drawn concludes, "the intrinsic meaning of the work dries up," workers no longer see work as the source of their self, and they become cynical. But cynicism is the response to disappointment when the sense of what is right and proper is taken away. That sense in human work tells us to be in touch with work as the paramount source of reality. Ultimately we live in a physical world: The plumbing has to be repaired, the wires drawn, people dealt with in their embodiment before we can revel in the world of images. Images don't feed the world; working bodies do. It is contact with the physical world that we sense can ultimately be relied upon as the whetstone against which to sharpen the sense of one's self and a foundation on which to build a solid and meaningful social structure.

The Basis of Social Reality in Work

A paradox—the demand that we accept two contradictory dogmas of what is real—is built into any experience we can have of modern organizations from the very beginning. This comes from the conflict between work and job, or between the experience of physical reality and virtual reality.

Job defines what we are supposed to do in interaction with reality as scientific management experts see it. Actual work, however, is defined by what we find ourselves as having to do as we work to come to terms with factors in reality not captured in the job description or by the virtual reality on the computer screen.*

Inevitably the reality we "work out" in our interactions with the objects we belabor contradicts how things "are supposed to work out" according to the definition of the job or what the computer says is real.

*Compare the section on Edmund Husserl in Chapter 5 on "The Thought of Bureaucracy."

This casts doubt on the validity of the organizationally created social structure that is designed to support our jobs or virtual realities and in which we are expected to feel at home. The result is what has been characterized as "the homeless mind."[30]

Formal social structure, in its claim to provide a totally meaningful world for its inmates, challenges our very experience of work. This experience suggests to me nothing less than that my working constitutes me as a self, through the integration of present, past, and future into a specific dimension of time. I realize myself as a totality in my working acts. I am enabled to communicate with others through working acts. By controlling my work from the outside in, bureaucracy also controls in the most primordial sense who and what I am and what is real to me.[31] If meaningful action is conduct motivated in terms of a preconceived project[32]—i.e., the "working out" activity that realizes a plan—then bureaucracy also tries to control all meaning in my world.

Bureaucratic Society

The theory of bureaucratic society, then, makes these assumptions:

1. The social knowledge we have of each other in bureaucracy as the official society is based on reference to jobs or, lately, a computer-programmed virtual reality. We learn to know each other in terms of second-order constructs: our jobs or images on a screen.
2. Job design and reality design are out of our hands. They are in the hands of organization designers, managers, and computer programmers.
3. Social reality is no longer self-enforcing, based on the mutual assumptions of its creators and participants; it must be enforced by management discipline. (It is more difficult to run a constitution than to make it.)
4. It follows that inmates of the bureaucratic society lack the sense of deep immersion in their social relations that comes from their natural growth out of mutual experience based on the solidity of physical work: encountering objects or human beings.
5. Actual work, however, continues within and outside of official job descriptions or computer realities. This means primary social relations continue to be created, and so do competing definitions of self and reality. From this follows that the plausibility and legitimacy of bureaucratic society are fragile and shaky. They are secondary and are vulnerable to attack based on primary working and social experiences.
6. To ward off challenges from primary social experiences, bureaucratic society must attempt to become totalitarian: that is, to stamp out or otherwise render harmless all areas of autonomous experience within which natural social relations based on work can grow.
7. Everyday coldness, policing, and persecution of nonauthorized social actions and orientations are simply defense mechanisms of the bureaucracy. These are its attempts to maintain total control of employees' orientation toward its social structure as the basis for total control action. Nothing personal.

In short, social orientations within bureaucracy are always twofold: The official structure tries to wipe out natural social structure yet naturally growing social relations intrude into offical bureaucratic society. The injuries and social hurts experienced by clients and employees in and with bureaucracy are the result of this fact: The social individual working in or facing bureaucracy lives in the tension between artificial society and natural society.

In summary, social relations in bureaucracy and society can be characterized as follows:

In Bureaucracy	In Society
• Originate in management	• Originate in work
• Are laid down in job typifications	• Are laid down in ongoingly constructed mutual orientations
• Are secondary	• Are primary
• Are subject to challenge	• Are fundamental
• Need to be enforced	• Are self-enforcing

The two primary tools of social control are hierarchy and the division of labor. Hierarchy initially divides labor. But those doing labor are expected to co-laborate even while being denied access to each other. For approved knowledge of how they might co-laborate, they must turn to the superior who links them: Hence, hierarchy's power itself is based on the division of labor.*

Control Relationships

All of the often-complained-about structural characteristics of bureaucracy —like the division of labor, which gives no single functionary enough power to do anything alone but allows him or her to specialize, or the requirement that the functionary treat clients not personally but as cases—are derived from the imperative of control.

The division of labor, for example, has two purposes. On the one hand, it makes a functionary capable of developing highly specialized skills. The advantage of this may be that the bureaucracy can bring to bear on a specific problem an individual who has the ideal capabilities to resolve that problem. It makes possible the development of the expert. On the other hand, because of specialization, it is often impossible for one expert to solve an overall problem without the cooperation of other experts. And to mobilize this cooperation we need the manager.

We now have arrived at a most important insight into the whys and wherefores of the structural arrangements of bureaucracy. People's work is divided not only to make them expert and more efficient but also to make them dependent on managerial control.

*See the discussion of hierarchy and division of labor in Chapter 6, "Bureaucracy as Polity."

If you want to survive as a bureaucrat, you will never forget that the prime relationship you engage in is that between you and your manager, not that between you and your client. And that functionary–manager relationship is a control relationship. The successful manager never forgets this.

In many public service bureaucracies the choice between service and control is being made every day. A police officer on the beat may truly want to render a service to a citizen.[33] In fact, contrary to popular misconception, the kinds of behavior of which police are most proud and which they recall with great self-respect are instances of personal service they have rendered to citizens. An anonymous patrolman in a midwestern city provides an example:

The things you really do for people, you never get credit for.

I remember picking up this kid out of the gutter three times. High on dope. The fourth time, I start taking him in. His mother comes running up to me and says the kid is going into the army in a couple of days. The medical corps. He'll straighten out. He'll never be on the stuff again. I'm supposed to give him another chance. Three times before!

I must've been out of my skull. I let the kid go. Kid goes in the medical corps, gets his training. Now he's in medical school, becoming a doctor. Once in a while he still keeps writing me letters saying how I saved his life.

Imagine me putting that into my day report![34]

Here is a clear-cut case of an officer of a public service institution rendering an individual citizen a human service. No matter how laudable the patrolman's humanity might be, however, his act also represents a clear-cut breakdown of bureaucratic control. It is a threat against the very existence of the police department as a modern organization that is at least potentially under the control of legitimate political authority.[35]

Against this deterioration of control, managers who intend to keep their jobs as sergeant, lieutenant, or captain of police will defend themselves by such techniques as introducing the use of "shoo-flies" (internal police spies), tightening up on the number of times a patrol officer has to report in by radio, and demanding more written reports on how and on what time was spent. All these assertions of control, of course, take time away from service. But it is a choice a manager cannot help but make.

WHAT THE EXPERTS SAY

What people experience, experts should explain. In the preceding, we have seen that social relations—how humans encounter humans—differ radically between bureaucracy and society. How has this difference been explained by the experts?

Max Weber

The classic, and still leading, expert on bureaucracy is Max Weber, who also gives us a definition of social action outside bureaucracy that underlies much of current sociology.

Social Action

In *Economy and Society,* the theoretical groundwork for his sociology, Weber offers this definition of action and social action:

We shall speak of "action" insofar as the acting individual attaches a subjective meaning to his behavior—be it overt or covert, omission or acquiescence. Action is "social" insofar as its subjective meaning takes account of the behavior of others and is thereby oriented in its course.[36]

What does he mean, and how is what he means relevant for any attempt to distinguish between social action in bureaucracy and in society?

If we take Weber personally, his meaning becomes clear: I am engaged in action when I do something and attach some sort of meaning to what I do. For example, I may be swinging an ax and hacking away at a piece of wood. This behavior, in itself just a physical exercise, becomes action when I attach to my swinging and hacking the intention of ending up with some kindling for the fire.

So far Weber's point about action is merely definitional. He is simply saying to us: This is how I shall define "action" in a purely arbitrary way. But, of course, he has a hidden purpose, and this becomes apparent when we look at the definition of *social* action.

Social action is action not simply of the sort to which *I*, as the actor, attach my personal meaning. It is action in which I take into account the meaning that *others* may attach to it.

For example, if I am in the woods by myself and want some kindling, I may swing and hack at anything that comes along. If Joe is with me, however, I do not want him to misunderstand my wild swinging and hacking as an attack on him. I therefore chop in a very organized way at one piece of wood at a time, hoping Joe will recognize in my care and direction the meaning I attach to my action: "Hey, Joe, I'm chopping at this piece of wood, you see? Not at you!" When I so design my actions that I take into account how others might react, I have begun to transform action, with its purely personal meaning, into social action, which is intended to have meaning for myself and at least one other person.

From this, Weber progresses to the form "social relationship." "The term 'social relationship' will be used to denote the behavior of a plurality of actors insofar as, in its meaningful content, the action of each takes account of that of others and is oriented in these terms."[37] Now we have at least two actors, you and I, for example; and each of us acts in such a way that the other can understand the meaning of the action. I, for example, am now writing these words with the intention of having you understand them. And, you, to the degree that you want to engage in a reader–author (social) relationship with me, read with the intention of understanding me. To the extent that we each direct our actions toward the other, we are engaged in a social relationship.

Now let us ask ourselves to what extent bureaucrats are allowed to engage in either social action or social relationships with their clients. To answer the question, we can simply ask ourselves:

1. To what extent do bureaucrats intend to have their actions understood by clients?
2. To what extent do bureaucrats intend to engage in relationships with clients in which all action rests on mutual understanding?

In our ordinary human life, we treat people as people. We try to understand them and give them a chance to understand us. But what of the bureaucrats' position? Do they wait—*can* they wait—until they are engaged in a relationship of mutual understanding with their clients? The fact is that the machinery of bureaucracy must grind on long before that. What Weber meant to tell all of us working in and living with bureaucracy is that the pressures we feel from being unable to deal with clients as human beings are not occasional. They are not symptomatic of something gone wrong in bureaucracy. They are built into bureaucracy. They are essential to bureaucracy if the great claims of modern organization to greater efficiency and their ability to manipulate large masses of people are to be achieved. Bureaucracy *is* the rational organization of action.

That leaves us with one more of Weber's terms to understand. What is rationally organized action?

RATIONALLY ORGANIZED ACTION

Weber clarifies the character of rationally organized action in another essay, "Some Categories of a Sociology of Understanding," in which he distinguishes between social action, defined as "action based on mutual understanding," and "institutionally commanded action."[38] The first type of action is most developed in that sociohistoric stage of development traditionally called "community." It is also called "communal action" (*Gemeinschaftshandeln*). "We shall speak of communal action," writes Weber, "wherever human action is related in terms of its subjective meaning to the behavior of other human beings."[39]

"Institutionally commanded action" (*Anstaltshandeln*)[40] gradually replaces communal action as community becomes "society"—that is, as human relationships become "socialized." In this new form the actions human beings engage in are designed by others. Individuals are expected to obey society's rules even if they did not have a chance to contribute to their design. In a final stage there is the probability that they can expect to be *forced* to obey.

In the first kind of action, two individuals are considered to be of the same mind, sharing an understanding of each other, because they have contributed to that understanding. In the second type of action, two individuals are of the same mind because they are *forced* into it.[41] This is the kind of action already prefigured in society. Society imposes general rules for proper social behavior, but personal discretion is allowed, providing plenty of room for actions based on mutual understanding. As society becomes more bureaucratic, however, rationally organized action finally collapses that room: In its never-ending search for control over its functionaries, bureaucracy must destroy discretion.

Rationally organized action thus dominates the step that follows community and society in the history of human existence. These stages and their dominant types of action can be portrayed as follows:

community   = communal action based on mutual understanding.
society   = social action: general rules mixed with discretion for exercise
               of understanding within the rules.
bureaucracy = rationally organized action: design of all action from above;
               shrinkage of discretion.

The insight that bureaucracy is a new type of social relationship, first outlined by Weber, is subsequently developed in three directions. Talcott Parsons and the functionalists accept rationally organized action as a necessary condition of the large-scale organizations into which human beings have fitted themselves for survival in the twentieth century.[42] Jürgen Habermas, a successor of both Weber and Karl Marx, criticizes the decline of true social relationships of a personal kind and penetrates the farthest of any academician into the consequences of the new form of human relationships in spheres such as education, technology, and politics.[43] But the third direction in which Weber's insight is developed contributes most intimately to the understanding of our personal experience with bureaucracy. This direction is pursued in the phenomenological sociology of Alfred Schutz.

Alfred Schutz

Phenomenology in this context refers to nothing more than a technique for reducing our experience of life in bureaucracy to its basics. Phenomenology begins with ordinary everyday experience, brackets out the accidental and unessential, and ends up by exposing the fundamentals of any experience.

Where Weber distinguished between social action as constituting ordinary social life and rationally organized action as constituting bureaucratic life, Alfred Schutz asks how such differences are experienced by ordinary human beings. He observed that such ordinary experience divides relationships I have with you into two types: In one I perceive you and myself as part of the same group, as part of a "we"; in the other I perceive you as alien to me, as part of a "they." Phenomenology thus points to two essential and different types of human relationships: the "pure we-relationship" and the "they-relationship."

WE-RELATIONSHIPS

In the pure we-relationship I create my social life with others who have intentions similar to mine. In the they-relationship the social world has been preconstructed for me and my contemporaries, and the problem becomes to get to know them in terms of the significance and role already assigned them by the system. It is easy to see that the we-relationship describes the situation between close friends, whereas the they-relationship describes that between bureaucrat and client, with the bureaucrat being forced to think of the client in terms predefined by the bureaucracy.

The same distinction can be observed between creative or revolutionary political action and institutionalized political action.[44] In creative politics at least two individuals must go through the effort of determining what each of them wants or intends. If their goals or intentions are similar, they then can work out a shared social act that will bring them together, laboring toward those goals. Once this act has worked for them in achieving their shared goals, they may want to repeat it under the assumption: We have done it once, we can do it again. But at that point, institutionalization of politics begins. The second time around, the problem of achieving a want or intention does not have to be apprehended anew. All the participants have to do is identify the want or intention. If it fits into the category of a want or intention previously accomplished by a political action, all they need to say is: "It fits under Political Routine No. 1001B; let's do Political Routine No. 1001B." Typical routines of action replace original and creative action. Bureaucracies and specifically their organizational structures are such routines frozen into permanently repeated patterns; that is, they are institutions. What makes social life appear human is a kind of intimacy I gain from interacting in depth with my consociates—the members of the little world whose center I am and which I enlarge by including you in the we-relationship. In fact, the more I make an effort to understand you in your complexity and the closer to you I feel, the more meaningful and satisfying life in the social world appears to me.

THEY-RELATIONSHIPS

They-relationships tend toward just the opposite pole. Routines, stereo-typing, recipes for action coded in work rules—and the evenhanded application of these to *all* comers—dominate they-relationships. The relationship between bureaucrat and client is easily recognized as the extreme example. Not that human relationships of a personal sort are never used, but they represent a deviation. The bureaucrat who becomes deeply involved in the life of a client is regarded as either undependable or corrupt.

When we think of bureaucracy in the value-free sense, neither condemning nor approbating, we think of the organization of human labor into methodically applying overall institutional goals and functions. The essential characteristics of such a human apparatus can be defined in terms of the inner logic it must come to possess if it is to carry out its predetermined purposes. These terms will be spelled out in the next section, but it already is evident that bureaucracy is the ideal type of the Schutzian they-relationships of the world of contemporaries, located at the polar opposite end from the we-relationships of consociates. In the world of contemporaries, Schutz writes, "we never encounter real living people at all."[45] It is not the face-to-face we-relationship in which "the partners look into each other and are mutually sensitive to each other's response."[46]

Schutz's concept of the they-relationship corresponds to Weber's concept of action that is not social. If we recall the example of the clerk in the license plate office, pressed by office rules and the number of clients, Schutz's concept helps us understand more closely the situation the clerk is in:

I cannot assume, for instance, that my partner in a They-relationship will necessarily grasp the particular significance I am attaching to my words, or the broader context of what I am saying, unless I explicitly clue him in.[47]

For me, as a hard-pressed clerk, there just isn't enough time to penetrate through the cloak of anonymity that having to treat people as cases has thrown over them. "As a result, I do not know, during the process of choosing my words, whether I am being understood or not. . . ."[48]

Few bureaucracies have standards for the functionary's behavior that test the client's understanding of what the functionary has done or said. Schutz points out, "In indirect social experience there is only one way to 'question a partner as to what he means,' and that is to use a dictionary. . . ."[49] This again argues the one-directionality of communication in a bureaucracy. Functionaries are allowed to utter any statement they like from within a repertory assigned them by the organization. They need not see to it that this organizationally approved statement is understood. On the other hand, clients have to bend over backwards to learn the bureaucratic language.

Two Separate Worlds

According to Schutz, the worlds of we-relations and they-relations remain distinct. As a client dealing with a bureaucrat, our ideal type of they-relationship, I am not allowed to know him intimately "unless, of course, I decide to go to see him or to call him up; but in this case I have left the They-relationship behind and have initiated a face-to-face situation."[50] As Schutz indicates, travel between the two worlds involves a special effort on the part of the client to gain personal access to the functionary. Of course, an infinite number of devices—ranging from failure to hand out a telephone number to claims of bureaucratic secrecy, purportedly intended to protect the client's anonymity—protect the bureaucracy and its functionaries from becoming accessible to what Weber called social action and Schutz calls the we-relationship:

In the We-relationship I assume that your environment is identical with my own in all its variations. If I have any doubt about it, I can check on my assumption simply by pointing and asking you if that is what you mean. Such an identification is out of the question in the They-relationship.[51]

Ultimately in the world of contemporaries (here used to include the world of bureaucracy), "we never encounter real living people at all. In that world, whether we are participants or observers, we are only dealing with ideal types. Our whole experience is in the mode of 'They.'"[52] In other words, we are dealing only with cases. But cases are artificial constructs that bureaucracy requires real people to become before they can be considered for service. The motorist must have an insurance form, a driver's license, and an application form, and must be free of driving tickets before qualifying for a license plate; that is, before flesh-and-blood uniqueness can become a generalized case that the bureaucracy is pre-designed to handle. In Schutz's words:

Observation of the social behavior of another involves the very real danger that the observer will naively substitute his own ideal types [case characteristics] for those in the mind of his subject. The danger becomes acute when the observer, instead of being directly attentive to the person observed, thinks of the latter as a "case history" of such and such an abstractly defined type of conduct. Here not only may the observer be using the wrong ideal type to understand his subject's behavior, but he may never discover his error because he never confronts his subject as a real person.[53]

The results of the functionary–client relationship can be disastrous. A mother and her children applying for welfare may even suffer and die because the mother is one child short of becoming a "case." A patient is denied treatment at a hospital, not on medical grounds, but on grounds of being an insurance card short of qualifying financially for admission.

But these are extreme cases. More widespread, and affecting us all, is the ever-present pressure of a multitude of bureaucracies demanding that we think and act at all times like cases.

In conclusion, Schutz can show us, through his exposition of they-relationships, that in bureaucracy social life has ended. And he shows us the reasons why. If we first define what social life consists of—what Weber called social action and Schutz the we-relationship—then it becomes possible to measure the distance away from these standards of social life that human beings are forced to go.

Michael M. Harmon

DECISION-RULES AND KNOWLEDGE

The distance between extreme they-relationships and we-relationships can be portrayed on a spectrum suggested by the work on decision-rules of public administration theorist Michael M. Harmon. Five kinds of rules, Harmon says, are or can be employed in making and legitimating decisions in public organizations: hierarchy (unilateral decision), bargaining or market rules, voting, contract, and consensus.[54] There is one major benefit in thinking of how different decision-rules work in organizations: It becomes obvious that we get different kinds of knowledge depending on which decision-rule we use.[55] Consider the decision-rules distributed over a spectrum, as in Figure 1.2.

The kind of knowledge mobilized by the hierarchical setup permits only the knowledge of the superior, not the subordinate, to become the official basis for action.

As we move to contracting, each contracting partner has an autonomous power base and is respected for what he or she says on the grounds of that base. An exchange of knowledge is possible, though only on the basis of an assumed zero-sum game rule: What you win, I lose. Knowledge tends to be highly controlled still: I only let you know what I believe to be in my interest to let you know. Over this relationship, to keep individuals from killing each other, looms in the contractual system an umpire with enough power, as Thomas Hobbes said, to keep them all in awe. Hierarchy is still there, but knowledge arises from the contracting partners, not from the top down.

In bargaining, we move a step further from situations of domination and distrust. It is conceivable to think of two natives of different countries meeting on a desert island and bargaining food for services, or the like, without necessarily having a third party watch over them to threaten death and destruction if a bargain is not kept. Perhaps rational perception of one's own self-interest can function as a disinterested third party, if neither bargaining partner considers it in his or her interest to break off bargaining altogether. Very likely, however, bargaining also holds a hid-

Figure 1.2: Decision-Rules

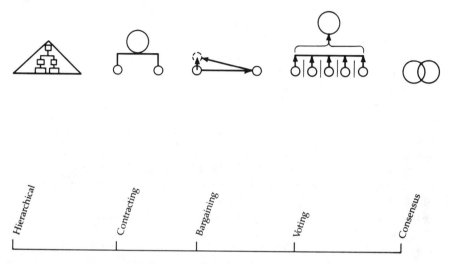

den hierarchical agenda: Each partner is likely to want to get the better of a bargain, thereby raising him- or herself to a superior position relative to the other (represented by the dotted circle in Figure 1.2).

Voting also mobilizes knowledge and, especially, judgments of bottom-line individuals; however, the separation of voters from one another prevents, at least during the act of voting itself, any communication about the definition of problems or solutions. As public administration specialist Frederick Thayer points out, democracy is a hierarchical system. Quite clearly he is right: The division of labor in the act of voting separates people from one another, and representative government itself constructs a hierarchy at each election. While knowledge may flow upward in elections (that is, in *political* action), official *governmental* action is shaped by knowledge that flows downward from those authorized to aggregate it and use it.

Consensus as True We-Relationships

Only consensus operates on the possibility that a true we-relation is possible; that is, on the assumption that knowledge can be shared among participants in a situation and that this knowledge is not simply additive (you tell me what you know, I'll tell what I know) but synthetic. Many heads in a consensual relationship are better than one, not simply because there are more sources of knowledge but because qualitatively superior problem definition can arise from such relationships.

Ultimately, Harmon argues, all parties gain from relationships in which assessment of a situation and the process of working out solutions are shared by all. "Even managers may get a surprise: they may actually gain power to solve problems by slackening the reins of topdown control over employees," Harmon says.[56] Much of organization development and of Japanese management rests on consensual decision-rules. In fact, "decisions" as such tend to be avoided and become unnecessary as "insight" into problems suggests the solutions.

In amendment to Harmon: Insight must be added to consensus. Otherwise consensus is empty or trivial. Consensus must contain realistic information to the organization. Consensual employees might be engaged in groupthink, each expressing what he or she thinks the others want to hear. Only if what is expressed is related to work—if there are what might be called work-based consensual decision-rules—does the organization get a realistic database for its social structures designed for information processing. If the users of consensual decision-rules are workers and if they are able to give words to what they do, the organization gains in access to direct knowledge of the work—as distinct from reports rammed into parameters of jobs predesigned by hierarchy.

With work-based consensus rules there is at least a chance that everybody will be open to individuals' talk about their work experiences. To the extent that these can be expressed in speech, mutual understanding of work is fostered, and processes and structures can be developed to provide coordination and supports so the individual can do the work well.

It is clear, of course, that such building of social structure from the bottom up endangers bureaucracy's control of social relations from the top down. There are trade-offs here between control on the one hand and point-of-production effectiveness on the other.* Yet, where control and work are assigned their proper realm, controls can also deliver a tight service or support structure so that workers can be free to do what they judge must be done.

BUREAUCRACY AS SOCIETY

Bureaucracy replaces society. This claim may seem farfetched—but only at first. Examine the place of bureaucracy *in* society. At first, bureaucracy is only a tool. It is intended to be the extension of my hand as taxpaying citizen. Through the extension I reach out to other citizens who become the clients of bureaucracy.

Bureaucracy, the Divider

Bureaucracy, initially, is a bridge between citizens as taxpayers and citizens as clients. It links those who have something to give with those who expect to receive—taxpayer with welfare recipient—as distinct individu-

---

*See also the redefinition of work in Chapter 5.

als. But bureaucracy also links me as taxpayer to myself as car driver in need of a license and license plate, as the victim of crime in need of police protection, as a citizen of a nation needing defense against other nations. The New York State Motor Vehicles Department, the Los Angeles Police Department, and the Defense Department in Washington, D.C.—all are links between me in one role (taxpayer, productive worker, voter) and me in my other roles (driver, crime victim, target for international attack).

When we think about the size of the huge machinery needed, a sense of a vast absurdity breaks through into our consciousness: The machinery intended to *link* me with my fellow citizens is also the machinery that separates me *from* them. The bridge has become a chasm.

In the realm of welfare, bureaucracy exists not only to channel funds from me to people whom taxpayers like me have decided are worthy of getting our help. The welfare bureaucracy in its size and complexity puts a vast physical distance between me and the welfare client. The welfare bureaucracy makes certain that I, as taxpayer, will never be confronted face to face with a welfare recipient.

Bureaucracy separates the giver from the taker, the giver from the bureaucrat, and the bureaucrat from the client. All three relationships cease to be personal, emotional, and social and begin to be impersonal, "rational," and machinelike. Here is the practical meaning of Max Weber's original insight that "bureaucracy is *the* means of transforming social action into rationally organized action."

Practical Attitudes toward and in Bureaucracy

To what practical use can our insights so far be put? We can outline for ourselves as social actor, as citizen, as functionary, and as client—all of whom may be one person in separate roles—the type of attitude natural to each role. Once I can think clearly about the reality of the social interaction in which I must engage, I may hope to extricate myself from various difficulties and perhaps become more successful in my dealings with bureaucracy.

Social Relationships

If I want the benefits of life as a social actor I must take a specific attitude toward others. In society, the social relationship is the fundamental type of action. It involves at least *two people* who talk with one another about a *shared reality* and who interact with one another to construct or maintain that reality.

In more precise terms, any social relationship requires five elements:

1. Two discrete individuals,
2. each capable of orienting himself or herself to the other as if he or she were that other,

3. who share a common perception of a shared world,
4. who communicate about the world, and
5. who interact mutually to gain or maintain control of that world.[57]

Each of the words used here has a very special meaning in phenomenology. By "two discrete individuals," I mean people capable of social contact. They must be authentic and undamaged individuals, having an existence in their own right and free in a profound sense of such dependency-making forces as bureaucracy.

Figure 1.3: Elements of Social Interaction

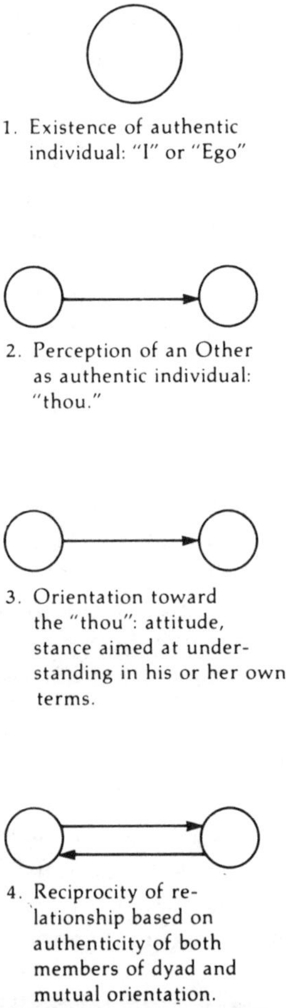

1. Existence of authentic individual: "I" or "Ego"

2. Perception of an Other as authentic individual: "thou."

3. Orientation toward the "thou": attitude, stance aimed at understanding in his or her own terms.

4. Reciprocity of relationship based on authenticity of both members of dyad and mutual orientation.

Source: Derived from R. P. Hummel, "Are There Groups in Organizations?," paper presented to the fifth scientific meeting of the A. K. Rice Institute, Washington, D.C., April 2–4, 1981.

Figure 1.4: Inner Referents of Social Action

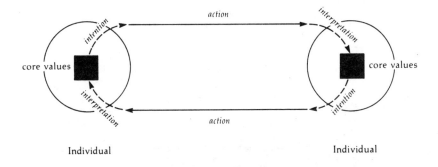

Graphically, the picture of external human interaction that emerges in society can be drawn as in Figure 1.3.

Internally, however, the social relationship requires the existence of a core of values within the individual. To these the individual refers what he or she does. An action referred to values is a meaningful action. Similarly, in trying to understand what the action of another means, the individual perceiving the action first refers that action to his or her own values and, if the result is not satisfactory, begins checking what the action might mean in terms of the values of the other.[58] Social interactions require the drawing of a more complex picture than that in Figure 1.3. Figure 1.4 reflects the fact that the social actor must be adept at coming to terms with his or her own inner values and with those of another.

POLITICAL RELATIONSHIPS

The political attitude is more sharply focused on the ability to recognize human tensions. Political relationships are a variant of social relationships. In general, political relationships are those social relationships having to do with constructing solutions to acute social problems. A political relationship involves the following elements:

At least two people
who perceive and communicate
shared tension
between human needs and social facts, and
who initiate a relationship to resolve that tension.

Graphically, the political relationship can be depicted as in Figure 1.5. Any truly political situation can be understood in terms of at least two individuals, each capable of perceiving a shared tension and orienting action toward the other to satisfy needs expressed in that tension. A political tension is not necessarily a tension between individuals but arises from the perception of a gap between existing solutions to human needs

Figure 1.5: Elements of Political Interaction

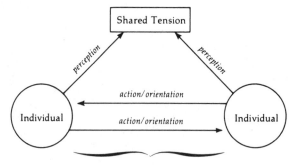

Interaction to Satisfy Need

Source: From Ralph P. Hummel and Robert A. Isaak, *Politics for Human Beings,* 2nd ed. (Monterey, Calif.: Brooks/Cole Publishing Co.-Duxbury Press, 1980), p. 17.

(social facts*) and new human needs. Political consciousness is the formulation of that tension in terms that can be communicated.

BUREAUCRATIC RELATIONSHIPS

The bureaucratic attitude is neither primarily social nor political but physical. Thus would things treat things, if they had any consciousness at all. In contrast to full social and political relationships, bureaucratic relationships are truncated. A bureaucratic relationship, or the bureaucratic field of action, consists of these minimal elements:

1. An individual (the manager) and a pseudo-being (the functionary),
2. the first orienting himself to the second as if it were the exclusive task of the latter to orient himself to the first,
3. both lacking a common perception of a shared reality but organizationally restricted to living in worlds apart,
4. the first speaking a language at the second that is totally instructional and one-directional and that does not allow mutual redefinition of the relationship, and
5. both prohibited from reciprocal interaction for constructing a shared reality, the first retaining a monopoly on initiating reality construction for the second.[59]

One-sided though the bureaucratic relationship is, its very one-sidedness is demanded by what people expect from bureaucracy. We do not want functionaries to act on their own volition and from a position of independence. We want managers, whom we empower with authority, to be able to define tasks, to possess or control superior technical knowledge of what the tasks are all about, to be able to give orders one way and see them carried out. All of this seems, from the point of view of the bureaucratic solution to such expectations, to require the subordinate to tune in

*Whether objectivations or reifications.

to the manager, to attempt to understand the manager's intentions and language rather than impose his or her own intentions and terms, to be passive rather than active in an initiating sense.

But not even this much activity is required of the functionary. Tuning in, understanding, even acceptance are necessities of social action, not of bureaucratic action. The functionary simply learns proper responses to specific orders. The functionary refers to the rule book. He or she learns routine types of action embodied in the job description. In exceptional instances, the functionary seeks authoritative interpretation of an order from above. Lacking is the effort involved in voluntary and intentional acts of interpretation and understanding. It is not required that functionaries understand either their orders or their actions, but merely that the latter reflect the former.

That the major cognitive, social, and political powers of the functionary are not utilized but are, rather, suppressed is both the strength of bureaucracy and its greatest handicap. A future form of organization that can both enforce socially legitimate policies through organizational structure *and* mobilize knowledge-based social and political power of those working in such structure will overwhelm modern bureaucratic organization.

SUMMARY

What is the immediate practical use of being able to recognize one's own location in different types of relationships—social, political, and bureaucratic?

First, our ability to do well in life or in situations depends on bringing our expectations into congruence with realities. If I identify my situation to be a bureaucratic one, I will not make the mistake of expecting to be treated as a fully contributing social equal or of expecting that my sensitivity to human tensions will be rewarded by the bureaucratic structure. I can even ask myself the very practical question: Does my personality best fit roles of social, political, or bureaucratic action? If I am mainly concerned with understanding others, a social role might be advised. If my sensitivity is toward the recognition of tensions between human needs and social facts, a political role might be best. If I am by nature a truncated human being, limited in understanding and consciousness of political tension, but enabled by nature or training to perceive human behaviors in the same cold light as I see the behavior of things, a career in purely bureaucratic functions of modern organizations promises success.

Second, however, the ability to place myself in the kind of reality that surrounds me—social, political, or bureaucratic—and to tailor my expectations and actions accordingly does not automatically lead to passive acceptance of what is. Human satisfaction is limited by the truncated relationship such as the bureaucratic one. This may encourage the political activist to appeal to the suppressed dimensions of bureaucracy—the social and political potential of its members—to work his will, whether for good or evil. A form of organization that suppresses the foundation in the working knowledge of the human capacity for interaction with other human beings is forever vulnerable to new social and political formations.

Third, from the viewpoint of the bureaucrat defending bureaucracy, there may indeed be in all this the message that he or she must stand constant guard over the possibility of independent social and political relations arising within the iron cage of tough one-sided rules and relationships. But the bureaucrat, also, will be aware that to stick to bureaucratic relations alone is to deprive himself or herself of immense power to mobilize the working knowledge of subordinates and to accomplish things that are difficult or almost impossible within the one-sided, top-down bureaucratic relation.

Even in the bureaucratic relationship, there is a residue of political and social relations that mobilize the willingness of subordinates to fit themselves and their work into the organization. It may well be that, if any work gets done in bureaucracy, it gets done not because of the force that structure imposes from above but because of the social and political capacities that human beings bring to their jobs—the capacity to know their work, the capacity to communicate in such a way that a piece of work is defined for mutual co-laboration, the ability, in other words, to do what all humans do: to construct a work reality out of one's own capabilities.

NOTES

1. Max Weber, *Economy and Society: An Outline of Interpretive Sociology*, 3 vols., eds. Guenther Roth and Claus Wittich, trs. Ephraim Fischoff et al. (New York: Bedminster Press, 1968), p. 987.

2. Interview conducted by the author. All such interviews in this chapter were conducted in the period 1974–1976, except where noted.

3. Ibid.

4. Weber, *Economy and Society*, p. 975.

5. A social worker in New York City, anonymity requested. Interview conducted by the author.

6. Written report to the author, May 1974.

7. All data presented in this case from State of New York, Office of the State Comptroller, Office of the Special Deputy Comptroller for the City of New York, "Trends in Public Assistance Caseload and Expenditures in New York City with Comparisons to Selected Counties in New York State," Report No. 36-85, Nov. 27, 1984, submitted to the Financial Control Board of the City of New York. My thanks to Norman Gertner, chief analyst for economic and revenue forecasting, Office of the New York State Special Deputy Comptroller for New York City, for explaining the methods used in forecasting public assistance caseload.

8. Weber, *Economy and Society*, p. 1401.

9. Ibid., p. 1393.

10. Henry Jacoby, *The Bureaucratization of the World* (Berkeley: University of California Press, 1973). Originally published in German in 1969. My thanks to Dwight Waldo for calling this work to my attention.

11. Contrast the victory of modernization in China today with Weber's own description of the antimodern cultural barriers of traditional China at the turn of the century. See Max Weber, *Gesammelte Aufsätze zur Religionssoziologie*, 3 vols. (Tübingen: J. C. B. Mohr, 1920–21), vol. I., pp. 308–309 ff.

12. I have taken the translation of this passage directly from Max Weber, *Gesammelte Politische Schriften*, 2nd ed., ed. Johannes Winckelmann (Tübingen: J. C. B. Mohr, 1958), p. 310. In the English translation, in *Economy and Society* cited above, the translators use the term "public ownership" instead of Weber's "'socialization.'" While his use of the term "socialization" undoubtedly signified "public ownership," the translators took an unjustified liberty. Weber meant socialization, with direct reference to Russia and socialism. His use of quotation marks always indicates that he means to use a term ironically or not in the sense in which it is routinely used. Here the use is ironic. Weber meant to indicate that what was taking place in Russia in terms of "socialization" was not socialistic in Marx's sense but was a case of conversion to state capitalism. See also *Gesammelte Politische Schriften*, p. 505.

13. Written report to the author, June 1975.

14. Here the regular print contains the demand for logic; the italicized part, the demand for visibility. Talcott Parsons, *The Structure of Social Action* (New York: McGraw-Hill, 1937), p. 58.

15. Personal conversation with author.

16. Official rules become so structurally embedded in everyday regulation of performance that the functionary spends more time looking over his or her shoulder at the rules than looking forward at the product. The assumption that visible work constitutes the totality of what goes on in modern organizations is, however, an illusion. The manager who succumbs to that illusion simply blocks out part of the reality, which is, at least in part, constructed by his subordinates. As one commentator writes: "The organization is what members make of uncertainty and the formal organization."—Stewart Clegg, *Power, Rule and Domination: A Critical and Empirical Understanding of Power in Sociological Theory and Organizational Life* (London: Routledge & Kegan Paul, 1975), p. 130.

17. Michael P. Smith, "Alienation and Bureaucracy: The Role of Participatory Administration," *Public Administration Review* (November/December 1971), p. 660. For further research into the bureaucratization of the teacher, begin with the older but still valid analysis by Willard Waller of what teaching does to teachers in *The Sociology of Teaching* (New York: Wiley, 1932), pp. 375–409.

18. A report on Eliott Eisner et al., "What High Schools Are Like: Views from the Inside" reported in Fred M. Hechinger, "An Inside Look at High Schools," *New York Times*, Sept. 9, 1985, pp. C1 and C7; citation from p. C1.

19. Eliott Eisner in Hechinger, op. cit., p. C7.

20. Charlotte Krepismann in Hechinger, op. cit., p. C7.

21. David Schuman, *Policy Analysis, Education, and Everyday Life: An Empirical Reevaluation of Higher Education in America* (Lexington, Mass.: Heath, 1982).

22. See the work of Emile Durkheim.

23. See the work of Max Weber on charismatic leadership.

24. This is Martin Heidegger's position. See the sections on Heidegger in Chapters 4, 5, and 6. Adopting it now would be premature.

25. Alfred Schutz, "On Multiple Realities," in *Collected Papers*, vol. I, *The Problem of Social Reality* (The Hague: Martinus Nijhoff, 1967), pp. 207–59; citation from p. 227.

26. Roger Jehenson, "A Phenomenological Approach to the Study of Formal Organizations," in George Psathas, ed., *Phenomenological Sociology: Issues and Applications* (New York: John Wiley & Sons, 1973), pp. 219–47; see p. 226: "By such standardization of the scheme of typifications, the organization attempts to establish a congruency between the typified scheme used by each actor as a scheme of orientation and that of his organizational fellow-

men as a scheme of interpretation, with the expected result that the chances of success of human interaction in the organization will be increased."

27. Operator in wood-pulp bleach plant quoted in Shoshana Zuboff, *In the Age of the Smart Machine: The Future of Work and Power* (New York: Basic Books, 1988), p. 201.

28. See especially the thesis that no working reality can be totally programmed into a computer suggested by Charles Perrow, "Normal Accident at Three-Mile Island," *Society*, vol. 18, no. 5 (July–August 1981), pp. 17–26.

29. Ibid., p. 339.

30. Peter Berger, Brigitte Berger, and Hansfried Kellner, *The Homeless Mind: Modernization and Consciousness* (New York: Random House—Vintage Books, 1974), p. 184: "In everyday life the modern individual continuously alternates between highly discrepant and often contradictory social contexts. In terms of his biography, the individual migrates through a succession of widely divergent social worlds. Not only are an increasing number of individuals in a modern society uprooted from their original social milieu, but, in addition, no succeeding social milieu succeeds in becoming truly 'home' either." If we read "original" in terms of the power of humans to originate their own social world by reference to shared work, then we have a reading of this last sentence fitting to our present context.

31. This argument is further developed in Chapter 5; see especially the sections on Edmund Husserl and the redefinition of work. The wording in the second to last sentence of this paragraph is taken almost verbatim from the felicitous formulation of a student of Husserl's, Alfred Schutz: "As will be shown very soon, the wide-awake self integrates in its working and by its working its present, past and future into a specific dimension of time; it realizes itself as totality in its working acts; it communicates with Others through working acts; it organizes the different spatial perspectives of the world of daily life through working acts."—Schutz, op. cit., p. 212. With Schutz, p. 226, I consider the world of work, as organically created in working, the paramount reality.

32. Schutz, op. cit., p. 145.

33. For the motivations of police, see my "Teaching Human Beings: A Socio-Psychological Role Model of Relationships with the New Student," paper presented at the 1976 annual meeting of the New York State Political Science Association, Albany, N.Y., March 26–27.

34. Personal interview with the author, August 1975.

35. For numerous reasons the cop on the beat exercises immense discretion, and the costs of supervision to limit that discretion are usually considered too high. On patrol officers' discretion, see James Q. Wilson, *Varieties of Police Behavior: The Management of Law and Order in Eight Communities* (Cambridge, Mass.: Harvard University Press, 1968), especially Chapter 2.

36. Weber, *Economy and Society*, p. 4.

37. Ibid., p. 26.

38. Max Weber, "Ueber einige Kategorien der verstehenden Soziologie," in *Gesammelte Aufsätze zur Wissenschaftslehre*, ed. Johannes Winckelmann (Tübingen: J. C. B. Mohr, 1968), p. 471. The fact that Weber here defines social action in the same way he defines social relationship in *Economy and Society*, and thereby vitiates the distinction between the two, should not be held against him. Great men are allowed to be inconsistent, and besides it is difficult to engage in social action without waiting to hear a signal from a partner and thus engaging in a social relationship.

39. Ibid., p. 441 especially; also pp. 452–64.

40. Ibid., p. 467.

41. Ibid., pp. 465–66.

42. The tone for this acceptance was set in Parsons's own classic, *The Social System* (New York: Macmillan, 1951).

43. Perhaps the fundamental essay in which Habermas develops these implications is "Technology and Science as Ideology," in Jürgen Habermas, *Toward a Rational Society: Student Protest, Science and Politics* (Boston: Beacon Press, 1970).

44. This distinction is further developed in Ralph P. Hummel and Robert A. Isaak, *Politics for Human Beings*, 2nd ed. (Monterey, Calif.: Brooks/Cole Publishing Co.-Duxbury Press, 1980), especially Chapters 2, 3, and 12. See also the more recent recovery of the "action" concept as the essential creative attribute of human beings in social and organiza-

tional relationships as developed by phenomenologists in public administration, policy study, and planning: Michael M. Harmon, *Action Theory for Public Administration* (New York: Longman, 1981); Robert B. Denhardt, *In the Shadow of Organizations* (Lawrence: Regents Press of Kansas, 1981); Bayard Catron, *Theoretical Aspects of Social Action* (Ph.D. dissertation, University of California—Berkeley, 1975); Frank Fischer, *Politics, Values and Public Policy: The Problem of Methodology* (Boulder, Colo.: Westview Press, 1980); David Schuman, *Policy Analysis, Education, and Everyday Life* (Lexington, Mass.: Heath, 1982); and the work of John Forester and Howell Baum in Pierre Clavel, John Forester, and William Goldsmith, eds., *Urban and Regional Planning in an Age of Austerity* (New York: Pergamon, 1980). For general surveys of the phenomenological movement that began in the early 1970s in political science and public administration and in the mid-1970s in planning and public policy study, see R. P. Hummel, "Doing Phenomenology in the Social Sciences: The Rise of Intentionalism," *Policy Perspectives*. Fall 1981, pp. 111–123, as well as R. P. Hummel, "Phenomenology in Planning, Policy, and Administration," book review, *Polity*, vol. 15, no. 2 (Winter 1982), pp. 305–14.

45. Alfred Schutz, *The Phenomenology of the Social World* (Evanston, Ill.: Northwestern University Press, 1967), p. 205.

46. Ibid., p. 202.

47. Ibid., p. 204.

48. Ibid.

49. Ibid.

50. Ibid.

51. Ibid.

52. Ibid.

53. Ibid.

54. Michael M. Harmon, *Action Theory for Public Administration* (New York: Longman, 1981), pp. 5, 9, 93, 95–96, 101 ff.

55. The following discussion is based on running discussions between members of the Institute for Applied Phenomenology, including Michael M. Harmon, Sandra Fish, and Ralph P. Hummel, though only the present author should be held responsible for the final interpretation presented in this understanding of Harmon's decision-rules.

56. Personal communication with Michael M. Harmon, Feb. 6, 1986.

57. This summary and the subsequent discussion are based on Hummel and Isaak, *Politics for Human Beings*, especially Chapters 2 and 14.

58. This section is based on the work of Max Weber and the phenomenological philosopher Edmund Husserl. Weber defined meaning in terms of action referred to values (*Wertbeziehung*). Husserl set out to show that for every type of object in the outer world, the individual would need to have recourse to a specific inner attitude suitable for understanding that object; the term "intentionality," used by Husserl, refers to that attitude. For the relation between Husserl and Weber, who cites Husserl, see R. P. Hummel, "Max Weber as Phenomenologist," paper presented at the sixth annual meeting of political science departments of the City University of New York, New York City, Fall 1980.

59. Adapted from the description of the bureaucrat–client relationship ("bureaucrat" can be substituted for "manager" and "client" for "functionary") in R. P. Hummel, "Toward a Human Cost Audit of Modern Organizations," paper presented to the Conference on the Phenomenological Analysis of Asymmetrical Relations, Wright State University and Ohio University, Dayton, Ohio, May 20–22, 1977. See also Hummel and Isaak, *Politics for Human Beings*, pp. 329–31.

2

Bureaucracy as the New Culture

Since bureaucracy has a "rational" character, with rules, means-ends calculus, and matter-of-factness predominating, its rise and expansion has everywhere had "revolutionary" results . . . as had the advance of rationalism in general.

—Max Weber[1]

The modern world today is split by culture conflict.

The culture war is about values.[2] Is there anything on earth that can oppose the modern values that dominate humanity? Can modern values be successfully fought at all?

Though modern values dominate from above, human values spring up again and again from below. Wherever work is done to satisfy human needs, there what is judged worthwhile are the moves required to achieve actual work* and the social relations needed to support them. Over and against them loom the rationalist and functionalist values that hold artificial systems together. The confrontation looks like this:

Society/Bureaucracy Conflict

Social Values[3]	Bureaucratic Values[4]
justice	stability
freedom	discipline
violence	reliability
oppression	calculability of results
happiness	formal rationality
gratification	formalistic impersonality
poverty	formal equality of
illness	treatment
love and hate	
salvation and damnation	
victory and defeat	

*As distinct from the moves necessary to do a job defined from above.

In economics, in the distribution of scarce goods, demand for satis-faction of human needs works itself out as a conflict between quality and quantity. Modern organizations produce quantity, but people eventually demand quality. When what is produced is not what it was sought for, people rediscover that quantity is no substitute for quality. A car that does not transport is not a vehicle. Garbage pickup that leaves garbage behind is not a service. And formal access to jobs when there are no jobs is not justice. Inside organizations, this values confrontation looks like this:

Quantity/Quality Conflict in Organizations[5]

Important to Quantitative Organizations	*Important to Qualitative Organizations*
Bigness . . . because it gives economies of scale.	Belief in being the best.
Low-cost emphasis . . . because survivors make it cheaper.	Belief in the importance of the details of execution, the nuts and bolts of doing the job well (emphasis on the actual work well done).
Peace at all costs . . . because keeping trouble-makers down ensures following the plan.	Belief in the importance of people as individuals.
Analysis as the solution to everything . . . because if you can take it apart into numbers you know what's going on.	Belief in superior quality and service (emphasis on putting things together).
Decision-making as more important than follow-through . . . because, if you make the right decisions, things will fall into place.	Belief that most members of the organization should be innovators, and its corollary, the willingness to support failure.
Control over everything . . . because things and people out of control introduce the unpredictable.	Belief in the importance of informality to enhance communication.
Growth as a hedge against insecurity, even in industries one knows nothing about.	Belief in and recognition of the importance of economic growth and profits (in industries known to managers).

In politics the attack on modern values would also seem to have a chance. Political campaigns appeal to social values: Citizens, not systems, vote. But here the set of values, the political culture itself, is split, and the values that link people to one another in the net of society (values of social conscience) run up against the values that set them against one another (values of rugged individualism):

Political Culture Wars[6]

Values of Social Conscience Assert:	Values of Individualism Assert:
America is a *national community* that marches ever onward and upward toward greater *equality* and *social justice* under the leadership of *Great Presidents*.	America is a nation of *individuals*, each of whom engages in *hard work* in healthy *competition* to acquire *property* that becomes a *right* to be defended against all comers.

Can substantive values from the economic and political cultures successfully oppose the formal and instrumental values of modern culture? On the surface, substantive values would seem to be at an advantage: They have concrete content and are about end-states that people would like to enjoy: quality products, effective public service, a politics that balances social justice and individual achievement. All modernity has to offer is instrumental values: the means logically calculated to get to human ends.

THE CULTURAL SUPERIORITY OF MODERNITY

The problem is that the overall modern culture at large indoctrinates its members to believe first of all in instrumental values and only secondly in human values. How is this done?

We do it every time we tell ourselves that what is real is what is measurable and scientifically observable, not what we feel, vaguely sense, uniquely experience. Modern instrumental values lend themselves well to such reality definition; not by accident are they called "rational." *Ratio* or reason, the rational mind, defines the categories for what can be considered real, not emotion or a feel for what is right and appropriate. Max Weber specifically characterizes the attitude of not only the bureaucrat but of the modern organization toward reality as *sine ira et studio*, without passion or prejudice.

The rational calculation of markets, production, and risk in fact has produced modern economics, with its emphasis on the calculation of everything so that gains can be reinvested and yet greater market share won.* Modern reinvestment capitalism rests on faith in modern values; what is measurable *is* real for the industrialist and business owner.

The rise of rationalistic private organizations was accompanied by the rise of rationalistic public organizations. These regulated and governed

*For further development of this theme, see "What the Experts Say: Max Weber," later in this chapter.

the economy, removing unpredictables such as contractors who did not keep to their contracts or robber barons who held up goods going to markets. Again, what became valued was the kind of governing organization that enabled producers sending goods to market to calculate and predict their costs and gains. Another win for rationalistic, calculable, instrumental values.

We recognize government bureaucracy, though we may have forgotten its original role in evening out the playing field for economic competition and growth. Of this form of modern organization Max Weber wrote:

Experience tends universally to show that the purely bureaucratic type of organization—that is, the monocratic variety of bureaucracy—is from a purely technical point of view, capable of attaining the highest degree of efficiency and is in this sense formally the most rational known means of exercising authority over human beings.

And here comes his partial tally of rational values:

It [bureaucracy] is superior to any other form in precision, in stability, in the stringency of its discipline, and in its reliability.

How does bureaucracy serve the economy?

It thus makes possible a particularly high degree of calculability of results for the heads of the organization and for those acting in relation to it.[7]

Right away we can see that when human values are asserted against modern values, people will say: That is very well, but do you really want to live without mass production of goods and mass delivery of services? What's a little bureaucratic oppression when measured against the precision of airplanes that fly on time? On the quality/quantity issue: Yes, you want a car that works well and gets you there, but don't you also want cars that are cheap and available to everyone? On the political values issue: Yes, social justice and equality are nice ideals and we should strive toward them, but don't forget economic value is produced by individuals working hard in competition yielding, yes, inequality, but also the creation of goods and property. From there it is only a small step for an alliance between those supporting businesslike values and those supporting the values of bureaucracy that help business compete on a controlled and predictable playing field.

No wonder we moderns value modern values: Our supply of economic goods and our style of government administration of social and economic peace hinge on them.

THREE PREDICTIONS ABOUT CULTURE WARS

The purpose of this chapter is threefold:

1. To show how cultural battles of the forces arrayed against modernity work themselves out in practice (see the section entitled "What People Value").

2. To give depth to the understanding of what is at stake in the different values systems (see the section entitled "What the Experts Say").
3. To give reasons why the various reforms and revolutions attempted against modern organization are bound to fail (see the section entitled "Bureaucratic Culture").

A beginning can be made by becoming aware of the values that are at stake in the two most salient arenas of cultural battle: economy and politics.

This chapter advances three theses about the increasing irresolution of what is to be valued in the politics of the organization as well as the politics of the nation:

1. Quality will not triumph over quantity; modern organization will save itself by redefining quality in quantitative terms.
2. Conscience will not triumph over practicality; politicians and reformers *both* will simply learn to treat issues of conscience as currency with which to win allies and oppose foes in the political marketplace.
3. At best, modern organizations—especially government bureaucracies—will link political pressures for social reform to greater rationalization and scientification of the tools of administration. The model for this is bureaucracy's alliance with populism/progressivism at the turn of the last century, resulting in the rise of scientific management and private and public merit systems. But the elective affinity between the individualistic and antisocial values of economy and the instrumental control values of bureaucracy is dominant.

Examples of each type of conflict may yield some insight into the battles and their likely outcomes.

WHAT PEOPLE VALUE

People may reject an action because it does not work or because it is considered morally wrong. In both cases, values are at bottom of the judgment. Actions that do not work are judged worthless only against a standard of practical success. Actions that are held to be wrong are judged as without worth when held up against a standard of moral rightness. Modern organizations, as institutionalized patterns of action, today are under attack on both grounds.

Citizens and workers both claim inadequacy of institutional working patterns on the grounds of practical failure. Citizens judge resulting goods or services as ineffective. Workers complain that mandated operating procedures, while technically correct, force them to engage in working acts that are inappropriate to the task at hand.

Similarly, in the moral sphere, organizational acts may meet modern standards of successful instrumentality. They may serve general agreed-upon goals. But they may still be assaulted as frustrating the aspirations of minorities or even a majority. There is the case of women who are kept from full career actualization in the military by arguments that certain tasks technically call for implementation by males. There is the case of the stepwise but slow, and sometimes totally impeded, rise of minorities through the Civil Service System. This system, though "rational" and even based on the scientific study of jobs and scientifically validated qualification tests, may still frustrate the aspirations of minorities and the economically, and therefore educationally, disadvantaged. And so on.

What is it like to be caught up in modern organizations that, though they pursue technical values appropriate to them, frustrate the desire for practical success (beyond mere technical correctness) and the moral sense of justice?

From the 1980s into the 1990s, the country launched into two types of reform: reform in the *way* products and services were delivered and reform in *to whom* and *through whom* they would be delivered. The first reform originated in the economy. There, middle-class buyers came to judge products like cars by their quality when availability based on quantity was no longer an issue. The second reform originated in the social system and was moved through politics into law, where America's neglected and disadvantaged managed to mobilize America's social conscience. The way these reforms worked themselves out in practice can be illustrated through several experiences of what people have come to value in the quality/quantity struggle and the political culture struggle.

People Who Value Good Work: The Quality/Quantity Conflict

People on the outside assess what modern organizations produce in terms of social values and the bureaucratic redefinition of these. People inside face this conflict in terms of quality *versus* quantity.

This is especially clear in production industries. There physical reality stands up against the mere mental calculations that reason and science produce as blueprints, training and tools for handling that material.

JUDGMENT IN PHYSICAL WORK

One of the most calculated working operations is car assembly. Quantitatively every part should be the same and every assembly operation should be the same. But a retired assembly worker had this to say about that:

They've got it all standardized, but still, every fender is different. You've got to use your body a different way to get it on. Push with your shoulder, while pulling back with your right hand, and wiggling it with your left. Every fender ought to go on the same way, they think. They give you just so much time, the same amount of time for every fender. But that's not the way it really works.[8]

A tire mounter at Ford Motor Company gives us added insight into how work feels from the inside out:

I started out on truck tires. I made 60 to 80 jobs a day, and this times six. We put in six days a week. A job's a whole truck. And six tires to a truck, plus spare. *There was a trick to putting the rim in, so that it had a little click. You had to be very fine to know.* So you would put this clip around and then you stand over it, and I would just kick it over—boom!—in there. This I had to learn on my own. Didn't nobody teach me this.[9]

The importance of *bodily experience*—the contact with the physical through the five senses—emerges as an essential value in work wherever the physical is encountered. But what happens when the scientific study of work comes up with disembodied rules and blueprints according to which work has to be done? Then the crafts worker, and even the industrial worker operating a machine, must make *judgments of translation*— that "little click"—to convert quantitative instructions into qualitative moves of the hand. These do not come from mathematical formulas but from the sense of touch.[10]

JUDGMENT IN SMART WORK

In the extreme, what happens when the computer, as the ultimate bureaucracy, detaches operators of physical production processes altogether from physical reality by mathematizing everything? Shoshana Zuboff deals with this question in her study of the computerization of work. Having demonstrated the value of *physical judgment* in crafts work and even in industrial work, she points out that *judgment in general* is valued in the totality of the organization as an integrated workplace.

Where physical work and computerized work are both required in one production process, for example in a paper mill, both *physical judgment* directly involved with the work and detached *mental judgment* may be required:

We all get involved in the problem so we all know what happens. A couple of us stay at the terminal, and a couple of people go out and check things [in the physical plant]. First we look it all over on the computer. Then, you see what you need to do outside. Or, if there's a little time, someone runs to the door, and a person at the terminal will yell, "Check this and that" while you're running out the door.[11]

When the computerized control room was first glassed off from the physical plant in this paper mill, Zuboff reports, the door between mathematized reality and physical reality was literally mangled by angry operators desperately oscillating between the computer and the physical processes it controlled.

Once computer work is accepted next to physical work, as an *arena of judgment over mathematized abstractions* as against an *arena of judgment over sensory experience*, what becomes valued is the computer operator's ability to *imagine* the physical processes represented by his or her data. Without such imagining, he or she cannot judge what are the realistic moves to be made to control the physical processes. Consider highly technologized organizations with high diffusion of information through information systems. There *teams* of operators—from the computer area, from the industrial machine area, and from the hands-on crafts area—are required to exchange judgments in all three areas and produce what David Carnevale and I call the *synthesizing judgments* of "smart work":[12]

This kind of work pulls together knowledge about all three kinds of work: hands-on work that survives from the pre-industrial past, industrial machine work that still produces most of our goods, and computer work. . . . Smart work involves a good feel for each of the subtypes of work that allows someone, or several someones, to pull together a new set of skills for those who see to it that work gets done (*pace* managers).[13]

LOSS OF JUDGMENT IN BUREAUCRACY

There are, of course, modern organizations in which physical contact is absent. We know them as the paperwork bureaucracies of government but they also exist in the private sector: in bureaucratic units such as staff analysts, the payroll department, accounting. Here the discovery of smart work means this: It is not that physical reality is not there; it is simply that organizations have developed according to inner standards in detachment from physical reality.

But in such detachment, crucial judgments about the meaning, impact, and effect of work cannot be made. The solution is to reattach bureaucratic organizations to physical reality. Where the physical reality is made up out of bodies that carry social meaning—human beings—this means to reattach the organization to its clients. This can be done by placing emphasis on the *judgments* of line functionaries who actually have their hands on physical material to be worked on or on the "social material" of clients and customers.

In the words of a U.S. Naval Hospital's executive officer implementing a successful Total Quality Leadership* program on Okinawa, this connection requires a twofold approach. Statistical tools such as "customer surveys can be the tools by which needs are determined and prioritized" but improvement depends, among other factors, on "implementation of programs *designed by the work force* with approval by the organizational leadership." And it can be done through statistical tools such as customer surveys.[14]

THE COLLISION OF QUALITY AND QUANTITY

Without consultation with those with their hands on the pulse of patients, a hospital's leadership is as disabled from making sound, reality-based

*The navy's version of Total Quality Management.

judgments as the individual physician who is kept ignorant of relevant resources and commitments of the hospital. The core of any proper response is consultation with those with their hands on the material and clients. Finally, there must be *integrated judgment* of the "what" of what needs to be done (quality) by all members of the productive or service organization.

To do this, however, brings judgments appropriate to the internal functioning of the organization (and the corresponding power structure) into conflict with judgments made from the viewpoint of the external outcomes of such functioning. External outcomes constitute the "what" of what an organization does; in Latin, the appropriate word is *"quale,"'* the origin for our "quality." Internal operations are evaluated by the measuring sticks of modernity: measures of time, of space, of intensity of work or magnitude of work. Quality now encounters and confronts quantity. This encounter between modernity, and its detached and formal organizations, and humanity, with its involvement in substantive needs, cannot be a happy one.*

Modernity's entire ability to control the world rests on its ability to abstract *from* the world. Science and mathematics are the tools for such abstraction. Around science, mathematics and their offspring, technology, an entire power structure has grown up. It is ready to defend not only this knowledge system but the inhabitants of that power structure itself: managers.

In the words of one of our students, a meteorology specialist in the U.S. Air Force:

When our version of TQM (total quality management) came in, we were all enthusiastic. We went through the entire 14 points [of quality advocate W. Edwards Deming]; we found out how the whole team could work together, and our manager got respect for what we were doing. Now I've checked back with my unit, and I find what was the first thing the new manager did when he took over?—Get rid of TQM.[15]

This raises the issue of power. But if power is an obstacle inside organizations, power also complicates the picture when it is applied to organizations from the outside: from society at large. In the United States, this complication works itself out in terms of a conflict between political values that then spills over into bureaucracy.

People Who Value Politics: The Social Obligation/Individual Rights Conflict

Outside of modern organizations lies the political environment. There people supposedly have the power to master and rule organizations.

---

*For a fundamental discussion of the reasons for this unhappy encounter, see "What the Experts Say: Martin Heidegger," later in this chapter.

There also another struggle is going on. It is between groups in American society who want policy to be based on principles of social obligation and those in society who see individual accomplishment and relevant rights as the foundation of the republic. How will this battle affect the chances for de-bureaucratization?

The battle is over which values it is appropriate for the nation to adhere to. Today the struggle is expressed as a battle of terminology used in political discourse. Power may lie with those who possess individual rights to property. It may be based on economic property or political positions won through individual effort. But an attempt can nevertheless be made to devalue such rights and property. Advocates of a values system of social obligation attempt to redefine the worth of just such political goods to be fought over. Once values such as social justice and equality are elevated in public discourse, and individual rights and property lowered, candidates can be fielded in campaigns over such a difference and power won at the voting booth. Social obligation advocates aim to win victory not so much through discourse over power as power over discourse. This is a case in which the word is mightier than the sword. Consider an example in the redefinition of political values:

White, Male, Middle-Aged Managers
and the Politics of Meaning

In a diverse class of men, women, Caucasians, African Americans, and students with Hispanic surnames, the following exchange took place during a discussion of affirmative action policy.

"The fact is," says a white, male, middle-aged manager, "I still get evaluated by my unit's efficiency. I'm not going to pay attention to all this affirmative action stuff."

"Maybe you'd better," says the white, male, middle-aged manager sitting next to him. "I'm your affirmative action officer."[16]

Before going on, you might want to join with some friends or colleagues in discussing this: What social values and what organizational values are at stake in this case? Set an arbitrary limit of 10 or 15 minutes for this discussion. Then discuss something else: the level of emotion and passion evoked by the discussion.

THE POLITICS OF INTERPRETATION

Note how the case can be read in at least two ways. We can unquestioningly accept the traditional meaning of the words. Or, we can try to promote an awareness that the meaning of some words is changing—and can be purposefully changed.

An interpreter immersed in established meaning might rest his or her interpretation on standard dictionaries. These hold that the words "diverse," "white," "male," and "middle-aged" are merely neutral and objective adjectives used to identify and distinguish members of the group.

Here diverse means different or varied. White is a color. Male describes the sex of a participant, and the term middle-aged approximates his chronological age. An interpreter from this tradition would be astonished to be told that he or she is using the words in a political way.

However, there are people interested in redefining words to achieve cultural change. They would argue that established meanings, far from being nonpolitical, simply stand for values undergirding a political establishment.[17] Some of these interpreters call attention to the fact that "diverse" can be given an explicit political meaning also. Its use may alert proponents of "diversity" to what they might consider the author's sensitivity to the value of having representatives from many different ethnic, racial, gender, and other groups in any given situation. At the same time, the words "white" and "male," especially in combination, have become code words valued negatively by some of those fighting for minority and women's rights. Thus, Prof. Becky Thompson of Brandeis University, in a manual distributed by the American Sociological Association, equates "white" with "racism" and "male" with "sexism": ". . . it is not open to debate whether a white student is racist or a male student is sexist. He/she simply is."[18]

It is clear that the same words can be read from quite different points of view. The first point of view assumes that words have an unchanging, objective, and nonpolitical character. What characterizes the second point of view is the recognition that words have political meaning; and using words—discourse—is a form of power. From this point of view, to change the value of a culture means to gain control of the meaning of the words in the political discourse.[19]

In an immortal exchange between Humpty-Dumpty and Alice in Wonderland:

Humpty-Dumpty:	When *I* use a word, it means just what I choose it to mean. . .
Alice:	The question is whether you *can* make words mean so many different things.
Humpty-Dumpty:	The question is which is to be master—that's all.[20]

What, for example, if people can be gotten to accept that the assertion that whites are racists and males are sexists is no longer open to debate? Then a true change in the meaning that human beings accord to words has been achieved. Whites and males are put in an inferior position in a reshuffled hierarchy of political values. In all political struggle, change in what is valued is undertaken in the power interests of specific groups organized for political contests over scarce goods. A victory in the politics of meaning also means victory in the struggle for the material conditions of life. Access is rerouted to education, opportunity to jobs, perhaps even property.[21]

THE POLITICS OF MEANING AND THE FUTURE
OF BUREAUCRACY

In today's political context, a case about affirmative action is not just about affirmative action. Affirmative action, which supports using public jobs to remedy employment discrimination,[22] itself expresses the intrusion of a social value into modern organizations.[23] The value is that of *social equity.* Under our list of social values juxtaposed against bureaucratic values, social equity probably falls under the heading of *justice,* though the intent of affirmative action is also to remedy previous *oppression* and correct resulting conditions of group *poverty.*

Strictly speaking, such values have no place in purely modern organizations. In fact *justice* of the kind here pursued, namely substantive justice that gives an employment advantage to members of some groups, runs up against *formal equality of treatment.*

To the extent that such incompatibility exists, our first white, male, middle-aged manager is correct: Dealing with having to place members of disadvantaged groups in his unit *might* take energy away from 100 percent attention to a key value of modern organization: *efficiency.*

Actually, some personnel experts disagree. For example, in *Griggs* v. *Duke Power,*[24] the Supreme Court continued previous demands that organizations produce scientifically validated tests for employment. It might be argued that this focuses managers' attention more on modern values of selecting and promoting by standards that are job-related rather than on traditional ones such as: Do we like the group the applicant comes from? On the other hand, the same case also says that lack of discriminatory intent, as partly shown by the presence of professionally developed tests, does not constitute a valid defense. This can be interpreted as saying that, even if selection tests are valid and job-related, resulting discrimination will not be tolerated. In short, the same political and legal pressure both strengthens continued rationalization and weakens it. The final outcome must depend on the balance between politics and the rationalistic spirit.

The complexity of the case perhaps shows this: A manager concerned only with task performance and efficiency is living in a world in which the battle between social values and bureaucratic values has not yet been resolved.

But, the case is not only about affirmative action defined as a legal system to remedy job discrimination. Note the descriptive adjectives applied to the actors: white, male, and middle-aged. The adjectives as applied by the author are not meant to be derogatory; they merely describe some of the characteristics of the actual actors. However, in the climate of culture change of the late 1980s and the 1990s, to be white and male was, in the view of some reformers, to be part of the problem. Similarly to be middle-aged might mean that a white male was an entrenched and difficult-to-change part of the problem.

As in any culture change, the upward valuation of some groups and individuals was accompanied by the downward valuation of other groups and individuals. Even though opposition to age discrimination was itself a value pursued by reformers in theory, its practice might be directed against older incumbents of jobs simply because their long service placed them in positions of power. (Note that in this case, one white, male, middle-aged manager, however, seems to have adapted to the reform policy, while the other has not.)

Can the values of social conscience find an ally in bureaucracy for a decisive battle against traditional society? For an answer to this we need something like a map to the future. Can a theory of culture do the job?

A THEORY OF ORGANIZATIONAL CULTURE

The use of studying culture is to find out what people value. Values give meaning to people's actions. Meaningful actions we can deal with. When a man rushes at me with a sharpened axe, it helps me to know whether I am on the New York City subway or at a reenactment of medieval battle scenes. In the one case, the act is likely to be deadly in intent because I know that I live in a culture in which it is possible for a police series to run on television under the motto, "Let's do it to them before they do it to us!" In the other case, the act's meaning—and its consequences—are likely to be shaped by what is valued by people playfully reenacting violence, not reproducing it.

Modern organizations are human relationships organized according to rational principles. If we know these principles, we can predict what people are likely to do. In the words of public administration theorist Jay D. White, "The greatest force for ensuring predictability is the establishment of the norms, values, and rules that make up the formal and informal structure of our organizations. The bureaucratized model of organizations is the classic example of an idealized system of explicit values, consistent norms, and formally stated rules.[25] This means those of us working in or with bureaucracy spend most of our time *interpreting*[26] what actions are required of us and what actions are addressed at us according to our understanding of a few underlying values that give meaning to norms and rules. It *pays* to know (1) the bureaucratic culture, in both its private and public versions; (2) the general culture of modernity with its emphasis on the value of science and rationality that underlies bureaucracy; and (3) the political culture that encompasses and limits the rationalism of bureaucratic culture.

In all these worlds, the individual needs to find out *what* is going on. But what is going on can be understood only by discovering the values according to which typical individuals in a situation understand the facts of their world. Take this scenario:

A middle manager is called upon to "do something, quick" by her executive assistant who bursts into her office announcing: "Your people are killing each other on the fifth floor."

The manager rushes into the elevator, takes it down to the fifth floor, flings open the door to the claims bureau and finds a fistfight in progress among ten of her employees.

What is the first thing the manager says? Take your pick:

a. "Get me a consultant to do a scientific study to explain what happened here!"

b. "Get the operations research department to do a trend projection on how long this is going to go on!"

c. "What the hell is going on here?!"[27]

The manager concerned with understanding what it is that is going on—is it a rehearsal for the medieval battle reenactment? Is it a fight over the new compensation system? Is it a fight over who gets to succeed her if she doesn't settle the fight?—will seek to get a grasp on the reality before her by trying to get at its meaning. But understanding meaning is neither an explanatory or predictive scientific enterprise; it is a question of interpretation. Interpretation is possible when we understand the underlying motivations, beliefs or norms, and values that people try to achieve or defend. These may be highly particular to a given situation—for example, the fifth-floor battle scene—but there are general values according to which all people in a given culture act. And the fact is that most of us have never consciously tried to discover the values that are the means to answering the question that arises in our daily lives: What is going on here?

Ingersoll and Adams: Patterns and Metamyths

The question "What is going on here?" can be answered by simple interpretation. Or it can be answered from a critical standpoint. Either can be useful. Interpretation gears me into the outer world, but in terms of the meaning of social patterns that I already share with people in that world. Critical examination allows me to picture an alternative to such patterns, weigh preferences for mine or the others' pattern, and prevents me from being thoughtlessly caught up in a current pattern enthusiastically advocated and endorsed by everyone else.

The organization culture movement has been characterized by just such thoughtless enthusiasm.[28] Nice pictures of a wonderful world of work were painted—and then rammed down workers' throats without further examination. The result: short-term ecstasy over being able to step outside the humdrum world of modern routine, long-term reversion to modern routine. Even in the heyday of cultural innovation, no one is ever encouraged to wonder at the fact that the new and wonderful culture remains in the service of traditional modern goals: profit making in the private sector and economy and efficiency in the public sector. No one among the advocates, consultants, and academics endorsing new management systems, now advertised as full-blown entire culture renovations, ever grows suspicious of the fact that new cultures, such as that of management by objectives and the current total (read: totalitarian) quality management systems, are installed against the background of thousands of people being fired.

Out of the resulting need for a critical view, this theory of organizational culture has emerged:

A theory of organizational culture in our day must be a theory describing and explaining the tension between at least two cultures: the pseudo-culture that is imposed by the hierarchy (today: the culture of quality) and the culture that quietly stands in the background ready to absorb and modify the imposed culture (the culture of quantity).

This theory is most clearly expounded by organization theorists Virginia Hill Ingersoll and Guy B. Adams.[29] For them, although the overarching culture lurking in the background is modernity itself, the pattern most directly related to practice is the "managerial metamyth." No matter what values are espoused in any attempt to differentiate one agency or business from the next, the managerial metamyth persistently asserts these beliefs as to what is right and proper:[30]

1. Eventually all work processes can and should be rationalized, that is, broken into their constituent patterns and so thoroughly understood that they can be completely controlled. (Note the obsession of, for example, Demming's fourteen points with this, despite its endorsement of quality.)
2. The *means* for attaining organizational objectives deserve maximum attention, with the result that the objectives become lost or forgotten. (Note the obsession of quality management *systems* with the means of capturing workplace knowledge rather than with that knowledge itself.)
3. Efficiency and predictability are more important than any other considerations. (Note the justification of the quality culture movement in terms of profit payoffs in the private sector and economy payoffs in the public sector.)

While Ingersoll and Adams caution that "there is no suggestion [by purveyors of the managerial metamyth] that this is the way things actually work" and that "this is a set of beliefs about how things ought to be," the managerial metamyth "tends to be used as a justification and a guide for organizational action."[31]

Operational presence of this myth as a guiding force can explain a number of paradoxes in the organizational culture movement. Why, for example, can an early advocate of excellence cultures, Tom Peters, conclude in his third book with a call for quantity contradicting his own espoused values of quality? "I offer one last demanding piece of advice.

Quantify. I am attempting to quantify almost everything. It can be done, no matter how apparently qualitative the attribute. Therefore I urge you to set a tough, quantitative target for 'differentiators,' as I call them, to every product and every service you provide. Specifically, I suggest ten for every 90 days—and frankly, that's far too low."[32]

Ingersoll and Adams will detect in the wording further evidence of what they call the managerial subculture, in which managers are always tough, demanding, and savvy.[33] As a consultant, Tom Peters is close enough to managers to know to appeal to this. But the key points here are these. Once we appreciate the hidden presence of the managerial meta-myth, we can understand why Peters seems to be subverting the values of his own qualitative excellence culture.* In addition, we are alerted to the likelihood that so-called qualitative cultures, widespread in the last ten to fifteen years, really mean quantity when they say quality. It is simply naive for social scientists to take the self-advertisements of the business community, consultants, and lately of government—that they are pursuing quality—as the final word on what they are really doing.

There is, however, a problem with the concept of examining cultural claims in terms of espoused pattern and hidden metapattern.

As Ingersoll and Adams themselves put it, "To the extent that technical rationality demands instrumental meaning structures and disallows intrinsic meaning maps, it impedes the meaning–giving potentialities inherent in human nature. But one finds intrinsic meaning structures in individuals, and even pervading organizations, where the managerial metamyth holds sway. The linkage is not clear. . . ."[34] As Ingersoll and Adams themselves suspect, making that linkage clear involves a deepening of the culture discussion into human psychology.[35]

Howard Schwartz: Narcissism and Culture

People can enjoy their work in ways that encourage identification with the organization. Ingersoll and Adams concede this, but they attribute this possibility only to "emergent systems." In these, people's working values would *become* the values of the organization. But Ingersoll and Adams are unable to imagine that there is an equally intrinsic joy in accomplishing purely technical work comparable to the intrinsic motivation that comes from doing work one's own way. "Imposition of rationalized systems, on the other hand," they write, "can extinguish that motivation, to say nothing of de-humanizing the workplace."[36]

This judgment ignores a crucial fact: It is precisely the genius of modernity to be able not only to insinuate itself into appealing to fundamental human needs but to raise some needs, even though patholog-

*See the list on page 67.

ically, above others. This is a question for psychology. Howard Schwartz suggests that when it comes to organization culture, psychology comes first and values later. Modern organization, Schwartz argues, first seduces the individual into precisely what Ingersoll and Adams recognize as "identification with the organization." In modern times, it is only in and through identification with the organization that consciousness of what one believes to be good and true is allowed to evolve. This calls for an amendment to our theory of organization culture, which now must read:

Culturally, modern man lives in organizations in a tension between a rationalistic–quantitative culture and corrective cultures that are a superficial response to the psychological deficits that the modern culture produces.

A theory of organizational culture in our day must be both a cultural theory of values and a psychological theory of how those values are created and processed. The cultural theory alerts us to the need to distinguish between at least two cultures: the pseudo-culture that is imposed by the hierarchy and the culture that quietly stands in the background ready to absorb and modify the imposed culture. The psychological theory of culture alerts us to the individual's psychological distortion of values that come in to the psyche and the distorted production of values that go out.

As a product of the Enlightenment, the modern organization tempts us psychologically with the image of a perfect "good" world that will be ours when the bad stuff is gotten rid of or gotten away from. This is literally Schwartz's argument. The image of a perfect "good" world even tells us the way to get there: It is technique.* If only we sharpen our skills enough and focus enough on the details of our work, we can achieve what Schwartz calls the "organization ideal." In short, we must change ourselves to reach the ideal state of being that the organization potentially already is; to the extent that it is not, it is our fault: We have not perfected ourselves. In the psychoanalytic approach to the study of organizations, this is called identification with the organization.[37] However, psychology also tells us this: The attempt to reach such an ideal is always doomed; therefore the human costs are not only high but to a large extent in vain.

For the psychoanalytic observer, understanding such self-idealizing organizations involves understanding the psychological complex of narcissism. The Narcissus of Greek myth looked so long into his own image mirrored in a stream that he fell in love with it. The modern organization tempts us with a perfected image of ourselves into placing our love in that image.

This is the explanation of how what seems to be extrinsic motivation can appeal to fundamental intrinsic needs—such as that for healthy self-love (exaggerated into pathology)—in the human being.

Turning the argument of culture upside down, Schwartz concludes

---

*See the discussion of technique in Chapter 5.

that: "A main function of culture, that is to say, is to give content and direction, to render sensible our longings to return to narcissism and to avoid the anxiety arising from our mortality."[38] The picture of the organization ideal, he writes, will be familiar to all teachers of organizational behavior:

This is an organization in which everyone knows what he or she is doing, in which there is no conflict or coercion, in which communication is open and direct, in which people want to do what needs to be done, in which every member is solely concerned with and works diligently to promote the common good. As I argued in Chapter 1, the picture is of an organization that has never existed and never will. But somehow it is of the utmost importance to students to be able to believe in it.[39]

Though Schwartz follows this up with deep-reaching studies of General Motors and the National Aeronautics and Space Administration, we can come to a tentative conclusion: The cultures advocated in the organizational culture movement sound suspiciously like the organization ideal. Their image is highly motivating because it reaches deep into the human psyche. But anyone who surrenders himself to their siren call will live in the tension between reality and an ideal that never has been nor ever will be. A more complete basis than this cannot be found to condemn the fantasy nature of imposed organizational cultures and their advocates.

A word needs to be said about what follows next. In earlier editions, each chapter's sections on "Experts" introduced the underlying approach supporting and sustaining the analysis. As experts like Ingersoll, Adams, and Schwartz rise in our own time, often combining and synthesizing knowledge across fields, the official experts in the "Experts" section of this and some other chapters recede into background. However, the background is the ground on which new experts stand. The founding experts are retained for their fundamental understanding of what is at stake in the battle between modern organization and the human soul. Specifically, three experts—Max Weber, Martin Heidegger, and H. Mark Roelofs—show how modernity retains superiority in its defense against the quality movement and social values mediated by the political culture.

WHAT THE EXPERTS SAY

Max Weber: The Culture of Private and Public Bureaucracy

The method of understanding what people do by digging down to their basic values was first and foremost developed by the sociologist Max Weber. Weber asked: Without which assumptions does the behavior of people in a given culture make no sense? He applied this question to modern capitalist enterprises. He found a specific set of values according to which modern capitalists—as distinct, for example, from ancient Roman capitalists—guided their actions and made sense of their world. Similarly, he discovered a basic set of bureaucratic values in general according to which those in bureaucracies, private or public, guided their behavior. Entrepreneurs, of course, use bureaucratic organization for some of the same purposes as do governments. Out of this research emerge imperatives of capitalism and imperatives of bureaucracy without which capitalist and bureaucratic life, complementary parts of modern culture, make no sense.

Max Weber: The Imperative of Capitalism

Those of us interested in understanding the conflict between bureaucratic and human values can learn something from the fact that bureaucratic norms surround us everywhere—not only in public service but in the bureaucratic components of private enterprise.

All business people at all times have always wanted to make money. But there is only one way to succeed in business today, and that is to recognize that modern capitalism is a specific way of making money superior to previous forms of doing business. The proof of the pudding lies in the fact that an entrepreneur not using modern business practices simply cannot compete against one who does. There seems to be a central set of rules—a modern capitalist imperative—which, if followed, puts the modern business person at an advantage over the more traditional predecessor.

The owners of my favorite doughnut shop on Manhattan's 14th Street understand this imperative of modern business perfectly. If the doughnut shop is to stay in business and overcome slow days when income is low, the enterprise needs to accumulate money to increase its margin of security. This money can then be directed into two channels: It can be put away as a cushion against bad times, and it can be invested in another doughnut machine to increase sales and further profits. Growth and security are intimately related.

But to know how much of a cushion is needed or how much profit can be reinvested, operating costs (rent, labor, materials, depreciation of machines) must be calculated. In addition, the owners have to determine how many doughnuts must be sold to break even. How many customers have to go in and out of the shop each hour, on the average, to let them reach their break-even point?

The owners of the shop, in other words, are highly modern business people. They understand that profits are not just to be spent, but are a guarantee for the stability and growth of the shop. And they understand that sound use of investment and reinvestment can be achieved only through calculating everything—not only materials, machines, and labor, but also customers and consumption.

They have understood the imperative of modern capitalism: capital stability and growth through sound reinvestment achieved by the calculation of everything. This imperative can be analytically divided into two parts, the goal and the means. The goal is growth of capital. The means is calculation—or, to use a term with which we are already familiar from our discussion of bureaucracy, rationalization. In other words, bureaucratization of business practices becomes the means through which capital growth as the imperative of modern capitalism is achieved. The private bureaucracy of the accounting office is the first pillar supporting capital enterprise.

This is an important point for understanding the imperative of public as well as private bureaucracy. The imperative of bureaucracy, from the first, has always been control. It was through the bureaucratization of his accounting methods, personnel selection and use, and market calculations that the first modern capitalist became truly modern and therefore superior to his less calculating predecessors.

Max Weber contributed mightily to this understanding of both modern capitalism, with bureaucracy as its control instrument, and modern public bureaucracy as the control instrument of the political system. Bureaucracy in both cases is the outgrowth of a unique Western belief that everything in the world could be calculated and thereby be brought under human control. This attempt to bring the world under the command of calculating reason—rationalization—becomes not only an inner tool for capitalism but an outward condition. Weber reminds us of the rationalistic control component of the overall bureaucratic imperative, for example, in his definition of the manufacturing type of modern capitalism as "orientation to the profit possibilities in continuous production of goods in enterprises with *capital accounting*."[40]

So much for the internal norms of capital enterprise. To the extent that accounting spells control, they are entirely within the range of the list of bureaucratic norms drawn up at the beginning of this chapter.

But elsewhere Weber's extensive research[41] also establishes that modern capitalism can exist only in an environment in which general rationalized norms, including bureaucratic ones, become the external conditions of existence.

In drawing up his summary of the conditions under which modern capitalism can develop, Weber includes these three points:

1. Complete calculability of the technical conditions of the production process, that is, a mechanically rational technology.
2. Complete calculability of the functioning of public administration and the legal order and a reliable, purely formal guarantee of all contracts by the political authority.

3. The most complete separation possible of the enterprise and its conditions of success and failure from the household or private budgetary unit and its property interests.[42]

These points summarize the dependence of the capitalist imperative—profit making through capital reinvestment—on the concurrent development of modern technology, modern bureaucracy, and modern economics.

Max Weber: The Imperative of Bureaucracy

The imperative of bureaucracy is control. This is true, for historical reasons, whether bureaucracy is master or tool.

CONTROL THROUGH RATIONALISM

In capital enterprises, the first office to be bureaucratized was the accounting office. Rationalistic methods of accounting, embedded in regularized procedures and office structures, which are themselves susceptible to rational oversight, allow entrepreneurs to "account for" any and all operations of their enterprises and how each affects the other. The final measure of such accounting is "the bottom line"—the profit–loss statement. The bureaucratization of accounting is the starting point for bringing financing, raw-material supply, machine and labor operations, and sales into a tight relationship with profit outcome. By demanding the rationalization of the labor process—that is, its description and organization in quantifiable terms—the accounting office could adjust the labor process as a means to maximize profit as an end. The logical and effective linking of means and ends in this way constitutes the very definition of the concept of modern rationality.* Bureaucracy becomes the practical carrier of the rationalization process inherent in Western civilization.

But what makes this emphasis on rationalistic control the imperative of bureaucracy when applied to public service? The answer seems to be that modern bureaucracy was specifically conceived as a control instrument to be applied to public service from the very beginning. In this sense, it has always been more master than tool.

One of Weber's contributions is that he calls attention to the need that capitalism, as an economic enterprise, has for the bureaucratization of the social and legal world. The outstanding value that bureaucracy offers to capitalism is that it makes the behavior of labor, fellow capitalists, and consumers predictable. Especially in law, bureaucracy freezes into relative permanence behaviors that are in the interest of capitalist entrepreneurs

---

*For some amusing and not-so-amusing deviations from this rationality, especially in contemporary business, see William J. Haga and Nicholas Acocella, *Haga's Law* (New York: Morrow, 1980).

to have permanent. The previous types of capitalists, with their innate tendency to play for high risks and take their money and run, come to an end when not only the methods of production but also the stabilization of the external environment make reinvestment of capital for ever-expanding growth a good risk. On the behalf of this growing class of entrepreneurs, state bureaucracies set norms of contract among entrepreneurs and marshaled the power to enforce them. They also regulated the ways in which workers could and could not sell their labor and began regulating markets to protect entrepreneurs from foreign and domestic fluctuations.

The central value that public bureaucracy offers private enterprise is stability against the tendency, found in previous types of administration, to allow flux through the arbitrary and unpredictable application and enforcement of policy. Such previous policy was, of course, the policy of kings, nobles, and landholders. Thus from the very beginning, bureaucracy served the purpose of limiting and regulating the exercise of political power by providing conditions of stability favorable to the exercise of economic power.[*]

Bureaucracy ensured this relative permanence in contractual, labor, and market conditions through its structure. Instead of being left to the good will of individuals, policies became embedded in offices or, more accurately, became the operating procedures of permanent offices which, if followed, guaranteed the income, status, and institutional identity of their temporary occupants.[†] By making the structure of administration inflexible, bureaucracy made an ever-changing world permanent. To accuse later bureaucracies of inflexibility is therefore to ignore the origin and nature of bureaucracy as an administrative concept.

When Max Weber first analyzed the central characteristics of modern bureaucracy, he also isolated its central values by a comparison. But his comparison was with the dominant system of administration that preceded it. Weber's famous six characteristics of bureaucracy (which are discussed below) mean little and reveal none of their value biases if they are read out of context—that is, without comparison with the preceding forms of patriarchal and patrimonial rule.

An overall view of Weber's six points shows that his theme was to contrast a new form of administration, moving toward permanence of control, against the occasional, haphazard, and often unpredictable form of arbitration associated with feudal kings and ancient empires. Each of the six points describes conditions that will prevail if a permanent and predictable administration of control is achieved. To bring out this emphasis on control through comparison more strongly, I have below taken the

---

[*]The ultimate replacement of politics by administration was in this sense a tendency built into bureaucracy from its inception. See also Chapter 5.
[†]On identity as the ultimate reward for bureaucrats, see Chapter 3.

central ideas of each paragraph, explained them in terms of the control aim, and related them to comparisons against older forms of administration that stem mainly from Weber himself. The full text is available in a number of reprinted versions.[43]

CHARACTERISTICS OF MODERN BUREAUCRACY

1. Bureaucracy is characterized by "fixed official jurisdictional areas."[44] *Jurisdiction* literally means to speak the law. Jurisdictional areas become areas of the exercise of law. These are clearly defined, systematically differentiated within a system of legal–rational legitimacy, and assigned to specific offices. They are the beginning of a rationalistic *division of labor.*

In its own internal structure, bureaucracy is initially a rationalistic model of patterns of behavior that it is designed to impose on the outside world. Once the world itself has become ordered, bureaucracy is intended to reflect that order in its internal structure.

In contrast, the precursors of modern bureaucracy are patriarchal and patrimonial systems—rule by the father. Premodern organizations that survive today include the family, especially the extended family of some ethnic groups, political machines, and the Mafia. In such premodern organizations, the law is what the father-ruler says it is, within the confines of tradition.[45] Areas of responsibility may be delegated, but not systematically, and they are subject to the arbitrary will of the father as sovereign. The vague and overlapping boundaries of jurisdiction reflect the lack of clear social organization. This is frustrating, especially to the rising classes of modern entrepreneurs, merchants, and industrialists who require stable laws and administration regarding labor, raw materials, markets, and contracts binding one another.

1.a. Bureaucracy is characterized by "official duties."[46] Duty is defined by law and by superiors in their capacity of office holders. A favorite saying of functionaries is, "I just did my duty; nothing personal." The psychologically compelling source of duty is an external one. Functionaries are obedient to rationally traceable, external command.

In contrast, work in premodern organization is done out of a sense of personal obligation. The source of the sense of obligation is conscience; that is, it is *internal.* A favorite saying of subordinates is, "I owed it to him; I couldn't live with myself if I didn't pay my debt to him." Subordinates act as if they obeyed an inner voice. In premodern organization, the reasons why someone is obeyed cannot be traced rationally by comparing actions to a list of prescribed duties; they become a matter for depth psychology.

1.b. In modern bureaucracy, authority is "distributed in a *stable* way."[47] Here Weber elaborates on Point 1: The emphasis on stability favors predictability and control. To the bureaucrats it means they can expect to see different types of orders always come from different places: The payroll department orders you to submit timecards; personnel rules on your fitness for the job; line supervisors give task commands. In a different sense, the bureaucrat learns to associate distinct forms of behavior with occupancy of distinct offices. Authority is clearly structured into permanent offices.

A further subpoint is that "authority . . . is strictly *delimited* by *rules* concerning coercive means."[48] Rules, in other words, are in existence and are published before administrative behavior takes place. The range of sanctions is strictly limited and assigned to specific offices.

In contrast, under premodern rules, authority is centralized in the paternal ruler and either not clearly distributed, if delegated, or not distributed at all. A contemporary example is the unstable fate of a White House staffer whose authority not only may overlap with that of others, but who has no permanence since the president may relieve him at any time; nor are his functions usually clearly delineated or clearly understood by others. Contrast this with authority distribution in any of the permanent cabinet departments.

In contrast to the delimitation of authority by rules, consider the family as a leftover of premodern organization. Here rules may not exist until a child engages in behavior not approved by the parent. Rules are often *ex post facto*. Notably, the purpose of administration in the family is not primarily control but growth. The range of coercion is infinite to provide for a vast range of possible behaviors and family needs: The Roman head of household could kill the child; the parent today can torture the child psychologically to develop control mechanisms of guilt and shame even as the child grows through individuation to material independence. Any member of the family can apply psychological torture to any other member; there is no official office of torturer, though there tends to be a chief executioner. In traditional families, it is the father.

Similarly, in the political machine, rules regarding reward and punishment for graft collection or political payoffs are never published. They change with the recipient, though an ethic related to them is understood.

1.c. Bureaucracy is characterized by "continuous fulfillment of . . . duties."[49] Such an arrangement favors the client's expectation that the administration of rules and behaviors in a functional area is permanent.

In contrast, premodern organization offers no such reliability, fulfillment of duties being dependent on the whim of part-time administrators whose interests in administration and assigned authority are ever changing. Such lack of continuity makes it impossible to develop expectations of finding the same market conditions, the same enforcement of contracts, the same administration of freedom of commerce, or a labor supply from one day to the next. This in turn makes impossible the rational calculation of means and ends for entrepreneurs or, for that matter, the rational planning of state tax levies to continue to support the administration without interruption.

Second, permanent assignment and fulfillment of duties give rise to "corresponding rights."[50] Rights are habituated expectations on the part of people that they will be rewarded in exactly the same way for an exact repetition in their performance of assigned duties. Without clear definition of duties and guarantees of the continuous application of sanctions and rewards to ensure their fulfillment, there can be no development of rights for either the functionary or the citizen.

In contrast, in patrimonial and patriarchal systems, exactly because they lack administrative structures to continually exercise duties, there are no "rights," only privileges bestowed by the ruler and left to the holders to assert as best they can.

Third, those employed to carry out duties must "qualify under general rules."[51] Again this provision enhances both the orderliness of administrative structure and the orderliness of administrative behavior in the environment. Functionaries picked according to their qualifications by standard rules can be expected to behave in an orderly and standardized fashion. Further, such standards can now be task-related rather than remaining ruler-related. In summary, in bureaucracy: (1) There are qualifications related to the task; (2) these qualifications are established in regulations; and (3) they are universally applied.

In contrast, in premodern organization: (1) There may not be task-related qualifications, loyalty to the ruler taking precedence; (2) there are no official regulations, only ad hoc rules stemming from the ruler's temporary will; and (3) the ruler's will varies from case to case. No way to run a railroad.

2. Bureaucracy is governed by the "principle of office hierarchy . . . levels of graded authority . . . a firmly ordered system of super- and subordination."[52] Again orderliness favoring control is fostered. Whereas jurisdictional areas provide a vertical division of labor, hierarchy provides a horizontal division between levels of administration concerned with matters of different scope and importance. It is also the control mechanism that holds the vertical division of labor together. This latter point is of great importance to bureaucratic control: The division of labor weakens the possibility of anyone acting successfully on his or her own, especially in situations where the division has been carried to such an extent that one functionary's action completes only a fraction of an authorized administrative act. At this point the individual functionary becomes dependent on guidance from the next higher office as to when and how to perform his or her action in such a way as to integrate with the actions of other functionaries. It is this dependence, based on the division of labor, and

the management of that dependence by ever-higher offices in the hierarchy that constitutes a law of causality for the immense power of modern bureaucracy. Functionaries are forced to look upward for the ultimate norms and rewards governing their actions. In doing so, they must provide a higher office with information on which sanctions can be based; they thereby surrender the management of their actions. The structuring of offices into a pyramidal hierarchy in which the highest office is the ultimate judge and manager guarantees central control over all offices.

In summary, hierarchy means the clear delegation of authority descending through a series of less and less powerful offices, the clear status knowledge of where you are located in the hierarchy, and the principle of supervision by the office next higher up.

In contrast, premodern organizations show an overlapping delegation of authority, with the higher office not necessarily more powerful, responsible, or authoritative. There is also uncertainty about what one's own place and authority and responsibility are from case to case. And there is a continuing struggle for power as a normal condition of officeholding, a continuous circumvention of higher-ups. Politics remains a fact of everyday work life.

Dependence on hierarchy for guidance and reward in one's own actions, and therefore dependence as a style of survival, cannot develop in premodern organization. Without the dependence, premodern organization fails to develop a means of control that is reliable over a long period of time and can encompass the immense vastness of geographical or demographic space covered by bureaucracy.*

The interaction between the division of labor on rational grounds and the management of divided labor by hierarchy is the basis for the scope, intensity, and controllability of modern bureaucracy as the power instrument without compare.

3. In bureaucracy, management is "based on written documents."[53] Written records make visible both what bureaucrats are ordered to do and what they actually do. Rationally organized administration, suiting means to ends—including the correction of such administration based on written reports from below—thus becomes possible. In private business, written methods of accounting are an example, as are computer methods, which are equally visible because they are retrievable. Examples in public service include records and reports. Administration activities are recorded

*Charismatic authority, for example, can be more intense than bureaucratic legal–rational authority, but it is usually short-lived and yields to eventual rationalization. Traditional authority may encompass vast areas, but it is subject to fragmentation as office-holders develop their own power base on a psychology of independence from higher-ups ultimately demonstrated by force—knights versus the emperor, feudal lords versus their Liege lord, and so on.

and survive personal willfulness, incompetence, dishonesty, and the departure or death of functionaries. Activities are at least potentially *open to supervision* from above—the hierarchy—and ultimately from outside—the public. There is here the promise of administration as a politically controllable enforcer of orderliness in those areas of human activity assigned to it.

In contrast, in premodern organization, communication and command tend to be by word of mouth and by humanly fallible memory. Personal control over bias of perceptions and understanding, personal determination to put personal interests aside—these guarantee reliability. Where such honesty is absent, administration breaks down.

Without permanent records, activities are difficult to inspect and analyze for the purposes of future correction and control. Control from one center becomes doubtful given the lack of formal regulation, evaluation, and feedback.

4. Bureaucracy's office management requires "thorough and expert training."[54] Here Weber not only repeats his earlier observation that modern bureaucracy requires employees who qualify under general rules, but emphasizes that office management as an activity itself becomes specialized and rationalized.

In contrast, in premodern organization, the qualifications of employees are mainly the confidence and trust of the ruler—e.g., the boss, the machine. The question is not so much "Can you do the job?" but primarily, "Can you be trusted?" This does not mean that a political boss, for example, will purposely hire incompetent people; rather, he or she will seek out competent people but make sure that, first of all, they can be trusted. The myth of the hack is just that—a myth—often perpetrated by professionals.

5. Bureaucracy requires the "full working capacity of the official."[55] Weber contrasts bureaucracy with the previous, premodern state of affairs in which the reverse was true: "Official business was discharged as a secondary activity."

Here Weber reemphasizes implicitly the primacy and continuity of administration over other, personal interests. Officials discharge administrative duties as their primary effort in life. This effort not only excludes time for personal or other interests, but suggests the development of an inner loyalty to and therefore inner dependence on the institution: Bureaucracy becomes a way of life.

In contrast, in premodern organizations, the available work capacity of the individual is given primarily to private endeavors. The office is second, at best. Officialdom is a source of private or social honor and income, not of institutional status and identity. Given such orientations, we can hardly expect officials to favor the rationalistic ordering of society according to general rather than individual interests.

6. In bureaucracy, management of the office follows "general rules."[56] General rules are rules codified in the interests of all or of those in whose general interest a bureaucracy is set up. Specifically avoided are rules favoring some as against others. Thus management itself becomes predictable; expectations of functionaries become regular; and a general atmosphere of orderliness and predictability is fostered—even within the structure of bureaucracy itself—with an aim toward projecting this onto the outer world.

In contrast, in premodern administration, management tends to be ad hoc, guidance occasional and spotty, the expectations of functionaries uncertain, leading them to look outside the office for security and support. A classic example of this is the type of administration that leads to corrupt police departments.

In summary, a restudy of Weber's brilliant analysis of modern bureaucracy should place the characteristics he cited in the light of the past and the light of the purpose for which this form of administration was created. The ultimate imperative of control is reflected in each of the characteristics of structure, behavior, and implicit psychology he cites.

Martin Heidegger: The Challenge of Quality

As early as 1903–1906, Max Weber warned against the tendency of the growing scientific culture to consider those things more real that could be measured and placed under a rule or law showing things occur in patterns or with some regularity. Especially when you or I are engaged in trying to *interpret* what other people mean when they act out toward us, knowledge of laws and human behavior "mean nothing to us."[57] Even social science's ability to show that a certain behavior is distributed uniformly throughout the world doesn't get us "one step closer to the interpretation" of that behavior.[58]

At the same time, the mathematician and philosopher Edmund Husserl, whom Weber read,[59] issued a related warning. Given natural science's increasing reliance on mathematics—bringing physical phenomena under mathematical rules—modern culture was getting out of touch with things physical.[60]

Nowhere have the warnings that science gets us out of touch with things human and things physical been more fulfilled than in the current crisis of industrial production in the United States. Parallel to this crisis, we experience a crisis in the delivery of physical products and human services by government agencies—a crisis more subtle, but a crisis nevertheless.[61]

The industrial crisis of modern organizations cannot be denied. Ironically, mathematics as the study of the bottom line helped us recognize it. Product market share decreases as the "scientific management" of American production lines steadily increased management control over workers' time and space.

By the late 1970s, after American consumers revolted against American automotive and other products by turning to the Japanese, quantitative studies showed each American car had 3 to 5 defects against a Japanese car's 0.7 to 1.5 defects; American air conditioners were 63 times as defective as Japanese products.[62]

American industry's response? Companies raced for survival. They tried to leave behind the idea that all human beings and all things could be managed from the top down according to general rules or laws. They fixed their eye on a new knowledge: one based on individual interpretation from below of what was going on between people and between people and things. Copying the Japanese model, American managers started listening to workers in worker–management participation programs.

As early as 1982, 41 percent of companies having more than five hundred employees reported having worker–management participation programs. By 1984, only a few years after the industrial crisis dawned on American business, 2.3 million workers were said to be taking part in such programs.[63] As the quality movement spread, becoming ever more all-encompassing in its claims, a version called total quality management took the lead, coming under attack in the private sector as early as 1992. At the same time, while the private sector was having second thoughts, the movement spread through all the armed services and to the federal and state governments. A General Accounting Office survey of 2,800 federal government installations found total quality management "alive and well" at 1,900, or 68 percent, of them in 1992. The National Governors Association found the system in some form present in 36 states.[64]

Across the board, modern organizations, while praised for doing well in the delivery of quantity, were defending themselves for doing badly in tuning in to qualitative needs of human life.

How could this happen? A few voices had warned against the culture of quantity for many years. One such voice was that of the philosopher Martin Heidegger, who took great pains to explain the hidden values of science and to juxtapose values of human life equally hidden in and by modern culture.

The Scientific Imperative

Assume that all we know can be got by listening to general laws of nature.[65] This is not how you and I experience getting to know things.

We, as ordinary human beings, get to know things in their individuality: my friend Jay here and my friend Michael there; this car door, which slams differently from that of my other car. But, if it were true that all human knowledge can be got from general laws, this would greatly simplify things. Then all friends, all cars, all things living and dead could be, if not understood, then explained—perhaps controlled?—by reference to a few natural laws, like the law of gravity or the law of self-preservation.

Modern science promises exactly such knowledge by reference to laws. And, at least in physical matters, science seems to have delivered. So that you and I, who don't know much about how to discover general laws, would be well advised to surrender our knowledge enterprise to an elite of scientists. From this it follows that there should be an elite of politicians, of legislators, of entrepreneurs, of bureaucrats, certainly of the clergy—of all those who have developed special methods of gaining access to general laws, whether "given" by nature, by the body politic, or by God. There have, of course, always been elites. Elites are those few who rule by claiming special access to knowledge of what is right and wrong and how to impose it on others. But, once science infests a culture, the necessity for such elites—knowledge elites—becomes obvious to all.

It is the achievement of Martin Heidegger to have shown us that human beings have not always assumed that their lives could be understood and regulated by general laws and to have shown us what orienting ourselves toward general laws makes us miss in the quality of human life.[66]

Two Assumptions of Modern Knowledge

Since Galileo, we have assumed that:

1. Knowledge of individual things comes from general laws *outside and above* the things instead of from *qualities inside* the things.[67]
2. Only that can be known which responds to ideas about reality that can be *preconceived*. This notion that reality has to be approached in terms of preconceived hypotheses the Greeks called *mathesis*. It is in this sense that all knowledge of modern science is *mathematical:* The knowledge is obtained by testing or challenging reality to respond (or not) to preconceived ideas about it.[68] Both before modern times and in today's postmodern beginnings, the alternate approach is to let nature—and human beings—speak for themselves in their own terms.

Assumption 1: Top-down Rules Outweigh Bottom-up Knowledge. The organizational consequences of assumption number 1 is scientific management. This organizes work from the top down according to general rules or laws about production generated by scientists and engineers. Today this type of organization is being challenged by the reality that overorganization of workers' time and space from the top down denies them a sense of the quality of the items that pass by on the production line. Without time and space to develop a bottom-up knowledge of *what* passes by on the line, there is no opportunity to judge what is appropriate behavior toward these objects. The result is a loss of quality in production. In public bureaucracies, of course, acceptance of the procedures of production ordered from the top down has produced the key strength of modern bureaucracy: top-down control. But there also, it has long been questioned by street-level functionaries whether their work can really be done simply by following the rules and without tuning in to the needs of the clients at hand.[69]

Assumption 2: Reality Is That Which Responds to the "Mathematical" Approach. The organizational consequence of assumption number 2 is hierarchy. We believe there is no other form of knowledge but the kind reflected in the elite of scientific management: Engineers and bosses know best. It is assumed that all that can be known and done is already *prefigured* in the hypotheses that science and management can make. Reality is determined by testing and shaping its behavior according to such prefigured hypotheses. In bureaucracy, this assumption of science supports the belief that all eventualities can be provided for ahead of time in the design of work. What is needed is a clear policy. This must be founded on a solid, scientific understanding of the principles of human behavior. This is then implemented in a logically derived program designed to manipulate one set of human variables to obtain a change in another set. So it is assumed that, if we throw money at people, human welfare will set in. There is one trouble with this assumption that all human behavior can be provided for ahead of time by sound scientific laws translated into sound policies and programs. The trouble is that putting all human behavior under scientific laws leaves no room for human innovation. (In fact, this technological view of science [the logic of technique] denies the discovery mode of science itself: the mode of thinking that great scientists allow themselves to enter into so they can get a feel for their subject matter *before* they decide on a research path expressed in terms of hypotheses to be tested. Heidegger's phenomenological perspective emphasizes processes of getting in touch with nature in its own terms *before* we challenge it to show itself in our terms by testing it.)

The bureaucratic consequence of accepting science as the underlying determinant of what is real in modern culture is to neglect all realities that do not respond to the scientific/bureaucratic "knowing it all ahead of time" approach. So, for example, all knowledge of any new action on the part of clients can, of course, not be provided for in a predesigned policy or program. It follows that it is bureaucracy's task to stamp out new action wherever it should show itself: as anyone engaged in launching a new business knows after encountering government rules. *Any* unplanned innovation is a threat not only to bureaucratic control but to the entire modern culture that prides itself on being able to anticipate *all* eventualities in the sense of being ready for them *before* they occur. Such innovation must be brought under control because it threatens the steady-state empire of modernity. Out of this grows the bureaucratic imperative for control.

The technological consequence of the scientific/mathematical preordering of reality before it is allowed to show itself is similar to the organizational consequence. Technology comes to be perceived as a vast storehouse of knowledge in which are laid away recipes for dealing with all possible natural and human problems.[70]

The political consequence brings home the fatality of this approach. Politics comes to be seen as the administration of human problems according to general rules, either scientifically established or, for the moment, promulgated by force or authority. Politics ceases to be a process by which people themselves become aware of how they shape their problems to begin with. (See the discussion of politics as administration versus politics as evocation in Chapter 6.)

In the meanwhile, the bureaucrat especially will find himself or herself caught up in an increasingly intolerable tension between people's demands for quantity in products and human services and these very same people's demand that the mass of such products satisfy the qualitative needs of human life. Such tension will be reflected in politics.

H. Mark Roelofs: American Political Culture

Any modern society defines the qualitative needs of its members through politics. Bureaucrats are supposed to be the instruments of politics to carry out the political will of the society. When bureaucrats turn to politics, what can they expect?[71]

But should a bureaucrat turn to politics at all?

When a bureaucrat does turn to the political culture for advice, he or she finds not a point of reference but road signs pointing in contrary directions. Say an administrator is concerned with political support for the federal government's main welfare program, Aid to Families with Dependent Children, which serves 4.8 million families or 13 million people. But: "The country reacts to them with a split personality," observes one newspaper report. "It frets that almost one American child in four now lives in poverty. But it also frets over the perception that their mothers, or at least some of them are behaving in unacceptable ways—not working, not studying, having children when they are too young and poor to support them."[72]

Survey researchers, almost since polling began, have observed this split personality.[73] It reflects a deep-seated split in what Americans value politically. On the one hand, politicians are able to call on altruism; but this can soon be reversed by egotism. Americans, given a chance, will come out in favor of broadly generous and deeply caring policies to help their fellow man, woman, and child, who cannot help themselves. These same Americans can be turned possessively selfish, exhibiting an "others be damned" attitude on these very same social policy proposals.

Political theorist H. Mark Roelofs explains why Americans swing wildly between altruism and individualism. He observes two sets of political values, some of which are directly opposed to each other. Minimally, this means that federal bureaucrats and others wanting to maintain their mission and their funding are well advised to pay attention to where the pendulum swings in any given presidency.

Consider the two sets. One set of values defines Americans' social conscience. The other set stands for what Americans believe worthwhile in the daily work of making it in America:

Social Conscience Values	Individualistic Values
Equality	Individualism
Social justice	Competition
Community	Hard work
Great leadership	Property

Under the social conscience set, Americans believe that America is a national community that marches ever onward and upward toward equality and social justice under the leadership of great presidents. Under the individualist set, Americans believe that a person has worth if, as an individual, he or she works hard in competition with other individuals to acquire property that can then be rightly defended against all comers—including government.

The Political Imperative

The political imperative in America is to do good without stepping on anyone's property. The political imperative for bureaucrats is to implement the public interest without offending anyone's private interests, especially not the private interests of powerful politicians who control the public purse. These, after all, have worked hard in competitive campaigns to earn "property" in public positions which must not be challenged.

Clearly the values of the public interest (as expressed through social conscience) and private interests are to a major extent incompatible. The individualist work ethic and its resulting claim to property, or political spoils, produce unequal achievements; this outcome results in inequality and divides the national community.

For the bureaucrat the question becomes how to gain and maintain the *power* to perform *public service* by allying himself or herself with either the social conscience values or the individualist values—whichever is at the moment most relevant to a desired outcome. The practical meaning of the bureaucrat's much-vaunted political neutrality is the ability to exploit *any* political value in order to implement his or her own. This means juggling and combining elements of three sets of values: the bureaucratic set, the individual conscience set, and the individualist set.

In stable times, when individualism is dominant, it would be unwise for a bureaucrat to link himself or herself to presidential aspirants espousing visionary causes.

In times when rugged individualism is interpreted as selfish and an obstacle to the great communal goals, however, the tools and values of modern organization have in the past been placed in the service of presidentially led visionary reform. See, for example, the link between the Progressive Movement at the turn of the century and rationalistic and scientific management theory, yielding America's first modern bureaucracy—one based on merit and encased in the Civil Service System.

How does this relation between bureaucratic values and the dual sets of political values work itself out today? Say you are a bureaucrat. You know that reformers are in the White House. You now have an opportunity to forge an alliance based on the formal fairness of bureaucratic values and the substantive fairness of the political values of equality and social justice. The problem is that reformers in their righteous pursuit of visionary values are likely to step on the toes of legislators whose career depends on protecting the political property rights in their position. Playing footsie with the president may easily displease those in Congress who fund your bureau.

A way of illustrating the tension among the three sets of values is to apply the schema to an analysis of the Clinton administration based on some early data.

THE CLINTON ADMINISTRATION AND THE POLITICS OF MEANING

The political battles of the Clinton administration present a perfect example on how the political culture split affects American politics and bureaucracy. In political institutions, the values work themselves out as follows.

Roelofs observes that the individualist values are embedded in America's *effective* political institutions,[74] the reservoirs where power lies. When power holders operate there, they can appeal to the fact that they have *earned*, through *hard work* in campaigns, *property* in small baronies that control power in the political arena. The values to which they appeal validate and legitimate their *right* to trade in power. Institutions thus possessed are, for example, the subcommittees and committees of Congress, through which legislation must flow, or the presidency.

America's relatively *ineffective* institutions, on the other hand, lack this power base but have been designed to enshrine the hopes and aspirations of America's social conscience. Typical of such institutions are political parties, whose power, especially when compared to parties in other countries, is a myth.

In stable times that myth remains what we call "mere" myth. For example, working through political parties is *not* an effective way to fulfill individual needs. A better way is to lobby through political baronies that give access to legislative power: Campaign contributions and the political payoff are standard there. The trick in this realistic politics is to find the means to influence individuals who have earned their political position (property) in the hard work of elections and control the subcommittees and committees of Congress.

However, myth also has a powerful, evocative side; its appeal can be compelling when citizens lose faith in the values that support the normal operations of politics. Roelofsian culture theory, therefore, also can help us make sense of unstable times.

A crisis of legitimacy arose in the early 1990s. A clear sign was the appearance of a third presidential candidate: Ross Perot. Against a background of economic dislocations for the predominantly white middle class and rising social expectations of the disadvantaged, the wheeling and dealing of lobbyists and the people's purported representatives ran up too blatantly against the mythical self-image of a national community of equality and social justice. Such crises historically have redefined the terms of the political discourse: what could be said and what could not be said.

Redefining the terms of the political discourse is itself a political move; it is the politics of meaning. The politics of meaning attempts to redefine what political "goods" normally mean.

Thus, President Bill Clinton appealed to the mythical side when he called taxes "contributions" to a national communal effort to rid the country of an enormous deficit. A similar appeal to community is contained in calling spending "investment." Spending on national infrastructure, for example, can be redefined as no longer constituting government pork-barrel largesse that benefits only the powerful or those successful at lobbying; instead, it can be depicted as benefiting the nation as a whole.

The trouble is, of course, that people can be pried loose from commitment to such national communal values by competing politicians. These merely need to cite chapter and verse of unequal contributions and unequal distribution of the investment, that is, by pointing out the presence of selfish individual values in a program sold on the grounds of social conscience. Thus, while 58 percent of Americans approved the Clinton presidency in January 1993 (with 20 percent disapproving), approval ratings went down to 46 percent, with disapproval up to 44 percent, by May. Similarly, support for President Clinton's economic plan dove from 59 percent at the February unveiling to 35 percent at the end of May with opposition at 45 percent.[75]

The entire early part of the 1990s, beginning with the 1992 presidential election, can be seen as an exercise in the politics of meaning. A third campaign (Ross Perot's) specifically critical of politics-as-usual, based on "What's in it for me?," disabled both of the two standard parties from racking up a majority. The result: a government backed by a plurality not a majority, the administration of Bill Clinton.

In turn, the Clinton campaign had also run for change and against politics-as-usual. It had promised the solutions typical of the social-conscience side of the political culture. There would be a return to a selfless national community on behalf of which a great leader could espouse social justice, including rights for minorities but also fairly shared tax burdens and equally fairly distributed governmental benefits for everybody.

CULTURE SPLITS IN THE PRESIDENCY ITSELF

In the case of the Clinton administration, however, the application of the social conscience/individual interest pattern alerts us to the following picture. Viewing the top of presidential government from this perspective shows that the split in the American political culture reached straight into the highest intimate circle, into the presidential family itself.

Sustained by pressure for a greater role for women in government, the president's wife, Hillary Rodham Clinton, emerged as a leader on issues of social conscience, such as health care for all. In turn, her husband was called upon to engage in skills long practiced as governor of Arkansas: the negotiation and compromise so necessary among the political barons of the American system if anything were to get done at all.

The result was a picture of contradictions. With exception of perhaps only one president—Woodrow Wilson, who was strongly criticized for sharing power with his wife—earlier presidents riding the culture's mythic wave had done so singly. These included George Washington, Abraham Lincoln, Teddy Roosevelt, even Franklin Delano Roosevelt, and perhaps John F. Kennedy. Any culture split would have to be sustained, fought out, and integrated within a single individual. Inevitably that individual would then be able to present only one face to the crowd: leaning either to be the visionary social-conscience side of the culture or the realistic baronial side.

Now a maritally shared but culturally split presidency was attempted, and not only the American public but the political barons appeared confused as to whether they had a visionary or a baronial presidency on their hands. Those with visionary expectations were disappointed: "With the public, there's a growing sense of betrayal," said one independent political analyst.[76] Baronial politicians saw incompetence. Even analysts consulting with Clinton's own party while defending him were critical: "It's a reflection of his being beaten up on all sides, his own party, the opposition party. He's taken a number of hits, some of them self-inflicted. He needs to understand the political culture of Washington, whether he likes it or not."[77] Bill Clinton's presidency was declared doomed by most political observers, less than half a year into his term, unless his economic plan survived a very close vote among the barons in Congress. (It did.)

On the one hand, the presidency now conveyed a series of policy demands cast in moral terms that tended by their very nature toward the absolute and non-negotiable. On the other hand, the presidency showed itself pressed and on occasion able to back off from the rhetoric of absolute demands and willing to compromise. The presidency was on a collision course with itself, not only in embodying different values segments in two individuals (one unelected) but in giving the force of authority to opposed segments of the cultural values system. Specifically referring to the uncompromising, combative, and visionary influence of Hillary Rodham Clinton on the presidency, one critical commentator wrote, "Returning to moral judgment as a basis for governmental policy must inevitably mean curtailing what have come to be regarded as sacrosanct rights and admitting a limit to tolerance. And that will bring the politics of meaning hard against the meaning of politics."[78]

OPPORTUNITIES FOR BUREAUCRATS

For bureaucrats, understanding the two sides of the cultural coin is crucial. Knowing the system is made of many small baronies tells the bureaucrat that, for example, to finance his or her agency, he or she must also learn to make deals and play the individualist-value game of politics.

And, what does knowing about the extraordinary power of mythical institutions in abnormal times teach? In the past being aware of the power of myth has enabled bureaucrats to piggy-back their modern institutional values on the backs of recurring drives for reform undertaken by visionary presidents.

But the long-term future is also clear. The collision of social conscience and individualism runs through stages, Roelofs suggests. These stages are (1) an initial incongruence (when myth can no longer conceal operational reality); (2) a spillover of the conflict into violence or other forms of vehemence, rage, and political breakdown; and (3) horror, exhaustion, or distraction. This last stage leads to reassurance that somehow, despite all contradictions, both sets of values can coexist. There is a decline of political consciousness into normalcy.[79]

In short, bureaucrats, like any citizens looking to the long term, should expect that a time will come again when: "Comforting myths are rebelieved and old practices resumed." How is this possible? Marking values collisions are presidential assassinations, the demonizing of entire segments of the population such as in the actual Civil War or class wars or ethnic or, more recently, diversity wars conducted against the white males of the traditional power structure. How is it possible to forget such wars of civil sacrifice? "This is possible because the old practices are the only available ways in which American citizens conduct practical life and because it is easy to rebelieve the myths. It is not in the nature of myth to be falsified by experience."[80]

BUREAUCRATIC CULTURE

How are the culture wars likely to turn out? Who will be the winners, who the losers?

For a prediction, the following trends and tendencies must certainly be considered.

First, modern organization, with its emphasis on formalism and detachment from substance, contains the tendency toward depriving actions, people, and events of their social meaning and toward judging these by their functionality.

Second, contemporary American politics also contains a tendency toward functionalism. An example is the translation of the drive for social justice into the merely technically "just" values of equal access to jobs. The campaign for this equality is fought in terms of substantive outcomes organic to society—people expect better education, better jobs, better income. However, the only way that victory can be declared is to implement these outcomes in modern organizations. And there all values are functional to a system founded on detached knowledge and systems values. The legal and administrative translation of political campaigns tends toward functional equality. Thus, for example, all individuals *functionally qualified for a job* are mandated to have equal access to that job.[81]

The foundation for this is the assumption that from the organizational point of view, people are interchangeable functional elements of a system and that the qualitative differences between them do not make a functional difference. "Everywhere bureaucratization foreshadows mass democracy . . . ," Max Weber already wrote.[82] But, following his example, we must put the "equality" of that mass democracy in quotation marks; it is not based on any presumed intrinsic value of the individual but merely on his or her competence when measured by the parameters of a job. With this kind of equality, individuality and personal dignity, the bases for equality in essentialist philosophy and modern society, disappear: Women, men, the races, ethnic backgrounds, religions, styles of private life are now all equally irrelevant and meaningless to the organization where only functional competence counts. As Weber observed: "The whole pattern of everyday life is cut to this framework."[83]

Third, the battle between quality and quantity *inside* organizations involves two factors, at least one of which plays into the hands of further modernization. The one that does not is this: rising belief in a distinct and autonomous knowledge base of those who actually have their hands on th ˑ work—line functionaries. The factor that does play into the hands of further increase in rationalism is this: the rising belief in the utility of statistical knowledge passed upward and downward and laterally throughout the organization through information systems. Faith in this utility does rest on an error: the assumption that hands-on knowledge can be translated into information systems data. But the organization does have the power to *force* such mistranslation.[84]

These three factors, and their elements, theoretically might be combined in any number of ways. Yet, in the real world, such culture choices are made by social "carriers." Cultural carriers (*Kulturtraeger*) are social groups that have a material interest in one or the other set of values as tools of knowledge and power and that exercise power to bring them to bear.[85] Using this theory of the advance and development of values and knowledge in social institutions, we can draw the following deductions from the above three points:

First, the drive toward valuing actions, people, and events by systems *functionality* rather than substantive *meaning* is supported by any and all modern organizations, which already dominate the world.

Second, the groups acting as carriers of *substantive* values such as *social* equality and *social* justice have been historically willing to allow these to be defined in legal, that is, *formal* and *functionalist*, terms as defined by systems. As a result, even where substantive values are represented (such as in affirmative action), access to jobs has been limited by administrative values such as competence to do a job. There is no reason to think that ultimately these carriers will have any choice but to functionalize all their substantive demands that they expect to see implemented.

In addition to this, the *political* opposition to modern values is split. Part of American political culture insists on *individual rights*. Faith in these is the engine of the economic activity in a capital-reinvestment economy. Yet individual rights limit the possibility of winning substantive values on behalf of groups. And, if recent Supreme Court decisions are any indicator, the carriers of rights may be in the ascendancy. This further limits the potential of advancing substantive *social* values such as *equality* and *social justice* for minority and other disadvantaged groups. Not only do organizations functionally subvert such substantive claims but the political opposition hedges them in.

Third, the battle between quality and quantity inside organizations pits a relatively less powerful and less organized working class against a managerial class. As Max Weber noted, "Bureaucratic administration means fundamentally domination through knowledge" of a certain sort: "technical knowledge" and "experience in the service."[86]

The managerial class' claim to power rests on quantitative knowledge and experience in manipulating the political power bases of the organization in imposing that knowledge.[87] Even when the validity of that knowledge is exaggerated "to the point of fantasy,"[88] there may be nothing subordinates can do to stop managers from imposing their power. In the words of the then head of the National Aeronautics and Space Administration, monitoring of quality does not depend on the number of employees involved in it, but on what the reporting mechanism is: "In other words, if they find something wrong, what can they do about it?"[89]

The managerial class has already sustained large-scale firings—one million managers and their staff in the private sector in the 1980s—under the leveling onslaught of management information systems. It cannot be expected that the remaining managers will give up their residual power base by admitting the importance of line-functionary knowledge in making the synthesizing judgments needed where the hand meets the material. Nor can the managerial class long permit claims by customers and clients that they are quite capable of competently judging what is good for them.

The salvation of all those with a power interest in the quantitative knowledge system lies in creating crypto-quantitative distractions such as greater variety, customization, and computerized demand systems that trigger swift, small-scale production of batches for specific localized use. These produce quick turnarounds in demand/supply cycles for both products and services. None of these, of course, say anything about *what* a product or service *means* to a customer or client in actual application or use—its quality. The distractions serve to control such meaning by preempting evaluative standards just as traditional advertising and marketing did.

The Lineup of Power and Values

The power alliances that are likely to form are these:

The Battle Line of Values

On the modern side:	*On the revolutionary side:*
• Any and all modern organizations	• Qualitative organizations
• The implementation policies of social groups	• The political organizing and campaigning promises of social groups
• Managers	• Line functionaries

All the weighty carriers and their values are arrayed on the side of modernity.

Qualitatively oriented organizations still must perform according to the measurable standards of the stock market, if they are in the private sector. If government organizations, they must perform according to the quantitative standards of legislatures. (It is no accident that Total Quality Management came to be used everywhere as a cutback and retrenchment tool, just as Management by Objectives used to be.)

As for groups standing for substantive social values, their problem is a lack of awareness to modernity's translation and cooptation potential. It is simply too difficult to imagine implementation of social values without their translation into modern values: for example, of social justice into administrative equality of treatment. As a result, when carriers of social values take a "revolutionary" position *vis-à-vis* modernity, they are able to sustain that position only in the grassroots stage of organizing and campaigning. When it comes to governing, modern realism sets in.

Similarly, line workers know that organizations cannot deliver unless these workers apply their unique and autonomous knowledge of how things really work in the delivery of quality goods and services to clients and customers. But the practice and theory of their knowledge cannot ascend into an effective power position unless permitted to do so by managers. (Shoshana Zuboff finds that the main tool for this, access to the computer's database, is denied workers by managers. But the real problem is this: Hands-on knowledge does not translate into hands-off knowledge that can be put into a database.)

These are some of the internal dynamics between modernity and its humanist* opponents. They may help account for the fact that modernity has infinite capacity for coopting challenges and foreclosing alternatives.

NOTES

1. Max Weber, *Economy and Society: An Outline of Interpretive Sociology*, 3 vols., eds., Guenther Roth and Claus Wittich, trs. E. Fischoff et al. (New York: Bedminster Press, 1968), p. 1002. Weber's emphasis.

2. On definitions of culture, see J. Steven Ott, *The Organizational Culture Perspective* (Pacific Grove, Calif.: Brooks/Cole Publishing Co., 1989), especially pp. vii, p. 51 on the vast variety of definitions of culture, and Chapter 7 on the origins and development of central concepts of organizational culture.

3. Jürgen Habermas, *Toward a Rational Society* (Boston: Beacon Press, 1971), p. 96.

4. Max Weber, *Economy and Society*, pp. 956–58; cf. pp. 224–41.

5. Paraphrased from Thomas J. Peters and Robert H. Waterman, Jr., *In Search of Excellence* (New York: Harper and Row, 1982), pp. 42–44.

6. This summary taken freely from H. Mark Roelofs, *Ideology and Myth in American Politics: Portrait of a National Political Mind* (Boston: Little Brown, 1976) and H. Mark Roelofs, *The Poverty of American Politics: A Theoretical Interpretation* (Philadelphia: Temple University Press, 1992). The split between America's self-definition as a communal nation whose values

*For an argument that humanism may not be enough in the confrontation with modernism, see Chapter 7.

derive from social conscience and as a nation of rugged individuals in constant competition over property and its ensuing rights has, however, also been observed by applied researchers. These range from Lloyd Free and Hadley Cantril, *The Political Beliefs of Americans: A Study of Public Opinion* (New Brunswick, N.J.: Rutgers University Press, 1967), finding Americans divided to a "schizoid" level between operational liberalism and ideological conservatism, to John Nalbandian, "The Supreme Court's 'Consensus' on Affirmative Action," *Public Administration Review*, vol. 49, no. 1 (Jan.–Feb. 1989), pp. 38–45, finding the Court operating in a tension between social equity and individual rights.

7. Weber, *Economy and Society*, p. 223 for all three quotations above. On the shift from substantive to formal values, see also: Michel Foucault, *The Order of Things: An Archeology of the Human Sciences* (New York: Random House—Vintage, 1973).

8. Quoted in Ralph P. Hummel, "Behind Quality Management: What Workers and a Few Philosophers Have Always Known and How It Adds Up to Excellence in Production," *Organizational Dynamics*, vol. 16, no. 1 (Summer 1987), pp. 71–78; citation from p. 75.

9. Interview with Ned Williams in Studs Terkel, *Working* (New York: Random House/Pantheon Books, 1974), pp. 174–77; citation from p. 174. Italics for emphasis.

10. See the discussion of the nature of mathematical knowledge under "What the Experts Say," subsection on Martin Heidegger.

11. Shoshana Zuboff, *In the Age of the Smart Machine: The Future of Work and Power* (New York: Basic Books, 1984), pp. 199–200.

12. Ralph Hummel and David Carnevale, "Of Mice and Managers," review of Zuboff, op. cit., *Public Administration Review*, vol. 52, no. 2 (March/April 1992), pp. 213–14.

13. Ibid., p. 213.

14. Terrell Bean, "Program Evaluation: Customer Survey as a Measurement of Total Quality Leadership," research project submitted in completion of requirements for the MPA degree, Programs in Public Administration, University of Oklahoma, July 4, 1992, p. 15 ff.

15. Student, Offutt Air Force Base, 1993; anonymity requested.

16. Exchange between two civilian managers in the U.S. military, Tinker Air Force Base, 1989, as recorded by the author.

17. For some examples: Bina Goldfield, *The Efemcipated Handbook* (New York: Westover Press, 1983); Cheris Kramarae and Paul A. Treichler, *A Feminist Dictionary* (Boston: Pandora Press, 1985); Francine Wattman Frank and Paula A. Treichler, *Language, Gender and Professional Writing: Theoretical Approaches and Guidelines for Nonsexist Usage* (New York: Modern Language Association, 1989); U.S. Department of Labor, *Job Title Revisions to Eliminate Sex- and Age-Referent Language from the Dictionary of Occupational Titles* (Washington, D.C.: U.S. Government Printing Office, 1975); Paula S. Rothenberg, *Racism and Sexism: An Integrated Study* (New York: St. Martin's Press, 1988).

18. Quoted in Patricia Collins and Margaret Anderson, eds., *An Inclusive Curriculum: Race, Class and Gender in Sociological Instruction* (Washington, D.C.: The American Sociological Association, 1987) as cited in Henry Beard and Christopher Cerf, eds., *The Official Politically Correct Dictionary and Handbook* (New York: Random House—Villard Books, 1992), p. 91. It may be noted that, inasmuch as politics is talk, to attempt to foreclose debate before it starts is a profoundly antipolitical act.

19. The assumption that the insights of discourse theory ultimately lend themselves to control, however, may itself be questioned. To the extent that language is the home of human beings and not the other way around, the belief that language can be brought under control is already a surrender to the control-orientation of modernity whose people and products are to be brought under control. On the application of literary theories to issues of administration: Jay White, "Taking Language Seriously: Toward a Narrative Theory of Knowledge for Administrative Research," *American Review of Public Administration*, vol. 22, no. 2 (June 1992), pp. 75–88.

20. Thanks and a tip of the hat to George D. Beam, "Ethics in Public Administration: Thinking and Doing—Book Review Essay," *American Review of Public Administration*, vol. 22, no. 2 (June 1992), pp. 145–55, for this citation from Lewis Carroll, *The Annotated Alice* (New York: Branhall House, 1960), p. 269.

21. By the way, the reference to the white males as middle-aged would be interpreted by some advocates of minority and women's rights as going beyond descriptive utility and constituting a negative value in the author's presentation: ageism. Reform and radical

groups using the redefinition of meaning as a political tool and weapon look at language not as the apt naming of things as they are, as for example Thomas Hobbes had it, but as the place where the future is defined. The politics of meaning as a movement is therefore associated with postmodern discourse theory, which sees language itself as a text that can be infinitely reinterpreted. See, for example, Ronald Schleiffer, *Rhetoric and Death: The Language of Modernism and Postmodern Discourse Theory* (Urbana and Chicago: University of Illinois Press, 1990).

22. "Specifically, [affirmative action] favors achieving the value of social equity in recruiting, hiring, and promoting qualified people from different social groups in proportion to their percentage of a relevant and qualified labormarket." Donald Klingner and John Nalbandian, *Public Personnel Management: Contexts and Strategies,* 3rd ed. (Englewood Cliffs, N.J.: Prentice Hall, 1993), p. 120.

23. This would not be the first time this has been done: veterans' preferences also constitute the intrusion of a value from society at large into organizations.

24. *Griggs* v. *Duke Power Company,* 28 L Ed (1971).

25. See already the distinction between the system's "functional rationalization" and individuals' "substantial rationality" by Karl Mannheim in *Man and Society in an Age of Reconstruction* (New York: Harcourt, Brace, 1940), p. 49.

26. In turn such a translation is translated into the more familiar terms of the individualist side of the political culture, so that definition of job parameters is taken as a definition of individual rights. The courts are as guilty of this confusion as anyone else when they uphold a "property right" in job positions.

27. Weber, *Economy and Society,* p. 226.

28. I am as guilty of this as anyone in academe or consultancies.

29. Virginia Hill Ingersoll and Guy B. Adams, *The Tacit Organization* (Greenwich, Conn.: JAI Press Inc., 1992).

30. Ibid., p. 40.

31. Ibid., p. 41.

32. Tom Peters, *Thriving on Chaos: Handbook for a Management Revolution* (New York: Harper & Row—Perennial Library, 1988), p. 72.

33. For the much more complex picture of the managerial subculture, see Ingersoll and Adams, op. cit., pp. 49–51.

34. Ibid., p. 247.

35. Ingersoll and Adams write, just preceding their own observations on the limits to their theory, that there is a difference between *instrumental motivation* whose rewards tend to be externally controlled and *intrinsic motivation* which is "generated by the pleasure of the task itself or by the satisfaction of being a contributor to something greater than oneself." Here I pursue the third possibility that both types of motivation are in some sense "intrinsic" to the human being.

36. Ibid., p. 246.

37. As, again, Ingersoll and Adams already have said.

38. Schwartz, op. cit., p. 18, citing E. Becker, *The Birth and Death of Meaning,* 2nd ed. (New York: Free Press, 1971).

39. Ibid., p. 21.

40. Weber, *Economy and Society,* p. 164. My italics for emphasis.

41. Including the three-volume collected essays in the sociology of religion, *Gesammelte Aufsätze zur Religionssoziologie* (Tübingen: J. C. B. Mohr, 1920–21), which actually, in Weber's own words, constitutes "a universal history of culture."

42. Weber, *Economy and Society,* p. 162.

43. The standard source of reference for the essay on bureaucracy is Max Weber, *Economy and Society,* pp. 956–1005. But the essay is reprinted in numerous readers, especially in the areas of sociology, public administration, and management science.

44. Weber, *Economy and Society,* p. 956.

45. For classic cases relevant today, read Mario Puzo, *The Godfather* (Greenwich, Conn.: Fawcett, 1969), for patriarchal rule in the Mafia; and Mike Royko, *Boss: Richard J. Daley of Chicago* (New York: New American Library, 1971), for a thinned-down version of fatherly rule in a contemporary political machine.

46. Weber, *Economy and Society,* p. 956.

47. Loc. cit.
48. Loc. cit.
49. Loc. cit.
50. Loc. cit.
51. Loc. cit.
52. Ibid., p. 957.
53. Loc. cit.
54. Ibid., p. 958.
55. Loc. cit.
56. Loc. cit.
57. Max Weber, "Knies und das Irrationalitätsproblem," part II of "Roscher und Knies und die logischen Probleme der historischen Nationalökonomie," in *Gesammelte Aufsätze zur Wissenschaftslehre,* 3rd ed. Johannes Winckelmann, ed. (Tübingen: J. C. B. Mohr [Paul Siebeck], 1968), pp. 42–105; citation from p. 70.
58. Loc. cit.
59. Loc. cit., pp. 77, 102, 109, 110. See also R. P. Hummel, "Max Weber as Phenomenologist," paper presented at the Fifth Annual Conference of Political Science Departments, City University of New York Graduate Center, New York City, Fall 1980.
60. Edmund Husserl, *The Crisis of European Sciences and Transcendental Phenomenology—An Introduction to Phenomenological Philosophy,* David Carr, tr. (Evanston, Ill.: Northwestern University Press, 1970).
61. See R. P. Hummel, "The Two Traditions of Knowledge: Quality Management and the Crisis of Quantity," cited below, note 84.
62. On cars: data from study by James E. Harbour submitted to senior executives of Ford, General Motors, and Chrysler in the fall of 1980; reported in Thomas L. Freidman, "Autos: Studying the Japanese—U.S. Analyst Cites Their Cost Cutting," *New York Times,* Feb. 27, 1982, pp. 29 and 31. On air conditioners: data from David E. Sanger, "Another No. 1 Rating to Japanese: Quality Study Is Disputed," *New York Times,* Aug. 25, 1981, pp. D1 and D6.
63. 1982 data: New York Stock Exchange survey; reported in William Serrin, "Giving Workers a Voice of Their Own," *New York Times Magazine,* Dec. 2, 1984, p. 136. 1984 data: William Serrin, "Giving Workers a Voice of Their Own," *New York Times Magazine,* Dec. 2, 1984, pp. 125–37.
64. Federal and state data reported in John Larkin, "Total Quality Management Holds Ground," *PA Times,* vol. 15, no. 11 (1 December 1992), pp. 1 and 10.
65. The entire discussion of the scientific imperative is based in the main on two sources: Martin Heidegger, *What Is a Thing?,* W. B. Barton, Jr., and Vera Deutsch, trs.; analysis by Eugene Gendlin (South Bend, Ind.: Regnery/Gateway, 1967); and Heidegger's understanding of Immanuel Kant's *Critique of Pure Reason,* see Kant, *Critique of Pure Reason,* Norman Kemp Smith, tr. (New York: St. Martin's Press, 1965), especially B xi through B xiv.
66. Heidegger's attempts to show us the quality of human life as it extends beyond modernity and technology is a theme throughout his work, but it emanates critically and philosophically from his earlier work and poetically from his later work.
67. This is best expressed in Heidegger's analysis of the meaning of Galileo's experiments in allowing balls of different weight to fall from the Leaning Tower of Pisa; see Heidegger, *What Is a Thing?,* pp. 88–90.
68. Heidegger, op. cit., pp. 65–80. To the Greeks, Heidegger writes, "The μαθήματα, the mathematical, is that 'about' things which we already really already know about. Therefore we do not first get it out of things, but, in a certain way, we bring it already with us." Op. cit., p. 74. This is an accusation difficult to understand in regard to our popular impression of how science works: Certainly science *tests* its assumptions against things; but the accusation makes sense if we remember Kant's point that science approaches nature like "an appointed judge who compels the witnesses to answer questions which he himself has formulated." Kant, op. cit., B xiii. Nature is asked to respond to those questions, and *only* those questions, preconceived by science. Heidegger's accusation is easier to understand and accept when we look at the cultural impact of the scientific attitude: Certainly managers, especially adherents of scientific management, approach things, tools, and us as workers with the idea that they already possess the general principles by which they can successfully

manipulate us; it is we who must adjust to the principles, not the principles to us. This might seem a corruption of the true scientific approach; but Heidegger goes on to say that science itself is already corrupt when it does not allow things to show themselves in their own terms.

69. See R. P. Hummel, "Bottom-up Knowledge in Organizations," paper presented at the Conference on Critical Perspectives in Organization Theory, Baruch College, City University of New York, Sept. 5–7, 1985.

70. Martin Heidegger, *The Question Concerning Technology and Other Essays*, William Lovitt, tr. (New York: Harper and Row, Torchbooks, 1977), pp. 15–19 ff.

71. This section is based on H. Mark Roelofs, *Ideology and Myth in American Politics: A Critique of a National Political Mind* (Boston: Little, Brown, 1976); Roelofs, *The Language of Modern Politics: An Introduction to the Study of Government* (Homewood, Ill.: Dorsey Press, 1967); Roelofs, "Critique of Pure Politics," paper delivered to the 1982 annual meeting of the American Political Science Association, Denver, Sept. 2–5, 1982; Roelofs, "The Biblical Contribution to Western Political Thought: A Phenomenological Perspective," paper presented at the annual meeting of the Canadian Society for the Study of Religion, Montreal, June, 1985; and Roelofs, *The Poverty of American Politics*, cited in note 6.

72. Jason DeParle, "Policy Rift: Campuses Buck Clinton on Welfare," *The New York Times*, "Week in Review" section, October 25, 1992, p. 4E.

73. Lloyd A. Free and Hadley Cantril, *The Political Beliefs of Americans: A Study of Public Opinion* (New Brunswick, N.J.: Rutgers University Press, 1967).

74. Roelofs, *The Poverty of American Politics*, cited in note 6.

75. Gallup Poll cited as USA TODAY/CNN/Gallup Poll in Adam Nagourney and Richard Benedetto, "Clinton Sputters: Supporters Wonder What Happened," *USA Today*, May 25, 1993, pp. 1–2A.

76. Charles Cook quoted in Nagourney and Benedetto, "Clinton Sputters," cited in note 75, p. 1.

77. Democratic consultant Victor Kamber cited loc. cit.

78. Michael Kelly, "Saint Hillary," Sunday magazine of *The New York Times*, May 23, 1993, pp. 22–25, 63–66; citation from p. 66.

79. Roelofs, *Ideology and Myth in American Politics*, pp. 43–44.

80. Ibid., p. 44.

81. In turn such a translation is translated into the more familiar terms of the individualist side of the political culture, so that definition of job parameters is taken as a definition of individual rights. The courts are as guilty of this confusion as anyone else when they uphold a "property right" in job positions.

82. Weber, *Economy and Society*, p. 226.

83. Weber, *Economy and Society*, p. 223.

84. On the autonomy of worker knowledge: Ralph P. Hummel, "The Two Traditions of Knowledge: Quality Management and the Crisis of Quantity," in Donald J. Calista, ed., *Bureaucratic and Governmental Reform* (Greenwich, Conn.: JAI Press, 1986), pp. 277–93; p. 287: "Quality remained as a concept denoting tight control over measurable tolerances in the process of production or tight control over the range of discretion permitted in the delivery of private or public services. Quality did not retain its original and primary base of direct experience of the individual with people or things that could give rise to claims for a realm of quality requiring a distinct type of knowledge."

85. The concept that social ideas need carriers for their implementation is adopted from Max Weber. See especially his *The Protestant Ethic and the Spirit of Capitalism*, tr. Talcott Parsons (New York: Scribner's, 1958).

86. Ibid., p. 225.

87. See also Joel Kotkin and Yoriko Kishimoto, "Theory F: All Those Studies on Japanese Management Overlook the One Ingredient That Makes It All Work: Fear," *INC.*, April 1986, pp. 53–60.

88. Nobel Prize-winning physicist Richard P. Feynman, after investigating the crash of the space shuttle Challenger, as quoted in John Noble Wilsford, "U.S. Acts to Speed Recommendations of Shuttle Panel: Aides Say Reagan Is Pleased With Report and NASA Will be Ordered to Comply," *The New York Times*, June 11, 1986, pp. A1–B6; quotation from p. A1.

89. Charles Mohr, "NASA Chief Argues for Replacing the Space Shuttle," *The New York Times*, May 28, 1986, p. B5; quoting James C. Fletcher.

3

The Psychology
of Bureaucracy

*The bureaucratization of all domination very strongly furthers the devel-
opment of . . . the personality type of the professional expert.*

—*Max Weber*[1]

Psychologically, the experience of knowing and feeling—cognition and
emotion—is radically different for the bureaucrat from knowing and feeling among people in society. This is so because bureaucracy's structures
force bureaucrats into behaviors that alter the psyche's processes by
which knowledge is acquired and by which emotions are felt. The individual no longer retains the right to judge what is right and wrong. The
individual no longer is accorded the ability to judge when work is done
well or done badly. Above all, bureaucracy claims the right to determine
who or what we are; no longer are we allowed to work out our personality; we are assigned an organizational identity as we let the organization
be our conscience and define what is real. The individual as such disap-
pears and is replaced by a bundle of functions: a role. Emotionally we
agree to this dissolution of our conscience, our ego competence, and our
personality when we first agree to enter the state of passionless and
mind-numbing rationality demanded by bureaucracy's norm of neutrality.
When we are asked to give up our personal feelings for the people and
things we work on, we surrender the prime human emotions: love and
hate.

Yet human beings have great difficulty working without a sense of
what they are doing (reality), without a sense that what they do affects
others for good or for ill (morality), without an inner sense of who they
are (personality), and without feelings for the things they belabor or the
people they work with or the work itself (intentionality). Imprisoned in
reality structures that can enforce such working conditions from without,
people in bureaucracy make up their own reality from within. Fantasy

comes to dominate. This is something that the designers of bureaucracy did not foresee in their deep belief that rationalism could conquer all. A psychology of work rises up against the psychology of organization. The psychology of organizations overall focuses on the dilemma that different, and at times antagonistic, psychologies are required for organizing and for actually accomplishing work.

In sum, the psychological experience of bureaucracy is this:

1. Bureaucrats are asked to become people without conscience; judgments as to right and wrong are to be left to the supervisor, the manager, or the organization as a whole. Those who submit become people without heart: not only does their sense of moral judgment atrophy but so do their feelings for others. Those who cannot quite submit suffer from complex convulsions of their psyche, including guilt over doing things of which their conscience does not approve or from shame at doing things of which they know others would not approve.

2. Bureaucrats are asked to become people without a sense of mastery; judgments as to whether they do their work well or badly are to be left to those in the hierarchy or to the organization's rules, not to direct experience with the reality of things itself. Those who submit become people without head: Ego function, their sense of knowing what it takes to get a piece of work done, atrophies. Those who cannot quite submit suffer from conflicts: How can they respect themselves when they submit daily to orders and judgments of superiors that contradict their own experience of the world and the work they do? Especially professionals—but also anyone with a strong sense of what works—begin to question who or what they are and face the choice of exit or hanging their head in shame, confusion, and doubt when confronted with doing something right or doing it according to orders or rules.

3. Bureaucrats are asked to leave their emotions at home. Yet all that human beings do—in relating themselves to other people, the objects of their work, the working itself—carries with it feelings. We love our work when we do it well. We feel affection for a boss who enables us to succeed in what we are good at. We have feelings for those we work with—love or hate, like or dislike, envy or good will—and we feel for those who are our clients—compassion or disdain, superiority or inferiority, and so on. The proper bureaucratic response to the injunction against any open display of emotion is to repress emotion to where it cannot be felt. As a result, unconscious feelings silently accompany all our relations with people and things at work—at times distorting, at times supporting our ability to get work done.

4. Finally, bureaucrats experience, in moments of accidental or organizationally planned personal crisis, their dependency on the organization for identity. Who or what I am is at all times dependent on who or what the organization says I am. To the extent that I have already given up moral and mastery judgments along with my true feelings, there does not seem to be much left of me in the face of the organization. My personality is no longer my own; it has been replaced by what I am for the organization: Organizational identity comes to replace self-identity. This is more than a psychological problem; I feel myself challenged by modern organization in my total ability to be a human being.

The following sections explore these difficulties. We ask first: What is the typical psychological experience of the bureaucrat? Second: How have experts interpreted, or how would they interpret, this experience? Third: What psychology of bureaucracy can be constructed today?

WHAT PEOPLE KNOW AND FEEL

A functionary:

When I first joined the traffic department, I felt I knew my job. My job was taking out my crew—I had two helpers—go out with the truck, and we'd see a street sign down, and we'd put it back up. We had all kinds of signs in the truck. We'd do maybe 40 signs a day, and when we got tired, we knocked off. Maybe an hour or two early.

Then they said: Put it on paper. So we knocked off maybe three hours, did maybe 35 signs or so, and the rest was paperwork. I guess if it wasn't on paper, they didn't feel it was done.

Then they brought in an efficiency expert. The section boss one morning hands me a piece of paper: "You will put up this and this many signs a day, or we'll know the reason why." I looked at the piece of paper, and took it out in the street to my crew. Then we rolled in the street for 20 minutes, laughing our heads off. Their quota was 20 signs a day. We'd been doing 30, 40 before they started screwing around. Paperwork, reports, efficiency experts. Now we do 20 signs, and knock off.[2]

A manager:

I'm a banker. That is, I work for the _____ bank. We lend money. To big companies, too. When the company doesn't come through on a loan, we go in and take them over. I've fired an entire board of directors and the entire top management in one afternoon.

Anyway, we go into this one company. There's me for my bank, and representatives for four other banks. This outfit really was stretched thin on loans. They hadn't paid off for almost a year. They made computers. We asked: What's your total output for the year? They said: Well, it varies. We asked: What does one of your units sell for? They said it depends on the market. These guys just didn't know what the hell they were doing. We fired them.

One vice-president came in not knowing what was going to happen. He thought he was there to give the plan for the next year. We told him he was fired. He didn't even hear what we told him. He just went on giving his plan for the next year. I don't think it hit him 'til he got home.

The other vice-president just put his head down and cried.

It makes you wonder. You feel you are somebody because you've got a lot of power. You've been running the lives of, say, maybe 300, 400, a thousand people. Suddenly you're out. You're a nobody. How could it happen to you? It can happen, though.[3]

These interviews reflect typical bureaucratic experiences with knowing and feeling. But, in their interpretation, the storytellers also illustrate four popular fallacies about bureaucracy. These fallacies are the direct result of failure to understand the distinct psychology of bureaucracy.

The first is the fallacy of the superego. Here the functionary assumes, because he has intimate contact with the work that needs to be done, that he can remain the best judge of whether that work is done properly according to social standards of moral right or wrong.

The second is the fallacy of the ego. This assumes that bureaucracy can and will allow an individual to achieve and maintain full mastery over a piece of work apart from other individuals and judge whether it is done badly or well.

The third is the fallacy of misplaced emotion. This leads the inmate of bureaucracy—public or private—to falsely assume he or she can lead a purely rational work life—until confronted with a situation where emotion becomes overwhelming.

The fourth is the fallacy of identity. This leads bureaucrats—whether public or private—to assume that after they have given their all to the organization they will be permanently granted an identity. This comes from the social experience that the more one exercises one's personality, the more one "has" one's personality. Organizations' needs change, however, and, when the identities constituted by a cluster of previously needed functions are no longer needed, they are dissolved—and the people who carry the identities with them.

The fallacies are held by many. They are uttered in what amounts to typical folksayings among bureaucrats. What are the assumptions of such fallacious sayings? What truths do they nevertheless contain? How does psychology evoke these truths?

The Fallacy of the Superego

In the case of the sign repairman, he presumed he could best judge what constituted an honest day's work. He knew the job. He presumed he could judge the standards for the job: You do as much as you can, and when you get tired you knock off. His motivation was an inner one. So was his measurement of tiredness. His standards reflected a sense of social usefulness of the work to be done and a sense of social fairness: When signs are down, you help motorists by picking them up, and you give an honest day's work for the dollar.

THE DENIAL OF JUDGMENT

Judgment in work situations can be of two kinds: situational and social. Situational judgments have an inner and an outer horizon. Outwardly, the standard for judgment as to how well or how badly one performs is the definition of the job—the way the organization sees the work. The inner horizon and standard for judgment is the work itself—the way a piece of work must be approached in its own terms if it is to yield to human manipulation. In regard to the first standard, the worker assumes, in a typical folksaying, that, "As long as I do my job [as defined by the organization], nobody is going to bother me." In judgments referring to the work itself, the folksaying is, "I know my work, nobody can tell me what to do." The first folksaying is the refuge of the ingrained and successful bureaucrat. The bureaucrat who relies on the second belief as a standard tends to get in trouble with the organization—for work often contradicts the organizational definitions of the job.

There is also social judgment. Despite their implicit surrender to organizational values implied in the job contract, some employees persist in using society's values as the ultimate standards for judging whether they are doing right or wrong on the job. Industrial managers and workers may show qualms over polluting the larger environment beyond the company's gates. Civil service workers may refuse to carry out legal orders of their bureaucracy that they feel are not legitimate—for example, when a public health doctor is ordered to sterilize a welfare mother. During the Watergate affair, some high administrators allowed themselves to be fired or resigned rather than carry out what they perceived as legal but nonlegitimate presidential orders.

On the other hand, the well-integrated organization man or woman will do anything a superior orders, including breaking into the headquarters of an opposing political party, rifling confidential psychiatrist's records, subverting the election process, putting into question the continuity of American democracy itself, and similar trifles. For such people, effectiveness in organizational terms takes precedence over any higher law. Of the Watergate offenders, Judge John J. Sirica wrote, "There seemed to be no limit to the contempt in which the White House men held the legal process. . . . They seemed always concerned about politics, never about whether their actions were right or wrong."[4] The point, however, is that the structure of modern organization and its system of rewards and punishments make such behavior perfectly normal: A situation is created in which what works is appropriate and moral issues are irrelevant.

What does this mean psychologically? In Freudian terms, standards for behavior in society are stored in a structure of one's psyche called the superego. The superego stores, after some interpretation, society's norms of what is right and wrong. In society, the work you do for and with other individuals is very much tied in with how they will personally feel about you and your worth; consequently, the superego contains standards both for social relations and for work. Modern bureaucracy, however, is specifically a type of organization that intends to separate work from personal relationships.

In bureaucracy the individual functionary is asked to surrender part of the superego to the hierarchy. He or she must not only, as Max Weber says, "subordinate himself to his superior without any will of his own,"[5] but must agree to become subordinate to an external, alien superego.

Functionaries are thus persons with externalized superegos. This term, "externalized superego," expresses two thoughts. Functionaries still act according to the norms and standards of a superego. But, the ultimate location of the superego containing these norms and standards, and possessed of a will to apply them, is not their psyches but the office of their superior.*

The fallacy of the superego is then a carryover from the previous solid assumption of subordinates that they are best suited to judge their own work, an assumption that is, however, disputed by the bureaucratic context. It divides into two subfallacies—the subfallacy of the individualist and the subfallacy of the professional.

THE SUBFALLACY OF THE INDIVIDUALIST

The subfallacy of the individualist rests on the functionary's carrying over from society a self-concept that has no place in bureaucracy. The self-concept of the individual in society is that of a personality—those unique characteristics that make a person stand out from all others. The self-concept of the functionary in bureaucracy, however, is never allowed to develop in terms of separateness and uniqueness, but only in terms of integration and similarity (or functionality) in relation to the rest of the organization. What the functionary *is* the organization intends to design exclusively from above.

This is especially important to the question of norms and standards contained in the superego. In normal society, I, as an individual, judge myself, often harshly, according to my own standards, which make up the superego. My superego, it might be said, looks at what I do and, when I fail to measure up to its standards, punishes me severely through a variety of psychic pains—guilt, for example. My inner superego constitutes a sense of my own worth: It is a measure of my self-esteem. There is, of course, the esteem of others. They have their norms and standards, and they often try to impose them on the lone individual who deviates. There is, however, a tremendous difference between saying that in society others "occasionally" or even "often" correct the behavior of individu-

---

*It would be a mistake to now see the superego of the subordinate placed in the psyche of the superior. Superiors simply carry out actions dictated to them by the job definition associated with their office. They are not their subordinate's personal superego; they are his or her official superego. Were the managers to be removed, others would carry out the dictates of the organization approximately in the same manner and certainly within the same definition of the function of the superego, which is that it is always the superior office that exercises the legitimate right of imposing and judging standards, not the subordinate within his or her own mind.

als and observing that in bureaucracy all correction is ultimately carried out by an agency outside the psyche of the individual.

Consider the individuation process in society. Society exists before we are born into it. We learn, or internalize, its norms. But as we mature into individuals, as we go through the process of individuation, we adjust, change, and overturn much of what we have learned. Our superego, finally, comprises learned norms and norms we ourselves have developed in our own experience with life. The new norms themselves are then passed on or back to society as new generations take their norms from us as parents, teachers, and fellow members of society.

In addition, social norms and individual norms always stand in a relation of reciprocity to one another; there is a chance that in my social relationships I can affect the norms of others.

Now consider what chance I have of doing so in a bureaucracy should my personal work experience lead to new work standards that I want to discuss with my superior in an open social relationship. Here I encounter one of the great shortcomings of managers if not of bureaucracy itself. Managers view a correction of work standards suggested from below as a challenge to their control. This is a human failing. But ultimately there is also an institutional failure built into the bureaucracy concept—though never in terms of that specific bureaucracy looking at itself. The institutional failure becomes apparent when a particular bureaucracy has just recently reviewed its goals and its methods, found them in keeping with its overall purpose, and is then confronted with suggestions from below. If these suggestions contradict the just-reviewed goals and methods, not only must they be rejected, and if necessary suppressed and action stamped out, but the survival of the responsible subordinate is put in question. Functionaries know this well. The possibility of this kind of reaction to suggestions from below is always there. And because they have little experience in judging norms themselves and are subject to having their own work judged by others according to the norms of others, functionaries are likely to avoid the area of norms altogether.

All of which is to say that in pure bureaucracy norms are effectively dictated from above and accepted from below—all the time. There is a difference between the impact on the individual's superego of this situation and the human situation where one is expected to bring to all social relations, and to society at large, the benefit of one's own norms and judgment—the individuated superego. The individualist moral conscience has no place in bureaucracy.

THE SUBFALLACY OF THE PROFESSIONAL

The subfallacy of the professional is expressed in the folksaying: "I am a professional and must be judged on professional grounds." The hidden assumption here is that the professional, as distinguished from the functionary and the manager, is subject to internal norms, not to an externalized superego.

This assumption is subtly wrong. It expresses a last attempt by a human being to retain both humanity and individuality. But such an attempt is not viable in the bureaucratic world. As a result it causes many difficulties for the professional and those who have to work with him or her.

In the words of Dr. Robert Jarvik, the developer of an artificial heart, commenting on a Food and Drug Administration review of one model, surgeons would have to "sit on their hands while the F.D.A. shuffles paper."[6] Jarvik had already left one hospital, where paperwork delayed his use of the Jarvik heart, to go to another. This might seem to be an example of asserting professional independence on behalf of human concerns over bureaucratic ones; but not necessarily so. The assumption of professional independence is wrong for two reasons. First, professionals need institutions to work in: Doctors, for example, the more specialized they are and the more they consider themselves professionals as a result, need a hospital. But institutions are run by bureaucrats—by managers. Therefore managers, responsible for the existence and continuity of the institution, will either have the ultimate word over the professional's worth to the institution, or the institution will be threatened with organizational decay and untimely death. If these are to be avoided, professionals will have to adjust their inner norms to the dictates of the usual bureaucratic superego. Physicians' acceptance of diagnosis related groups (DRGs) is an example.[7]

The professional's assumption of independence and psychological integrity is also wrong because of the existence of hidden superiors. Professionals exist by the tolerance of a crypto-hierarchy of fellow professionals. Without the approval of this hierarchy, professionals can be disbarred as lawyers, expelled from the medical association with likely loss of license as doctors, or defrocked as priests. Professional associations are externalizers of the superego in their own right; they constitute the conscience for individual professionals who go astray and exercise the power of punishment.* Thus the professional has a great psychic affinity to his or her colleagues in bureaucracy.

Lawyers, especially, have always been members of a bureaucracy: They are officers of the court. Over time, bureaucracy has attempted to strengthen its hold over these professionals who, as defense attorneys, are expected to represent the human interests of their clients. Of course, law itself—the practice of law—has nothing to do with human interests but is a rationalized model of what human life would be like if it were

---

*Professionals do present a special case, if only because of their infinite capacity for self-deception.

conducted by lawyers. Yet many lawyers enter their profession with the idea that they can do some human good; they believe that they can not just apply law but obtain justice. As a result, lawyers in general have defended their relations with clients even when these are known to be of dubious character. In 1984 the Comprehensive Crime Control Act and the Tax Reform Act made it possible for the government to seize money paid lawyers if clients had illegally obtained it and required lawyers to report cash payment of $10,000 or more. A survey by the National Association of Defense Lawyers found that in two years most lawyers had undergone challenges to their fees from federal prosecutors; three-quarters of them were subject to litigation over fees or subpoenas, ending up with the lawyers disqualifying themselves from representing the client.[8] Under pressure from health and legal institutions, the bureaucratization of physicians and lawyers was well on its way, raising the specter that no one would stand for the patient or client.

To summarize, in society, the individual must live up to his or her own inner standards, contained in the superego. A typical folksaying would be: "You've got to be able to live with yourself." The expression indicates the limits the individual puts on willingness to accept social standards when these conflict with individual standards.

In bureaucracy, the individual must live up to external standards. If there is a conflict, he or she can be sacrificed—the strength of bureaucracy as a control institution cannot. Inner standards must be left at home before entering the office; office standards become a replacement superego for the human being during the eight hours a day spent as a functionary on the job. Beyond this, the fact is that many functionaries "become" their organization. They are the identity it gives them. They cease being private persons with private personalities. If they internalize bureaucracy's external norms, they never also internalize the right to make normative demands on their surroundings. In their public identity they become dependent on the organization because they internalize a set of norms the actual and only origin of which remains external. Only their superiors can change these norms or have power to maintain them. In the extreme, therefore, the functionary has an externalized superego, while the citizen has an internalized superego. In the case of the functionary, part of the psyche has been removed and placed outside.* Where? Not in superiors, for these may change, but in their offices. Together, these offices up and down the organization constitute what is called "hierarchy." Organizational hierarchy begins to perform for the bureaucrat the functions of the superego. Hierarchy is the bureaucrat's externalized superego.

---

*This is the origin of the psychology of dependency that characterizes the organization man (or woman).

The Fallacy of the Ego

The sign repairman in our case study complains about two demands typically made by bureaucracy. The first is for information from below: "Then they said: put it on paper. So we knocked off maybe three hours, did maybe thirty-five signs or so, and the rest was paperwork. I guess if it wasn't on paper, they didn't feel it was done." The second demand is for obedience to control from above: " 'You will put up this and this many signs a day, or we'll know the reason why.' "

Aside from the fact that each demand reduced the amount of work done in the putting-up-signs department, as experienced by this particular repairman, what was the basis for his objections?

The Denial of Mastery

Psychologically, a demand for information and a demand for control mean that an individual surrenders mastery over a piece of work. Someone is saying, "You are no longer master over your fate. Give us the information about the challenge you face. We'll judge what is the proper response, and we'll tell you what to do."

Such instructions are a direct attack on the individual's ego, a structure of the psyche charged with exactly the functions that our sign repairman's superiors now arrogate to themselves. The ego receives information from the individual's environment in the form of a challenge. The ego judges how the challenge relates to the organism's ability to handle it. The ego designs responses that take into account both environmental demands and human needs.[9] Ultimately, the ego is master over the individual's survival within an environment.

How can an attack on such mastery be justified? The fact is that the power of a modern organization to cope with challenges larger than any ever met before rests exactly on its assuming mastery over the actions of all its employees. The organization handles huge tasks; an individual handles limited tasks. The organization has a vast horizon; the functionary has a limited horizon.

The sign repairman's complaint about the denial of mastery stems directly from his limited horizon. Within that limited horizon he sees it as his task to put up signs, as many as he can, as well as he can. Any order from above that reduces his sign output, he sees not only as an attempt to supersede his mastery but as bad mastery. Yet, from the viewpoint of the organization at large, less work from him might actually mean more work overall from all departments of the organization. This is especially true when less work from him means less uncontrolled work.

For example, imagine that our hero presses happily ahead day after day putting up as many signs as his crew's strength will allow. One day, a Friday, they put up forty signs. On "Blue Monday," when the crew is tired and hung over, they put up fifteen and knock off at noon. On Tuesday, stirred by guilt they make it up: They put up a total of sixty-five signs.

Now assume there is a section of signpost painters who scrape and paint signposts from which signs have fallen. To let the paint dry, they are always supposed to be one day ahead of the repair crew.

Various problems can arise if the repairers are allowed to set their own quota. If the painters' quota is smaller, the repair crew will be falling over painters while putting up signs. Signs are likely to get splattered with paint, and so are the repairers. Motorists won't be able to read the paint-covered signs. No one will like it. And the repair crew will put in for an additional uniform-cleaning allowance.

Moreover, such problems will not arise in a predictable fashion. Let us say the quota for painted posts is thirty a day. On Friday collisions between painters and repairers might occur at a maximum of ten posts. On Monday there will be none. By Tuesday the repair crew will have caught up with the painters again and be exactly a day behind. The reader who intends to be a manager can envision further complications, beginning with the day when the repair crew comes into the garage demanding a gallon of cleaning fluid for their clothes and extra wash-up time.

Even at this simple level of coordinating two crews, each crew's horizon, their view of how work is best to be done, does not extend to encompass that of both crews together. Once labor is divided and becomes specialized, it must be coordinated. Such coordination is best done by an office superordinated to both crews. In this way the function of evaluating work to be done—the environmental challenge—is shifted from the level of those actually doing it up to the supervisory level. So is the ultimate decision of striking a balance between organizational capability to respond and the demand of the environment for a response. And so, finally, is the task of designing the response.

Because workers on the scene are intimately involved and acquainted with the nature of the immediate work at hand—which means they have more detailed and close-at-hand knowledge than anyone else can have—they always perceive the removal of the final decision-making power from their egos to the "organizational ego" of a superior office as a psychological insult.* Yet, if bureaucracy survives as the most successful control institution yet invented, it does so exactly because it does not leave mastery to each and every individual employed—especially not to the individual on the line.

From the functionary's point of view, this is a major paradox of work-

---

*I use the term "insult" here in both the popular and the medical sense. In the medical sense it signifies an injury or impairment of an organic function.

ing in bureaucracy: If I know more about my work than anyone else, why is it that I cannot be allowed to manage my own work? The problem, of course, is that the functionary's definition of the work is circumscribed by a limited horizon. The organization's definition of the job, with its larger horizon, must supersede the individual's if the organization is to remain what it is—an organization.

The individual worker is conditioned by organizational structure to misperceive what life in the organization is all about. It is never about getting the work done. It is always about integrating yourself with the rest of the organization so that the organization can get the job done. When there is a conflict between getting work done individually and the demand for integrating one's self with the organization, the primacy of the latter is and must always be asserted—again, if the organization is to survive as a control instrument.

The Fallacy of Misplaced Emotion

A vice-president of a computer company invests his work, his hopes, and his emotions in that firm. Bankers judge the results, find them lacking, and coldly—without fear or favor, love or hatred—dismiss the vice-president and his colleagues. Emotion bursts out. The vice-president puts his head down and cries.

Emotion is normally repressed in modern organizations. Yet in social life, our very sense of self rests from the beginning on emotion. Psychoanalysts who deal with the pain reported by inmates of organizations focus on what the individual "takes in" from his or her organizational environment.[10] One major source of pain arises when we are disappointed in other individuals whom we have taken into our psyche and allowed to become part of our self. Relations with bankers are no exception. Loss of relations with fellow managers also evokes emotional pain.

Taking others into our self is a fundamental human tendency. Freud speaks of the child's original experience of being the center of a loving world. This gives the child a sense of cosmic significance. A love of others arises from which the child gets a sense of self; this he labeled "narcissism."[11] Others orient themselves toward the child. This makes possible a mutual chain of love: The child loves these mirroring others and opens itself up to them, permitting it to bask in their love for it. The experience of that love is one of love for oneself.

It is easy to see how, while love for others permits self-love, rejection by others becomes self-rejection. Psychoanalyst Melanie Klein takes up this problem. As we continue to live and work with others, according to Klein, we run into those who have needs other than providing love for us; these, too, are internalized. Their rejection of us becomes internalized as our rejection of ourselves, to form a stable part of our personality. In the words of psychoanalytic organization theorist Howard Schwartz, "It is thus that a permanent wound to our narcissism is created, thus that we cannot permit ourselves to be what we are, that the locus of our identity shifts from who we are to who others will permit us to be. . . ."[12]

Partial self-rejection, then, is a normal wound we all sustain as we grow up, and we learn to live with it. In our adult working life, we encounter people who remind us of internalized others. We work with them. We cannot avoid them. These will reopen wounds of self-rejection.

This is the pain of loss of self that work-oriented psychoanalysts try to deal with and try to alleviate. Modern organization is not accidentally or only occasionally populated by people who have no love for me. Modern organization prides itself on promoting emotional neutrality. Love is one of the most dangerous emotions for a rationalized organization, if not *the* most dangerous. Max Weber pointed this out in his studies of charisma.[13] Love is therefore institutionally driven out of all formal relations in a modern organization. Yet it persists personally—along with other emotions. When the rational cover over the subterranean emotional fabric of organizations is torn off, the fallacy of assuming we can misplace our emotions without personal cost is exposed.

The Fallacy of Identity

The vice-president of an organization is fired. The man who fired him comments: "He thought he was there to give the plan for the next year. We told him he was fired. He didn't even hear what we told him. He just went on giving his plan for the next year." Another vice-president in the same situation "just put his head down and cried." A federal civil servant at the G-16 level discusses with friends the possibility of applying her fifteen years of top management experience to the private sphere. Then she admits she probably will not take the leap: "I am afraid that outside the office I won't have any identity at all."[14]

Psychologically, something very serious is going on in all three instances. In the first case, there is an inability to even admit the reality of the firing; in the second, a breakdown; in the third, a sense of dependency on the institution and fear of other institutions despite a clear display of superb competence within one's institution.* Are these atypical cases?

In our workaday world we distinguish between who a person is in and of himself or herself (personality) and the role the person plays in an institution (identity). There is a difference between who I am for myself— my personality—and what I have to be for others—my institutional role

*The résumé of the civil servant in question reads like the life history of an Horatio Alger. Contrary to popular assumptions about civil service bureaucrats, many of them climb to the top through a display of considerable energy, initiative, and even courage within the institutional framework—as was the case in this instance.

identity. Furthermore, each one of us knows that I am much more free in determining who I am in society than in bureaucracy.

To the extent that we surrender who we are to what the organization intends us to be, we lose our personality and take up institutional identity. If we do this over the life of a career, when we retire, we suddenly find ourselves without institutional identity and with only an atrophied sense of self to fall back on. In a moment of existential panic, we face the reality that without the institution we are nothing. Only people with considerable strength are able to retain their personality within the outer mask they must put on to display their institutional identity.

To the extent that bureaucrats are typically unconscious of the externalization of their superegos and the fragmentation of their egos—as reflected in the false assumption that they are still possessed of these— they commit the ultimate fallacy of identity. While they are institutionally employed, bureaucrats assume they have personal identities, or personalities, in the same way that they had personalities when still within society. That is the fallacy of identity.

This fallacy is twofold. The first part we commit when we assume that we are independent of bureaucracy. Bureaucracy is what ultimately dictates our norms and assigns us our jobs. We are deprived of self-judgment (superego) and mastery (ego) and we refuse to acknowledge it for the simple reason that it is too painful to do so. The fallacy expresses itself in the folksaying heard again and again at social parties in answer to the question, "Who are you?" Typically, those of us imprisoned in the fallacy of identity reply: "I am a professor at the University of Oklahoma," or "I am an autoworker at the Ford Rouge plant," or "I am the secretary of state." What is wrong with all these statements is that while we may "be" these things when we are in our office or on the assembly line, we are not these things outside our office or away from the line. For without the institutional environment, we cannot know what we are to do or whether what we do is right or not, and worst of all we lack the power that only institutional structures can give us to exercise the quasi mastery that our role entails. The secretary of state vacationing in a mountain cabin and away from a telephone is not the secretary of state.

Second, the fallacy of identity involves a confusion between personal personality—the patterns of behavior we have learned and that remain at our beck and call no matter where we go—and institutional identity—the patterns of norms and behavior that have meaning and can be exercised only within and through cooperating institutional structures. Identity in this sense is not personality. Individuals who surrender their personalities, who they are, to institutional identity, what others make of them, give up something that can never be recovered. To send a well-conditioned functionary out into the world of society, which was originally formed and continues to be formed by the interaction between autonomous individuals, is akin to amputating a man's head and sending him off to fend for himself.

A THEORY OF BUREAUCRATIC PSYCHOLOGY: THE WORK BOND

Take any human being. Now remove his or her ability to judge what is socially responsible. The result is a sociopath. Then remove the ability to master challenges from the environment. He or she does not survive. Yet modern organization strips the human being of control over both these abilities. How does the functionary so deprived nevertheless survive?

The functionary survives, socially and physically, exactly because bureaucracy exercises the functions of superego (conscience) and ego (mastery) activity on the person's behalf.[15] As long as the individual remains inside, the same agency that takes away the use of certain individual psychological capabilities also exercises them *for* him or her.

The functionary exists as long as he or she establishes strong bonds with managers or offices, into whose hands two-thirds of the original individual psyche has been placed. This may be represented as in Figure 3.1.

After the externalization of superego and ego, the functionary must identify or bond with the hierarchy and division of labor or their representatives: the functionary's superiors. If not, he or she ceases to exist. Since the manager is the closest representative of the powers of hierarchy and the division of labor—externalized superego and ego functions—the manager becomes the object for such bonding. Identification and projection establish the bond.

Bonding also derives from the organization's need to get work done. Under the imperative that only the responsible manager shall judge the propriety of a piece of work and the methods and tools to be used, which leaves functionaries with little more than their id energy, the organization itself welds the manager and functionary into one work unit. The functionary cannot work without the manager, and the manager is similarly dependent on subordinates: Without their energy the work cannot get done.*

The new unit of analysis comprises both the manager and the functionary in a work setting. Psychologically, I have called this the "work bond." The work bond refers to the structure that is the simplest unit of the modern organization that can get work done. This structure is welded together not merely by external reinforcements but actively by a psychological bond between manager and subordinate. The bond stems from the

---

*The manager who insists on working along with subordinates is generally considered a "bad" manager from the organization's point of view. The "good" manager is expected to make judgments designing the work and then leave the actual expenditure of energy to those below.

Figure 3.1.: Externalization of Superego and Ego

I. PSYCHE IN SOCIETY

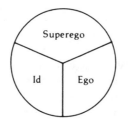

Superego = Moral judgment

Ego = Mastery

Id = Energy

II. PSYCHE IN ORGANIZATIONS

A. Superego Externalization

Test Question:
What happens to
an employee who
brings personal
values (con-
science, judg-
ments of right
and wrong) to
work?

Hierarchy (manager,
supervisor, foreman)
assumes superego
functions on behalf
of employee.

B. Ego Externalization

Test Question:
What happens to
an employee who
insists on
using own tools
or methods
at work, or who
attempts to
experiment?

Division of labor (in-
cluding job design)
determines range of
ego mastery over work,
shapes mastery func-
tion, assumes ego
functions on behalf
of employee.

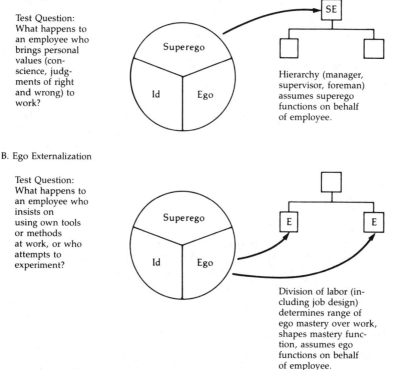

positions of mutual dependence into which the manager and functionary
have been placed by the organization. The bond is the very human attempt to salvage lost personal integrity by placing portions of what was
lost in one other person and identifying that person as part of one's self.[16]
The manager and the functionary in the work bond become, together, a

Figure 3.2: The Work Bond

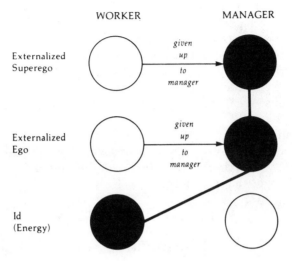

WORKER   MANAGER

Externalized
Superego   *given up to manager*

Externalized
Ego   *given up to manager*

Id
(Energy)

reconstructed self. What does human nature in bureaucracy look like? Investigate the work bond. Pictorially, the work bond can be depicted as in Figure 3.2.

Workers who do not integrate themselves into the work bond may engage in a misplaced narcissism: the desperate search for a lost self conducted in the wrong place—within the self. But from the viewpoint of individualistic psychology, the psychic activities necessary to maintain the work bond are similarly pathological. Identification with the manager is regressive, reawakening early childhood ways of bonding before the capacity for loving existed. Projection is the attempt to bridge the gap between the self and a lost object in one great subconscious leap of faith; when the lost object is one's own ego or superego, an entirely new form of projection must be developed. The relation between functionary and manager is hardly one based on any sense of reality. It is, from the bottom up, a projected relation constantly subject to sudden, unforetellable, apparently irrational corrections from above. People who fit well into the bottom half of the work-bond dyad are those trained in society to be masochists. They love punishment and the power of the punishers. Those who fit into the top half had best be sadists.

Visions of the snakepit open up when the lid of organizational structure is lifted. From the viewpoint of an organization psychology looking at the new bonds and psychological processes with cold and "neutral" eyes, what emerges are entirely new concepts of what a psyche is—along with an entirely new view of what psychology is. However, as the work of B. F. Skinner has shown, such a psychology would merely accept conditions as they are, having lost its critical perspective. But then, did not Freud and the individualists lack such a critical point? How many laudable human characteristics constituting the group psyche of the age of community were swept under the scientific rug in the triumph of individualism? The entire question of whether there is an absolute once or future human nature has not been answered. And yet, if human experience is not to be totally ignored, we owe it to those suffering the transition from the individualist age to the bureaucratic age to record their agonies from their perspective.

A beginning toward a critical understanding of bureaucratic psychology can be made by reacquainting ourselves first with the experts in modern society's psychology and then with those who observe how bureaucracy changes that psychology.

WHAT THE EXPERTS SAY

The bureaucrat's psychology is radically different from that of the man or woman in society. This assertion stands supported by three groups of experts. First, the picture painted of normal people in society by leaders of traditional psychology does not mesh at all with the reality of the bureaucrat's psyche. This point is made below in applications of two traditional psychologies to the bureaucratic reality—Freud's individual psychology and existential psychology. Second, entirely new psychologies have had to be constructed to match the new reality while denying our human experience of it. "Organizational psychology" now treats the institution itself as possessed of a psyche, in which case human beings become mere subcomponents that must be integrated into the organizational psyche. And as bureaucracy penetrates into society, B. F. Skinner's behaviorist psychology tries to explain behaviors inconsistent with earlier models of an integrated psyche standing apart from the conditions that surround it. These new techno-psychologies,* whether of bureaucracy or society, emphasize the two characteristics most striking in our discussion of bureaucrats in the preceding section—their lack of personal psychic integration and their psychic dependence on the environment.† The third school explicitly takes the individual psychologies originating in the social context of the nineteenth century and updates them to apply to the context of

---

*Skinner refers to his psychology as "human engineering" and as a "technology of operant behavior."

†Representative examples of these new psychologies, which generally deny that the self has any problem at all in modern organization because they deny either that there is or that there ever was a self, may be found in Edgar H. Schein, *Organizational Psychology* (Englewood Cliffs, N.J.: Prentice-Hall, 1965), and B. F. Skinner, *Beyond Freedom and Dignity* (New York: Bantam/Vintage, 1972) and *Science and Human Behavior* (New York: Free Press, 1965). Critiques of these two approaches, present in the first edition of this book, were omitted in the second edition to make room for new psychologies and are not repeated here.

modern organizations. This movement is affiliated with the neo-Freudian social psychiatry of Harry Stack Sullivan, object relations, and a new phenomenological psychoanalysis.

Freud and Individual Psychology

The most striking event of the bureaucratic age is the disappearance of the individual. This becomes clear when we juxtapose Sigmund Freud's image of humans against today's reality.

ELEVATING THE EGO

As Freud saw the history of the psyche, it developed through two stages. In the first, the communal stage, the individual was submerged in the mass. His or her psychic structure, to the extent that separate components could then be considered as already differentiated, consisted of a dominant superego, a weak ego, and a repressed id. Graphically the constellation might be depicted in this way:

Superego

Ego   Id

This constellation asserts the supremacy of communal norms through the superego. The ego, as autonomous integrating center for the individual to adapt to reality, is correspondingly weak: All the allowable patterns of adaptation have already been worked out by the community and are dictated through the superego. Similarly, the superego, at this stage almost entirely congruent in its norms with the will of the community, sharply represses or punishes any asocial attempts by the instinctual drives, death-dealing and life-loving, to assert themselves. The id is repressed. It can gain satisfaction only through tightly circumscribed, culturally approved social channels.

In contrast, we may observe, as Paul Roazen has done, that in applying his psychology to the people of his time, "Freud's whole therapy is aimed at liberation and independence."[17] The concern of Freud's ego-dominant psychology is with the maturing of the individual into an autonomous source of intelligence and power from whom society in turn draws its strength. Gone is the idea of each member's subjection to the community. Here also lies the difference between society and community, the form of social life that preceded it.[18]

In the second stage of development, the social stage, the psychology of the single human being is restructured. The ego rises to the top, pushing the superego aside when its socially derived norms get in the way of individual survival. And the id is freed to express itself in channels approved by the ego in its attempt to mediate between the outer and the inner world. This is not total freedom, as is psychosis in which the id runs wild, but in contrast to the restraint and submission to both the laws of nature and of humans characteristic of the communal stage, individuals in modern society did radically make over the world in their own image. We need think only of the vast destruction wreaked on nature and the vast construction of both material and social empires. The psychological structure of individualist man can be depicted as follows:

Ego

Superego   Id

Here ego is dominant. "The ego has a unifying function, ensuring coherent behavior and conduct. The job of the ego is not just the negative one of avoiding anxiety, but also the positive one of maintaining effective performance."[19] And what Freud did not do for the dominance of the ego, having developed his ego psychology late in life, his successors did.[20] With the ego dominant, society's standards, as enshrined in the superego, were subject to revision and adaptation to the needs of individuals. In contrast to the communal era, the superego now becomes dominated by the ego. The id remains often repressed, but when its needs are fulfilled, they are more likely to be channeled through the ego than through the superego.

Freud considered the growth of the individual not only crucial to the individual himself but essential for society at large:

The liberation of an individual, as he grows up from the authority of his parents, is one of the most necessary though one of the most painful results brought about by the course of his development. It is quite essential that that liberation should occur and it may be presumed that it has been to some extent achieved by everyone who has reached a normal state. Indeed, the whole progress of society rests upon the opposition between successive generations.[21]

Exactly for the reasons that politically Freud was a European liberal and that scientifically he made the individual his unit of analysis,[22] his ego-dominant image of humans stands in stark contrast to our age. There, the individual person created himself or herself in the company of other humans. Often the individual would be, in the words of Thomas Hobbes, alone, alive, and afraid. But then freedom was defined in terms of being left alone by others to work out one's own fate. On this definition both the political philosophy and the theology of liberalism met.[23] Today the prevailing political and social reality is that of the corporation. The unit of analysis now is the disindividualized individual at best, as in the works of B. F. Skinner, or the organization itself, as in the works of Edgar H. Schein.[24]

FRAGMENTING THE EGO

With the separation of the superego from the rest of the psyche and the fragmentation of the ego, the possibility of the individual resubmerges into the mass from which it only recently emerged. The concept of the individual derives from the Latin word *individuus*—"indivisible." The individual as such did not exist in the world of community; he or she was molded too much by the social environment. The individual arose only with the development of modern society, owing his or her existence to the idea that humans could grasp hold of their world, including the social world, and reshape it in the individual's own image. This was the idea of early modern science, technology, and industry, and it carried over into the early social sciences.

Freud's psychology, despite its group context (which he did not at all deny), was an "individual psychology."[25] The task of Freudian psychoanalysis and therapy to this day remains, at least avowedly, the reestablishment of the functioning individual. If analysts or therapists are asked to whom they owe their direct obligation, they reply that it is to the individual whom they analyze or attempt to heal.

But man or woman the indivisible is now no longer so. Especially not in bureaucracy. He or she is man or woman the divisible. Whether or not he or she is still a human being in some absolute sense need not be asked here. All we require is an understanding of why the bureaucratic human looks so inhuman to us as outsiders. He or she looks inhuman from our perspective to the extent that we still operate under the definition of "individual" that emerged with the rise of society, the form of social organization within which we still perceive ourselves to live apart from working hours. Similarly, the more our own perceptions reveal the penetration of bureaucracy's human-concept into society at large, the less surprised we are at the divisible human.

The cutting edge of that penetration is revealed in a television commercial in which a young woman who feels she is in fact three women is regarded as perfectly normal—and requires the "normal" equipment of such a fragmented individual, i.e., three types of watches to go with her three incarnations. This acceptance of the split personality is quite new, as reflected in the fact that in the 1950s a young woman was subjected to considerable psychiatric treatment when she had a similar experience. The story is told in *The Three Faces of Eve*,[26] which also became a popular motion picture.

In contrast to both preceding pictures of the structure of the psyche in other eras, perhaps this is the best that can be done for the image of the bureaucratic human:

Externalized Superego

Fragmented Ego

Id
(in the service of the organization)

While this image has a faint resemblance to the communal psyche, under the dominance of a superego, it bears no resemblance at all to the structure of the individualist human. The individual has simply disintegrated under the immense power of bureaucracy and his or her need to make a living in it because one cannot make a living elsewhere in the shrinking arena of society.

THE PROBLEM OF INDIVIDUALIST PSYCHOLOGY

Yet there is a problem with traditional psychoanalysis's focus on the individual. Increasingly, in the doing of work, it is useless to speak of individuals in separation from other individuals. Work today is organized work, whether the hierarchically organized work of the modern organization or the teamwork or program management of postmodernity. The corporation in-*corporates;* the organization *organ*-izes. In an echo of medieval times, we are speaking here of bodies [*corpus*] and organs [*organon*]. Nowhere except in psychological analysis does it become more clear that the natural process of in-*corporation* and *organ*-ization is reversed when the center of analysis stops being the individual and becomes the corporation or organization. Traditional psychoanalysts can still talk of the individual incorporating the outer world: internalizing it. But today it is the outer world that incorporates the individual. It takes the individual into its organized body; there it absorbs and redistributes what used to be individual functions. In the face of that reality, how inadequate is an orthodox psychoanalysis founded on the primacy of the individual?

The problem for any individual is not that he or she may feel pain because part of the organization rejects him or her—a rejection that is felt as self-rejection. The problem is that the organization, which incorporates the individual into its functioning whether for profit or control, *systematically denies all love* to the individual. Using orthodox psychoanalysis's own foundation assumption about how individuals find self-love through the love of introjected others, I can only conclude that organization members find themselves in a system that is the absolute enemy of the human need for love that orthodox psychoanalysis stipulates.

THE PROBLEM OF PSYCHOANALYSIS

We can now understand why it is that traditional psychoanalysis, as a human way of dealing with our reality, finds itself on the defensive when it is challenged to explain contemporary life of human beings incorporated by organizations. The conditions of modern organization are so totally and absolutely inimical to the condition for human psychic health presumed by psychoanalysis that traditional psychoanalysis would have to declare itself to be unable to deal with such conditions if it were to be honest with itself. This, however, would mean the end of an individual-centered orthodox psychoanalysis—which those committed to it must, of course, deny.

There are two ways to go. Either the basic assumption of orthodox psychoanalysis must be reexamined. This means a philosophical reexamination of its metatheory—the theory behind psychoanalytic theory. Or, orthodox psychoanalysis must take into itself an additional way of looking at the world: that is, a second basic assumption. Psychoanalysis has, indeed, chosen the latter course as we see in such successor psychologies as object relations theory[27] and social psychiatry.[28]

Individuals, however, cannot wait. The question for the individual is more acute. It is not how a method of knowledge can adapt itself. It is how individuals who have learned to rely on themselves and love themselves can adapt to a world in which they must adapt, officially at least, to the total absence of love. Such a world does not simply question my ability to love myself; it questions my entire being. The experience of life in modern organizations is bigger than, and qualitatively different from, that portion of life that orthodox psychoanalysis can deal with. The basic question of late modernity is not a psychological one but a philosophical one. It is the perennial question of what life is all about. The question is not concerned with the origins of pain but with what it means to be alive today in an organized world that incorporates us into itself.

Between Experts: The Problem of Existence Meets the Problem of the Psyche

The bureaucratic experience is marked not only by pain but by loss. Modern organization does not merely attack our psyche; it puts in question whether we can still have a psyche. Modern organization challenges not simply our psyche; it puts in question what kind of *being* we have: who or what we are. The bureaucratic experience is not most fundamentally the experience of deadened feelings that explode into pain. The pain arises precisely because we face being nothing and nobody. We recognize this in occasional confrontation with that nothingness: on being disciplined, fired—and, more subtly, even on being hired. Our response is to seek deeper and deeper refuge in exactly that which is able to question our existence: bureaucracy. Once bureaucracy has already incorporated us, once our hand and minds have constituted it as a voluntary externalization of self, it becomes a necessary externalization of self without which there is no self.[29]

An Employee Deals with a Firing

When a dismissed employee tells us of her attempt to counter the loss of self occasioned by her dismissal, she is not simply recounting a tale of the loss of self-love but a tale of an attempt to reattain *existence*. Take the story of her firing as told by Cynthia Confer[30] and of her attempt to counter not only its psychological but ontological effects: the threat not only to self-love but to having any being at all:

I didn't really mind getting fired. The company had been in trouble for a long time. What I did mind was passing my boss every day in the hallway and his being unable to look me in the eyes, say hello, much less smile. I still had two weeks to go before I'd actually have to leave. He'd see me coming down the hall and he'd turn away.

What did she feel?

Why, it makes you feel like you're nobody—a nonentity!

What did she do about it?

I felt hurt, and angry, and a whole bunch of things. Insulted mostly, mostly insulted. I don't know what precipitated it, but I just lay in bed one night, not sleeping at all, and thinking about it, and getting very excited about going in and talking to him about it. I—you know—I just got feeling really happy about it. Even if—well, what could they do: fire me? [laughter] So I spent almost all night doing that, trying to decide what I was going to do and getting just so excited I couldn't sleep. Happy! You know.

And I just went in the next morning, right the first thing at eight o'clock, and walked in his office and said, "Jack, I'd like to talk to you sometime, when do you have time?"

And he said, "Well, how about right now?"

And so I just sat down and—I remember it was December 14, I remember the day—I said:

"Jack, I want to talk to you about this whole situation. Jack, I don't *care* [I talked just like that, full of emotion] I don't care about being laid off. We *all* have known for years we're going to be laid off, always waiting for the other shoe to drop, and I don't hold that against you at all and nobody here in their right mind does. But! I can't *stand* the way you're treating us." And I remember him just staring at me, like, "What?"

How did the manager react?

The first minute or two, he didn't have any reaction. I had to keep on going under my own steam. He finally said, "What do you mean?" And I told him about his avoiding us in the hall and that stuff.

"We don't exist anymore," I said, "after you've given us our notice. . . . Maybe the rest of the people here don't mind but it bothers me. We've always had a good relationship for six years now, and it makes me angry when you treat me like this, and all of a sudden you won't speak to me, etc. etc." I was very emotional.

How did the manager respond?

He *relaxed!* He leaned back in his chair, put his feet up on the desk, heh, and smiled. And so I knew at least he wasn't going to say: Get the hell out of there! [Laughter.] And he said, "Cindy, that's the *only* way I know how to deal with it. Do you know what hell I've been going through here? This place is . . ." He swore and said everything and he was the classiest guy you'd ever want to meet. He said, "This has been putting me through hell." I can't remember what swear words he used. He said, "Coming in here just drives me into little pieces; I have to go to a shrink, because I'm so screwed up over this. The only way I can deal with what I have to do is, after I lay people off, I can't—I act as if they don't exist any more. I can't handle it." And I said, "But that's just *exactly* the wrong thing." We went on and on about that. It was incredible. He talked to me like I was his sister or his mother or something. I couldn't believe it.

How was it all resolved?

Finally he said, "Is this what you want out of life?" And I said, "No!" I said, "I'm going to move to Maine and live in the country, and have the simple life. That's all I ever wanted." And he said, "Me, too. This is just b——s—t! You know what I'm going to do? As soon as I get *my* walking papers—which, of course, are coming after yours—I'm going to go to California and sell Mercedes!" And you know, he went and he did!

The narrative is full of a number of psychological and organizational points. The manager's *numbing of his senses*—to the extent not only of not looking at others but not seeing them anymore—fits the purposes of emotional neutrality of any bureaucracy. The manager's example leads, even on the firing line. The modern organization "wants" the manager to set this emotionally neutral example; as long as emotions can be repressed at the dying of an organization, employees can be expected to go through their routines.

The *pain* of the firing experience arises only when the fired employee faces up to what the deadening of experience will ultimately do to her. Rather than perpetuating the bureaucratic routines through emotionless following of the daily tasks, she feels compelled to face up to the change that the organization has forced her into. Her strong emotions reflect both pain and hope.

But, most important, the employee's decision to stand up for herself—and to do this by confronting her boss and saving him also from the inhumanity forced upon him—is not an issue of psychology at all. It is an issue of *basic humanity*.[31] Cynthia Confer undertakes the rescue of her being. And she undertakes that rescue by accomplishing it in the company of others. She speaks on behalf of her co-workers and she enables her manager to speak the unspeakable: to damn the company and plan to save himself.

In no better way than through the words of human beings confronting annihilation by the bureaucratic machine can we express the quiet daily heroism of men and women living in the modern age.

However, the analysis of the problem of *existence* requires an approach beyond the analysis of the individual psyche.

Ernest Keen: Existential Psychology

The crisis of the individual penetrates all traditional psychologies—that is, those psychologies that either have not sold out to organizational masters and distorted themselves or those that recognize the new organizational reality and voluntarily abandon the concept of the individual.* While it is not possible here to survey the scope of that crisis, it is possible to examine specific problems of individualistic psychologies in the face of the bureaucratization of the world.

PRESENTING A FALSE SELF

Existential psychology is concerned overall with what existential psychologist Ernest Keen termed the three faces of being[32]—the faces an individual turns onto his existence. A very conscious concern of existential psychologists is that at least one of these faces of being is so overemphasized by the pressures of the modern world that the individual's essential integrity is permanently challenged. The three faces of being are as follows:

1. Being-in-the-world. This is the way I experience myself as actively engaged in the world. It is my direct experience of the world through my involvement in it. I am the active subject working my way out in the world. Maslow might say that this is the me that is actualizing itself in the world. What is important is that my experience in the world is, in this state of being, direct, not reflective. I am not looking back at myself in action from a detached distance. I *am* in action.
2. Being-for-oneself. This is the way I see myself by doing what I did not do in the state of "being-in-the-world"—through reflectively looking at myself as an

---

*The psychology of Abraham Maslow is of the first type, although its distortion was accomplished by others. For an outline of Maslovian "third force" psychology, see Abraham Maslow, *Motivation and Personality* (New York: Harper & Row, 1954). For examples of the second type, see the behaviorism of B. F. Skinner and the organizational psychology of Edgar H. Schein.

object. "Out of this experience of oneself 'as object' comes the notion of 'self-concept' and the casting of oneself into substantive terms so that there is some kind of solid 'me' or definition which one can use to make decisions about what to do, how to act, etc."[33]

3. Being-for-others. This actually means how others see me as an object. But since I can never directly experience how others actually perceive me, being-for-others means presenting myself to others in terms I expect will be acceptable to them. "Oneself is experienced through the eyes of others, and one becomes the object of 'the other.'"[34]

In a well-integrated individual, there is a balance between these three states of being. But life in bureaucracy forces me to overemphasize an aspect of myself that others—specifically co-workers and superiors in the hierarchy—will like. When this presentation of a face to others is in conscious conflict with what I know myself to be, I am said to be "lying-for-others." The first experience of lying-for-others occurs when I, as a child, discover that I can present myself to my parents in a way that differs radically from what I perceive I am. This is an important stage in growth because I previously believed, as Jean Piaget among others has pointed out,* that my parents could read my thoughts. The problem becomes serious because "there comes a time in the life and lying of the child when he comes to believe his own lies."[35] It is this problem that modern man faces in bureaucracy: He must so much be what others expect him to be that he loses his own self. Keen gives a specific example:

Suppose, for example, that a salesman is encouraged by his company to be aggressive. His supervisor is aggressive and this supplies a model for the salesman. Because of the power structure, satellization around the supervisor occurs and the individual internalizes the value "aggression = good" as a criterion against which to measure himself. He comes, then, to see himself as aggressive (whatever that might mean to him) and to feel that he is not being the "real him" when he is not. Idealization of one's self around this concept and guilt for not living up to the idealized image grow together in the vicious circle of lying-for-oneself. The guiltier one feels, the more adamant is the affirmation of the standard, and vice versa. Soon the salesman has identified with the role to such an extent that his immediate perception of the world is changed. Neutral persons become potential sales targets; relationships are subordinate to the goal of sales.[36]

It is easily understood how an organization might be very happy with such an employee, but anyone concerned with what might happen to him in his journey from society into the world of bureaucracy can only shudder. Keen here asserts what within Freudian analysis we have understood as a loss of integrated self—through the absorption of external

*Jean Piaget is best known for his cognitive psychology emphasizing child development. Typical examples among a large array of works are *The Language and Thought of the Child* (Cleveland: World Publishing, Meridian Books, 1955) and *The Construction of Reality in the Child* (New York: Basic Books, 1954). For an introduction to Piaget's concepts, see Barry J. Wadsworth, *Piaget's Theory of Cognitive Development* (New York: David McKay, 1971).

superego standards—and foreshadows what below we describe as the dynamic of the bureaucratic psychology. That is, he answers the question: Why do bureaucrats, though they suffer in bureaucracy, feel forced to return again and again? Keen's answer is that once I have absorbed for my state of being the external standard set by bureaucracy, I cease to have a state of "being-for-myself"—cease not only to "be" myself, but cease even to "have" a self. For this reason, the bureaucrat cited in the preceding section expresses the constant fear: "I am afraid that outside the office I won't have any identity at all."

THE BUREAUCRATIC PERSONALITY

Who lives in modern organizations? What is their personality? What is their situation? How do the two interact to make the organization fail or function?

Since the psychology of organizations was refounded in the 1970s, the most developed new model for exploring such questions, in both the public and the private sector, has become an organization-structural variant of psychoanalysis: psychoanalytic organization theory.[37] This is also the least understood approach. It is subject to the easy popularization that the psychology of Sigmund Freud has suffered in general; it is easy to make fun of, evoking concepts like sex, mother, and childhood. For both these reasons, this section not only reports some of the findings of this approach but tries to show how organizational consultants use it.[38]

Psychoanalytic Organization Theory

What makes people in modern organizations tick? This question is treated in psychoanalytic organization theory as both a question of personality and a question of the prevailing conditions that shape it. Much is known about how organizations impose values and what pathways they construct for social relations. Until recently little was known about how the individual unconsciously processes such values and such structures—or how such processing then feeds back into organizational values and structures. In the words of psychoanalytic organization theorist Howard Schwartz: We knew little about how the emotional "snakepit" related to the idealized "clockwork" of organizational structure. Worse yet: We did not *want* to know anything about it![39] What is probably the most advanced of psychoanalytic organization theory explores this question of the unconscious life of individuals in organizations—*but in relation to a theory of organizations*. This is *not* a traditional Freudian solution of putting the organization or the employee on the couch.

How this type of analysis works is depicted first in a case involving a consultancy. Then we can evaluate the power of insights produced by application of a single one of its concepts. And then we can summarize some of its findings.

A CASE OF A PSYCHOANALYTIC CONSULTANCY[40]

How does a psychoanalytically oriented organization consultant work on what goes wrong in an institution? In following the case below, we can, up to a point, fantasize that as we read its facts we could do a social or a cultural analysis. What happened in one state's department of human services can be explained to some degree as a function of hierarchy and the division of labor. To some degree it can be seen as a conflict of values. A restructuring might be the solution. Or a good dose of the proper values, announced by the director and trained into staff. But this is not enough to right the wrong.

The psychoanalytic approach does not merely add depth to such analyses; in this case, at least, it provides an insight without which social or cultural reconstruction would have failed. In order to make possible the reader's concurrent evaluation of the case according to social or cultural insights, the psychoanalytic insight is presented only toward the end. The reader is asked for patience in following the case step by step. The case:

A state department of human services acquired a number of new programs to administer in addition to its own. The new director, Jack Smith, wanted to draw up a departmentwide mission statement. However, he ran into departmental problems: "inadequate sharing of resources, poor communication between agencies, and a general lack of vertical and horizontal information-sharing." Subordinates expressed widespread acceptance of Smith, saying "Jack has background with the department, and that makes a difference!" or "He's one of us." Yet their unwillingness to share resources and information persisted.

In group sessions, the psychoanalytically oriented consultant looked for feelings. He found them. The stories people told were full of suppressed anger and resentment toward two previous directors. The directors had called staff members "stupid" and "incompetent" in front of others. They were remembered for shouting at them. One director, it was recalled, derided managers of staff for perceived disloyalty and insubordination.

The harvest of discontent persisted into the reign of the new director. Instead of focusing joint efforts on a man they liked and a mission they could themselves design, staff kept on complaining about the past. At a retreat, program divisions complained that support divisions were too preoccupied with control and, consequently, were unresponsive to the needs of the programs. Support divisions felt programs were withholding information, were uncooperative and ungrateful, and tended to pin blame for problems on them. One head of a support division put it this way: "Programs go around with the attitude: What have you done for me lately?"

The consultant identified the cause of the problems as the fact that the two prior leaders were still present in the minds of employees. Bad feelings and defensive reactions stimulated by the previous directors had become institutionalized and got in the way of working with the new director they liked. Projecting their previous treatment outward onto the environment, staff referred to themselves as "survivors" of an unappreciative and often hostile public and victims of sadistic leaders.

The consultant interpreted this behavior in terms of the technical concepts of *projection, object loss,* and *persecutory transference.* Surface self-examination by the participants could not reveal a psychological truth: You must mourn even someone you hate. Furthermore, the psychoanalytic approach expects resistance to such mourning. The consultant explains:

Projection—the psychological tendency to reject bad feelings and place them outside oneself, and, then, to act as if they belong to someone or something else—makes grieving hard to do. With each group session and during the retreat itself, participants criticized and told painful stories about the previous two directors. "They were buddies of the governor," some said. "They lacked leadership skills, and they misunderstood the program divisions," others proclaimed. "Polk was corrupt and Holmes treated people badly," they agreed. Finally, and most pointed for the consultant, "Jack Smith inherits the baggage of Holmes and Polk," several suggested.

The consultant's conclusion: "Mourning the loss of someone loved and cared for seems understandable, but grieving for someone despised is unimaginable to many*. . . . DHS members had to confront and let go of these negative feelings from the past, which affected their relations with one another and with the new director. They had to undo the *persecutory transference* that left them cynical and with little hope of positive change."

The technical terms used here may, like all professional language, exclude the noninitiated. However the terms remind the expert that one phenomenon such as anger or grieving is embedded in an entire psychological dynamic that must be understood to make a diagnosis and suggest a solution. A cultural approach might simply have focused on getting members to discover shared values for a mission statement. The psychoanalytic approach discovered deep-seated injuries that had to be healed first. Only then could reasonable discussion of values and missions ensue: "*Mourning the loss* of a despised leader was essential to their constructing more realistic (and less pessimistic) perceptions of themselves as

*It is in fact, however, a process of grieving for oneself, what psychoanalysts call object-loss. Heinz Kohut calls this the loss of the selfobject.

an agency, and to repairing emotional injuries . . . that influenced their view of the current leadership."

Without psychology—in this case, a psychoanalytic understanding—of the mental processes of people involved, it is not possible to understand oft-cited paradoxes and pathologies of modern organizations. This can be illustrated by pointing to the power of a single concept.

RITUALISTIC BEHAVIOR AS A KEY TO BUREAU-PATHOLOGY

The power of an approach can be evaluated by the depth of its insights. In the case of psychoanalytic organization theory this can be shown by exploring how a single concept—that of *ritualistic behavior*—can explain how bureaucracies become their own worst enemies.

Begin with a simple question. What sustains the surface equanimity of the bureaucrat—his or her constant display of even-handedness?

A cultural interpretation trivializes how this is created and maintained. It says simply: They act without fear or favor because these are their values.

When we look at the psychology of the bureaucrat, we are pointed in a different direction: down into the realm of feelings. Is even-handedness simply due to an iron discipline? Is it due to reason, which "controls" any outbursts of feeling? On the contrary, we find that feelings themselves are working and writhing just below the surface to maintain the image of instrumental rationality we observe when we see the cold and neutral bureaucrat. These are exposed in psychoanalytic organization theorists' concept of ritualistic behavior.[41]

Since Max Weber is it well understood that government bureaucracy's original purpose was that of stabilizing the economic environment.* We will understand if this value of stability is echoed in the orientation of the functionary. Just as the organization attempts to stamp out all instability in the environment, the organizational operator is asked to focus on stable practices such as the habitual observance of an established form or process for doing things and the repetition of such acts. But in terms of the health of the individual—his or her own ability to gear successfully into the reality of the environment—excessive devotion to such habits is what Michael Diamond calls *"dysfunctional and obsessional practice."*[42]

The practices mentioned function as a defense that allows the individual to evade normal anxiety. But normal anxiety is very much part of human existence. It arises from confronting the great life dichotomies of life and death, love and hate, stability and growth, and the resulting juxtaposition of meaning and meaninglessness, self and dissolution. To sidestep confrontation with these leads to a greatly curtailed life and personality. Yet, as the study of bureaucratic culture has shown, bureauc-

*See the discussion of this under "The Imperative of Bureaucracy" in Chapter 2.

racy tries to place its inmates clearly on one side of these life dichotomies.

The mission of bureaucracy explicitly devalues the conflict and uncertainties that these existential dichotomies create in the world. The method of bureaucracy is to raise to primacy in our attention the *means* to flatten out such instability.

Ritual in social life affirms the dichotomies and confronts them in celebrations such as a christening or a b'rith, a rite of passage from puberty into adulthood, a wedding or wake. These produce a feeling of completeness—"a whole act, a finished sequence, the achievement (at least for a while) of satisfaction, satiation, perhaps serenity."[43] *Ritualistic behavior* denies the dichotomies of life, repressing the ambivalent feelings they create that threaten one's self.

We may say that the bureaucracy is an appealing workplace that attracts people already inclined toward ritualistic repression of healthy feelings toward life's openness and contradictions, and we may also say that it will train newcomers in such repression.

The concept of ritualistic behavior as typical of bureaucrats' emotional state also gives us insight into bureaucracy's intolerance for healthy conflict in the environment it was created to stabilize. Given its selected operators' trained intolerance for ambivalence in the life status of the self, it is unlikely that their imagination will be able to tolerate such ambivalence in their field of endeavor. Economic growth and entrepreneurial innovation, in an environment which the bureaucrat has strict orders to stabilize, are perceived not only as a threat to the mission of a regulatory agency but as a personal threat to the individual operating it.

There is here an explanation of one of the great conflicts of organizational culture: between bureaucratic values and social values.* The bureaucratic values include those of formal rationality, formalistic impersonality, and discipline. These serve as a means to repress healthy concerns with one's fate as expressed by social values: justice, freedom, violence, oppression, happiness, love and hate, and ultimately salvation and damnation. The result is that "Exaggerated ego defenses and ritualistic actions perpetuate the organizational culture by encouraging resistance to insight and change."[44]

Diamond, in his case studies, goes on to show that the entire range of values, actions, and personality formation of people is tainted by distortions of reality relations such as *ritualistic behavior*.

But there is an even larger lesson to be drawn from exploring bureaucracy through the concept of ritualistic behavior. As already pointed out, some of the effects of such distortions reinforce the modern organization's mission. But it would be superficial to conclude that a mission of enforc-

*See the first page of Chapter 2, "Bureaucracy as the New Culture."

ing environmental stability can be reinforced by simple parallel rigidity in the thinking and feeling of the enforcers. Carrying out such a mission may require much personal sensitivity and flexibility. With these tools the enforcer can respond to challenges emanating from control operations and adapt his or her tactics. A rigid controller may in fact be too inured to what is going on to produce the desired rigidity in the environment.

Thus personal pathologies stimulated and home-grown by the government bureaucracy's mission and methods end up being counterproductive.[45]

The bureaucratic personality subverts the bureaucracy!

The exploration of bureaucratic pathology exposes not only the incompatibility of government bureaucracy with healthy personality formation among its clients but the incompability of the bureaucratic personalities it produces internally with its own mission. This is not a minor insight.

Psychoanalytic Findings

Among the research findings of psychoanalytic organization theory, there are now so many they cannot be presented in brief summary. The findings below, however, may be considered typical.

Bureaucratic Personalities: Psychosocial Analysis

If we want to know what kind of personalities to expect in bureaucracy, we can begin with personalities shaped in early childhood and ask which of these are going to be recruited and supported by bureaucratic social structures.

MICHAEL A. DIAMOND AND SETH ALLCORN: PERSONNEL SELECTION BY DEFENSIVE TYPE

Psychoanalytical organization theorist Michael Diamond and collaborator Seth Allcorn suggest that the bureaucratic machine is a particular kind of stressor that exacerbates human anxiety. Such anxiety is built into us all in childhood because we at one point had to deal with the loss of the mother and the resulting loss of interpersonal security. Since such bureaucratic structures as hierarchy and division of labor strictly control relations, which in turn produce regression among personnel, experience in such structures is likely to reawaken childhood defenses against anxiety. Bureaucracy selects certain defensive personality types—and it selects them for either management or the rank and file. There prevails an unconscious selection process in bureaucracy that reinforces and reproduces the bureaucratic structural and normative status quo.

Managers: Because of its power, hierarchy attracts as managers those people who already have an extraordinary desire to control events and contain feelings of anxiety. Among these types are: the *perfectionist*, the *arrogant–vindictive*, and the *narcissist*.[46] Their behavior is structurally supported or tolerated by their position. Perfectionists are allowed to carry out rigid and self-righteous attitudes. The arrogant–vindictives are allowed to carry out an "I win, you lose" attitude. And the narcissists are allowed to express the kind of convulsive self-importance of which Max Weber already spoke in characterizing bureaucrats. It may be guessed that, from the viewpoint of the average employee, these are wonderful people to work for, but the reality—both from the human and the organizational point of view—is worse than that; for the bureaucratic structure also selects for survival specific defensive types among employees—easy sheep for the slaughter.

Employees: Because of the lack of autonomy and power built into subordinate positions, organizations will be bottom-heavy with people who tend to rely on *self-effacing* and *resigned* tendencies in dealing with security from anxiety.[47] *Self-effacing* employees tend to look to others to take the lead in meeting their security and safety needs. They minimize their own sense of having been effective in an accomplishment. And they find sustenance in the belief that they are sensitive, lovable, and deserving of being loved. Naturally such an individual is extremely vulnerable to manipulation by perfectionist, arrogant–vindictive, or narcissistic superiors. *Resigned* employees bring to work past experience in dealing with anxiety through suppressing all awareness of internal conflict and even of anxiety itself. They simply withdraw from events and from people. They want to be left alone. Since bureaucracy is not designed to leave anyone alone, this type eventually comes into conflict not only with others but with the organization itself unless sustained by the jurisdictional autonomy.

Diamond and Allcorn's model of personnel selection in bureaucracy hinges on Diamond's discovery of a fundamental irony. Bureaucracy, he argues, is the modern human being's most perfect instrument for dealing with the kind of anxiety[48] that comes to all human beings when they face loss of a beloved other: This could be the mother in childhood or other loved figures in adulthood. Bureaucracy stabilizes all personal relationships. However, bureaucracy does this at a cost. Stability of fixed roles is offered as a substitute for real people-to-people relations that human beings construct on their own.[49] The impersonality of role relationships also takes all emotion out of human relationships. In short, bureaucracy deals with everyone's craving to love and be loved, but it does this by successfully suppressing into the unconsciousness of its members that there even is such a craving. As long as this cold machine faces stable conditions—of environment, of personal relations, or of work—all may be well. However, when any kind of stress enters the machine—as it will, for example, in firings or budget cutbacks—the human element is ready to explode. Then, all the defensive tendencies, learned early on to guard against the anxiety of loss of interpersonal security, collide with one another. Manager psychologically beats up on employee and employees try to defend themselves, or managers find employees unable to deliver what is needed.[50] Such stressful events need not be an organizationwide crisis; *any* manager–employee encounter is potentially loaded with the collision of incompatible defenses to anxiety. Whenever the thin layer of organizational protection of security is scratched, an explosion is possible. In short, the Diamondian irony of modern organizations is this: Designed to reduce interpersonal insecurity in work operations, bureaucratic structure tends so much to suppress basic human needs for self-constructed interpersonal security and love that bureaucracy actually heats and stirs a hidden cauldron of insecurity always ready to erupt.

KAREN HORNEY'S NEUROTIC TYPES AND BUREAUCRACY

Bureaucracy, because it takes over basic functions of the self-reliant and loving individual, tends to attract what in society would be called individuals who have neurotic responses to challenges to self-reliance and love. Psychoanalyst Karen Horney suggests that there are three types of such neurotic responses: turning toward people (dependency); turning against people (dominance); and turning away from people (detachment).[51] I would like to suggest that bureaucratic structures tend to attract different types of neurotics into different levels of the hierarchy, as illustrated in Figure 3.3.

People Who Turn Away from People—Top Administrators: There simply is no time for the top administrator to deal with real people. This is the fate of his or her role. Organization of reality here must be in terms of concepts and numbers. A cold, self-loving personality would be ideal for this role. What Freud said of the leader holds of the top manager: The leader loves no one but himself.

People Who Turn against People—Middle Managers: While many middle managers actually succeed in their role by informally nurturing, even "mothering," their subordinates, the formal role requires attitudes, skills, and behaviors of turning against the needs of subordinates when these conflict with the needs of the organization. People attracted are types who can play roles of dominance. They need other people, but they need them to dominate them.

People Turning toward People—Employees: Structures requiring obedience to command and to impersonal rules select from society and nurture within the organization those people who have a need to depend on others. Such employees need to be led through guidance in getting work

Figure 3.3: Distribution of Defense Types in Hierarchy

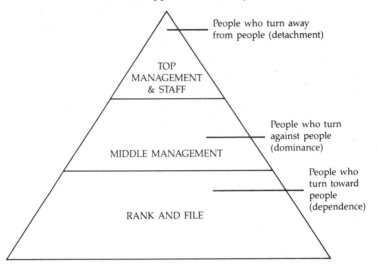

done, initiating the construction of work relationships, and initiating the satisfaction of personal love needs: sense of belongingness, being appreciated, being taken care of. Others (for example, professionals deriving a great deal of a sense of autonomy from their professional status and values) have a difficult time. At the least, they live in constant conflict between their need for professional autonomy and the required dependency. But any worker who retains any sense that he or she is best able to judge, from personal and intimate experience, the work at hand has the same problem. The danger is that the organization designed to take personal relations out of work tends ultimately to remove all work out of its organized (emotionally repressed) impersonal relationships.

Douglas LaBier: Power Positions and Technical Positions

What kind of people are attracted to wield the power in government bureaucracy and what kind of people are attracted to do the work?

Psychoanalyst Douglas LaBier found that "The answer lies in the observation that different roles call for more or fewer irrational attitudes."[52] For example, people handling power relations between individuals tend to manifest more irrational attitudes. Those involved in getting work done, such as auditors, tend to come from a more normal range. LaBier's suggested distribution of different types attracted to different levels of the hierarchy are illustrated in Figure 3.4.

LaBier says that power roles attract a different kind of person than work roles: "Certain roles are more likely to select and support the devel-

Figure 3.4: Distribution of Passions at Work

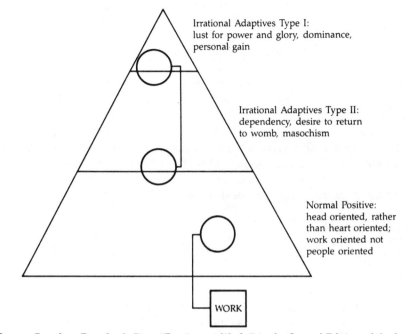

Irrational Adaptives Type I: lust for power and glory, dominance, personal gain

Irrational Adaptives Type II: dependency, desire to return to womb, masochism

Normal Positive: head oriented, rather than heart oriented; work oriented not people oriented

WORK

Source: Based on Douglas LaBier, "Passions at Work," in the Second Edition of the book.

opment of irrational attitudes. These include various 'power positions' found throughout government, such as policy formulation, high adminis- tration, or positions of assistant to presidentially appointed administra- tors."[53] While LaBier suggests that a power-hungry type is usually found at the very top, for example, among presidential appointees picked to push programs through very quickly, and a masochistic type among the middle levels of the bureaucracy, we can probably generalize that domi- nance/submission relations occur generally wherever the maintenance of power and not getting work done is the prime object of a pairing of roles.

Irrational Adaptive Type I: These persons show a lust for power and glory, desire to subjugate and/or destroy others, and greed for personal gain—all of which have come to dominate the person to a pathological degree. That is, the behavior is really beyond their control.

Irrational Adaptive Type II: These persons show passive dependency, a desire to return to the womb, and submission to masochistic humiliation. This dependence and submissiveness are also pathologically ingrained.

Normal Positive Type: These individuals are, by traditional psychiatric criteria, normal. However, they are not fully healthy, having failed to develop "such qualities as love of life, concern for others, affirmation of truth"[54] (characteristics of the heart) while having overdeveloped particular concrete technical skills—such as those of accountants—favoring accomplishment of work. Their character fits the bureaucratic setting where the rationalism of head work is prized but not the vagaries of the judgmental heart. These people tend not to be found in power positions.

Finally *irrational nonadaptive* and *normal negative* types simply do not fit well into bureaucracy. The first type because its members show emotional disturbances (rather than keep pathology under wraps). Unlike the irrational adaptives, their pathology simply does not fit into the role requirements assigned to them, which gives rise to conflicts and observable symptoms. The second type because the work environment also stimulates the "negative or unproductive sides of their character; traits like loyalty, fairness, authority, and assertiveness turn into submission, dominance, withdrawal, and destructiveness."[55]

Existential Analysis

THE ANXIOUS PERSONALITY
AND THE BUREAUCRATIC DRIVE

The psychological analysis of bureaucratic personality rises and falls on the validity of the individualist perspective. That perspective sees the bureaucrat's psyche as sick or distorted; yet from the technological and organizational perspective, the bureaucrat is functional. Similarly, while some inmates of bureaucracy find the bureaucratic experience psychologically devastating, an administrator might argue that many seem to find in bureaucracy the satisfactions of their life's work. A value relativism pervades both viewpoints. Unless the critical perspective, and its experiential and empirical results, can be based on something more solid than what could be attacked as arbitrarily chosen values, a valid psychology of bureaucracy can ultimately *not* stand. Because of this problem, raising to the forefront the concept of anxiety as the prime motivator in bureaucracy takes on crucial importance.

Many industrial and organizational psychologists have pointed out that modern organizations must satisfy primarily the physical and psychological needs of inmates for survival and existence. Here the names of the organizational humanists come to mind: Maslow, Herzberg, McGregor, Argyris, and others. Why the needs for survival and existence are basic—and the experiential testimony of people in bureaucracy also bears out that they are—does not become evident, however, until we take a critical perspective. What this perspective allows us to see is that bureaucracy creates the bureaucratic personality by attacking existence. It begins by disintegrating, if not forever destroying, the social personality. This explains the sense of loss experienced by those who are recruited from society into bureaucracy, the feeling of emptiness at work, and the inability of retired bureaucrats to get along outside the institutional context.

Bureaucracy gets its power exactly because it creates for us an existential dilemma by promising to solve our existential crisis. The individual is deprived of the feelings of human solidarity that a healthy superego provides and denied the sense of individual self-being that the independent exercise of mastery over a piece of work brings about. He or she does not merely become dependent on organizational structures for a sense of "ersatz" interpersonal inclusion—the sense of society—and for a sense of having a self provided by the replacement identity of the role. The individual is also continuously at the mercy of the institution to fulfill these needs. Yet anxiety is pervasive and profound. It is based on the knowledge that, in any matter of crisis, the organization will put its own crass survival before the meaningful existence of the employee. The arrangements for getting work done provide in subtle ways daily experience of the essentially dispensable, interchangeable, and replaceable roles that employees play in the larger picture. Employees are not simply afraid of losing their jobs, a real fear that managers exploit; they are pervaded on a minute-to-minute and day-to-day basis by a vague feeling of dread—nothing you can put your finger on, a dread that must in fact appear irrational but which is always there. Employees of modern organizations are in fact afraid not of anything specific but of the general and ever-present possibility of having the essential nullity of their importance in the values hierarchy of the organization exposed to themselves and to others. Anxiety as the dread of nothingness keeps me with my nose to the grindstone. The grindstone reassures me that I have a nose and that there is a "me."

Support for the anxiety concept comes also from a quite different source, the philosophical work of the phenomenologist Martin Heidegger. Heidegger characterizes the condition of human beings in modern society as an escape into institutions and anonymity away from the one fact of life that no human being can look straight in the eye: that on the other side of or below the foundations of institutions there is nothingness.[56] The social world is made by humans. The psyche is a social product. The psyche, in our context, is an institutional product.

Modern organization constantly places us in contact with nothingness in two ways. First, at the point of transition between society and bureaucracy, we suddenly sense that the ground for our lives has been torn out from under us. It is an experience no one is likely to forget, even if we do not understand it. Secondly, the day-to-day management of modern organizations continually brings us into contact with nothingness: It is a managerial technique to deprive us of the grounds for assuring ourselves of existence (self-assurance) in order to continually recreate the need for the assurance that managers and the institution can provide.

Bureaucratic Ontology: Psyche versus Being

Psychological approaches to bureaucratic personality tend to focus on the problems of organizational attack on the self, raising problems of insecurity. At bottom is a focus on anxiety. Bureaucracy is seen as the modern person's way to create stabilized conditions in the world and at work. These promise to get the person away from the anxieties of interpersonal insecurity that Thomas Hobbes's state of the war of all against all represented. At the same time, it is the contribution of psychoanalysis to have shown that new insecurities are created by bureaucracy, turning people back to anxiety. The psychoanalytical, like the general psychological solution, however is to heal either the assaulted psyche or fix the offending bureaucratic structures or both. Anxiety is seen as an illness of the psyche that can be cured—either by healing the psyche or by improving environmental conditions. This assumes that the bureaucratic assault is an assault on the integrity of our *psychic structure*. Such an assault questions whether we "have it all together." But the assault may be more basic. It may be an assault against our being. This puts in question whether modern institutions allow us to have any existence at all. It is the final question of whether we are "out of touch with ourselves." The second possibility is *not* a psychological problem. It is an ontological problem. Psychology studies what makes us tick. Ontology studies who or what we are (from the Greek *ontos* + *logos* = the logic of our being). This distinction forces us to ask whether we are dealing, inside modern organizations, with neurotic anxiety or existential anxiety.[57]

The ontological approach argues that anxiety is not a disease but *the* most fundamental human condition.[58] Psychological descriptions of anxiety are quite accurate: We sense ourselves as filled with a nameless dread of *nothing* in particular; unlike fear, anxiety has *no* object; *nothing* in particular seems to trigger it.[59] This is exactly the existential ontologist's point: Human beings normally must confront the fact that beyond their own existence there is nothingness. We live our lives as beings confronted by the abyss of nonbeing. Throughout history, humankind has tried to find refuge from the threat of nonbeing—but in no culture or civilization, the ontologist argues, have human beings ever *denied* their existential suspension between being and nonbeing. Modernity is the first culture to deny there is a problem. Bureaucracy is the most advanced institutional attempt to hide the problem. Bureaucracy—as organization theorist Robert Denhardt has pointed out in regard to one problem of being/nonbeing, namely mortality—promises immortality.[60] Individual members may come and go but in the programs and structures of the bureaucracy they will live on forever: "Contemporary organizational thought provides a comprehensive, although often disguised, scheme of moral behavior to which the member's actions can be related; by following this code, we presume our soul will be granted continuity."[61]

MARTIN HEIDEGGER: COGNITION WITHOUT THINKING

As an ontologist, Martin Heidegger looks at this personal problem on a larger scale. He is critical of modern science, modern technology, and modern organizations exactly because they pose one central danger: They enable Man to lose touch with his own being. What is wrong with bureaucracy is exactly that it attempts to radically reduce anxiety. Reducing anxiety absolutely is the absolute denial of the prime human condition. The member of the human community who denies his or her anxiety in the face of the daily confrontation with nothingness is also out of touch with the one great human power: the ability to leap ahead of ourselves into the dark, to leap from moment to moment into a future that can never be known fully ahead of time, to leap into our own potential—the ability of Man to create himself.[62] Instead we proceed by taming nature through science, manufacturing a world of our own design through technology, and controlling everything including human beings by an administration that treats everything as things. Thus we foreclose our own possibilities. We have tended to think that nuclear extinction is our greatest danger— and we have looked to technological solutions like Star Wars (the Strategic Defense Initiative). Yet Heidegger argues that we are in the greatest danger today, exactly when the nuclear bombs do not explode:

We do not stop to consider that an attack with technological means is being prepared upon the life and nature of man compared with which the explosion of the hydrogen bomb means little. For precisely if the hydrogen bombs do *not* explode and human life on earth is preserved, a change toward feeling homeless in the world moves upon us.[63]

What is the basis for this change? ". . . our inability to confront meditatively what is really dawning in this age."[64] We have not merely stopped emoting, we have stopped thinking. In a world in which everything is provided for, there is no more room for Man to think about providing anything for himself. In this age, science, technology, and organization still claim to be able to provide total security—despite all indications to the contrary: random nuclear war, runaway technologies no longer under control, rampant insecurity in organizations. All that is demanded is enough time and money. All things can be fixed, and Man becomes a thing among things. We may conclude that the paradox Man confronts is this: In the bureaucratic world we have created a barrier against the anxiety of having to confront nothingness. Yet, nothingness—Cindy Confer, among others, called it being a "nonentity"—intrudes into our daily lives as the condition of our modern being.

Is the experience of anxiety over being treated like a nonentity a *disease?* We sense it is not. It shows itself not as a disease but as a condition we find ourselves in. Anxiety—as silent suffering or in full cry—is the human condition in the bureaucratic world. But who suffers? We suffer, not bureaucracy. Anxiety is ours, yours and mine. It belongs to us. It is one of the very few things we can call our own in this world. But that makes it something to be treasured. We can treasure it as a sign. Signs point from where we are to where we might be able to go. As a sign, anxiety shows us our present condition: that of false security within the bureaucratic order. As a sign, too, it points beyond that order: to a place where anxiety is once more in our hands rather than we in the hands of anxiety disguised as security.

In sum: Those who see anxiety in these terms will care for and take care of others. But they will not be satisfied merely with easing pain psychologically, nor will they obscure its origins organizationally. Neither as a healer nor as an architect, but with the word will they proceed. This means thinking—even before assuaging pain. In fact, it is thinking that builds on the pain. It also means thinking before rebuilding. The ontological position is that the "psychological" problem of bureaucracy is not one of emotions or irrationality, nor even of rationality. Neither the emotional nor the cognitive psychology of the modern individual is at stake. What is called for is a new kind of thinking, deeper than emotion and harder than rationality, that cuts like the sword through the false peace of bureaucracy.

NOTES

1. Max Weber, *Economy and Society: An Outline of Interpretive Sociology*, 3 vols. Guenther Roth and Claus Wittich, eds., E. Fischoff et al., trs. (New York: Bedminster Press, 1968), p. 998.

2. Interview with the author, May 1975. Anonymity requested.

3. Interview with the author, May 1975. Anonymity requested.

4. John J. Sirica, *To Set the Record Straight* (New York: New American Library, Signet, 1980), p. 180.

5. Weber, *Economy and Society*, p. 968.

6. Quoted in Philip M. Boffey, "F.D.A. Sets Rules on Artificial Heart Implants," *New York Times*, Jan. 9, 1986, p. A15.

7. My thanks to Cheryl Smith, then medical records administrator of Penobscot Bay Medical Center, Rockport, Maine, for permitting me to contribute to a seminar on DRGs and ethics, 1984, Penobscot Bay Medical Center.

8. See Marcia Chambers, "Criminal Lawyers in Study Say New Laws Inhibit Case Choices," *New York Times*, Nov. 21, 1985, p. A20.

9. In Freud's own words, the ego is "an intellective activity which, after considering the present state of things and weighing earlier experiences, endeavors by means of experimental actions to calculate the consequences of the proposed line of conduct . . ." (Sigmund Freud, *An Outline of Psychoanalysis* [New York: Norton, 1936]).

10. Personal conversation with psychoanalyst Douglas LaBier, November 1985.

11. The discussion of the growth of self-love here is taken from Howard S. Schwartz, "Immoral Actions of Organizationally Committed Individuals: An Existential Psychoanalytic Perspective," Draft 1.1, circulation draft of paper delivered at the annual meeting of the American Society for Public Administration, April 13–16, 1986, Anaheim, California.

12. Schwartz, op. cit., p. 7.

13. See the sections on charisma in Max Weber, *Ancient Judaism*, Hans H. Gerth and Don Martindale, trs. and eds. (New York: Free Press, 1952); *Economy and Society; The Religion of China*, Hans H. Gerth, tr. and ed. (New York: Free Press, 1964); and *The Religion of India*, Hans H. Gerth and Don Martindale, trs. and eds. (New York: Free Press, 1958). See also R. P. Hummel, "Charisma in Politics: Psycho-Social Causes of Revolution as the Preconditions of Charismatic Outbreaks within the Framework of Weber's Epistemology," unpublished Ph.D. dissertation, New York University, 1972.

14. My thanks to Professor Charles Hayes for this case.

15. I derive this theory from the first edition of this book. It is developed in R. P. Hummel, "The Work Bond," paper delivered at the first annual scientific meeting of the International Society for Political Psychology, New York City, Sept. 1–4, 1978.

16. See, for example, R. P. Hummel, "Freud's Totem Theory as Complement to Max Weber's Theory of Charisma," *Psychological Reports*, 35 (1974), pp. 683–86, and "Psychology of Charismatic Followers," *Psychological Reports*, 37 (1975), pp. 759–70.

17. Paul Roazen, *Freud: Political and Social Thought* (New York: Knopf, 1968), p. 247.

18. For an understanding of what communal life is like psychologically, see the example Bruno Bettelheim draws from contemporary *kibbutzim* in *Children of the Dream: Communal Child-Rearing and American Education* (New York: Avon Books, 1970). See especially his concept of the "collective superego" in contrast to the individual superego of the individual in society, pp. 142–43.

19. Roazen, *Freud*, p. 234.

20. Ibid., p. 233 ff.

21. Sigmund Freud, *The Standard Edition of the Complete Works*, James Strachey, ed. (London: Hogarth, 1955), vol. 9, p. 237.

22. Roazen, *Freud*, p. 248.

23. For the definitive work on the meaning of modern liberalism since Hobbes, and on the elective affinity of Hobbesian-Lockean politics and Lutheran-Calvinist theology, see H. Mark Roelofs, *Ideology and Myth in American Politics: A Critique of a National Political Mind* (Boston: Little, Brown, 1976).

24. See B. F. Skinner, *Science and Human Behavior* (New York: Free Press, 1965), and Edgar H. Schein, *Organizational Psychology* (Englewood Cliffs, N.J.: Prentice-Hall, 1965). Thus, for example, psychiatrist Gregory Zilboorg, in commenting on "this sacrifice of the individual" speaks of a "disindividualized concept of the human personality" and the "rather sickening phenomenon of the disindividualization of man in favor of his serving the social, or mass machine." (Gregory Zilboorg, "The Changing Concept of Man in Present-Day Psychiatry," in Benjamin Nelson, ed., *Freud and the 20th Century* [Gloucester, Mass.: Peter Smith, 1974], pp. 31–38.)

25. Sigmund Freud, *Group Psychology and the Analysis of the Ego* (New York: Boni and Liveright, undated), p. 1.

26. Corbett H. Thigpen, and Hervey M. Cleckley, *The Three Faces of Eve* (New York: Popular Library, 1957).

27. On the object-relations approach, see, for example, the *SASP Newsletter* issued by the Society for the Advancement of Self-Psychology, New York City, and Jay R. Greenberg and Stephen A. Mitchell, *Object Relations in Psychoanalytic Theory* (Cambridge, Mass.: Harvard University Press, 1983).

28. On social psychiatry, see the work of Harry Stack Sullivan and Erich Fromm; see also the work applied to private bureaucracies by Michael Maccoby and the work applied to public bureaucracies by Douglas LaBier. See also the article by Michael A. Diamond, "Organization Psychiatry," *The Bureaucratic Experience*, 2nd ed. (New York: St. Martin's Press, 1982), pp. 134–37.

29. See Michael A. Diamond, "Bureaucracy as Externalized Self-System: A View From the Psychological Interior," *Administration and Society*, vol. 16, no. 2 (August 1984), pp. 195–214.

30. Interview with Cynthia Confer, Jan. 13, 1986, and completed Feb. 23, 1986, for the following quotations.

31. I would like to thank Professor Michael A. Diamond of the University of Missouri-Columbia for raising, in reviewing parts of the introduction to the third edition, the issue

that the fundamental problem of the psychology of organizational life is not simply the pain of inmates but is a question of "basic humanity."

32. I am taking this phrase from the title of Ernest Keen's summary of existential psychology, *Three Faces of Being: Toward an Existential Clinical Psychology* (New York: Appleton-Century-Crofts, 1970).

33. Ibid., p. 59.

34. Ibid., p. 59.

35. Ibid., p. 46. Keen continues: "This is a highly subtle and yet very important phenomenon. When the child presents himself to his parents as 'good' and knows he is 'bad,' that is not a lie-for-oneself. But when a child invests so much in the being-good-for-his parents that it becomes an overwhelming concern, then his honesty in confronting himself is likely to suffer. Extremely punitive parents, therefore, undermine the child's honesty with himself. The experience of guilt can be so threatening that one effectively loses control with what one really feels or desires. In the place of this honest reckoning of oneself emerges an 'idealized self,' as Horney (1950) has called it, which may come to dominate one's entire being." Keen here refers to Karen Horney, *Neurosis and Human Growth* (New York: Norton, 1950). An interesting application of this theory of child development would be an investigation of the childhood of former President Richard M. Nixon, with whom the press experienced the great difficulty of finding the "real" Nixon.

36. Ibid., pp. 330–31.

37. The school is well represented in Manfred F. R. Kets de Vries and Associates, *Organizations on the Couch: Clinical Perspectives in Organizational Behavior and Change* (San Francisco: Jossey-Bass Publishers, 1991). Notable in the field of public organizations are Howell Baum, Michael Diamond, and Howard Schwartz, all of whom are represented in this chapter.

38. Among previous attempts at innovative departure in this field by the present author, the concept of the "work bond" is now contained in the new section entitled "A Theory of Bureaucratic Psychology," just preceding the section entitled "What the Experts Say." For the deductive model of what personality characteristics one could expect to find based on a theory of organizational socialization—"Bureaucratic Personalities: Socio-Psychic Analysis"—see the previous three editions. The model of "Existential Analysis," arguing that Man's basic problem in bureaucracy is not psychology but ontology, stands; it is appended to the psychoanalytic section.

39. Howard Schwartz, *Narcissistic Process and Corporate Decay: The Theory of the Organization Ideal* (New York: New York University Press, 1990), p. 8. Schwartz's students rejected learning about the snakepit, though they agreed it matched the reality of their organizations; instead they demanded to learn more about the idealized clockwork image usually passed off in college courses as organizational reality. Schwartz supports my suspicion that what we teach students in business colleges and public administration programs is, literally, ideology.

40. The entire case is condensed from Michael A. Diamond, *The Unconscious Life of Organizations: Interpreting Organizational Identity* (Westport, Conn.: Quorum Books, 1993), Chapter 10, "Examples of Leadership Transition and Object Loss."

41. This concept has been explored by several organization theorists looking at public service organizations, including Howell Baum, *The Invisible Bureaucracy* (New York: Oxford University Press, 1987); Howard Schwartz, *Narcissistic Processes and Organizational Decay* (New York University Press, 1990); and Michael Diamond, cited below.

42. All citations in this section are from Chapter 2 of Michael Diamond, *The Unconscious Life of Organizations: Interpreting Organizational Identity* (Westport, Conn.: Quorum Books, 1993).

43. Diamond, Chapter 2.

44. Diamond, op. cit.

45. It is possible that there is less rigidity and pathology in private sector modern organizations, where ultimate judgment hinges on the accomplishment of mission and less on method.

46. Michael A. Diamond and Seth Allcorn, "Psychological Responses to Stress in Complex Organizations," *Administration & Society*, vol. 17, no. 2 (August 1985), pp. 217–39.

47. Loc. cit.

48. Michael A. Diamond, "The Social Character of Bureaucracy: Anxiety and Ritualistic Defense," *Political Psychology*, vol. 6, no. 4 (December 1985), pp. 663–79.

49. Michael A. Diamond and Seth Allcorn, "Role Formation as Defensive Activity in Bureaucratic Organizations," *Political Psychology*, vol. 7, no. 4 (1986), pp. 709–32.

50. Michael A. Diamond and Seth Allcorn, "The Role of Unconscious Actions in Work Relations," paper presented to the 1984 annual meeting of the American Political Science Association, Aug. 29–Sept. 3, 1985, New Orleans; specifically, see Table 2 outlining types of work relations.

51. Karen Horney, *Our Inner Conflicts* (New York: Norton, 1945), pp. 48–51, 53–55, 63–67, 73–77, and 79–81.

52. Douglas LaBier, "Passions at Work," in R. P. Hummel, *The Bureaucratic Experience*, 2nd ed. (New York: St. Martin's Press, 1982), pp. 141–47; citation from p. 142. See also LaBier, "Emotional Disturbances in the Federal Government," *Administration & Society*, vol. 14, no. 4 (February 1983), pp. 403–48; and LaBier, *Modern Madness: The Emotional Fallout of Success* (Reading, Mass.: Addison-Wesley, 1986).

53. LaBier, "Passions at Work," p. 143.

54. Ibid., p. 145.

55. Ibid., p. 146.

56. Martin Heidegger, *Sein und Zeit [Being and Time]* (Tübingen: Max Niemeyer Verlag, 1976 [originally published 1927]). See also *Heidegger and Psychology*, special issue, *Review of Existential Psychology and Psychiatry*, vol. 16, nos. 1, 2, and 3 (1978–1979).

57. Neurotic anxiety is merely an overdetermination of the ego from the outside, opening the ego up to the flood of forces emanating from the id. Existential anxiety is seen as the human condition. Freud: "In view of the dangers of [external] reality, the ego is obliged to guard against certain instinctual impulses in the id and to treat them as dangers" [pp. 81–82]. Ego fends off this danger by mobilizing a limited amount of anxiety [p. 71], which mobilizes unpleasure [p. 70] as a signal that something must be done to control "the unpleasure which the instinctual process was threatening to produce" [p. 71]. Sigmund Freud, *Inhibitions, Symptoms and Anxiety*, Alix Strachey, tr. (New York: Norton, 1959 [originally published 1926]), pages cited. Heidegger: "Warum sich die Angst ängstet, ist das In-der-Welt-sein selbst." Heidegger, *Sein und Zeit [Being and Time]*, cited, p. 287, paragraph 40.

58. R. P. Hummel, "Heidegger, Freud and Anxiety in Organizations: Consultants and the Crisis in American Psychoanalysis," paper presented to the annual scientific meeting of the International Society for Political Psychology, June 1983, Toronto.

59. Sigmund Freud, *A General Introduction to Psychoanalysis*, Joan Riviere, tr. (New York: Pocket Books, 1969 [originally published 1920]), pp. 402 and 404; and Freud, *Inhibitions, Symptoms and Anxiety*, p. 91.

60. Robert B. Denhardt, *In the Shadow of Organization* (Lawrence: Regents Press of Kansas, 1981), Chapter 5, "Organization and Immortality."

61. Ibid., p. 83.

62. Martin Heidegger, "The Origin of the Work of Art," in *Poetry, Language and Thought*, Albert Hofstadter, tr. (New York: Harper & Row, Colophon, 1971), pp. 15–87; reference to p. 71; see also Heidegger, *Sein und Zeit [Being and Time]* on the concept of "throwness" [*Geworfenheit*].

63. Martin Heidegger, *Discourse on Thinking*, John M. Anderson and E. Hans Freund, trs. (New York: Harper Torchbooks, 1969), p. 52. I have taken the liberty of retranslating the last clause, originally rendered as: ". . . an uncanny change in the world moves upon us." The original German word for "uncanny" is *unheimlich* [unhomely], which Heidegger uses to refer to Man's sense of not feeling at home in the world.

64. Loc. cit. Heidegger distinguishes meditative thinking from calculative thinking.

4

The Language of Bureaucracy

Bureaucratic administration always tends to exclude the public, to hide its knowledge. . . . The treasury officials of the Persian Shah have made a secret science of their budgetary art and even use a secret script.

—Max Weber[1]

Language used to separate countries; in and around bureaucracy it separates people from one another. All modern organizations, public or private, seem deaf to customers and clients. Functionaries are prevented from speaking with one another. Managers' speech separates them from employees. The thinking that language reflects also differs among all of these; most irritatingly bureaucrats seem to think differently from the thinking necessary to conduct everyday life. It seems a miracle when bureaucrats say, think, or do anything useful to ordinary citizens at all. Listen to the experience of a client.

HOW PEOPLE SPEAK

Clients: A Man on Social Security

Pasquale Plescia went by bus from California to Washington, D.C., to find out about delays in his Social Security checks:

"Well, I'll tell you something about this town. They got a secret language here. You know that? Bureaucratese. Same thing we used to call double-talk. These government people, they don't hear you. They don't listen. You start to say something and they shut you out mentally, figuring they know right away what you're going to say before you say it.

I knocked on doors here for two weeks but everyone's so busy with paperwork, they got no time for nothing else. I go to see one Congressman—a priest, so I figure he's got humanitarian interests—and his aide says I got to write him a letter first. Another one won't let me in 'cause I'm not in his constituency. Another gives me a press release and says, 'This is the Congressman's position on Social Security.' No kidding, that happened. So I go down to HEW [then the combined Department of Health, Education and Welfare]. They've got 180,000 people working for HEW, and you know what? They've got nobody to make a complaint to.[2]

Bureaucratic Language

Pasquale Plescia captures what bothers us most when we try to communicate our needs to bureaucrats. He asks, Why won't they listen to me? They tell him to write a letter or fill out a form. If you want something from bureaucracy, or even from a congressional staffer acting bureaucratically, you've got to say it on its terms. Write a letter, fill out a form. Bureaucrats don't seem willing or able to think themselves into our language: We are expected to think ourselves into theirs.

Bureaucracy also has its own way of thinking. This is what enables bureaucrats to "shut you out mentally." At bottom it is this that prevents us from being understood by the local neighborhood bureaucrat in his or her capacity as an official, though the person inhabiting the bureaucratic role may understand us very well. The typical demand: I'd like to help you, but the rules say you've got to answer a few questions for us first.

The answers to such questions determine the basic judgment as to whether you are real to the bureaucracy. Yet this judgment seems to be made by reference to some abstract and hidden standard that is not of this world. In a way, these standards are more real than you are. The bureaucrat looks up to them. He or she compares your situation to the standards for action. Through such *reasoning by analogy*, the bureaucrat determines whether you qualify for his or her attention—and ultimately for the program's benefits.*

What happens to a person who, like Pasquale Plescia, acts out of the ordinary, sidesteps the local office and takes the bus to the top of the hierarchy, thus failing to follow normal procedures? He does not fit the normal profile of a client deserving action. Result: "They don't hear you." For the bureaucrats you don't exist.

In short, language and thinking in bureaucracy strike us as strange because they seem designed to prevent understanding, which is what speech and thought are basically for.

Understanding, bureaucracy seems to tell us, is a one-way street: If your behavior or your speech doesn't fit our program, there's nothing we can do for you.

*What makes Max Weber's secret language secret, in the epigram at the beginning of this chapter, is that it refers to a program model of which the ordinary listener is unaware. What the ordinary listener does in such cases is place the words uttered in his or her own context, which, however, is unlikely to be the same as the program-model context of the "secret" language. What is secret about such language is not its words—these are publicly uttered. What is secret is the referential context for the meaning of such words.

As a result, the words that bureaucrats utter seem to be directed *at* us ("Talk our way, or die!") rather than being a bridge that both sides construct to serve as a medium *between* us. Instead of being two-way or reciprocal, bureaucratic language is one-way or *one-directional*.

And, because we don't know its source in bureaucratic thinking, there seems to be no rhyme or reason for it. Such language seems to be arbitrary. Its challenges are peremptory. And ultimately there seems to be no willingness to admit to an original cause or present context that can give such language its sense: It is context-free or *acausal*.

These are observations that can emerge out of the most cursory of contacts with bureaucratic language and the thinking that lies behind it.

Pasquale Plescia clearly has discovered two outstanding characteristics of bureaucratic language: *one-directionality* (the speaking without listening) and *acausality* (the contextless detachment that makes bureaucratic language seem a secret language).

What Language Reveals about Thinking

But Plescia has insight not only into bureaucratic speech but into the thinking it implies.

When he says, ". . . they shut you out mentally, figuring they know right away what you're going to say before you say it," he suggests a prior knowledge on the part of bureaucrats as to what can be said. This is precisely correct.

Whatever can officially be said—and heard—in an agency is predetermined by the policy it is assigned to carry out. That policy is translated into a program. Such programs define what can be considered by individual bureaucrats as legitimately and legally part of their concerns.

In short, policies and programs predefine what can become real for bureaucracy. It is the bureaucrat's task to silently ask one question about demands by clients: Do these fit into the reality defined by the boundaries of policy and the official functions authorized by programs? But this means a constant mental shuttling back and forth between what is before the bureaucrat in any given instance and what is behind her or him: the blueprint of the program. It is the program that must always be obeyed. It becomes the referent point for what is authorized to happen. In their constant reference to the program, the dead hand of the program takes on greater reality for bureaucrats than does the life unfolding in front of them.

The thinking behind what is said does not emerge out of any present context but out of a preoccupation with comparing what is in front of the bureaucrat with a predetermined model of it. The bureaucrat's thinking, loosened from any overriding concern for actuality though still touching actuality lightly as one pole in its shuttling back and forth, anchors itself solidly in a policy or program model. It becomes thinking by *analogy*.

Thinking by analogy is always a reasoning by comparison. In it, one thing or event is compared and found to be similar to another. The logic of this comparison does not simply say that each event or thing in a pair is equal in importance to the other. In analogy, one thing is always phrased in terms of being "analogous to." "Analogous to" implies that a lesser thing is similar to a greater thing, a thing we are more certain of or know better. So an actual apple is referred in analogy upward to the ideal of an apple. Analogous speech also is speech whose sparks fly upward, strengthening what is spoken by referring it to a higher model.

In bureaucratic analogous reasoning again, a lesser thing is referred upward to a greater one. The referent point is always the abstract and general model of the program being administered, not the concrete and particular needs of people in reality.

When such thinking is expressed as speech, the words point in two directions at once. The speaker *seems* to be addressing us. But, at the same time, he or she is addressing with greater reverence a hidden source that must be satisfied by what he or she says. We may suspect this source is the agency's policy or program; Pasquale Plescia has given us the clue to this in observing the all-too familiar phenomenon of "double-talk."

Bureaucrats are engaged not only in a *reasoning by analogy* but in a thinking that espouses the reality of the policy or program model's abstract *ideal* over the reality of the actual. Anything they may say to us must also and first address the imperatives of the policy and program model they represent.

Pasquale Plescia's pointing finger is precisely on target: Only a person who has his or her inward eye always on what a model in the mind's eye permits is able to shut out mentally what does not belong in that model. Only such a person can "figure to know right away what you're going to say before you say it." For such a person, what is allowed by the program model can be pre-dicted—literally, said ahead of its being said. Speech that does not fit the program model must simply be ignored. It is programmatically unreal: ". . . they shut you out mentally."

Plescia, puzzled as he is at the inhumanity of it all, is well on his way to understanding it all. The contextless nature of speech, the talking at (its one-directionality), the reasoning by analogous reference to a hidden model, the false concretization of programmatic ideals as more real than a real person—these characteristics constitute the type of thinking mandated for bureaucrats. They are exposed through the more elaborate investigations of experts on language and thought: Wittgenstein, Searle, Husserl, and Heidegger, below.

But Plescia also testifies to the assumptions we make about speaking and thinking in ordinary social life. Here *what* I say is given meaning by a context I share with others (is *contextual*). In the flow of speech people listen to each other (*two-directionality* or *reciprocity*). Similarly, my thinking is not abstract and general and it is neither referential nor reverential of abstract models; rather our thinking in real life is *concrete, refers to the particular,* and is deeply *immersed in experience.*

So far, we can summarize the speaking and thinking models of bureaucracy and society in these terms:

Speech and Thought Observed in Bureaucracy and Society

In Bureaucracy	*In Society*
Speech is	**Speech** is
acausal (contextless)	causal (contextual)
one-directional	reciprocal
Thought is	**Thought** is
analogizing	concrete
general	particular
referential	immersed in
to abstract model	experience

The Newly Hired: Ambivalence and Ambiguity

Top-down language also greets newcomers to modern organizations, whether private or public, as double-talk. Wherever double-talk is heard, the hearer should suspect analogous thinking: the mental reference by the speaker to addressing the standards of a hidden model even while speaking to the listener. Referential as the terms are to hidden models, they lend themselves to being interpreted in one way by those they address while withholding their reference to the policy or program model. I, as a client, cannot know what my words mean to the bureaucrat.

Ambivalent language is also used to mislead—and gain power over—newcomers. An example: the manager's "suggestion." The suggestion has a generally understood meaning in society: A suggestion there is not a command but a free gift: "Try this, if you like; it might work; no obligation." However in bureaucracy, a "suggestion" from the manager means "Do it my way!" The term is the manager's way of appearing to be social when she or he is really being managerial, engaged in the business of commanding the program to be carried out. At best the offering of a suggestion is a way of getting the listener to believe in the complete freedom of picking up the idea and then jump to what is really an order with the added verve of personal enthusiasm.

Similar double meaning is contained in a managerial "Don't worry!" This can be an evasive answer to your question, "Is this really what you want?" Note that the manager has neither told you that it is or that it isn't. He or she has recommended to you taking up a certain feeling tone. While you wallow in it—"Don't worry, be happy!"—the manager has a chance for thinking by analogy: to figure out whether what you have done is really part of the program. The real answer will come later on the performance evaluation.

Ambivalence and ambiguity are managerial tools. But such tools are often wrapped in the clear language that newcomers to organizations need and expect in order to be able to relate to the new reality. In the words of one career counselor speaking of recent MBAs: "Kids out of school are apt to take things literally."[3] Which seemingly clear word has an ambiguous meaning in the organization no newcomer can be advised ahead of time—except perhaps for the rule that the more general the words the less they refer to anything that you can later nail down in your defense.

To expect superordinates to clarify their instructions, however, is to overlook that their power is enhanced exactly to the extent that they can keep you guessing by *how* they say *what* they say. Exactly to the extent that a manager's words are vague, an employee must orient himself or herself more and more acutely and desperately toward discovering what it is the manager meant. (See also Chapter 6, "Bureaucracy as Polity.") This is such a generally valid rule that organizational communications expert James R. Killingsworth warns that, "Organizational talk is not made to be taken at face value by hearers. . . . As a text, it means what it says. As a pretext, administrative talk is a clue to still other, potential meanings."[4]

When a manager tells you, "You're being certified for our outplacement program," he or she is not simply using an apparently neutral or even upbeat expression for "You're fired." The manager is conveying information he or she is required to pass on but is doing so in words that evade personal responsibility for the act.

Killingsworth has produced a chart (see Table 4.1) that shows both the utility and the absurdity of vague, ambivalent, and ambiguous speech: Almost any phrase can be combined with any other in any column or at any level, thus achieving nearly total meaninglessness. The chart's utility comes from two facts. It contains bureaucratic vocabulary that must be taken seriously both by employees or clients. If they don't, they are not likely to survive in or with the organization. And it does not need to be taken seriously by managers. There's always a way of interpreting the meaning in many ways, and the person who has the power to interpret is in charge. The very fact that, in the chart, any combination of apparently differentially meaningful terms can be applied to almost any situation indicates how far detached organizational speech has come from referring to reality. Such speech can be used only in an organization in

Table 4.1
EMPTY TALK IN ORGANIZATIONS

Column I	Column II	Column III	Column IV
Gentlemen,	the realization of the program's goals	leads us to reexamine	existing fiscal and administrative conditions.
Equally important,	the complexity and diversity of the committee's areas of concentration	has played a vital role in determining	areas of future development.
At the same time,	the constant growth in the quality and scope of our activity	directly affects the development and advancement of	the attitudes of key members regarding their own work.
Still, let us not forget that	the infrastructure of the organization	requires the clarification and determination of	a participatory system.
Thus,	the new shape of organizational activity	insures the participation of key members in	new proposals.

Source: James R. Killingsworth, "Idle Talk in Modern Organizations," *Administration and Society*, vol. 16, no. 3 (November 1984), pp. 346–84; chart from p. 352, originally produced as a satire by Polish students.

which internal performance standards outweigh any contact with reality: that is, where job performance is more important than getting work done. All bureaucratic organizations—public or private—tend, because of their inner logic, to become detached from the boundary with outer reality, where work is done. In short, the detachment of modern organizational language from real referents indicates the general detachment of modern organizations from human social and physical reality.

The Uses of Jargon

People complain about bureaucratese, secret professional languages, and jargon because their use by members of a bureaucracy or profession keeps other people outside. Jargon prevents us from knowing what the jargon users are talking about. But one would assume that as soon as an outsider learns the insiders' language, the outsider will be one of them and know what the words mean and what is being talked about. That is true to an extent, but somehow a mystery remains.

The most obvious form of jargon is that of terms constructed from the first, or first few, letters of several words: acronyms. Some find a permanent place in the language; then the origins of the acronym may be lost forever. Today it is unlikely that many will know "radar" is an acronym, much less remember the words whose initials it represents. Acronyms are very much "now." Lacking word stems and roots that can be traced, they represent a loss of a society's or civilization's history. The term no longer functions like a word that grew naturally, often out of other words still present in it, so that its history is contained in it. For example, "acronym" itself can be traced to its origins and root meaning. These lie in the classical Greek words of *akros* (at the end) and *anyma* (name)—revealing "acronym's" meaning to be that of a word constituted by referral to the (front) end of several hidden words.

Acronyms handicap especially outsiders, even highly sophisticated outsiders. Here is what Nobel Prize-winning physicist Richard P. Feynman has to say about listening to testimony of the commission inquiring into the crash of the space shuttle *Challenger*:

The first thing we had to learn [as members of the commission] was the crazy acronyms that NASA [National Aeronautics and Space Administration] uses all over the place: "SRMs" are the solid rocket motors, which make up most of the "SRBs," the solid rocket boosters. The "SSMEs" are the space shuttle main engines: they burn "LH" (liquid hydrogen) and "LOX" (liquid oxygen), which are stored in the "ET," the external tank. Everything's got letters.

And not just the big things: practically every valve has an acronym, so they said, "We'll give you a dictionary for the acronyms—it's really very simple." Simple, sure, but the dictionary is a great, big, fat book that you've gotta keep looking through for things like "HPFTP" (high-pressure fuel turbopump) and "HPOTP" (high-pressure oxygen turbopump).[5]

While such alphabet-soup games may seem harmless, they slowed down the research into the causes of the crash by at least one of the brilliant scientific minds of the age. Feynman's cure to the problem of being hit with *one-directional words*—words whose meaning is controlled by the speaker—supports our suspicion that the cure to the monologic nature of bureaucratic speech is *dialogue*. Recalling his initial briefing at one of the space shuttle's suppliers, the Jet Propulsion Laboratory, he said:

It's called a briefing, but it wasn't brief: it was very intense, very fast, and very complete. It's the only way I know to get technical information quickly: you don't just sit there while they go through what *they* think would be interesting; instead, you ask a lot of questions, you get quick answers, and soon you begin to understand the circumstances and learn just what to ask to get the next piece of information you need. I got one hell of a good education that day and I sucked up the information like a sponge.[6]

Here Feynman outlines how dialogue works. You ask questions. Because you are on an equal power level as those questioned—a skill of

Feynman's was to convey this[7]—all sides are free to tune in to whatever everybody is talking about. What happens is not that *you* merely tune in to what *they* are talking about. Rather, in talking together, you construct common ground—the *what* of what you are talking about: "soon you begin to understand the circumstances." Out of that common ground, it becomes possible to move ahead: to "learn what to ask to get the next piece." This true dialogue enables you as a group to go farther in understanding than an individual would have gone talking to him- or herself or talking *at* others.[8]

A modern society, obsessed with the current meaning of words, with words that have "currency," will hardly mourn the loss of the ability to trace terms to their origins. The meaning of a term is understood in modern society, including modern organizations, to be defined by those who control present context: The term will mean exactly what they say it means, no more and no less.[9] And their power enables them to make it stick. Subordinates need to be well trained in the definitions of the terms ahead of use, to prevent redefinition in shared context with customers or clients. A group whose intentions are sharpened and coordinated by forced definition of words gains an immense advantage in action over a traditional group, whose words are surrounded by haloes, past connotations, and ongoing discussion and redefinition. However, the latter group is likely to have a greater depth of commitment when it finally does something.

Constant top-down innovation in the design of words gives terms a certain rootlessness. Loosening interpretation from any origin in the word itself enables arbitrary definition. This may be temporarily good for the powerful, but not good from the viewpoint of the powerless, who are made more powerless by the reinforced need to detect and bow to the superimposed meaning of language. (See the consequences of this for power games in the discussion below on Alexander Haig.)

Another part of jargon is the circumlocution and the newly coined word, the neologism. When innovation is carried out in circumlocutions, the intent, which is to talk around what really is going on, miscarries on occasion. The Vietnam War brought us "terminated with extreme prejudice," as when the Central Intelligence Agency dropped suspected enemy agents out of helicopters; the Gulf war brought us "servicing the target," meaning dropping a bomb on people on the ground. This literally leaves the victims speechless—and unable to debate that the meaning of the term really signifies "killing."* But such is war. Such phrases serve the purpose of detaching functionaries from what they are really doing. Yet a consequence may be to evoke a sense of being politically manipulated when true meanings of bureaucratically designed words percolate up

*Personal experience of the author.

among citizens on the homefront. Trust in what one's government is saying, so necessary to the support that comes from legitimacy, may decline. Misuse of trusted words is not without cost.

At worst, such terms represent a lowering into shallow technical terms of a high social intent. The American people probably wanted peace when they set up a Department of Defense. At one point, the Defense Department, perhaps recognizing it could not deliver peace, decided to stop using the word and substituted a phrase accurately representing what it technically could do: "permanent prehostility"[10]—always being ready for war.

The bureaucratic style of defining reality by manipulating words is not a monopoly of bureaucracy itself. Citizens who can tap into bureaucracy's power to enforce the meaning of terms have been known to seize that advantage. So, for example, when the affirmative action officer of a university tells a professor he cannot use the term "reverse discrimination" in a discussion of personnel issues ("It might legitimate the term"), she is taking advantage of her power position to prevent free speech.

In general, however, top-down definition of speech by interest groups accessing government power is ultimately doomed to disappointment as long as not *all* speech can be controlled. So much for imposed neologisms like "waitron" for a female waiter, circumlocutions like "vocally challenged" for mute, and technical jargon such as "core rearrangement" for the meltdown of a nuclear plant. Such terms, imposed without adequate public discussion and lacking the control of total repression, lead to radio shows such as Rush Limbaugh's and to dictionary satires such as these: "Waitron, there's a nonhuman animal in my soup!" or "Whoopsy daisy," remarked the plant operator, "I think this baby is a teensy bit above critical, and we could be seeing some core rearrangement here."[11]

A THEORY OF BUREAUCRATIC SPEECH

One way of defining bureaucratic speech, as distinct from social speech, is to see what is missing in it.

So far people who have testified to how speaking goes wrong in bureaucracy tell us these characteristics:

First, bureaucratic speech is *one-directional* in flow: We are expected to think ourselves as clients into bureaucrats' way of speaking rather than speech being a process of mutual determination of reality through speaking and listening: that is, *reciprocal*. As Pasquale Plescia said in an earlier example, ". . . they don't hear you. They don't listen." Even individual words are defined in a one-directional manner, and power can make the definition stick, as the use of jargon and neologisms shows.

Second, bureaucratic speech seems to rest on a specific kind of reasoning: *reasoning by analogy.* Unless you as a client meet characteristics of a predetermined program, bureaucrats in effect cannot talk to you at all. This was made explicit by Pasquale Plescia's experience with the Social Security bureaucrats. Bureaucrats seem to be engaged in a conversation internal to the bureaucracy, asking questions such as: Does this client fit the program? This is the primary conversation that goes on, and, while it is going on, conversation with living clients is put in abeyance. In contrast, ordinary speech for purposes of problem solving is not only two-directional or reciprocal but *causal:* that is, both partners explore in talking what the problem is about and why they should act on it. The causes of bureaucratic programs and of the resulting speech—language, grammar, and words—are specifically hidden from the secondary, one-directional "speech" that is accorded the client.

Finally, as already indicated in the second point above, joint *construction of reality*—the "what" of what is to be talked about—is specifically forbidden by bureaucracy's need to control the reality its programs predefine. Bureaucratic speech tries to impose reality. This was made explicit by Feynman's experience with jargon and the contrasting dialogue—which constructed the "what" or reality of the problem—with the engineers at the Jet Propulsion Laboratory. However unless speech control is total, subuniverses of reality still express themselves, often with pitiful caution, as in part of American society's rebellion against "political correctness."

The following lists of characteristics summarize the speech used in bureaucracy and society.

Speech in Bureaucracy and Society

In Bureaucracy	*In Society*
• One-directional	• Reciprocal
• Analogous (functionalist)	• Causal
• Reality-imposing	• Reality-constructing

FUNCTIONARIES: POLICE, FIREFIGHTERS

Functionaries themselves often don't understand the need for one-directional speech that forbids backtalk and for hiding the origin of a word or a policy when knowing it would cause orders to make much more sense.

Employees experience bureaucratic language always in the imperative voice and bureaucratic utterances as always coming from the top, that is, as one-directional: "When the orders come down, you can't talk back." Or in terms of the favorite gripe of the policemen I used to teach: "We're the guys who know what's going on in the street better than anybody. You'd think they'd want to know about that upstairs. But the hardest thing for us is to try and get to talk to them." Employees often tend to attribute causality to the commands they receive; that is, they assume there is both a reason and a person behind them. This assumption is erroneous to the extent that the officer in charge does not officially act on behalf of the office and the organization at large in personal terms. Nevertheless, the favorite line in a large East Coast fire department undergoing painful management changes was: "If it weren't for _____ [the fire commissioner] all these changes wouldn't be happening to us."[12]

The fact is, of course, that bureaucracies are designed to carry out orders, but the orders have their meaning defined in a context higher up and far removed from the work situation. "Retreat!" in the specific context of soldiers engaged in hand-to-hand combat with the enemy and knowing themselves to be winning is likely to mean to them, at the most, a call to disengage and fall back to established positions. That is the kind of sense the word makes in the context of their "work." But consider the general back at staff headquarters who issued the order after being informed of a massive enemy advance rolling up his army's left flank. To him, "Retreat!" meant something much more absolute and final, such as "Run like hell and don't stop until you get back home."

The overview that high position in hierarchy provides administrators must give them a different sense of what their commands are intended to convey than that allowed by the parochial view of an employee locked into his or her job by the division of labor and layers of superiors. The entire strength of bureaucracy as *the* form of modern organization superior in power to any other type of organization—one, for example, in which kinspeople pause in the midst of battle to dispute what their tribal chief meant—lies in the fact that language and speech acts are so structured as to forbid employees' asking "the reason why." Theirs but to do or die. Individuals are responsive to a narrow work context; the bureaucracy is responsive to a vast organizational context.

The experience with social speech was that people became personally attached to what they said. They made judgments, dependent on work and social contexts, as to whether one should be committed to carrying into action the implications in one's words. This caused all kinds of trouble: A soldier might not obey a general when ordered to shoot a member of his own family, a necessity perhaps in a civil war; a tax officer might not collect taxes from relatives; a road worker might not paint the yellow stripe down the center of a road during a rainstorm even though the performance of the road department was judged by how much paint was used up. When language was made impersonal (one function of jargon, which covers up any human values involved) and speech one-directional, a major problem of gaining obedience was solved. Impersonal language takes the burden of guilt off the executioner or the tax collector and the responsibility of making sense off the road worker. The inability to talk back, which can be a frustration, is also a relief: "There's nothing I could do even if I wanted, so I'll keep painting in the rain."

ADMINISTRATORS AND MANAGERS: A SECRETARY OF STATE

Words make power. This can be understood when we ask ourselves how we react to the words of the powerful. These individuals, especially if they run a bureaucracy, have us in their power to begin with: If I want to keep working for, say, the State Department, I will obey. But their control over the language used adds to their power—and in a way that the rest of us do not normally perceive as an exercise of power. That, of course, is the beauty of it: to be exercising power without seeming to.

Take the specialized words used by an American secretary of state and later presidential aspirant, a lifelong bureaucrat who, though a general, had never exercised a combat command. Some of the words and phrases used by this top administrator, along with some *Time* magazine comments, can be found in the box that follows.

Observe your reaction to this idiosyncratic use of what are mostly common words with a long and meaningful history in the social language in which we were raised: English. Amusement? Disgust? Confusion? Disdain? Perhaps all of these went through your mind. But now imagine you are somehow obliged to deal with the man who uses words in such a strange way. If you are a Russian diplomat, or a subordinate in the State Department, you *must* deal with the secretary of state. But the only way of dealing with him, especially if you are a subordinate, is by trying to understand what he means. You must try to understand him because you are in an inferior power position to begin with; if you don't try or if your attempt fails, you may act in the wrong way and you risk disfavor. So you turn your entire attention to the speaker and become a total listener.

Like most subordinates, you do not have a chance to ask the speaker, "What is it you meant?" Much less can you challenge him by saying, "What you have just said doesn't make any sense." What the powerful say makes sense because, like a character in *Alice in Wonderland*, they command it to make sense. I mean exactly what I mean, neither more nor less—and it is for you to find out what that is. So you look at the speaker's language use and at the contexts within which he speaks. You see what actions his words refer to, and what things. And after a while you think you have an idea of what he means by "careful caution," "definitizing," and "menus." Then you act on your understanding of his orders containing such usage, and, if nothing adverse happens, you assume you have understood him.

Note the strange and twisted attitude you must take toward a powerful speaker: You engage in a turning toward the other, but the other makes not the slightest effort to turn toward you.

Haigledygook and Secretaryspeak

Alexander Haig conducted a terror-ist campaign of his own—against the English language. His war of words with the Kremlin turned into a war on words, presumably much to the consternation of Russian translators. Herewith a lexicon of Haigisms:

Careful caution. A repetitious redundancy but preferable to careless caution. Similar to his "longstanding in time."

Caveat. An Al-verb, a victim of the general's verbification pro-gram, to which resistance is *ver-boten* for even the most insolent little noun. As in: "I'll have to caveat my response, Senator."

Contexted. The past tense of Haig's verbicose veins. As in telling Senator John Glenn that his question cannot be an-swered "in the way you con-texted it."

Epistemologicallywise. The only thing less clear than the meaning of this word is how many hyphens it should have.

Exacerbating restraint. A Push-mi-Pullyu, as in expressing the hope that the Soviets would do nothing "to exacerbate the kind of mutual restraint that both sides should pursue."

Menu. Used with careful cau-tion as in: "In each instance the menu—and I use that term guardedly—of assets available to the West will vary."

Nuanced and nuance-al. As when the secretary of solecism talks of "nuanced and funda-mentally sharp departures" and "nuance-al differences."

Posthostage-return attitude. An imploded word cluster that may be the result of reading too many NATO command manu-als in German.

Saddle myself with a statistical fence. A techno-cowboy's meta-phor that borders on the kinky.

The very act of definitizing an answer. A punishable act in most English-speaking countries.

This is not an experience I haven't been through before. Definitely not a non-Haigism.

Out of context these phrases make no sense; in context they make even less sense. Maybe, just maybe, the Haigledygook is deliberate. As the Secretary said at his press conference when asked to clarify a statement: "That was consciously ambigu-ous in the sense that any terror-ist government that is contem-plating such actions I think knows clearly what we are speaking of." Well, perhaps *they* do.

Source: *Time*, February 23, 1981, p. 19.

The mandated turning toward the other in language use, in which the other merely speaks over the shoulder *at* us, deprives us not only of participation in the construction of language but also of the ability to think independently and, ultimately, of the ability to take part in the construction of reality. But it does make our understanding a functional part of the whole.

This is, of course, exactly what the specialized language of bureaucracy, extending far beyond a secretary of state's idiosyncrasies, is intended to accomplish. From the viewpoint of citizens, legislators, and administrators—if we may change roles for a minute—we do not want bureaucrats who redefine the meaning of a law or a policy or a memo. We do not want independent thinkers to reshape what the polity has decided. And we do not want the illegitimate reconstruction of our social world by bureaucrats who are intended to be our servants, not our partners.

WHAT THE EXPERTS SAY

Wittgenstein: The Abolition of Language

In bureaucracy, we may be moving in a direction where language is not language at all. One of the strongest arguments on behalf of the death of language can be drawn from the philosopher Ludwig Wittgenstein. Language is communication, this argument runs; what goes on in bureaucracy is not communication but information. Communication is a two-way construction of meaning between at least two human beings; information is literally the molding and shaping of one human being by another. In fact, information does not necessarily involve human beings: Machines can "inform" one another.

COMMUNICATION AND INFORMATION

Language originates in the common life that human beings share as members of a community, Wittgenstein seems to argue.[13] Within this communal context, we engage in "language games.[14] That is, we engage in mutual interaction through language that is based on taken-for-granted rules silently agreed upon among ourselves. The fundamental agreement of the game is agreement in "what we do."[15] We might think of such agreement as a result of convention: "Okay, Joe, let's agree on not killing each other in this game by calling this a head and we all know heads are easily injured." But before I can even begin to agree with you on such definitions, I must already have an understanding of what a head is and what it means to be injured. That is, I must share with you my humanity. "If language is to be a means of communication there must be agreement, not only in definitions, but (queer as this may sound) in judgments."[16] As one Wittgensteinian commentator said, "Unless people agree in their reactions to colours they will not have the concept of colour they need to have to see certain behavior as 'agreement in reaction to colours'. Unless they agree in their expressions of, and reactions to, pain, they will not have the concept of pain they need to see behavior as 'pain behavior'."[17]

In summary, what makes language as a means of communication possible is the shared experience of being human. This shared experience Wittgenstein called "forms of life" [*Lebensformen*]. Forms of life are specific expressions of behavior among human beings that rest on the organic peculiarities of the species. In the words of another Wittgensteinian commentator:

Language, and therefore the higher forms of consciousness, depend, logically, for their existence on the possibility of common "forms of life." Hence, also, they depend, as an empirical matter of fact, on the existence of human beings regarded as members of a (fairly gregarious) species. To assert the existence of *such* forms of consciousness is in part to assert the existence, not of a single person, nor even of several separate persons, but rather, of people, that is to say of groups of individuals having not only common characteristics but also common (mutual) responses, interactions, etc.[18]

The relevant question to be asked about life in bureaucracy is whether such life still maintains the characteristics of human "forms of life" based on our biological characteristics as a species.

Specifically we can address this question to two kinds of "communication" within bureaucracy: (1) "communication" between bureaucratic structures and individual functionaries; and (2) "communication" between computers and individual functionaries or clients.

One of the leaders in modern organization theory, Herbert Simon, considers bureaucratic structures to be frozen decisions.[19] In other words, the office of the sales manager in a vacuum cleaner company is set up to perpetuate the decision that whenever a customer comes in to buy a vacuum cleaner there will be adequate sales staff to effect the sale. Setting up this structure once—the structure of the sales manager's office—for all time hence, or until another decision is made, obviates the need to have unqualified and ill-informed personnel run around, when a customer comes, searching desperately for vacuum cleaners, price lists, and the proper procedures for recording the sale so that inventory can be brought up to date, new machines ordered, and so on. In this sense, the office structure is not simply one frozen decision—the decision to sell—but many frozen decisions: on how to sell, what price to ask, how and when to reorder.

Nonhuman "Language"

The question that arises here is: Are the instructions contained in the frozen decision—i.e., the sales manager's office—really communication? That is, are they language? Or are they something else?

Let me tentatively suggest that the instructions so frozen are neither communication nor language in the traditional sense, but information. That is, for the very good reason of achieving predictability of behavior by the sales staff, the instructions encoded in the sales office are not subject to mutual agreement from below. They are one-directional. They shape behavior from the top down. As soon as, and because, it becomes detached from the original decision makers, who then become inaccessible to communication from below, information of this technical sort loses an essential characteristic of human language. The office in question is not a living thing, although it might be argued that it is usually inhabited by a living thing, the sales manager. But what characterizes the bureaucratic office is that its frozen decisions exist no matter whether there is a sales manager or not and no matter who he or she is. Even when the office is temporarily empty because the manager has been fired, the office "exists" and even "talks." It "talks" because many of its frozen decisions are encoded in price lists and work rules, which serve me as external guides to my behavior as sales clerk.

But does the office talk and exist the way human beings do? As a sales clerk, I am quite aware I can never talk back to it to inquire after the original decisions under which it was structured. One of these decisions was to have an office that would talk to me without having back talk. But, more importantly, in bureaucracy the office is specifically not the human being who fills it. Rule is impersonal. This means that even if I were to try to engage in back talk, I would be addressing a "partner" of intended communication that very specifically, and by design, lacks experience in the human condition. The office, after all, is the attempt to mechanize and automate both perceptions of what goes on in the sales process and instructions based on such inputs. Lacking human experience, the office as such can never become, under Wittgensteinian concepts of language, a partner for mutual agreement about a language game called "sales." Because the office is inhuman, it can only treat me as a thing like itself. I, who think of myself as a human being, am "thought of" and treated as an analogue to the machine—another machine. I can understand it only to the degree that I accept the rules it imposes on me, that is, to the extent that I become mechanical not only in my behavior but also in my conception of what language is. At this point whatever "talk" goes on between me and the office is no longer "language" in the Wittgensteinian sense. As Vesey notes, with tongue-in-cheek, about similar situations: "Arguments from analogy haven't a leg, even *one* leg, to stand on."[20] This is, of course, because offices, unlike humans, do not have legs. Given such a handicap we might, under Wittgenstein's premises, have assumed from the beginning that neither communication nor language is possible between human beings and the structures of bureaucracy.

But something does go on between the two, and if it is not language in the traditional sense, what is it? Here we may look to what Herbert Simon considers the ideal structure of modern organization, the computer, for an answer.[21] Don't computers speak to us? Don't programmers "program"—that is, "speak" to—computers?

Before proceeding to an answer, let us emphasize that the above argument on the linguistic relation between office structure and functionaries already demonstrates our main point: Language in bureaucracy is radically different from language in society. Wittgenstein's argument in fact suggests that language is not only different in bureaucracy, it is abolished.*

Nowhere does this become more clear than when people freeze business or public-service decisions into a computer and then make other people subject to the computer's instructions. Like the relationship between organizational structure and functionary, and for exactly the same reasons, the one between computer and functionary is not one of communication. The computer provides us with an especially clear-cut example of the difference between communication and information precisely because the last human element has been squeezed out of the computer, seen as an organizational structure into which decisions are frozen. An office, on the other hand, still seems to be occupied by a human manager, giving the impression of a human–machine symbiosis. In general, computer–human exchanges can no longer be understood in terms of how language used to link humans because a computer is not part of the human species.

A computer is as different from humans as humans are from dogs or stones. As one Wittgensteinian put it: "Why can we not intelligibly say of a dog or an infant that it is hopeful? Or of a stone that it is in pain? Why can we not say that a computer calculates?"[22] Pointing out that Wittgenstein himself asked this last question,† the same author summarizes Wittgenstein's reply:

A computer can reel out unimpeachable answers to the questions we feed into it. It may be tempting to think that here is exemplified the kind of competence that makes us speak of thought and intelligence in a mathematician. If the mathematician differs from the computer in *other* respects why should that undermine the similarity in their mathematical performance? Certainly if a man or a child writes down the answer to a mathematical problem this, in *itself*, does not prove that he has intelligence. To think of him as having mathematical ability we want him to be able to solve *other* mathematical problems. Whether or not his present perfor-

---

*Similarly, Jenny Teichman on the concept of "inaudible" language: "He [Wittgenstein] seems to be saying . . . that a language which cannot be used in communications is not a language at all (any more than infinity is a number)" (Teichman, "Wittgenstein on Persons and Human Beings," in Royal Institute of Philosophy, *Understanding Wittgenstein* [New York: St. Martin's, 1974], p. 145).
†In *Remarks on the Foundations of Mathematics* (Oxford, England: Basil Blackwell, 1956), Part IV, Section 2.

mance exhibits ability and intelligence depends on what he does on *other* occasions. But when we call a man who solves a wide range of difficult mathematical problems intelligent, we take it for granted that the symbols, formulae and simple operations he uses have meaning for him, that he understands them. We cannot take this for granted in the case of the computer. Merely responding to the problems fed into it with the correct answer does not show that the computer understands what it prints. . . .

In short, if the computer is to calculate it would have to have something like the human body, with arms, face, eyes, and enter into various activities in which the symbols and formulae it prints play a role. It is their role in these many activities, in shopping, measuring, accounting, engineering, that gives them the sense they have.[23]

In other words, without participation in the human experience, the computer is not capable of something like understanding. For the same reason, we can argue that the interaction between people and computers can never fully partake of the characteristics of communication, because one of the basic requirements for communication, the capacity for understanding on the ultimate grounds of sharing the human condition, is not available to the computer.

Similarly, the more human beings, who are dependent on modern organization for employment, adjust to the machine, the less likely they will remain capable of communication. As Wittgenstein points out, if a human responded to mathematical questions with the quickness of a computer and always came up with the correct answer, could carry out complicated formal transitions, and could work out involved mathematical proofs, but was "otherwise perfectly imbecile," then he or she would be "a human calculating machine."[24] In yet other words:

A person who produces such answers, whether in words, writing or print, is performing an activity in which thought and intelligence are displayed *only* if he lives a life in which this activity has a point and a bearing on other things he does, *only* if he has other interests—interests independent of producing these answers. In the absence of such a life even a being who is alive is not a human being.[25]

As we move from the society of human beings to the bureaucracy mix of functionaries and machines, we thus experience a sense of strangeness in the kind of language spoken there. According to the Wittgensteinian explanation, this is because structures of the bureaucratic type are incapable of producing human language, human communication, and human understanding.

Searle: The Separation of Language from Meaning

There is a very basic experience in bureaucracy in which we sense that speech there is radically different from speech in society. We reflect this when we call an institution's press spokesperson a "mouthpiece." We encounter a similarly strange experience when we see computer specialists "talk" to their machines. In both cases we sense that something strange is going on, but we don't understand why. In both cases we are right.

Detaching Meaning from Message

What we are observing when bureaucrats or bureaucratic structures (including computers) speak, or are spoken to, is often something unparalleled in human history—the separation of meaning from the message. It was of such language that bureaucratic practitioner and critic C. P. Snow wrote, "It was a curious abstract language, of which the main feature was the taking of meaning out of words."[26] Marshall McLuhan may glibly tell us that the "medium *is* the message," that the form of a message is its meaning; and he may be right: All communications media shape what they are capable of saying. But what is happening in bureaucracy is very specifically the separation of the message from both its content and its context.

Press secretaries of government institutions are very specifically understood by reporters *not* to be involved in what they are saying. They do lend, as the derogatory but very descriptive appellation of "mouthpiece" suggests, the mouth to the conveying of the institution's message; but his or her personal meaning is detached from what is said—the impersonal message. This is the function of the "good" bureaucrat's detachment from his or her acts. It is a sign of insufficient bureaucratization that news reporters held President Nixon's press secretary, Ronald Ziegler, personally responsible for the misinformation he distributed. On the other hand, Ziegler showed he understood the functionalist nature of official speech when he chose to characterize previous statements exposed by the press as falsehoods as "inoperative" instead of as "lies." A lie is a concept that belongs to the world of social language in which individuals are held responsible for what they say, and their intentions are expected to be congruent with their words. Within the world of bureaucratic language, "inoperative" is a perfect term for a statement that no longer functions in the bureaucracy's overall attempt to impose its will on its environment— that is, in a world where means and meanings no longer matter but program integrity does.

Nevertheless, those of us coming to bureaucracy from society are right in feeling there is something very strange going on in the way bureaucrats use language, though perhaps our sense of strangeness should be resolved through understanding rather than outrage. What can explain our sense of strangeness when confronted with bureaucratic language? For something to be strange, it must differ from what we are used to. How does bureaucratic language differ? If we could answer this last question, we could also understand our sense of being strangers in a strange land.

But first another example. Our sense of strangeness reaches a peak when we are spoken to by computers. Computers interest us here because they have replaced large segments of bureaucratic structures, are in fact often used *as* bureaucratic structures. A computer can, for example, replace a large section of a business's or civil-service institution's accounting or payroll office. To a large degree it is, in effect, the accounting or payroll office, and it is more bureaucratic in Max Weber's sense than any structure that preceded it. Precomputer structures are mixtures of people and machines in which people still visibly dominate even if, for the sake of bureaucratic control and stability, they are supposed to act like machines. For the segments that the computer takes over, this duality is resolved: The structure in which formerly twenty accountants performed calculating operations on a payroll is now a computer. The computer *is* the ideal bureaucracy.

When such a structure speaks, as we have said, the speech seems very strange to us—because all human components have been removed from the speaker. What is left is myself and the IBM terminal, myself and the printout.

Here, because the computer presents us with an extreme or "pure" example, we begin to see clearly the nature of bureaucratic talk—machine language—as opposed to people talk—human language.

The difference, as we have already indicated, is that in bureaucratic talk the message has to be so encapsuled and protected against the personal interests of its human carriers that it can stand by itself—apart from, and even despite, these human carriers. With the machine language of the computer, the designers of bureaucracy have finally reached that goal. There now is an impersonal language. And it is free from human interference. It is this fact that is unique in human history. No wonder we feel strange!

At this stage we may call upon the services of an expert linguist, John R. Searle, to deepen our understanding of just how serious this difference is.

A Retreat from Language

In ordinary human discourse, Searle argues, what is said (language) is never separate from the intentions of the person who says it (the speaker). The purpose of language, in fact, is to have the listener recognize the intention or meaning of the speaker.

Now, one of the strangest things about observing people who program computers—that is, who work with what computer specialists call "machine language"—is that they "utter speech," or construct speech, which the machine will then be able to use, without having in mind anything specific that they want to communicate. They are simply laying down the *means* of communication without reference to any specific *meaning*. Someone who wants to use the computer to communicate will come along later and use the means laid down—I hesitate to call it language for it is nothing of the sort in traditional terms—by attaching a meaning to it. This process of attaching meaning to the means of a language is one of the strangest experiences in which humans have ever engaged. Not that definitions have not been imposed from above for millennia. But the permanent, and very visible, separation of what is said, the signs and symbols, from what is meant has been experienced only for short spans at most, as when a child or a newcomer to a country uses a new word before learning the meaning attached to it. In the past such separation was always a handicap, a barrier to communication, but now the computer promises that separating means from meaning will encourage communication and make it more certain.

Some further exploration of Searle may deepen our understanding of this difference between what is said and what is meant. He writes:

Human communications has some extraordinary properties, not shared by most other kinds of human behavior. One of the most extraordinary is this: If I am trying to tell someone something, then (assuming certain conditions are satisfied) as soon as he recognizes that I am trying to tell him something and exactly what it is I am trying to tell him, I have succeeded in telling it to him. Furthermore, unless he recognizes that I am trying to tell him something and what I am trying to tell him, I do not fully succeed in telling it to him.[27]

That is, in ordinary human life the act of telling and the meaning attached to what is told are usually inseparable.* In contrast, the computer, and to a lesser degree the thoroughly bureaucratized bureaucrat, separates the two. Computer "language," as a pure example of an ideal bureaucratic "language," is not fully language until it is applied *by someone* to a *particular case.*† That is, it requires someone to come along and put what is a highly abstract and detached system of signs into a human context.

---

*In social life, having meaning attached to what is told us is best achieved by having the speaker remain personally attached to his or her words. For example, juries apparently tend to lend more credence to narrative testimony offered by a witness than to the same information presented in a non-narrative manner (for example, signed depositions), according to a research group headed by anthropologist William O'Barr of Duke University. (As reported in "Verdicts Linked to Speech Style: Anthropologists Say Subtle Patterns Influence Juries," *The New York Times*, Dec. 14, 1975, p. 88). Contrasting mock juries' reaction to narrative versus non-narrative information, the report concluded: "The result: The juries considered the narrative form of testimony to be more authoritative and stronger, even though the substance presented in the two varieties was indistinguishable." The narrative style, of course, is *social* speech. In contrast to bureaucratic speech, it allows speakers to become directly involved in what they say.
†I am putting the word "language" in quotation marks here to indicate that these are not languages in the traditional sense.

Such "language" is strange to us because most language we are acquainted with ordinarily appears in some sort of context related to a problem, interest, or activity in which we are engaged. Computer language, and to a large degree bureaucratic language in general, is in this sense "context-free." It lacks a context in the same way that a tongue would lack a context if I saw it going for a walk unattached to a head. And bureaucratic language thus unattached appears strange to us users of attached language in much the same way.

Linguists, who take language apart in their day-to-day work, have of course encountered language in this amputated form before. But, as Searle says, in real life, "speaking a language is everywhere permeated with the facts of commitments undertaken, obligations assumed, cogent arguments presented, and so on."[28] Those of us toying playfully and naively with computer "language," and the "language" of bureaucracy in general, might well be forewarned by the caution Searle addresses to his fellow linguists:

The retreat from the committed use of words ultimately must involve a retreat from language itself, for speaking a language . . . consists of performing speech acts according to rules, and there is no separating those speech acts from the commitments which form essential aspects of them.[29]

While Searle does not address himself to what we have observed—that people in ordinary bureaucratic life are now playing games with a language that involves the separation he fears—it is perhaps not too impertinent for us to read into his specific caution a general warning for ourselves as speakers, as listeners, and, above all, as human beings. The fact is that in everyday life we have begun to use "language" in a way that heretofore only linguistic analysts have encountered in their scholarly analyses that take living language apart. Modern use pries language out of its communal context of human beings sharing a common way of life (Wittgenstein) and reduces it to a mere tool (Searle). In modern organization, the consequences of such distortion appear in the clearest and cruelest form. But what makes such distortions cruel does not become fully clear until we ask what, in using language in such ways, we do to ourselves as human beings. This is a question of content raised by the philosopher Martin Heidegger.

Heidegger: Language as the Home of Being

With Martin Heidegger, we can focus on the cruelest aspect of bureaucratic language: that it reduces us to something less than human beings.

Modern science, the handmaiden of modern organization, has of course had a long-standing interest in language as a human *tool*. But this interest rises out of a hole that science has dug for itself when it comes to defining what a human being is. To science, a human being is an acting subject separate from other human beings. Given this assumption, it is no wonder that science shops around for a tool that human beings can use to bridge the gulf between them that science's conception of humans has created. This tool is language. Only through language, so science continues its assumptions, can human beings understand each other at all.

This gives organizers and managers of the modern organization of life a brilliant idea: By controlling speech, they can also control human understanding. Not only human understanding, but human beings' very way of being *with* one another: the ability to create a common world.

Language so conceived is a tool for control. As a tool, it focuses those interested in power, manipulation, and administration on the possibility of imposing their own will by seizing language as a hostage. Unless this hostage is released, we come to believe, we cannot live a shared life as human beings. There must be speech, but every effort is made to control who speaks to whom: never up the hierarchy, unless requested; and never across divisions of labor unless authorized by a superior who acts as the controller of speech.

Martin Heidegger puts a crimp in this blueprint for controlling human life through language control by tracing the origin of language. His thesis is that we already understand each other before language comes along. If so, this means not only that we are not dependent on language to link us together (as bureaucracy suggests). Also, the remedy for bureaucratic control over language is not simply lots of unleashed talk (as is suggested by advocates of process groups in which people speak freely).

Heidegger alerts us to a third way of thinking of speech apart from the controlled speech of bureaucracy and the facilitated speech of groups.

Heidegger's critique of the common definition of speech rests on his uncommon definition of what human beings are. In contrast to all assumptions underlying modern science, he does not believe each of us is an island entire and of himself. Rather he observes that, from birth on, we experience ourselves as a being that is in the company of others. The way we are—each of us—is already a being with others, a co-being.[30]

From Co-Being to Unhuman Speech

If we are not separate from one another, this deprives speech of its position in science as a *first* link that, only when spoken, creates the possibility of mutual understanding. Rather, it is because we already fundamentally understand each other to be fellow human beings that speech is possible—as the partial and particular expression that articulates our humanity in a given situation.

Heidegger speaks of communication as literally an "imparting" or division into shares of something we already have with others: our essential co-being. This sharing "articulates the constitution of an understanding being with others. It accomplishes the 'division into its parts' of our common situatedness and of the understanding of co-being."[31]

The implications for modern organizations are obvious. First, all claims to be able to control human beings *essentially* through controlling their speech deal with human beings at a very superficial level. Second, attempts to ameliorate such control by bringing bureaucratic inmates together in groups permitting free talk are equally superficial. Controlling speech does not destroy our common humanity; permitting speech does not have the power to restore it. Even in the worst of bureaucracies, human beings retain their potential to break out through the common understanding that underlies and constantly regenerates the course of speech. But equally so, the best of facilitated speech groups, in which speech flows ever so freely, does not necessarily restore speech as what Heidegger calls "the home of our being"—it may in fact encourage a flight into a false sense of communal being.

Language, in other words, is not a bridge that for the first time links separate beings; it is a testimony to the fact that we experience ourselves as part of each other to begin with. One proof is our experience that often we most deeply understand each other when we are able to be with each other in silence. This "being part of" each other is what is "imparted" in speech.

Speech that does not carry out this function, like bureaucratic speech, is unhuman to the core. Elsewhere,[32] Heidegger describes the kind of experience that human beings have when they are in touch with their deepest need. They want to engage in talk in which they can *express* themselves. "Self-expressive talk is a sharing. Its tendency toward being aims at bringing the listener into taking a part in the opened-up being toward that which is talked about."[33]

But bureaucracy also can claim that it responds to our needs. Here it is important to distinguish between the kind of needs that bureaucracy *can* respond to and those it *cannot*. Bureaucracy, by design, can distribute responses to those needs already defined. It must, however, carry out its paramount function of accountable program administration. To achieve this, it must do everything in its power to prevent *new* needs from being expressed that might affect the integrity of its programs. Bureaucracy is *the* enemy in human life to the human's potential for being all it has not already been defined as being—all it can yet be. As the institution of actuality, bureaucracy opposes potentiality. For example, it opposes politics as the art of the possible.* But potentiality—the ever-recovered and always reasserted ability to be—is the way in which the human being enacts itself. Bureaucracy, to maintain its own interests, must do every-

*See Chapter 6.

thing it can to sidetrack us from the road on which we become the being that is ever open to further being. That means it is in bureaucracy's interest to suppress speech that is expressive of human potential.

ORGANIZATIONAL BABBLE AS FLIGHT INTO INAUTHENTICITY

This is also a critique of one of bureaucracy's favorite techniques for raising *self*-consciousness of functionaries. In the prevailing literature, encounter groups and training groups (T-groups) are hailed as ways of breaking out of rule-bound consciousness. The question is never answered as to why bureaucracy is essentially unthreatened by such breakouts.

A Heideggerian answer is that a false self-consciousness constitutes itself in such groups. What is elicited in them is the superficial mutual "sharing" of one's being as defined by technical values. These values are, of course, entirely compatible with the ones a modern society can deliver.

Demanding and getting a fair and open hearing that one's technical knowledge, for example, be respected by managers and co-workers is hardly an earth-shaking content of speech that threatens bureaucratic values. (See Chapter 2.) So also the speech of outsiders. Say participation is elicited in focus groups. There it stays within an understood civility. Consumers, for example, do not presume to demand anything that the organization in essence cannot deliver.

What one *is*, expressed in such groups, is defined by a flight from authenticity: what one deeply knows oneself to be. Instead one takes one's cues from others and, in organizational psychobabble, flees from self into what one imagines yet others think of one. It is dangerous for a group facilitator to elicit more than the average understanding that social typification can bring; for, in a deeper understanding, the division from each other imposed by the organization—and thus the organization itself—might be put in question.

In summary, Heidegger's primacy of an experience basic to all thinking puts speech in its proper place. It rests in the experience of co-being. It *is* in speech that we reveal ourselves as the being that originally *is* with others. In this sense speech is, as he says, our home. But speech itself rests on and is made possible only by the extent to which we already share a sense of co-being. When that sense is destroyed or unnecessarily limited, co-being falls apart into false individualism. From it, inauthentic selves flee from their sense of loss of each other into a substitute for co-being: the crowd of anonymous others in which the self drowns itself in its own namelessness.

Clearly, as the epitome of institutionalization in modernity, bureaucracy promotes exactly such anonymity. Orders are to be obeyed out of the authority of an anonymous office, no matter whose name is on the door. This obscures co-being in which individual authenticity and being with others balance each other. It is no wonder that such conditions also water down language, if they do not, in terms of its most profound function, attempt to destroy it.

All this is not helped by proliferating opportunities for consultation, conferences and committees "to talk things over." "With the multiplication of talk about something there is not the least guarantee that understanding is brought further along. To the contrary: the far-flung talking things over covers over and brings that which is understood into seeming clarity, that is, the incomprehensibility of triviality."[34]

For an example, see the chart on idle chatter on page 162 provided by James Killingsworth. Suddenly a philosophic look into institutional speech shows us why it *must* be the way it is—with its necessary pathological effects that ordinary folk daily observe, including idle talk.

A specific example of idle talk is provided by the conversations between space shuttle *Challenger's* managers and engineers attempting to warn of defective O-rings. There, also, such talk satisfied the average understanding of things as far as they could be discussed in the existing power structure. When engineers reached the limits of that average, and what they had to say most profoundly was sensed to be a challenge to the structure, they simply retreated into a "Well, I've had my say"—and the shuttle exploded.[35]

THE BUREAUCRAT MEETS THE PHYSICIST

The tendency toward the triviality of normalcy is echoed by the media. These perform the function of reassuring us all is well with the world— especially when it isn't. An example is the evaluation of the investigating Rogers Commission by *The New York Times*.[36] The report fairly enough depicts two approaches to the space shuttle investigation: physicist Richard P. Feynman's and chairman William P. Rogers's, who admittedly "lacked any technical background for understanding the space shuttle."

"Right from the start, Dr. Feynman, a physicist known for his brilliant and original intellectual forays, was impatient with committee meetings, bureaucratic planning, formal hearings and detailed discussions of the best way to word reports. As far as he was concerned, the way to investigate a problem was to venture out as an individual and have long talks with the working level technical people who could explain to him everything they knew about the complex shuttle technology and its problems."

In contrast, Chairman Rogers is described as "determined to conduct what he called an 'orderly investigation,' with designated individuals and panels of commission members systematically looking into the major issues as they developed, tying up loose ends, and reaching a consensus."

Utilizing the authoritative tone of the semiofficial newspaper of record it takes itself to be, the *Times* then goes on to equate a reputation for being influential in the commission with effectiveness. How does that equation impose trivial normalcy? Feynman, who exposed frozen O-rings as a cause of the disaster, is evaluated as "by no means counted by others on the panel as among the most influential commissioners." "By most accounts, the most influential member of the commission, after Mr. Rogers, was Mr. [Neil] Armstrong, the former astronaut who now heads his own consulting firm in Charlottesville, Va." Such reporting neatly sidesteps the issue of what is most important in a scientific investigation: getting to the bottom of a physical phenomenon or being a good group communicator. Clearly doing the first is socially and organizationally ineffective unless one can do the latter. But the point is that groups may be unduly influenced by mere social concerns—Neil Armstrong's exploits "as the first man to step on the moon gave him enormous stature"—rather than by the issue at hand: What blew up the space shuttle?

For a society that values the compromise of social agreement above physical facts, the circle is complete, and with it the surrender to bureaucratic thinking. Critical thinking is suppressed on the job. Then there is attempted sidetracking of the one most profound critical thinker in the investigation. This is followed by public evaluation of the investigation in terms of mutual appreciation of participants. The society can go back to sleep, believing that the substantive results were the work of "a diverse group moving quickly and functioning as a team," as the *Times* would have it, rather than the result of the substantive probing of a single individual. Thus does bureaucratic speech lull a culture.

THE NATURE OF BUREAUCRATIC SPEECH

Bureaucratic speech estranges us from the experience of ordinary social life. Ordinary folk like Pasquale Plescia testify to this. But bureaucratic speech also alienates us even from the physical limits of life. Scientists testify to this. Why this alienation takes place must be explained by experts on what makes up meaningful human life existence as well as physical nature: philosophers. These examine the way speech expresses human life as an adventure in meaning-giving and the physical world around us, which becomes meaningful only once a human being approaches it.

That there are limits to the utility of bureaucratic speech even within bureaucracies is illustrated catastrophically by boundary-shaking events like the explosion of the space shuttle *Challenger*. (Smaller events, such as when a welfare office's actions make a client fare anything but well can simply be ignored.) Perhaps no more acute indictment can be found in contemporary science than the indictment by scientist Richard P. Feynman of the bureaucrat *par excellence* who headed the presidential commission investigating that crash.[37]

William P. Rogers, acting not out of malice but simply as the typical bureaucrat, did everything possible to keep speech within bureaucratic limits. Testimony was allowed to be *acausal;* those responsible for that bureaucracy's actions—or nonaction—would never be identified. Terms used in testimony were permitted of *one-directional* definition, so that even a scientist needed access to a secret dictionary to know what experts were talking about. *Reality-constructing* dialogue, absent in the official testimony, had to be built privately by Feynman taking on the role of an outsider to the commission.

If we remind ourselves of the contrasts between bureaucratic and social speech . . .

In Bureaucracy	*In Society*
Speech is	**Speech** is
one-directional	reciprocal
analogous (functional)	causal
reality-imposing	reality-constructing

. . . then we see that, typically, the bureaucracy shunned social speech and reveled in speech that would never get to the cause of the disaster: namely, its own practices.

"For a successful technology," Feynman concludes his report, "reality must take precedence over public relations, for Nature cannot be fooled."[38] But Feynman himself admits, ". . . I don't know what's natural in a bureaucratic system."[39] To some extent we now do: the triviality of normalcy that turns even the liberation of constrained speech into banality.

A bureaucracy, above all, must speak in such a way as to protect the integrity of the policy it was designed to carry out. But that integrity is always bureaucratically defined. That is, the meaning of the policy is translated into technical terms that the organization can understand. These lead to technical actions that the organization is technically capable of carrying out.

Yet, technical action and its speech are qualitatively different from practical action and its ordinary speech. The bureaucracy is filled with technical acts and language. But it is surrounded by an environment of practical people who judge all action and speech in terms of what that action *is* to them and what that speech *means* to them.

Thus, the bureaucrat finds him- or herself besieged by a world of speech acts that not only seems to be hostile but is hostile. The unexpected always comes along.

The unexpected appears as a world of chaotic turbulence to those who attempt to capture the world through bureaucratic speech. This is so for two reasons.

First, there are policy intents that actually cannot be translated into bureaucratic technique and its language. For example, when policy requires care, all the bureaucracy can give is control.

Second, even when policy is translatable into technical acts, policy always lags behind reality. The bureaucratic language encapsules such acts. It protects original policy intent in a technical way. But it will always be immune to one function of language that brings any language to life: language's ability to grasp what has not yet been grasped in the past, to seize the new as it emerges, to reassure us of order in our lives even as we leap from minute to minute into the unknown of the future.

Both to qualitatively different policy intent and to the future, the technical language of modern organization is, and must remain, immune if the control function of bureaucracy is to be maintained. No wonder bureaucratic speech has a deadening effect on the rest of us!

NOTES

1. Max Weber, *Economy and Society: An Outline of Interpretive Sociology,* 3 vols., Guenther Roth and Claus Wittich, eds. E. Fischoff et al., trs. (New York: Bedminster Press, 1968), p. 992.

2. Reported in the *Los Angeles Times,* reprinted as "He Forces Bureaucrats to Hew to the Line," *New York Post,* July 29, 1975, p. 62.

3. Career counselor Betty Harragan quoted in Mary Bralove, "Taking the Boss at His Word May Turn Out to Be a Big Mistake at a Lot of Companies," *Wall Street Journal,* June 4, 1982, p. 3.

4. James R. Killingsworth, "Idle Talk in Modern Organizations," *Administration and Society,* vol. 16, no. 3 (November 1984), pp. 346–84.

5. Richard P. Feynman, as told to Ralph Leighton, *"What Do You Care What Other People Think?"—Further Adventures of a Curious Character* (New York: Bantam Books, 1989), p. 126.

6. Ibid., p. 122.

7. In another situation, Feynman: "I was terrified. I hadn't realized my terrible power. I could see they were worried. They must have been told I was investigating the errors they had made! So right away I said, 'I had nothing to do, so I thought I'd come over and talk to the guys who put the rockets together. I didn't want everybody to stop working just 'cause I wanna find out something for my own curiosity; I only wanted to talk with the workers. . . .'" Ibid., p. 171. Elsewhere: "I said 'I just wanted to talk to a few engineers. There are so many problems to work on, I can't expect you all to stay here and talk to me.'" Ibid., p. 181.

8. Heidegger would call this a return to the understanding that comes from co-being; see section on Martin Heidegger, below.

9. Those detecting a reference to the usage of words in *Alice in Wonderland* are correct.

10. U.S. Department of Defense term reported Nov. 28, 1984, on "ABC Television News."

11. Innovative vocabulary and satires from original sources cited by Henry Beard and

Christopher Cerf, *The Official Politically Correct Dictionary and Handbook* (New York: Villard Books, 1992).

12. For the same reason that the police officers behind the composite quotation here must remain anonymous, I am extending the same courtesy to the fire commissioner in question.

13. The representation of Wittgenstein attempted here follows closely the work of Jenny Teichman, "Wittgenstein on Persons and Human Beings," in Royal Institute of Philosophy, *Understanding Wittgenstein* (New York: St. Martin's, 1974), pp. 133–48. The other major source is Ludwig Wittgenstein, *Philosophical Investigations* (Oxford, England: Basil Blackwell, 1953).

14. Wittgenstein, *Philosophical Investigations*, Part I, paragraph 241.

15. Godfrey Vesey, Foreword to *Understanding Wittgenstein*, p. ix.

16. Wittgenstein, *Philosophical Investigations*, Part I, paragraph 207. In this case judgment as to what a head is when I see it on someone else's shoulders. Such judgments can, according to Wittgenstein, only be based on shared concepts. And shared concepts, according to him, can emerge only out of a shared human nature and the behaviors that nature leads people to share. See also R. M. White: "The fact that human beings do in general react in the same way . . . is a contingent anthropological fact, but one without which language could never get off the ground. . . ." (White, "Can Whether One Proposition Makes Sense Depend on the Truth of Another? [*Tractatus* 2.0211-2]," in *Understanding Wittgenstein*, p. 26.)

17. Vesey, p. x.

18. Teichman, "Wittgenstein on Persons," p. 145.

19. See, for example, Herbert Simon's widely read article "Decision-Making and Organizational Design: Man-Machine Systems for Decision-Making," in D. S. Pugh, ed., *Organization Theory: Selected Readings* (Baltimore: Penguin, 1971), pp. 189–212.

20. Vesey, p. x.

21. Simon, especially p. 194.

22. Ilham Dilman, "Wittgenstein on the Soul," in Royal Institute, *Understanding Wittgenstein*, p. 165.

23. Ibid., p. 166. Dilman's italics.

24. Wittgenstein, *Remarks on the Foundations of Mathematics* (Oxford, England: Basil Blackwell, 1956), Part IV, Section 3.

25. Dilman, pp. 166–67. Human beings who behave like machines have been analyzed in modern psychology as early as Freud. Machinelike functionaries are no strangers to anyone who has visited a bureaucracy.

26. C. P. Snow, *Corridors of Power* (New York: Scribners, 1964), p. 371.

27. John R. Searle, *Speech Acts: An Essay in the Philosophy of Language* (London: Cambridge University Press, 1969), p. 47.

28. Ibid., p. 197.

29. Ibid., p. 198.

30. Martin Heidegger, *Being and Time*, John Macquarrie and Edward Robinson, trs. (New York: Harper & Row, 1962). However, translations are from the German *Sein und Zeit*, 15th edition (Tüebingen: Max Niemeyer Verlag, 1976 [original 1927]). To avoid difficulties with pagination, references are to paragraph numbers given in both editions. Co-being is treated by Heidegger in paragraphs 25–27; speech as sharing or taking part in joint being in paragraphs 34–35.

31. Op. cit., paragraph 34.

32. Ibid., paragraph 35.

33. Loc. cit.

34. Ibid., paragraph 34.

35. Thanks both to Patrick O'Hara of the John Jay College of Criminal Justice, City University of New York, and Mary Schmidt, cited in Chapter 5, for calling my attention to the collapse of engineers in crucial space shuttle conversations before the onslaught of powerful "partners" in speech.

36. This section is a critical evaluation of Philip M. Boffey, "Amid Disputes, Shuttle Panel Finally Forged an Agreement," *The New York Times*, June 7, 1986, pp. 1, 5. All quotations are from the article. Note how, even in the headline, the social values of disputes = negative value, agreement = positive value "normalize" the event and trivialize the fact that

dispute was critical to uncovering the substantive cause of the crash while agreement was precisely the organizational cause of failure to prevent the crash.

37. The indictment covers about half of the book under whose innocent title it is contained: pp. 113–237 of Feynman, op. cit.

38. Ibid., p. 237.

39. Ibid., p. 216. Feynman told William P. Rogers: "If a guy tells me the probability of a failure is 1 to 10^5, I know he's full of crap—but I don't know what's natural in a bureaucratic system."

5

The Thought of Bureaucracy

The primary source of the superiority of bureaucratic administration lies in the role of technical knowledge which, through the development of modern technology and business methods in the production of goods, has become completely indispensable.

—Max Weber[1]

Can bureaucracy design its own way of thinking? In what sense can we say there is such a thing as specifically bureaucratic thought?

Since the advent of the computer, which has been called the pure type of a bureaucracy, the answer *seems* clear. We think of bureaucracy as a programmed thinking machine. As clients, once our case is taken up by that machine, we expect it will be treated according to the same strictly logical rules as any similar case. But how do we become a case for the machine? How does the machine get its data, and how does it translate its calculating results back into reality?

This is the heart of the problem of bureaucratic thinking. Its inner *logic* works quite well; it just lacks *sensibility* to the outer environment.

To be the tool we want it to be, the modern organization admittedly has to get functionaries to reason in terms of a built-in logic. This logic commands them to apply general programs to specific problems as they come along. However, programs generally designed can apply only to problems generally defined.

What about *my* particular problem? So the client will ask. That particular problem must be capable of being reasoned to fit into the general type of problem for which the agency has a program. It is training in judging these problems of fit that is most important for the bureaucrat. He or she must learn to *reason by analogy:* comparing any particular case to the general problem to see if the case fits the program. Otherwise no further processing can be called for: The potential client is excluded from the program.

But reasoning by analogy is not as easy as it sounds. *Cases* are not naturally given in nature; *people* are. How can a bureaucrat elicit from a client that bundle of characteristics which can constitute the client in the eyes of the program as a case? This eliciting process requires not technical skill in analogous reasoning but interpersonal skills, social and psychological ones, perhaps even aesthetic ones. In short, the bureaucrat, in carrying out the thinking responsibilities of the modern organization, must have not only *logic* but *sensibility.* The bureaucrat cannot think by rules alone; he or she must have a feel for things. Nowhere does this struggle between inner logic and outer sensibility show up more than when bureaucracy does something that, seen from the perspective of real life, is really stupid. Consider the case of child-labor regulations and the batboy:

Batboy Is Called Out; U.S. Is Reviewing Law*

ATLANTA, May 27—Facing accusations that insensitive bureaucrats were trampling on the national pastime, the United States Department of Labor says it is reconsidering the case of a 14-year-old Georgia batboy who was sacked after his employment was found to run afoul of child-labor laws.

Shortly after a local newspaper published an article about the Class A Savannah Cardinals' new 14-year-old batboy early this month, a Labor Department official told the team that their employment of Tommy McCoy violated child-labor laws, which state that 14- and 15-year-olds must not work past 7 on school nights or 9 during the summer.

The club reluctantly dismissed the boy, who had papered the walls of his room with pictures of team members even before being hired, and put a 16-year-old in his job. Other minor league clubs, many in the same situation, ducked for cover amid fears of a nationwide crackdown.

The article set off a blizzard of local and then national publicity, and Labor Secretary Robert B. Reich issued a statement Wednesday that termed the application of child-labor laws to batboys "silly." A department spokeswoman, Mary Meagher, said today that the Department of Labor will not enforce any hourly violations in organized baseball pending a review of the law.

Mr. Reich said: "The application of child-labor laws in the case of 14-year-old batboys does, at first glance, look silly. It is not the intent of the law to deny young teen-agers employment opportunities so long as their health and well-being are not impaired."

The Cardinals' general manager, Ric Sisler, whose team has a 32–14 record in the South Atlantic League and a nine-game winning streak, seems to be making the best of things. The dispute has been a publicity windfall. Tommy threw out the first ball at the Cardinals' Wednesday night game, and Friday has been designated as "Save Tommy's Job Night" at the Cardinals' 8,500-seat Grayson Stadium.

If there is one thing that tends to go wrong with bureaucratic think-ing, at least from the viewpoint of clients and customers, it is this: Bu-reaucrats spend more time paying attention to bureaucracy's inner logic requirements than being sensible to the needs of people in the environ-ment. Bureaucrats come to think people exist to become cases, rather than case standards existing to help people.

This problem was recognized from the very beginning. Already to-ward the start of the century, Max Weber asks us about turning a bureau-crat into a machine. What do you think about this model of the bureau-crat?

The conception of the modern judge as an automaton into which legal documents and fees are stuffed at the top in order that it may spill forth the verdict at the bottom along with the reasons, read mechanically from codified paragraphs . . .[2]

In his own time, Weber found, such a model of judiciary bureaucracy, he goes on to say, was "angrily rejected, perhaps because a certain ap-proximation to this type would be implied precisely by a consistent bu-reaucratization of justice. Thus even in the field of law-finding there are areas in which the bureaucratic judge is directly held to 'individualiz-ing' procedures by the legislator." In short, bureaucracy had a political context.

As citizens and lawmakers we expect two orientations from bureau-crats. One is that they orient their thinking toward purely rational logic processing. This means to engage in comparison of an individual case to a politically authorized program model. It is *analogous* thinking. The other orientation, however, demands that bureaucrats process the logic of cases in such a way that something resembling our original policy intent emerges at the end of the program. We want the thinking to be technical and procedural, but the outcome to be practical and social. For the bureau-crat this means program integrity is to be consistently upheld through technical and procedural calculation, yet judgments must be made as to whether and how these calculations produce socially appreciated sub-stantive results. Max Weber already recognized that ". . . a purely techni-cal consideration ignores other wants."[3] Substantive results require *causal* thinking, implying knowledge of theories of social or physical causality that explain or give insight into how things are connected in reality.

Assume we could replace all human bureaucracies by computers. Society would still demand that judgments be made about what to put into the computer and about how what the computer prints out shall be applied to individual human beings. In short, we expect from computer processing exactly the kind of *sensibility* to the situation in which human beings are located that the computer does not possess.*

What we want from bureaucrats is *logic* and *adherence to program*

*See the section on Wittgenstein, Chapter 4.

models—but also *judgments of sensibility.* It is sensibility that makes possible judgment over how individuals fit into programs and how program outputs fit individuals—whether these are people or situations. Yet bureaucrats are totally untrained in sensibility.

HOW PEOPLE THINK

The dual demands on bureaucratic thought—and the tension they create—can be seen wherever inmates of modern organization work. The tension between inner logic and outside sensibility runs from the individual level to the level of entire organizations.

An individual:

I was working with two helpers laying out a ditch for a plumbing line. It was a hot day, and one of the guys was a little guy, about 150 pounds, and the ground was hard. So I set him to doing something else and I helped dig the ditch. I got written up for that: inappropriate supervision.

—Plumber on university staff

There are all kinds of reasons why the organization, for inner control purposes, might want to enforce its rules for supervision; what obsession with internal control, however, ignores in this case is the need for line personnel to make reality-based judgments at the boundary of the organization.

When entire organizations fail to make such judgments, the threat is that they will go out of existence—especially in the face of superior power of other organizations in the environment.

An organization:

The U.S. Air Force, which used to run separate units of bombers, fighters, transports, etc., now is experimenting with training people ahead of actual deployment in the mixed wings they would end up in eventually anyway. Any other air force that insists on the efficiency advantages of the simpler logistics and standardized training of separate wings will have a difficult time getting its act together if and when challenged by such sensibility to probable wartime reality.

Consider three detailed examples.

Force people to think like a computer. Does this make an institution more effective? Yes, in terms of its own inner standards of forcing outsiders to fit a general program or be ignored. Our first example will demonstrate this. Yet, is logic processing all there is to bureaucratic thought?

What happens when a client cannot be ignored because, for example, it is Mother Nature? What if, as in our second example, you are building a dam, ignore bottom-up warnings from lowly workers, and the dam collapses? Then imposing programmed thinking can threaten the very existence of your organization. Do you follow the program or tune in to reality?

Finally, what happens if you are a professional representing a planning organization and you have to administer that organization's program in the face of politically powerful constituents? Do you plan or do you politick?

Members of modern organizations are under two opposed pressures to tailor their thinking: to be logical and to be sensible. The one calls on them to be consistent, reliable, matter-of-fact in their processing of data and the other to make the program application fit individual clients and situations. The former requires a peculiar kind of logic. *Analogous reasoning* compares each individual case to a program model. But the second requires *sensibility*. This is judgment as to how the program model must be adjusted to fit the individual case. Good judgments of sensibility are especially crucial if support of the environment—physical or political—impacts future survival of the organization.

These are contradictory requirements. In terms of the expertise of the organization, Max Weber already observed, the bureaucrat will be tempted to focus his or her thinking on internal logic processing and to act according to the procedural requirements of this. But in terms of maintaining social effectiveness and ultimately social legitimacy, the bureaucracy must go beyond instrumental rationality to value rationality. It must be prepared to "rationalize" its actions according to the values and norms of the political environment: in terms of reasons of state, or, in the American case, the public interest or even the interests of groups and powerful individuals. "[I]n principle a system of rationally debatable 'reasons' stands behind every act of bureaucratic administration, namely, either subsumption under norms, or a weighing of means and ends."[4] To the extent that such reasons are not treated as central to the actions of a modern organization, its behavior becomes less predictable and its stabilizing influence in the society or polity is reduced. Weber himself suggests that mixed types of authority are more likely to be found than pure types. Nowhere is this more clear than in the focus on thinking.

In short, we can begin our probe into bureaucratic thought by discovering that the model for bureaucratic thinking is not as simple as a computer model would suggest.

Can Bureaucrats Think Like Computers?

Early in the computer era, economist and organization theorist Herbert Simon said bureaucratic structures were frozen decisions. He then recommended widespread computer use. This would get around the limited rationality of human beings in making such decisions.* The ideal bureauc-

---

*See the discussion of Simon in the section on Searle in Chapter 4.

racy would be a computer. Bureaucrats at their best would think like computers.

At a crucial point in the transition from human to computer bureaucracies it actually became possible for human beings to experience what it feels like to think exactly like a computer.

In the late 1970s, employees of New York State's welfare program were required to apply computer logic in admissions of clients. In a pilot project in Albany and New York City, a team of management consultants reduced welfare regulations contained in thousands of pages to 140 pages of decision-logic charts (see Table 5.1). Intake workers used to apply their own professional judgment, based on the study of rulebooks, in deciding how to proceed in client admissions. Now intake workers were guided through the regulations by following the set of charts. Each of these told them: If you get results A, B, C from your interview with the client, then go to the next appropriate chart A, B, C, respectively. The illustration shows a decision-logic chart to screen applicants for Aid to Dependent Children.

Table 5.1
A DECISION-LOGIC CHART

Conditions	Rules 1 2 3 4 5 6 7 8 Else
1. Does the applicant have (a) minor(s) whom he/she is living with UNDER THE AGE OF 18 OR BETWEEN 18 AND 21 who is/are regularly attending high school, college or undertaking an approved course of vocational or technical training, or is the applicant pregnant? DSS 1994, Section A, E. (See Notes 1, 2 and 3)	Y Y N
2. Is the minor deprived of parental support or care because of parent death and/or continued absence from home of a parent and/or mental or physical incapacity, or pregnancy, or unemployment of father? DSS 1994, Sections F, G, H, I, J, K, L. (See Note 4)	Y N N

Actions	Rules 1 2 3 4 5 6 7 8 Else
1. This is not an ADC case, these tables are not to be used. Explore HR category for possible assistance.	X X
2. This is a possible ADC case. Go to next table.	X
3. Ask Supervisor for assistance.	X (Else)

Source: Welfare Research, Inc., *Decision Logic Table Handbook* (Prepared for the State of New York, undated), p. DLT 2.

The idea is the intake worker simply looks at the two questions provided, registers the answers (three possibilities are open: Yes, Yes; Yes, No; and No, No), and then checks under the "Rules" heading for the next step to go to. In short, the workers were trained to think in terms of binary logic, just the way a computer "thinks." They experienced what it may feel like to be a computer. Using charts such as this one, the offices increased—short term—the accuracy rate for admitting welfare clients by more than 40 percentage points—from 51.5 percent to 94.6 percent. (Later the error rate went up again.)

The binary thinking process of the decision-logic chart, of course, does not include making the actual judgments of recognizing a person as a person. But it provides parameters for recognizing such persons as cases in its definitions. And it guarantees that, to some extent, each case is taken through the same steps for recognition or rejection. At each step the worker is expected to engage in the characteristic *reasoning by analogy* that marks bureaucratic thinking. In this thinking the model is the standard according to which a person can become a case to be processed.

The quality of such reasoning by analogy, which measures divergence of a potential client from a program model, will depend on the functionary's ability to tune in to the client: For before a piece of reality can be compared to a model, it is necessary to determine what that piece is. Otherwise qualified people may be left out.

How is the client to be persuaded to answer, and answer truthfully? This requires ability not only to tune in to the client but ability to get him or her to tune in to the questions. But the questions are now much more controlled. They are defined according to standards internal to the program model. They are placed in sequence according to the internal technical needs of decision logic. The function of judgment, freely exercised in an environment of discretion, allowing the functionary to decide how to tune in to *this* client at *this* time, is sharply curtailed.

At best, to the extent that the program deals with issues of *sensibility* at all, it is designed to be sensible to the "average" client in "average" situations. Not to *me* as client in *my* situation.

If I am the intake worker, the creation of conditions in which I can attune to reality depends more and more on my ability for social interaction skills, precisely in a program environment that devalues these skills. More than ever, although the charts indicate none of this is important, it is I and my skills that determine whether the proper answers are elicited, whether the client is enabled to understand what I am asking, whether he or she feels frightened and confused or able to respond.

This may account for the fact that the error rate soon went up again. The charts place the functionary under very tight program restrictions. The charts may even suggest to the individual that he or she is doing well as long as he or she simply sticks mindlessly to the charts. But the more the functionary does this, the more the questions will be divergent from the individual client's perspective and situation.

In short, the program can guarantee that nearly all those who do get on the Aid for Dependent Children will be qualified, but it cannot guarantee that those left off the rolls are *not* qualified.

But, who cares when it comes to welfare clients. Right? By definition they are powerless. The internal integrity of the program is more important. After all it is this that will please citizens and politicians who rail against welfare cheats. And these are more powerful than potential clients.

Already, in this logic, we see that, even where bureaucratic thinking seems to be at its purest technical best, it is—after all—concerned with ultimate political standards and power interests. Total programming according to pure standards of logic is an illusion. Logic processing is not sufficient for its *own* purposes: It cannot give the bureaucrat adequate access to reality for purposes of comparison to a program standard. And logic processing is not enough to keep the program within the policy aims that its technical standards claim to support. No bureaucracy is truly a computer, nor do citizens or legislators truly want it to be.

Why Logic Processing Is Not Enough

In the example above, we have not heard the voice of the client. But consider an example in which bureaucrats think programmatically but the client doesn't like it—and has voice to write a book about it.

A patient waits for a diagnosis in the emergency room of a hospital. Excruciating pain indicates a kidney stone, but the intern reads off a long list of possible diseases including an East African one. An East African one? This is Brooklyn, New York. East Africa? After the pain subsides, the patient walks out. He passes a computer. He looks at the printout. It is printing out lists of diagnoses. Aha! That's where the East African disease came from. The intern simply had failed to use good judgment, judgment that fitted the situation, and had unnecessarily troubled a patient with a low probability diagnosis that was *implausible* under the circumstances.*

The most immediate danger in the increased use of computers to administer programs—in this case, a diagnostic program—is that we begin to assume that computers think like us. But the fact is computers are logic processors; they are not able to think themselves into situations.† So it is exactly in those circumstances in which human beings have always had the most difficulty—in the making of judgments (does *this* act fit into *this* situation?)—that computers let us down.

*Author's own experience.
†See the section on Wittgenstein in Chapter 4.

Computers don't think exactly because they are unaware of the situations to which their logic applies. People who follow computers in their thinking don't think for the same reason: They believe reality is in the computer display or printout, not on the spot. To the extent that bureaucrats follow the grammar of institutional rules that demand action without thinking ourselves *into* the situation of clients, bureaucrats don't fully think.

The potential threat to modern organizations in limiting their processing operations to computer-like "thinking" is that such organizations cannot detect a threat to their own existence.

Mary Schmidt: Sensibility Ignored, a Disaster Results

Proceeding perfectly logically but without sensibility has already gone down in such folksayings as "The operation was a success, but the patient died." Such thinking may be counted as affecting only individual fates. But the effects can multiply. Then instead of individual loss, we have major catastrophes. Space shuttles blow up; nuclear reactors have meltdowns; entire product lines must be recalled; whole population groups are systemically excluded from public services.

Mary Schmidt, a planning consultant and organization theorist, looked into one such disaster—a dam collapse. A dam collapse is nothing like the exclusion of entire groups from the benefits of government. But it gives us an overseeable event that illustrates the basic thinking problem of modernity: the preference for technical thinking over substantive.[5]

Schmidt traced the cause of the Teton Dam collapse to major incommensurable differences in types of thinking. Line workers, who knew of actions imperiling the dam, faced and were defeated by the claim to superior knowledge on the part of engineers and managers.[6]

In 1975, as the Federal Bureau of Reclamation was filling a reservoir behind an earthen dam it had just completed on the Teton River in Idaho, the structure suddenly collapsed. Eleven people died, 3,000 homes were damaged, 16,000 head of cattle drowned, and 100,000 acres of newly planted farmland were flooded.

Investigators attributed the failure to inadequacies in the engineers' design and to overconfidence in the bureau, both ignoring safety factors. But Schmidt, in reviewing investigations of the dam collapse for a study at the Massachusetts Institute of Technology, found there was an entire batch of testimony that was unsought and unused. This was the testimony of grouters, the workmen who used cement slurry to fill holes and caves in the bedrock on which the dam was to rest.

In a letter written by three supervisors of such grouters, Schmidt found references to a series of judgments made by these lowly employees. These, in contradicting the judgments of their nominal superiors, the engineers, could have anticipated the dam collapse had attention been paid to them.

One type of action involved filling the holes and caves so the dam would have a solid base. Previous studies, in which water was pumped into the holes, showed they ran underground as far as 300 feet: The spot at which the water that was pumped in reemerged. Engineers insisted on what grouters called "salting" the hole, mixing salt with the cement slurry to make it set faster so as not to disappear into the farflung recesses of the holes. However, when the engineers set the salting at ten percent, as against a normal three percent, the grouters protested: "You're going to slug the hole." Meaning: The grout will set so fast that the hole won't be full enough. Meaning: The dam won't have a leg to stand on.

As with other disasters—for example, the space shuttle where the installers noticed a more than usual number of cracks in the O-rings but as yet had no statistical aggregates with which to impress the generalizing bosses—such hands-on knowledge was ignored. It has no place in the analogous reasoning of either the workers' bureaucratic bosses or their scientific bosses. The grouters' judgment that a hole was full based on a "feel for the hole" could not be absorbed in the abstract models of bureaucratic planning or in the abstract generalizations of science and engineering.

To take a related example: "The Bureau had made preliminary tests to analyze how fast the grout would set with various proportions of salt but could not discover a formula relating salt to setting time because of the complex interactions among many variables."[7] Yet, while the decision on whether to add salt or sand had to be left to the "low-skilled" grouters, their judgment—even though the dam rested on how well they had been allowed to do their job—was not solicited in investigations after the accident.

We can see that the thinking of the grouter is *concrete* (no pun intended), *particular*, and *immersed in experience*. In Schmidt's words: "The grouter's knowledge in practice is difficult to put into words. It cannot be measured and represented by formulas nor subjected to rules and standards. It cannot be taught in the classroom, but only learned in the field, by direct 'hands-on' experience in specific situations, under the guidance of a master craftsman."

As such, the knowledge of these line workers is not inferior to the knowledge of managers or engineers; it is simply different. But because their thinking does not fit the mold of being *analogizing, general*, and *referential to abstract models*, it also cannot be encompassed in the thinking of managers and engineers. Before such holders of power—even when these powerholders' knowledge is in danger of imminent failure—the subordinates in the hierarchy stand effectively mute and helpless. Giving words to their knowledge, Mary Schmidt explains their dilemma:

We posit that over time a grouter builds up a repertoire of strategies for treating various kinds of rocks in specific situations and acquires a kind of general knowledge. But since, as was said, each site, each hole, and even different stages of a single hole, are unique, he can never rely upon former models or general rules of thumb or recipes. If he settles into mindless routine, he will jeopardize the quality of his work. He must constantly be alert to the "back talk" of the specific situation.

This is what is meant by sensibility. The employee of any modern organization must think rationally; that is, in terms of the means that logically follow from the ends programmed into the organization. In dealing with events or individuals from outside the organizations, too, the employee must see to the extent to which these fit into the program. But in implementing the blueprints of the program, the events or people he or she admits to the organization become his raw material: To administer the program effectively, he must get to know and understand aspects of events and people that no programmer could have anticipated. This calls less for *logic* than for *sensibility*.

Of course, there is a solution for the bureaucracy where sensibility is devalued: Convince people that standards of logic should also be standards for their lives. This is what was attempted in the original investigations that sought to explain the dam collapse in technical engineering and procedural bureaucratic terms. Apparently there is sufficient submission to such standards by the culture at large to allow such judgment according to technical/bureaucratic values to be accepted.* Out of such instances arises the suspicion that bureaucratic thinking narrowly defined as logic processing *can* rule the polity. Yet where awareness of this has been raised, demands for the primacy of social values over bureaucratic ones is again reasserted.

A THEORY OF BUREAUCRATIC THINKING

We can summarize the characteristics of bureaucratic thinking. By design, at least, bureaucratic thinking (a) leans heavily toward the technical and yet (b) is ultimately subject to situational—social or physical—tests beyond mere inner logic. It lives in the tension between inner and outer validity.

Toward Inner Validity	*Toward External Validity*
• Analogizing	• Causal
• General	• Particular
• Referential to abstract models	• Immersed in experience

*See the conflict of bureaucratic and social values in Chapter 2.

Consider first pure rationalism. This is the extreme standard for the internal process rationality of a bureaucrat's institution. In this orientation, the bureaucrat *must* measure the reality of inputs from beyond the organization by whether they can be treated as an analog to an abstract model designed to capture such events in their generality. The program becomes the standard for what is real.

But next, the bureaucrat *may* be forcefully reminded of the power of social and physical reality with which he or she must deal. This power is possessed by those who make policy and by nature. This, at the other extreme, can sustain or fail to sustain the bureaucracy's inner reality. In dealing with this reality, the bureaucrat is called on to pay attention to why things are as they are (their causality) in particular. Reality is given to him or her as raw material on which to implement the institution's program. In dealing with that raw material, he or she is immersed in social or physical experience and must adjust his or her thinking accordingly.

As we will see later, these are distinct modes of thinking that must be treated in their complementarity if inner logic of a thought process is to have some relation to external reality: that is, to *have* external validity. (See "What the Experts Say.") First, however, to an illustration of how both forms of thinking are relevant to modern employees in everyday situations quite apart from major catastrophes.

John Forester: The Political Side of Bureaucratic Thinking

The need to engage in both logic-processing thinking and substantive thinking can also be illustrated by reference to the everyday experience of individual employees short of any catastrophe.

No matter how rational your training is, unless your bureaucracy has total control over its environment you must act in the face of power. So says planner and organization theorist John Forester. He suggests that in any social system—whether a political one or a modern organization—individuals trained in rational thinking, such as planners, will see none of this rationalism come to effect unless they also deal with the counterpoise of power.[8]

This is especially tricky because power distributes knowledge unequally across societies and organizations. Every society has systematic distortions of knowledge built in because it systematically distorts who can speak to whom and with what power. The individual professional who wants to survive in such an environment will have to do both his or her rationalistic thinking *and* weigh the tactics of political thinking. The first can tell technically how to get things done, the second can tell why others should help or resist in getting things done. Whatever the rank or professional standing of the front-line employee, he or she needs to get his or her plans both endorsed by and through the maze of power.

The systematic cure for systematically distorted knowledge systems is open communication. We have defined this as reciprocal and causal, two-way and constructive of reality; it includes revealing one's assumptions or models and taking responsibility for them.* But Forester points out that such openness is often not up to the individuals involved in a system; the entire system will have built-in tendencies to distort what people can say and what they can think. This he calls, following the philosopher and sociologist Jürgen Habermas, systematically distorted communications.

Planners are caught between the people who will build and the people who will live in the structures they plan—from city parks to buildings to entire cities. Some of these citizens are more powerful than others.

When something is planned for the community, its powerholders see no need to allow it to diminish their power. Builders, for example, will want to seize the occasion to make a profit and expand their power. Rich onliers to a planned park do not want their quality of life lowered by a place that attracts "undesirables"—noisy adolescents with radios, beer drinkers, the homeless. The interests and rights of the powerful are built into social systems.

The result is that the social system—with its rules for talk as well as for thinking—systematically distorts the talk and thinking that goes on in planning meetings.

Forester calls some of these distortions inevitable: information inequalities resulting from legitimate division of labor, transmission/content losses across organizational boundaries. But other systematic distortions are socially unnecessary; these include monopolistic distortions of exchange, monopolistic creation of needs, and ideological rationalization of class or power structure.[9]

Planners can deal tactically with *ad hoc* distortions—such as willful unresponsiveness, interpersonal deception, or interpersonal bargaining behavior (e.g., bluffing). "Clarifications can be requested; time for questions and cross-examinations can be allotted in hearings, reviews, or commission meetings; a sensitive chairperson can intervene to suggest that a speaker speak more slowly, more directly into the microphone, less technically, and so forth."[10]

But systematic distortions are built into the system. They are often tacitly and unconsciously accepted. They require first a raising of consciousness and then strategic remedies. "To isolate and reveal the power of such systematically distorted communications, critical theorists con-

*See the theory of bureaucratic speech in Chapter 4.

trast them with ordinary communication of mutual understanding that makes any shared social knowledge possible in the first place."[11]

A THEORY OF PRACTICAL
COMMUNICATIVE ACTION

Up to now we have spoken of speech and thought only in terms of processes. Forester speaks of practical qualities necessary to shape such processes. These make possible what he calls communicative action. For people to be able to speak to each other and hear each other at all, their speech must successfully make claims to factuality (truth), comprehensibility, legitimacy, and sincerity.

When a person's factual claim fails, listeners respond with disbelief. When his or her claim to saying something that is intelligible fails, they respond with confusion. When a person's claim to legitimacy fails, the result is lack of consent. When a person's claim to meaning what he says fails, people see a lack of sincerity and respond with distrust.

What are the remedies to situations when systematic distortion of communication produces systematic untruth, confusion, false claims to legitimacy, and insincerity? For each problem a practical question can be asked to cut through the problem. This is depicted in Table 5.2.

Forester further suggests that we need to go beyond asking these penetrating questions. The powerful cannot be put into a situation in which they are forced to answer our challenges unless we engage in a type of action that can be captured in one word: "organizing."[12] Put in a few more words: "This can be a planner's response to disabling distortions of practical communications: the careful, political organization of attention that can counteract these influences."[13]

Communication, therefore, is always a political act. Successful speech is not for the politically inept. But if this is so, and speech is closely related to kinds of thinking, then thinking is in a deep sense political also.*

AN AMENDED THEORY OF SPEECH AND THOUGHT

The research of Mary Schmidt and John Forester demonstrates that power interests suppress ways of thinking alternate to establishment ones, misshaping what can be talked about and systematically distorting what is said.

Our theory of organizational speech therefore must be amended to

*For an elaboration of this, see the discussion of thinking under Martin Heidegger in this chapter and the discussion of politics under Martin Heidegger in Chapter 6.

Table 5.2
CORRECTING COMMUNICATIVE DISTORTIONS: ORGANIZING PRACTICES OF PLANNERS

Practical Level	Type of Distortion (Criterion for Mutual Understanding Not Met)			
	Comprehensibility	Sincerity	Legitimacy	Truth
Face-to-face	Revealing meaning	Checking intentions	Determining roles and contexts	Checking evidence
	"What does that mean?"	"Does she mean that?"	"I don't need to accept that."	"I'll check to see if this is really true."
Organization	Minimizing jargon; creating public review committees	Organizing counteradvocates; checking with contacts, networks	Making decisions in a participatory manner; checking with affected persons	Using independent/critical third-party expertise
	"Clean up the language so people can understand it."	"Check with Stu to see if we can trust them on this."	"What has the neighborhood association had to say about this?"	"Check the data and calculations to see if these figures are really correct."
Political–economic structure	Demystification; counter-skills	Exposing unexpressed interests	Democratizing the state; politicizing planning	Institutionalizing debate, political criticism; democratizing inquiry; politicizing planning
	"All this really means is . . ."	"Of course they say that! They're the big winners if no one speaks up."	"Without political pressure, the bureaucracy will continue to serve itself."	"We have to show what can be done here."

Source: John Forester, *Planning in the Face of Power* (Berkeley: University of California Press, 1989), p. 151.

include political thinking. The list from Chapter 4 on p. 160 now must be updated to read:

Speech and Thought Observed in Bureaucracy and Society

In Bureaucracy (Technical)	In Society (Political)
Speech is	**Speech** is
acausal (functionalist)	causal (contextual)
one-directional	reciprocal
reality-imposing	reality-constructing
Thought is	**Thought** is
analogizing	concrete
general	particular
referential	immersed in
to abstract model	experience

Knowledge may be power, as Francis Bacon suggested. But a more general rule seems to hold. Whatever the knowledge system, its thinking procedures and its basic assumptions will be defended at all costs by those who benefit from it: knowledge elites. The knowledge system of society was admittedly political. The knowledge system of bureaucracy claims to be technical, and it is so internally. But when challenged from beyond its borders it defends itself just like any faith against heresy.

Today, modern quantitative knowledge systems are challenged by alternatives such as quality management.[14] It would be naive to claim that knowledge of any sort is value-free or to expect that those who hold bureaucratic knowledge will not use political power to defend it. Knowledge may be power, but power determines what can be knowledge in any system.

This theory, however, creates a special problem for modern knowledge. Modern knowledge legitimates itself on the basis of rationalistic thinking. This is what differentiates it from traditionalist thinking, which honors the return of the "eternal yesterday."[15] And this is what differentiates rationalism from charismatic thinking, in which thinking sinks or rises—depending on one's point of view—to the simple hope that a leader, endowed with God's grace, will do our thinking for us.

Of the rational basis of modern knowledge, and the type of authority that goes with it, Max Weber wrote:

Experience tends universally to show that the purely bureaucratic type of administrative organization—that is, the monocratic variety of bureaucracy—is, from a purely technical point of view, capable of attaining the highest degree of efficiency and is in this sense formally the most rational known means of exercising authority over human beings. It is superior to any other form in precision, stability, in the stringency of its discipline, and in its reliability. It thus makes possible a particularly high degree of calculability of results for the heads of the organization and for those acting in relation to it.[16]

But what if experience shows otherwise? Weber's internal process model* of bureaucracy may be alright as far as it goes. Yet, what if some other type of thinking aside from technical calculation is shown to be necessary for modern organization not just to be efficient but effective—as Weber already intimated? The grouters at Teton Dam and the engineers of the crashed space shuttle *Challenger* testified as much. What if all this emphasis on internal calculation served not only to produce efficiency and stability but a kind of deception enabling us to ignore what else it takes for bureaucracy to accomplish actual work?

Even while Weber was writing the words above, the mathematician and philosopher Edmund Husserl was writing his critiques of modern thinking as ignoring that kind of thinking that ties pure reason to reality. Philosophers can be helpful in doing what they do best: Think about thinking.

WHAT THE EXPERTS SAY

In thinking, as in speaking, we may be heading in a direction where thinking is no thinking at all. Instead, those who have thought most deeply about thinking—philosophers—suggest an inherent tendency in modern thinking to remove itself from ordinary life. Initially this is the source of the legitimate power of science. Beyond this it is the source of the power of elites.

By looking at the world through the lenses of only a few factors at a time, science wins clarity and coherence in forming a picture of how things work according to its assumptions about the world. Ultimately, however, playing with such pictures—analyzing them, reassembling them—becomes a technical preoccupation. The result is neglect of the problem of how applying such pictures helps us lead a more human life.

There is, from the beginning of modern science applied to management, a split in thinking. There are those who play with abstract pictures—in bureaucracy: managers. There are those who have to apply such pictures in real and complicated contexts for human purposes: workers.

Increasingly we recognize a disadvantage that the division into purported thinkers and mere doers gives us: in the aggregate, less knowledge than an organization is capable of. The claim of elites to power rests on the basis of having acquired a trained monopoly over thinking. With

---

*To use the fitting term of Robert E. Quinn. See his *Beyond Rational Management: Mastering the Paradoxes and Competing Demands of High Performance* (San Francisco: Jossey-Bass, 1991), p. 53–54 ff.

this monopoly comes a trained arrogance that casts a long and darkening shadow over the full reality of things. A mighty effort separating thinking from the immersion in doing was necessary in the early stage of science. People turned to science because of problems they had with controlling the conditions of daily life. Their task was to raise themselves out of the confusing manifold of sensations that constitute the ongoing flow of living; they sought to win a clear view. This was offered by the scientific perspective, which takes a look at only a few well-defined factors at a time. Today that clear perspective, but also its detachment from the flow of life, is dominant.

The problem now is how to rejoin science's findings back to the problems of real life. This is also the problem for bureaucracy: How can its functioning be thought back into how we live life?

To answer this question, we draw on three philosophers who probe the relevance of science—and its form of thinking—to life. Their insights fail to justify the obstinately recalcitrant knowledge elite that today dominates not only science but technology and modern organization based on a division of labor between those who think and those who do.

Immanuel Kant is the first to be critical of a split between the function of being in touch with reality and the function of analyzing what we are in touch with: the split between knowing and thinking. His insights challenge today's division between a management that claims it thinks while workers merely do. Thinking, Kant shows, is not possible without content that comes from doing.

Edmund Husserl, writing 150 years after Kant, gives us a further insight into what is wrong with our modern thinking. Accepting Kant's critique of thinking, Husserl predicted the current crisis of quality as the inevitable product of the conversion of science into technique.

In turn, Husserl's student Martin Heidegger suggests how we can rethink our thinking to escape from the modern preoccupation with technique that functions to the detriment of getting good work done. All these critiques are also critiques of the thinking of modern organization.

Kant: Thinking and Knowing

The most clearly recognized problem of today's organizations is the inability to produce products and services *for* human beings despite ever more sophisticated quantitative controls. This is the crisis of quality. It is ironic that this was anticipated as a result of modern thinking by a philosopher looking at the rise of science more than 200 years ago.

At first this is a story of the liberation of the mind: enlightenment. With the successes of the first modern experiments, wrote Immanuel Kant, a light dawned on all researchers into nature (B xiii).[17] Like the early geometricians who inspired all modern science (B xii), they understood the need to lift a clear picture of things out of a turgid and chaotic manifold of sense impression. The researcher achieves this not by leaping into the fray of things but by making clear to himself first what he is looking for. Instead of trying to read off all possible properties from things before him, he studies only those properties which his own preconceptualization (the hypothesis) alerts him to (B xii).

Only in this way would the picture, also called the concept, be totally clear: for the researcher, backed by empirical tests, could make it so. He is like a fisherman who constructs a net following factors that promise good fishing. The net is the searching concept the researcher dips into the sea of reality. The shape of the net determines what objects he catches. But for the net to prove itself, it finally must be dipped: It is good only when it is full.

Besides clarity the scientific procedure got a good grasp on those parts of reality it was designed to net. The experiment demanded that every concept be tested out against actual data given by reality and captured in the conceptual net. Pursuing the metaphor of the net, we might say, with today's commercial fisherman, that a net woven to precise specifications makes sure that only the fish for which the net was designed stay in it. Kant himself used the metaphor of the courtroom:

> Reason, holding in one hand its principles, according to which alone concordant appearances can be admitted as equivalent laws, and in the other hand the experiment which it has devised in accordance with these principles, must approach nature in order to be taught by it. It must not, however, do so in the character of a pupil who listens to everything that the teacher chooses to say, but of an appointed judge who compels the witnesses to answer questions which he has himself formulated. (X iii; N.K.S., p. 20)

Fans of the television series "Dragnet" may recall Sgt. Friday's injunction to witnesses: "Just the facts, ma'am, just the facts." He did not mean all the facts but only those facts that were relevant to a picture of the crime that was already in his mind, either confirming or disconfirming it.

By keeping a precise and clear construction of reality in mind, and forcing reality to respond (or not) to it, and measuring the degree of congruence, the modern scientist freed himself of the complexity, confusion, and fuzziness of being fully immersed in reality.

(Soon, impressed by those things science could do successfully, society itself shifted its values to honor those things. Things that science could not do were devalued by society also.)

The scientist had separated himself from the worker who did have to face the problems of tracing out the moves specified by a blueprint in all the fuzzy complexity and confusion of reality. Even and especially today, the management scientist can promise the worker: "If you precisely follow the procedures we have outlined for the limited set of factors in the blueprint, you will achieve the conditions of coherence and variance among those factors that we predict in the blueprint." But no management scientist can know the moves a worker needs to make to bridge the gap between the clear scientific picture and the complex reality.

Kant anticipated this in distinguishing between thinking and knowing. Today, in our organizations of strict hierarchy and division of labor, we believe the engineer or scientifically guided manager thinks while the worker *does*. Kant knew better and would ascribe to the worker the fact that he *knows*.

"To *think* an object and to *know* an object are thus by no means the same thing," Kant concluded in his *Critique of Pure Reason* (B 146). "Knowledge involves two factors: first, the concept, through which an object in general is thought (the category); and secondly, the intuition, through which it is given."

Clearly, since today's managers are cut off from direct sensory organizing (intuition) of reality, they only *think,* they do not *know.* In fact the problem often is that they think they know.

By the knowing of intuition Kant did not mean what today we popularly mean by a sudden flash of insight. He meant the way the mind organized and looked at sense data within the categories of time and space. This initial onlooking provides a view (literally: *Anschauung*) that makes a flowing reality stand still long enough for specific objects to be broken out of the complex flow. The objects then can be brought before the cold eye of reason to be analyzed into their component parts or related to one another according to a model or hypothesis.

But, unless the thinking part of the mind (reason) provides a picture ahead of time, what is broken out of reality cannot be organized for the purpose of further analysis. For this reason Kant concludes that, for anything to be understood, reason and intuition have to work together, for "Thoughts without content are empty, intuitions without concepts are blind" (A 51–52; B 75–76).

Because of this does Kant "distinguish the science of the rules of sensibility in general, that is, aesthetic, from the science of the rules of the understanding in general, that is, logic" (B 77; A 52). The former makes knowing possible, the latter is thinking—at least as far as modern science is concerned. Unless the two work together no reality-related knowledge is possible.

Where thinking and knowing are split, this has serious consequences in modern organizations. There it is indeed assumed that managers think while workers . . . Well, what do workers do? Workers *do*, don't they? With the crisis of quality recognized since Japanese management, quality circles, Theory Z, search for excellence, and total quality management, we realize what Kant had already tried to alert us to: In the search for quality, those with the aesthetic sense—who can say, "This feels right"—have a great advantage. But these, in the hierarchically split organization, are: workers.

Only those who approach reality directly through their senses *know* directly, i.e., have the sense or the feel—Kant would say an intuition—of it. Quality understood as *what* something *is* in relation to the working human being presents itself to that human being first. And that understanding can be communicated to management only in terms of words, concepts. Since concepts are considered clarified by numbers, worker knowledge tends to be qualitative while manager thinking tends to be quantitative.

Modern organizations separate the thinking function radically from working. Kant had already damned such a result. Management is confined to exercising "a faculty, therefore, which by itself knows nothing whatsoever, but merely combines and arranges the material of knowledge, that is, the intuition, which must be given to it by the object" (B 145).

If management, therefore, is dependent on what is communicated by workers about what they do, then management is truly in the dangerous position of being isolated in pure reason. Research may fill their concepts. But what can such research tell managers about instructing workers in the handholds of implementation that only working experience can give them knowledge of?

The problem for workers is that managerial minds, empty of working experience through which alone objects can be known, give them the orders as to how to do their work—and evaluate their success.

To understand our crisis in the effective production of private goods and public services, we needed to go no farther than Kant to find the causes. In organizations that split thinking and knowing, our managers live in a never-never land of concepts,[18] while workers are desperately trying to take blueprints, based on those concepts but irrelevant to working itself, into a recalcitrant but very real reality. But, oh no, why bother with philosophers?! They, after all, are so irrelevant to real life! Aren't they?

Husserl: The Thinking of Science, Technique, and Bureaucracy

Another way of understanding the thinking of modern organization comes from a second warning about the split between science and life issued toward the beginning of the twentieth century.[19] The mathematician and philosopher Edmund Husserl had begun to investigate how the split worked itself out in everyday life.

In the chaotic world between the two World Wars, it could escape no one that science, in becoming ever more sophisticated, had become increasingly irrelevant to basic concerns of leading a meaningful human life. Amazingly powerful and historically unique as a way of producing and controlling the material world from the outside, modern thought as epitomized in science did not, as Husserl pointed out, address such questions as the inner meaning of life, the reason or unreason of human beings, the human being as free subject.

Today we might say that science, in all the things it gives us, cannot answer the question "What's it to me?" In other words, science cannot demonstrate the necessity of the things it produces to being human. Only the human being can testify to any such need. But in our day that human being has surrendered its judgment to science: Anything science can produce we want. And so it is that the human being adapts itself to science rather than science being adapted to human needs.

In his book *The Crisis of the European Sciences*, Husserl pointed out the paradox in an ineluctable though somewhat Germanic question: ". . . can the world, and human existence in it, truthfully have a meaning if the sciences recognize as true only what is objectively established in this fashion, and if history has nothing more to teach us than that all the shapes of the spiritual world, all the conditions of life, ideals, norms upon which man relies, form and dissolve themselves like fleeting waves, that it always was and ever will be so, that again and again reason must turn into nonsense, and well-being into misery?"[20]

Science's role in these failures needed to be explained, especially in view of its influence on the design of modern organizations.

Husserl's critique can be put this way: We are committed as a culture to declare only that real which science can establish. But every time we conclude a scientific experiment, there is a pause. During this rest from science, ordinary human beings get along perfectly well without doing any science. In fact such pauses constitute the vast majority of the moments in which we live. Even science takes its point of departure from such ordinarily lived moments. And its findings, to be useful, must be capable of being translated back into the world of ordinary human life.[21] Science therefore is far removed as a way of thinking about the world from the way we actually live in the world—and so is any organization designed on scientific principles of understanding work.

But, how do these judgments about the existence of different types of thinking relate to the critique of bureaucracy?

How Do Ordinary Folk Think?

We have already observed a conflict between bureaucratic thinking and the ordinary thinking of everyday people, even of bureaucrats when they put on civil clothes and empathize with clients. Husserl's work suggests this conflict can be understood if we understand science and everyday thinking better. First, ordinary everyday thinking must be understood.

While thinking in the everyday world, each one of us experiences things from his or her own point of view. Things look different from the perspective of each one of us, though we assume that what we see are aspects of the same world.

These are two constituent assumptions about the nature of the world. Inasmuch as these assumptions—about perspective and the given oneness of the world—determine our thinking, ordinary thinking differs sharply from scientific thinking.

Scientific thinking grants no validity to subjective thinking. It insists on objective thinking as a necessary procedure for doing something the rest of us take for granted. It aims at *proving* the coherence of the world. And, with a vehemence the rest of us consider unnecessary, it seeks *total certainty.* Of these differences later.

Here the point is that ordinary folks have their own way of thinking. Science deprecates such thinking as lacking validity. We ourselves often subscribe to the idea that our thinking is more secure if it is scientifically tested. But daily life does not wait for science. Somehow we manage to open doors, grab coffee cups, walk—without engaging in a hundred experiments of scientific testing of our perceptions, observations, conceptualizations, and conclusions and prescriptions for action.

It surprises the scientist in us that we do not simply kill ourselves as we go barrelling around the next curve of our immediate future, without scientific test or rationalistic plan. But the fact that we survive proves that our ordinary way of thinking is just good enough for our purposes. This is exactly Husserl's point when he speaks up on behalf of the experience and thinking of ordinary people.

Not only does such thinking exist but it has its own legitimacy. Such thinking he concludes has its own standards of validity "which are just as secure as necessary for the practical projects of life that determine their sense."[22]

Science, Technique, and Bureaucratic Procedure

To the extent that bureaucracy expresses the same way of thinking about reality as does science, since both are very much parts of the modern world view, Husserl also speaks about bureaucracy. His argument requires following through a series of steps.

In modern scientific thinking we purposefully compare what we find in nature to models we already have constructed of it.[23] For more exact comparing we measure. Measurement enables us to create *formulas* determining how elements of the *model* relate to each other and how reality relates to the model: ". . . if one has the formulae, one already possesses, in advance, the practically desired prediction of what is to be expected with empirical certainty in the intuitively given world of concretely actual life."[24]

The totality of such a reducing of reality to measurement is the creation of a "formula world." Thinking of the real world in this way so far removes the scientist from real life as to create a concept that Husserl describes as "the formal-logical idea of a world-in-general."[25] We are reminded of $E = mc^2$. But we hardly need remind ourselves how distant that formula is from our everyday experience of the world as particular to, and meaningful only from, our varying perspectives.

Against immersion in the formula world even scientists have revolted, especially if their name is Richard P. Feynman. The Nobel laureate in physics wrote in this connection: "We know so very much and then subsume it into so very few equations that we can say we know very little."[26] But whereas the true scientist escapes into discovery, where instinct and knowledge both rule, there are enough equations for the bureaucrats of science—technicians—to immerse themselves in the details of calculation.

Eventually, Husserl shows, the original algebraic arithmetic of reducing reality to formulas is pushed to its "most extreme extension."[27] This world of figures becomes referential only to itself. Its functionaries—technicians—focus on problems internal to the coherence and consistency of the formulas with themselves. (Today we are well acquainted with this phenomenon in the internal tests for validity used in social statistics regardless of their relevance to the world; similarly bureaucrats use tests for the internal coherence and consistency of procedure without concern for its external adequacy.)

Scientists are reduced to technicians and become preoccupied with technique. Concern for the appropriateness of the models they use or their impact on the reality they study recedes into the background. (We can already anticipate the parallel to bureaucrats' preoccupation with procedure, selling short both the intent of policy and program outcomes in the reality administered.)

In the technization[28] of science, increased attention is paid to the comparing of models and reality. Science is reduced to "a sort of *technique*."[29] But "technique is . . . a mere art of achieving . . . results the genuine sense of whose truth can be attained only by concretely intuitive* thinking actually directed at the subject matter itself."[30] In short, technique may declare an operation a success, but this claim ultimately can be tested only if we look to see whether or not the patient died. Similarly, a bureaucracy may have used perfect procedure but the baby in the welfare office in the Introduction nevertheless died. In neither case is there bad technique or bad procedure, nor even are there bad people: There are only good technicians and good bureaucrats who have lost any sense of

*We will recall here, with Kant, that intuition or "onlooking" means the organizing of direct experience of reality.

the human purposes for which systems of science or bureaucracy are established.

As technique comes out of science, bureaucratic procedure comes out of policy. It is striking that technique in science functions just the same as does procedure in bureaucracy. The bureaucrat also has a model. It is the policy or the program. This defines ahead of time what can become real to him. The program or policy model is given; it is then the task of the bureaucrat to measure the distance or divergence that each relevant aspect of a client has from the model. Some potential clients too uncharacteristic of the model simply fall through the mesh of the net. And like fish falling through the net, they lack the required surface characteristics—size, qualities such as roughness—that can snag a mesh of the net. They never become congruent with their picture contained in the model. They are, in terms of the model, unreal and must be ignored. Potential clients that do match the model are serviced: They are real.

We find that bureaucratic reasoning is fundamentally by analogy. The functionary compares the attributes of a "case" against the parameters of a program. We can also say that, in its concern with the measurement of reality against models, scientific reasoning is by analogy.[31] Science is always a measuring of the divergence that actual objects have from the parameters of ideal models. Bureaucratic thinking and scientific thinking are very much of a piece. So are their limits.

LIMITS OF SCIENCE

From the beginning, Husserl shows, modern science distances itself from how ordinary folk experience reality. This is so because science is not concerned with the particular behavior of anything in particular. In contrast each ordinary human being is first of all concerned with things as they particularly affect that individual. Science—especially the queen of sciences: physics, on which modern sciences are modeled—is not concerned with any specific body. Instead it seeks to build the general formula governing the behavior of all bodies of that type. ". . . [O]ne is not concerned," Husserl writes of physics, "with the free fall of *this* body; the individual fact is rather an *example.* . . ."[32]

One of the staunchest proponents of science, Bertrand Russell, agrees with this evaluation: "It is time to say something about scientific method. Science is concerned to discover general laws, and it is interested in particular facts chiefly as evidence for or against such laws."[33] What a particular body is an example of is the formula or model constructed out of everything about any classified type of thing that can be captured in terms of its generality and measured in similar terms.[34] This approach gives science immense power to penetrate (explain), predict, and control things or events *to the extent that their behavior is dependent on general rules or laws.*

But that same science does not give us knowledge of what to do when a particular one of such things or events has to be handled on the spot. Science can design the general rules of jobs; it cannot advise how to apply such rules in the particular instance of work.

Such occasions science calls examples or accidents; but from the viewpoint of the ordinary client or the working individual, work is not an example and the world is full of such accidents. In fact, true managers are said to earn their money not through following routines but through using their brains to deal with the nonroutine. "We are not paid for doing what we are told to do, but for doing rightly that part of our job which is left to our discretion; and we rate our own and our fellows' jobs on our estimate of the weight of this discretionary element."[35] Elliot Jacques, to whom this observation is owed, found in one study that among all jobs, from the highest to the lowest, not one fails to involve some elements of discretion, some duty, essential to its performance that is not and cannot be specified in the instructions given to the holder.[36]

IMPLICATIONS OF HUSSERL FOR BUREAUCRACY

In summary, bureaucracy, like science, is distant from real life because its thinking tends toward distance from that of real life. This distance can be summarized in two ways:

1. Bureaucracy models reality. Its original modeling of reality becomes the standard for recognizing reality as something that is real *to* the model.
2. Bureaucracy, in time, becomes preoccupied with procedure. This dedication of its functionaries is entirely natural in view of human beings' tendency to immerse themselves in the infinite variety of technical problems that a technical approach opens up. But its focus on means rather than ends leads to a lack of concern with functionaries' own origin in real-life problems, for the solving of which the model was originally formed, and also the impact of the solutions.

As does technique in science, so does procedure in bureaucracy overshadow problem statement (policy intent) and solution (program outcome). Technique in science or logical procedure in modern organization truly is the art of achieving *precisely* what we want without due care for the human consequences.[37] To the extent that people allow themselves to become functionaries of bureaucracy, they fail to ask the question that concerns us all: Why are we doing all this? In turning from everyday thinking, bureaucrats fail to be what Husserl called "functionaries of mankind."[38]

Heidegger: Experience as Escape from Bureaucratic Thinking

How can we think our way out of scientific, technological, and bureaucratic ways of thinking? This question concerns Martin Heidegger.[39]

Thinking about it, he takes a different point of departure than does scientific thinking. Scientific thinking defines what we are in terms of essences: Ultimately the definition of any specific human being scientifically tends to be reduced to discovering the constituent parts or the rules for how the parts hang together: principles. These are supposed to be *essentials* that make up the human being. Knowledge of these, science hopes, can ultimately be reduced to a formula: for example, the genetic code. Man, however, does not experience life at the level of DNA.

In real life, even geneticists do not experience themselves in terms of the genetic code. The attempt to reduce human life to essential building blocks or formulas falls short of how we feel, sense, think our daily lives. Science falls short of covering experience.

Say this is fundamentally so. Then to use science to understand what human beings need, and to design methods of delivering it to them, can suit human beings at best only accidentally. There is no automatic meshing between our experience of what we need and what science can know about that experience.

But what if we then want to rethink scientifically designed delivery systems? The first step would be to obtain a picture of *experience*. It may then be possible to design delivery systems that fit human experience rather than change it.

Heidegger shows that the experience of being human points not to formulas but to just the opposite: openness, the undetermined nature of the human being. Human experience, far from being reducible to a closed formula, is wide open. Into this openness each of us throws him- or herself every day. This hurling oneself ahead of oneself requires resoluteness and courage; of this science knows nothing.

This is a point of departure from science. Heidegger's phenomenological approach—approaching things in terms of their own logic[40]—emphasizes experience as the basis of the human being's own self-understanding.

We are reminded that we are able to rethink ourselves in terms of our actual openness to future possibilities. For the human being, existence itself does not turn around this or that constitution of being but turns around the "freedom *for*" the ability to be. This has implications for organizations.

THE CARING ORGANIZATION

The lesson for organizations is clear. No organization can serve human beings if it proceeds from an already finished model of the human being; any organization in the service of human beings must allow these human beings to remain essentially open.

This does *not* mean a return to Social Darwinism and a noninterventionist state, government, or administration that lets an individual hang and twist in the wind as if he or she were alone in the world. Rather what is espoused is opening up a path on which each individual can recover his or her own freedom to be human *with* and *among* others.[41]

Nor does this mean a suffocating immersion in some kind of socialism: What Heidegger wants us to appreciate is our own experience that I feel myself to be most myself when I am suspended in the most caring relations with others, as in love or terror, guilt or courage.[42]

Also we are least ourselves when we treat others as objects. The task for the work of helping human beings be all they can be (for Americans there is here an echo of Abraham Maslow) therefore is not, as it would be if subject and object were separated by nature, to act as a kind of transportation medium that brings self and others together. The task is to help me develop for and by myself that form of self-awareness in which I recognize my original presence in the world as the being that is already in the company of others. Care opens up to that being with others.

POLICY AND PROGRAM IMPLICATIONS OF CARE

What is care? It is not possible to be myself unless I care for myself. What I care for when I care for myself is the maintaining and development of my innermost ability to be. That innermost ability to be is always oriented toward the future. The past has already made us what we are. We experience what we have become in the twinkling of an eye in the present. But what we are able to yet be is open only in the future.[43] Therefore I care most for myself when I orient myself toward what I can yet become in the future. Without a future, the being that I am would have no possibilities, only actualities already enacted. My innermost definition of my being is therefore the exercise of the utmost openness of myself toward my future. By caring about my being in future terms, I open myself to all the possibilities of being that only the future can open up for me.

This has direct consequences for my responsibility in caring for others. Others also have their future. If I deprive them of it, by defining them in terms of what they were or have become, I limit not only their future but their innermost ability to be. There are, therefore, two ways of caring for others: caring as a standing in for others until they can get back on their feet and caring as taking the place of others, in effect displacing them.[44]

This also has clear-cut implications for organizations. These perform the work through which a society cares for those in its midst who need help with their future. But this is all of us, whether this may involve concerns of national security (which ensures life itself) or the various forms of government regulation of the economy (which ensures the wherewithal for life) or the various forms of the so-called "caring professions": psychiatry, health, welfare, education.

The guideline for programs of care is to be true to the human being's innermost truth. This is that each human being comes into its own only when it is free to look to a future to be and enact itself in the direction of that future. An enabling organization can be judged according to two standards: Is it engaged in the kind of caring in which the organization stands *in* for people in order to allow them to get back on their own feet and conduct their own lives? Or is it engaged in the kind of deficient caring in which the organization *takes over* people's lives and converts them into permanent clients, that is, examples of models of clients contained in policy programs?

To this latter kind of caring belongs all bureaucratic organization. By its nature, bureaucracy is a delivery instrument for programs predesigned from beginning to end for people in terms of their past. Only such programs can be applied in a way in which those carrying it out can judge whether the tools they assign themselves have actually been carried through, which is what we mean by control.

This does not mean that *all* predesigned programs condemn clients to live up to the past. Programs can be predesigned that leave the actual working out of that program open *for* the client. This opening *toward* the client helps him or her orient him- or herself through its help toward the future. But such programs cannot be bureaucratically administered. They cannot be subjected to the ultimate judgment to which every bureaucracy is subjected: Did you or did you not follow the rules—carry out the instrumental means of the program the way they were predesigned? The answer to such a question will determine the extent to which bureaucracy has exercised proper control over the program and is accountable to policymakers but it says nothing about the *outcome* of a program.

All activities that determine the actual *outcome* of a program must be left to at least minimal participation by the enacting individual client helped by the worker.

Implications for Program Evaluation

In terms of prevailing statistical methodology of program evaluation: The evaluator of a program properly designed to help ensure the being of human beings is confronted, in the client's freedom to be, not with an *intervening* variable but with a variable unheard of in logic or statistics. Basing ourselves on phenomenology's fundamental insight into what makes us a human being—namely the freedom to be itself—we may call this an *originating* variable.

Beyond a certain point any supportive program cannot go. Beyond that point it is not possible to draw causal chains. Beyond that point no functionary of a program can be held accountable for what happens. What happens—that which comes into its own—is not up to the caring program but is up to what the client does with it. At that point all the caring program can do is get out of his or her way. This is well expressed in the epitaph for a program manager spoken in *The Soul of a New Machine:* "He set up the opportunity and he didn't stand in anybody's way."[45] Or, in the words of organization theorist David Carnevale: "Don't buy a fish for them, teach them how to fish. Don't try to control their lives, build capacity."*

But at that moment, the client ceases to be a client and again becomes what the caring policy originally wanted him or her to be: a human being capable of enacting his or her own future with an eye to preserving and enacting the freedom to be. At that moment, welfare programs take a turn and go beyond their own program standards: to produce either people faring well or faring ill. But so do defense programs. In a sense the quality of the original welfare program determines people's ability to pick up from where it leaves them off—to either fare well or fare ill, to be capable of defense or to be defenseless. But in a most profound sense that is *their* choice; no one can do it for them. I can procure for you the means to be happy but I cannot—nor can anyone—make you be happy. I can help find the support to recover your authenticity, but I cannot force you into being yourself. I can outline, through reasoning and pointing to your own experience, what it means to be but I cannot make you into a human being that confronts the choices and the terrors of what it means to face up to your being. Finally, I can teach you, but I can't learn you.

This also applies to rethinking the design of organizations internally. Workers can be enabled to do good work, but they cannot be forced to do good work.

THE NATURE OF BUREAUCRATIC THOUGHT

Critics of modern language and thought show the bias of these two human activities toward hierarchy. In speaking as in thinking, everyday activities are referred to abstract models. Modern organization, which organizes our thinking and speaking as much as any other activity, not surprisingly echoes this general bias of modernity. Unless a model can be found in bureaucratic policies or programs for a real individual trying to become a client, that individual can never come to exist for the bureaucracy as a client. Reality itself is defined according to ideal models. In bureaucratic speech, the client experiences this power to declare him or her existent, or a nullity, in terms of a number of demands by bureaucrats: Speak our language or get no help; answer our questions (according to some secret code unknown to you) or we will think you don't exist.

But the hierarchic bias in thinking—which declares those above

*Personal communication.

know better what is real than those below—also affects bureaucracy internally. The bias explains why managers are more valued than workers, why workers and managers communicate only with difficulty, why high-quantity organizations have problems getting workers to produce high-quality products or effective services. Always there is the judgment: Those who possess the abstract model assumed to govern reality know best—and must be obeyed.

Ultimately, if the resulting problems are to be resolved, there needs to be a new formulation in the speaking and thinking that define work.

Karl Everett: Care Workers and the Phenomenology of Work

One way of reformulating thinking in product or service organizations is to begin with experience. Experience is prior to logical thinking. In experience, each human being acts and knows his act. It is in the doing of things that he gets in touch with that which is experienced as the most fundamental manner of being: the ability *to do things*. It is this potential for doing things that most fundamentally constitutes our experience of life. Heidegger calls it the *possibility to be*. In working out our relations with the world, we work out who and what we most fundamentally are. We are the being that knows its own ability to be. Existence—our physical (or social) working out of our intentions and ourselves in the world—determines who I am, not some essence or code built into me from the beginning or a model imposed on me from the outside.

A Nurse: The Experience of Good Work

How we most fundamentally *are* in the world shows itself in the experience of workers themselves.

Organization theorist Karl Everett records the story of a nurse who, asked to tell of her best job experience, wrote this:

I had been taking care of a 16 yr. old diagnosed w/AML* for about a yr. (in and out of hosp. frequently). One night i [sic] went to check on her and she was awake. We sat and talked for a while, and then she asked me to do a favor for her. All she wanted was a hug, and i complied. It made me feel so wonderful to see a smile on this dying child's face, just for giving her a hug. Since then—she died, but i often think back on this moment, especially when in wanting to leave oncology nursing, and realize that the stress and hard work is worth it.[46]

It would be difficult to account for the nurse's judgment that helping a dying child was her "best" job experience were we to apply the standard scientific work definition as effort exerted to do or make something. At

*Amylotrophic leukemia.

best we would be able to say that the expenditure of emotional energy must have been draining.

The valuation of this experience as being among the "best," though, takes on meaning if we place it into a Heideggerian context.

Remember that, for Heidegger, our doing things reminds us even in our most mundane acts of our basic ability to be. Each act creates for us a reservoir of being; we become aware that it is this reservoir to which we can go again and again for renewed reminder of our possibility to be. Among our possibilities is the possibility of being unto death. It is a final possibility not only in the sense that it comes last in life but in the sense that death constitutes nonbeing. We all know we are going to die. This foreknowledge of our eventual nonbeing, when all our potential is exhausted, reminds us not only that there are limits to our being but that within such limits there are indefinite possibilities. Being reminded by death of our possibilities, we are called back to our possibilities in life.

Against this background, Everett is not surprised, as would a modern be, that the nurse would call an encounter with death and the dying her best experience.

We would interpret the nurse's "best" experience as "best" precisely because in it she faced the future nonbeing of her patient. She helped her face that nonbeing. In doing so she called her back to her remaining possibilities in the time left: including experiencing the love of a fellow-being who cared for her even unto the last possibility of death.

Also, in facing the future nonbeing of her patient—and in demonstrating that even then care can be given—the nurse also faced her own ultimate nonbeing. Encountering it she is reminded of her own possibilities. The fact that it is within her potential to give care to a fellow human being even *in extremis* asserts her in her fundamental way of being in the world, in her possibility to be.

This situation is not frustrating for the being of the human being who is called to the nursing profession. What is frustrating is what this nurse described as her worst experience: getting no help from the hospital administration to give due care to three patients who died within an hour of one another.

THE REDEFINITION OF WORK

The experience of this caring worker tells us something about how workers in general experience work.

Work is any activity in which a human being is free to work out his or her innermost possibilities to be.[47] In the world, of course, such freedom is constrained by having a job. But it would be a mistake to let the job definition define the work. Jobs are defined by time and motion study engineers and scientific management experts and, if not, by moderns who put the blueprint before the experience. These are stuck with the models of science. These models, especially those coming from the queen of sciences—physics—dictate that jobs be defined in terms of energy expenditure. In the nurse's example, this external definition runs straight up against the internal definition of work as care: care for oneself and caring for others, concern, too, for the implements with which we belabor physical or human bodies and beings.

The worker, no matter how much his or her job is externally supported or constrained, is concerned with taking care of himself or herself, giving due care or concern to his tools, and, as far as the job definition is concerned, giving as much care to it as is possible while taking care of one's own possibility to be.[48]

Everett, at the time the nurse's story was recorded, was conducting a study of burnout. Conventional management theory, based on science, would regard burnout as literally the burning out of the flame of energy that each of us has.

The phenomenological definition of work as Care, writ large, however, tips us off to another explanation: Burnout as no longer being able to work terminates our ability to care. In burnout we are at our wits' end in the most profound sense of experiencing an end to the possibility to be. What could bring an end to this? We may be suffering a deficit in inner resoluteness in our encounter with the world. But surely external conditions, which management claims to control, must be allocated their share of blame: specifically management's failing to deliver the necessary supports so that a human being can do care-full work, not just the job.

The notorious conditions in nurse jobs that prevent work include the demand that nurses dedicated to care spend more and more time on paperwork. This is necessary to show a profit and meet government regulations for reimbursements. Everett found that people who see no problem in shifting from care to paperwork *do not* burn out. It is only the best nurses who burn out, those who feel the tension between their possibility to be the best caring individual they can be and the negation of that possibility by the job. His prediction is that good nurses will be driven from the field, leaving a pool of nurses who flee into the inauthentic state of being that is provided by taking refuge in paperwork.

SUMMARY

Ultimately the exploration of speaking and thinking in modern organizations must tell us something about work. How far are these organizations from nurturing the kind of speech and thought essential to good work?

Clients and workers testify to the pathology of speech and thinking in these organizations.

Philosophers of language, of science, and of thinking itself assure us that clients' and workers' experiences of being shut out and kept down are typical, not accidental.

Bureaucracy *tends* to speak *to* itself and to think *for* itself. The cause is a very human proclivity to become preoccupied with the inner logic of our activities. Modernity feeds this proclivity; the devil *is* in the details. This explains why modern organization, in the end, does not speak to us nor, in thinking, does it care for us.

Things may be different where bureaucracy is still young. There it is still vulnerable to corrective external forces such as politics and nature. There its rationalist mode of thought lives in the tension between inner technical requirements and outer substantive performance standards. Still, bureaucracies age. Modernity as a state of mind itself grows older and hard. As modernity hardens, its organizations become insulated from society and polity. More often than not, the surgery is a success but the patient dies.

Workers are told to process data like computers; their sensibility in being able to elicit the needed data from reality is deprecated. Workers are told to just pour the grout and let the engineers take the rap; a dam collapses. Workers may find it simpler to stick to technical planning—and let someone else care whether the plan is politically viable. We recognize these as not accidental but essential characteristics of thinking life in bureaucracy.

Ultimately, the critique of speaking and thinking has to produce a payoff. Not only have citizens the right to ask, "How do bureaucratic speaking and thinking affect working?" but "What kinds of speaking and thinking are required to produce work that takes good care of us?"

All of us would like to believe we do good work. But it is clear now that the thinking that produces good work must meet three very difficult conditions:

1. It must be technically correct;
2. It must be careful of what it takes from and contributes to reality; and
3. Ultimately, it must be responsive not only to what the polity has authorized us to enact but to that which safeguards the future of the polity itself: the need to keep our potential of being human.

In speaking to accomplish work we must open up, not shut down, communications that keep us human. Being truthful, sincere, intelligible, and legitimate not only helps but is crucial: Without these we cannot know ourselves. In the same way, in thinking that aims at good work, we must not foreclose our future possibilities as members of the human species.

The conditions of pathology of speech and thought can now be combined in the picture we have been painting of organizational work.

Types of Speech, Thinking, and Work

Bureaucracy	Care-oriented Organizations
Type of Language acausal (functionalist) one-directional reality-imposing	*Type of Language* causal (contextual) reciprocal reality-constructing
Type of Thinking Analogous: relating "facts" to abstract models by measurement	*Type of Thinking* Field-constituting: including reason and science but both grounded in the felt sense of experience
Type of Work Defined as expenditure of effort on behalf of top-down goals	*Type of Work* Defined as taking care of our own and others' potential for being human while accomplishing job goals on the way

Here we have a picture that gives us three things: a definition of the pathology of speech, thought, and work in modern organizations; a direction to correct such pathologies; and a sense of the immense distance between where we are and where we need to be.

It is not the intention here to paint some ideal picture of the postmodern organization. The purpose here is critique. And, besides, modernity would only convert any ideal into another model that must be obeyed.

But we can begin to understand the magnitude of the task that stands before us. In any case, the resolution of that task is up to political formulation and decision—and there is a real question whether our present-day concept of politics is up to it. The fact that, in the modern age, we can separate the elements of life—social relations, values, psychology, speaking, thinking—from each other and from politics already indicates the depth of the problem for a politics expected to unify us in our being human.

NOTES

1. Max Weber, *Economy and Society: An Outline of Interpretive Sociology*, 3 vols., Guenther Roth and Claus Wittich, eds. Ephraim Fischoff et al., trs. (New York: Bedminster Press, 1968), p. 223.

2. Weber, op. cit., p. 979.

3. Weber, *Economy and Society*, p. 66. Weber does not emphasize the disjuncture between technical and practical knowledge, though he does say this: "For purposes of the theoretical (not, of course, the practical) definition of technical rationality it is wholly indifferent whether the product of a technical process is in any sense useful" (p. 67). It must be remembered

that it was Weber who pointed out that all systems of social reality construction rest on legitimating beliefs. In the case of technique, Weber recognized that, among moderns, faith in the calculative picture it paints of the world is based on a faith in science (p. 65). As long as people place their faith in the scientific tenet that only that is real which can be conceptually abstracted from experience and measured, there is no gap between science and reality or between the exercise of technique and practical results. Though Weber recognizes the tailoring of life to fit modern thinking and its institutions—"The whole pattern of everyday life is cut to fit this framework" (p. 223)—the task for exploring the possibility of the technique/life disjuncture is left to others, specifically Edmund Husserl and Martin Heidegger.

4. Loc. cit.

5. This segment is based on Mary Schmidt, "Grout—Alternative Kinds of Knowledge and Why They Are Ignored," *Public Administration Review,* vol. 53, no. 6 (November/December 1993), pp. 525–530.

6. U.S. Department of the Interior, Teton Dam Failure Review Group. *Failure of Teton Dam: A Report of Findings* (Washington, D.C.: Department of the Interior, 1976), Appendix C, p. 15.

7. Independent Panel to Review the Causes of the Teton Dam Failure, *Report to the U.S. Department of the Interior and the State of Idaho* (Washington, D.C., December 1976), pp. 10–12.

8. This section is based on John Forester, *Planning in the Face of Power* (Berkeley: University of California Press, 1989).

9. Forester, op. cit., p. 34.

10. Ibid., p. 35.

11. Ibid., p. 140.

12. Ibid., p. 152.

13. Ibid., p. 152. Forester develops strategies for organizing throughout his book.

14. For example, James E. Swiss, "Adapting Total Quality Management (TQM) to Government," *Public Administration Review,* vol. 52, no. 4 (July/August, 1992), pp. 356–62.

15. Max Weber, "Politics as a Vocation," in Hans H. Gerth and C. Wright Mills, trs. and eds., *From Max Weber: Essays in Sociology* (New York: Oxford University Press—A Galaxy Book, 1958), pp. 77–128; citation from p. 78.

16. Weber, *Economy and Society,* p. 223.

17. The form of references in this section is the standard one for Kant's *Kritik der reinen Vernunft* (1st edition, Riga: Johann Friedrich Hartknoch, 1781; second edition, Riga: Johann Friedrich Hartknoch, 1987), with A referring to the first edition followed by the page numbers and B referring to the second edition. The English translation referred to is the current standard one by Norman Kemp Smith: *Critique of Pure Reason* (New York: St. Martin's Press, 1965).

18. That is to say: they *officially* live there; in practice managers may use intuitive processes to get a hands-on feel for the situation they supervise, just as workers relate to their work situation. For a defense of managers' intuitive abilities: Ralph P. Hummel, "Stories Managers Tell: Why They Are as Valid as Science," *Public Administration Review,* vol. 51, no. 1 (January/February 1991), pp. 31–41.

19. This warning began with Edmund Husserl's *Logical Investigations* first issued in 1900 and continues with *Formale und transzendentale Logik* (Formal and Transcendental Logic) (Halle: Niemeyer, 1930), culminating in his famous *Crisis* (1937) cited below. It should be noted that Max Weber himself read *Logical Investigations* and developed his concept of "meaning adequacy" in relation to it.

20. Edmund Husserl, *The Crisis of the European Sciences and Transcendental Phemonenology: An Introduction to Phenomenological Philosophy,* David Carr tr. (Evanston, Ill.: Northwestern University Press, 1970 [original 1937]), pp. 6–7.

21. Ibid., pp. 130–31: "If we cease being immersed in scientific thinking, we become aware that we scientists are, after all, human beings and as such are among the components of the life-world which always exists for us, ever pregiven; and thus all of science is pulled, along with us, into the—merely subjective-relative—life-world."

22. Ibid., p. 125.

23. Ibid., p. 23. Kant already told us as much; see above, section on Kant. When Husserl was writing, the currently general usage of the term "models" did not come easily

to hand; instead he refers to models by a term drawing on the mathematical concept of limit: *Limesgestalten* or limit-shapes. However, he does on occasion use the term model for the same concept: "Sensible 'models' function in a similar way, including especially the drawings on paper in textbooks for those who learn by reading, and the like" (p. 26).

24. Ibid., p. 43.

25. Ibid., p. 46. With Heidegger, we can see in this attack on the formula world an attack on Platonic idealism.

26. Letter to Theodore A. Welton cited in James Gleick, "Tall Showman, All Genius," *The New York Times Magazine*, September 20, 1992.

27. Husserl, *Crisis*, p. 48.

28. Husserl, op. cit., p. 48.

29. Husserl's emphasis; *Crisis*, p. 46.

30. Ibid., p. 46.

31. The original misapprehension that everything in life can be scientifically investigated, Husserl tries to show, comes from an unwarranted assumption on the part of scientists that because bodily extension (*res extensae*) can be idealized into models of ideal shapes encompassing actual shapes then measured to constitute objective knowledge, all the fullness of life can be so measured. One of his purposes is to show that this is not possible: "The difficulty here lies in the fact that the material fullness [*Fuelle*]—the specific sense qualities— which concretely fill out the spatio-temporal shape-aspects of the world of bodies *cannot* [his emphasis], in their own gradations, be *directly* [his emphasis] treated as are the shapes themselves" (Husserl, *Crisis*, p. 33). Putting everything under the models of science, he concludes, is possible only in the same sense that everything can be put under the models of geometry: through "an objectification of the concrete causal world of bodies within corresponding limited spheres," i.e., models (*Crisis*, p. 36). When this happens, prescientific life's colors, tones, warmth, and weight become "in terms of physics, of course, tone-vibrations, warmth-vibrations, i.e., pure events in the world of shapes" or models (loc. cit.).

32. Ibid., p. 41.

33. Bertrand Russell, "The Art of Rational Conjecture," in *The Art of Philosophizing and Other Essays* (New York: Philosophic Library, 1968), pp. 1–36; citation from p. 19.

34. Loc. cit.

35. Elliot Jacques, *Measurement of Responsibility* (Tavistock Publications) paraphrased by Sir Geoffrey Vickers, "The Art of Judgement," in D. S. Pugh, ed., *Organization Theory: Selected Readings*, 2nd ed. (New York: Viking Penguin Inc.—Penguin Books, 1984), pp. 183– 201; citation from p. 200.

36. Vickers, loc. cit., summarizing the results of a study by Jacques.

37. My formulation, derived from Husserl, emphasizes concern with precision. In making precision the issue, rather than original problem or ultimate outcome, technicians can afford to ignore policy intent and program outcome and still feel they are being loyal to professional standards and values. This "sophistication" in technique damns all professionals. A second point: If readers wish to read an ethics into the term "due care," what this refers to here is merely an epistemological criticism. The technician does not exercise "due care" in the sense of searching for all the knowledge relevant to his or her acts. If he or she did so, he or she would discover this knowledge cannot be obtained through either science alone or technique. This is a cognitive, not an ethical, deficit.

38. Husserl, *Crisis*, p. 17: "In our philosophizing, then—how can we avoid it?—we are *functionaries of mankind.*" His emphasis.

39. The discussion here is based on Martin Heidegger, *Sein und Zeit*, 15th ed. (Tübingen: J.C.B. Mohr, 1984); *Being and Time*, John Macquarrie and Edward Robinson, trs. (New York: Harper & Row, 1962), paragraphs 54–60.

40. William Barrett, *Irrational Man: A Study in Existential Philosophy* (Garden City, N.Y.: Doubleday Anchor Books, 1962), p. 214: "Phenomenology therefore means for Heidegger the attempt to let the thing speak for itself. It will reveal itself to us, he says, only if we do not attempt to coerce it into one of our readymade conceptual straitjackets."

41. On co-being, Heidegger, *Being and Time*, §25–27. For Heidegger, communication is "im-parting" or division into parts: a sharing that "articulates the constitution of an understanding being with others. It accomplishes the 'division into its parts' of our common situatedness and of the understanding of co-being" (§34). Unless we experience ourselves

first in company of others, we cannot communicate what part we play in that co-being. Elsewhere (§35), Heidegger describes the kind of experience that human beings want when they are in touch with their deepest need. They want to engage in talk in which they can *express* themselves. "Self-expressive talk is a sharing. Its tendency toward being aims at bringing the listener into taking a part in the opened-up being toward that which is talked about." It is exactly an expressing of our innermost need that bureaucracy, if it wants to maintain its own duty to policy, program, and procedure, must prevent. Entering into a shared field of understanding out of which we approach a jointly defined problem can only lead to an undermining of the existential separation between those who hold the power of administration and those who wish to have their needs ministered to.

42. Michael Gelven, *A Commentary on Heidegger's Being and Time*, rev. ed. (DeKalb, Ill.: Northwestern University Press, 1989), p. 119.

43. See Gelven, op. cit., p. 200.

44. Heidegger, *Sein und Zeit* (Time and Being), §39–44 and 61–66.

45. Tracy Kidder, *The Soul of a New Machine* (New York: Avon Books, 1982), p. 274. The quote, originally applying to the relationship between an employee and a manager, also applies to clients.

46. This section is based on Karl Menoher Everett, Jr., *Stress, Burnout and Being: A Dasein Analysis of Nurses Seeking Authenticity and Health in Hospital Nurse Work*, unpublished doctoral dissertation (Norman, Okla.: University of Oklahoma, 1991).

47. See also Karl Everett, "What Is Work?" in *Dialogue—The Newsletter of the Public Administration Theory Network*, forthcoming. In the technical terms of Heidegger's *Being and Time*, work is defined through a definition of the worker as follows by Everett: "Worker as 'being-in-the-world', 'in which' other workers, equipment, and temporality are involved, is already and always engaged in preconceived projects, 'for which' the worker uses skills, knowledge, and equipment, 'with-which' the worker does actions, i.e., covert (thinking) and/or overt (performance), 'by which' serially connected tasks are done 'in-order-to' accomplish each successive projected project 'towards-which' the worker as Being strives 'for-the-sake-of-which' of Being authentically resolute towards Self and Self's potentiality-toward-Being FREE."

48. Everett, op. cit.

6

Bureaucracy as Polity

In a modern state the actual ruler is necessarily and unavoidably the bureaucracy. . . .
—Max Weber[1]

In a world of bureaucracy, administration replaces politics. As citizens accept bureaucratic values, they begin to judge the performance of politicians according to bureaucratic standards. Bureaucracies move into this field of opportunity. They begin successfully competing with political institutions. These now must measure up to rationalized standards in the shaping of issues and the making of policy. Inside bureaucracy itself, subordinates are told that politics has no place there; and everywhere they are discouraged from taking politics into the workplace. Yet they find politics whenever and wherever their managers make decisions. Politics seems to continue to exist within bureaucracy—except now citizens and the ordinary rank-and-file bureaucrat feel excluded from it. Bureaucratization conceals and denies the political experience.

At the same time, especially private bureaucracies are beginning to recognize the fact that their participation in a bureaucratic politics alone cannot solve problems of survival. Such problems emanate from those sources of "irrationality" that continue to exist in the increasingly rationalized world. Unrationalized international money markets and free trade cause troubles for American industry, accidentally giving a head start to the Japanese competition. Unrationalized citizens increasingly make new political demands on a system in which the bureaucrats thought they had figured out all the problems and were controlling all the answers. Here technology—rationalized science—seems to play a role: leading humanity into situations—such as the artificial prolongation of life or its artificial termination—for which there has been no previous human experience. As the fundamental questions of human life—What is it all about? What is the good life?—keep being reasserted, bureaucracies themselves initiate a third form of politics, neither traditionally political nor purely bureaucratic. (See section below, "Post-Bureaucratic Politics.") How can we make sense of these developments in the confrontation between politics and the bureaucratic experience?

In this chapter, we address this question in three ways:

1. We describe the bureaucratization of the wider political arena.
2. We describe the birth of a truncated bureaucratic politics within bureaucracy, a living paradox arising out of bureaucracy's own rationalizing tendencies.
3. After consulting two experts, Jürgen Habermas and Martin Heidegger, we try to describe the subtle and yet vague third-force political experience that crystallizes out of a reaction against both traditional interest politics and bureaucratic politics.

HOW PEOPLE POLITICK

The Bureaucratization of Politics

How do people experience the bureaucratization of politics?

PRESIDENTS

Even top politicians, the leaders of America, seem to notice that before they can get to an issue bureaucracy has already been there.
John F. Kennedy:

Sooner or later it seems that every problem mankind is faced with gets dumped into the lap of the president right here in the center of it all. But by the time it reaches here, the problem has been dissected, sanitized, and cast into a series of options—almost as though they were engraved in stone. What is missing is the heart behind them, what they mean in human terms.[2]

President John F. Kennedy's complaints—that problems have been "dissected, sanitized, and cast into a series of options" long before reaching the White House—do not stand alone. If agencies and staff purportedly under the command of the chief executive are capable of predecision making because of their superior knowledge and information about problems, they are also entirely capable of independent decision making and of entering the political arena to get their own way. Listen to what another president, Franklin D. Roosevelt, is reported to have said in conversation with one of his top administrators:

When I woke up this morning, the first thing I saw was a headline in *The New York Times* to the effect that our Navy was going to spend two billion dollars on a shipbuilding program. Here I am, the Commander in Chief of the Navy, having to read about that for the first time in the press. Do you know what I said to that? No, Mr. President.
I said, "Jesus *Chr*-rist!"[3]

Roosevelt is reported to have continued:

The Treasury . . . is so large and far-flung and ingrained in its practices that I find it is almost impossible to get the action and results I want—even with Henry

[Morgenthau] there. But the Treasury is not to be compared with the State Department. You should go through the experience of trying to get any changes in the thinking, policy, and action of the career diplomats and then you'd know what a real problem was. But the Treasury and the State Department put together are nothing as compared with the Na-a-vy.[4]

Thus a president of fifty years ago experienced in a very practical sense the error of Woodrow Wilson's statements of 1887:

Administration lies outside the proper sphere of politics. Administrative questions are not political questions. Although politics sets the task for administration, it should not be suffered to manipulate its offices. The field of administration is a field of business. It is removed from the hurry and strife of politics.[5]

Literary reports from practitioners—see, as a classic, C. P. Snow's *Corridors of Power*—established long ago that the permanent bureaucracy channels the currents that temporary political masters buck at their peril. Only recently has the dominance of bureaucracy over politics been recognized by American academic specialists. The bureaucratic experience of presidents is not unique. This is verified in a recent comparative study of bureaucracies here and elsewhere by B. Guy Peters. According to Peters, not only are agencies marked by "the ability of the permanent staff essentially to determine the agenda for their presumed political masters," but also:

Through the ability to control information, proposals for policy, and the knowledge concerning feasibility, the bureaucracy is certainly capable of influencing agency policy, if not determining it. It requires an unusual politician to be able to overcome this type of control within an agency.[6]

More sweepingly, Peter Woll comments in his study of the political role of bureaucracy in America:

The bureaucracy continues to run the government and often formulates its major policies, while the President and Congress play out the power game between them, and the courts stay in the background.[7]

While recent presidents (Jimmy Carter and Ronald Reagan) have attacked bureaucracy, through reorganization and budget cuts, their control seems not to have improved much. Whether from the liberal or the conservative perspective, there is every reason to believe that fiascoes such as Kennedy's Bay of Pigs decision and similar problems during the Iranian hostage crisis can be laid at the foot of the lopsided relations of power and influence between bureaucracy and the purported decision makers in the political realm.

In analyzing the disastrous invasion of Cuba at the Bay of Pigs, Arthur Schlesinger, Jr., a Kennedy adviser, pointed his finger at bureaucracy. As political scientist James David Barber reports, "The Bay of Pigs muckup, he [Schlesinger] suggested, had stemmed in large part from 'excessive concentration' on military and operational problems and wholly inadequate consideration of political issues."[8] If by this Schlesinger meant an overemphasis on means and a neglect of considering ends and overall purpose, we are on familiar ground. It is the typical problem that arises in any attempt to solve human problems when bureaucracy gets involved.

At times presidents are perceived as politically weak. Such was the case after Bill Clinton's plurality win over George Bush and Ross Perot. Then bureaucracies and parts of bureaucracies tend to run their own way. Thus, in 1993, the chairman of the Joint Chiefs of Staff visited *The New York Times* to campaign for his objection to using the U.S. military in Bosnia while his nominal commander-in-chief was heading in the opposite direction. Later in that year, the coordinator of American aid to the former Soviet republics had to be removed after he forecast the political demise of Russian leader Boris Yeltsin during a time when the president's policy was to support Yeltsin.[9] Later yet, the secretary of state had to reassure the world that America would still play a leadership role; a deputy had announced a recessional vision for America in which the captains and the kings depart.

At times, presidents seem desperate. Jimmy Carter engaged in a reckless attempt to rescue hostages in Iran (and his presidency) by sending in a helicopter mission over the advice and against the resignation of his secretary of state. Following Max Weber's rule that the only way to beat a bureaucracy is to create another one,[10] presidents since John F. Kennedy built up a major White House administrative staff. By Jimmy Carter's time, two veterans of his administration described even that staff as a "bloated and disorderly grabbag of separate and mutually suspicious staffs, units, councils, boards, and groups with strikingly different histories, purposes and problems."[11]

During Ronald Reagan's presidency, a special White House unit, set up to go around existing bureaucracy, was claimed (by the president) to have escaped presidential control; a marine colonel and other aides had delivered arms to Nicaraguan insurgents against congressional policy and purportedly without the president knowing it. To the extent that this operation failed in the sense of being exposed and endangering the presidency, it met Max Weber's dictum that "The choice is only that between bureaucracy and dilettantism in the field of administration."[12]

Clearly when there is an intellectually weak president, such as Ronald Reagan, but also under stronger leadership, the country can expect muffled wars between departments competing in a policy area, such as the State Department and the Defense Department. Such wars can usually be understood as contests over turf and power—each department head following the imperative of maximizing survival for his agency through constantly expanding its imperium—and the public be damned.[13]

The experience of chief politicians seems to be that they feel surrounded by bureaucracy.

1. Presidents seem to sense that bureaucracy gets to problems before they do, *predeciding* decisions by *defining* the problem.
2. Presidents seem to feel that bureaucracy unduly *controls solutions,* manipulating them according to its own interests, which may not be the president's intent or the public interest.

LEGISLATORS

Lawmakers sense a loss of integrity of the legitimate lawmaking bodies of the country, the legislatures, in the face of the private and public institutions the lawmakers are intended to control.

A speaker of the U.S. House of Representatives, Thomas (Tip) O'Neill (D-Mass.):

The House has always been a difficult body to lead; I do not believe, though, that even Henry Clay, despite the many problems he had with John Randolph of Roanoke who brought his hunting dogs on the floor of the House, ever had to deal with as many independent members as are found in the modern House of Representatives. The result has been a breakdown of party discipline and a refusal to follow party leadership, which leads in turn to congressional paralysis and an inability to act coherently as a legislative body.[14]

While the perception of a threat to the integrity of Congress is clear, the reference to members' growing "independence" needs explanation. This is forthcoming from another congressman, Rep. Barber Conable (R-N.Y.), who put the apparent independence of Congress members into context:

I'm scared. I'm scared. [So said Conable, the House expert on tax reform who later decided not to run again.] These new PACs [political action committees] not only buy incumbents, but affect legislation. It's the same crummy business as judges putting the arm on lawyers who appear before them to finance their next campaign.[15]

Conable was referring to growing control by modern institutions in the private sphere, especially corporations, over individual members of Congress through the use of political action committees (PACs).

Personal experiences are supported by measurement of their distribution. According to measurements of the percentage change in congressional campaign contributions between 1974 and 1982, Congress members' experience of the growing impact of PACs was backed by an actual 235 percent increase of PAC contributions compared with a 47 percent increase in contributions from individuals and candidates and a 176 percent increase from political parties. Senators were impacted by a 220 percent increase in PAC contributions versus a 68 percent *decrease* in party contributions and a 109 percent increase in contributions from individuals and candidates themselves.[16]

PRESIDENTIAL AIDES

So deeply accepted is the influence of private organizations on lawmaking that White House aides speak easily of teaming up with it. A White House aide, in 1982, speaking of coordinating spending by PACs and the Republican Party's national committee for twenty vulnerable Republicans:

If we can't buy half these races, we don't know our business.[17]

A former White House aide, in 1973, speaking of his experience under President Richard M. Nixon:

We don't have a democracy of the people now. We have a special-interest democracy. We have the auto lobby, the oil lobby. The individual has no way of appealing to the government.

The true democracy is where the individual is able to affect his own situation. That is not true in this country anymore. The big lobbies can do it, but the individual can't.[18]

So much for the influence of private bureaucracies. What about public ones?

POLITICAL SCIENTISTS

How do private organizations like corporations, public organizations like government bureaucracies, and politics fit together?

Economist and political scientist Charles Lindblom:

The large private organization fits oddly into democratic theory and vision. Indeed, it does not fit.[19]

Yet somehow private organizations and politics are made to fit. How?

Political scientist Theodore J. Lowi explains that lawmaking is achieved through what he calls a "triangular trade in politics" among private groups, public bureaucracies, and congressional committees. But to make political deals, each participant has to have a power base. It is easy to see where the power base of private groups, especially corporations, is: in money. But only Congress can make laws; it divides up this legitimate authority among its committees. The money groups can do nothing politically legitimate without the authoritative lawmakers; the lawmakers will not get reelected without support from the money groups. Each needs the other. Where does bureaucracy come in?

Political scientist Peter Woll suggests two reasons for bureaucratic power: First, Congress has delegated authority to government bureaucracies. It is hard to take this power back. Second, those who run congressional committees, where the deals are made, have a harder time lining up constituencies for each of the many policy problems that pass through the committees. In contrast, each specific bureaucracy already has a supporting group or several lined up to back its demands. That is how the iron triangle comes together. Woll:

Administrative policies often have virtually automatic political support which will in turn have significant impact upon Congress, for the groups that support the bureaucracy are more frequently than not very powerful economically and politically.[20]

We may conclude that modern organizations—bureaucracies, both public and private—are the leading forces in contemporary politics because:

1. Bureaucracies with their centralized command structure are *structurally superior* to fragmented political institutions and the entities that make a democracy: individuals. Democratic institutions are simply more *dis*organized, and cannot get their act together; so are lone individuals.
2. Bureaucracies have their *own competitive cultural base* in citizens' belief in modern values. Rationalism, efficiency, and formal equality are seen as producing a life of seeming stability, a refuge against the life of politics with its emotionally upsetting human passions and basic "irrationalism." Given the choice, citizens will often, in their attitudes and behavior, prefer stability to politics.

The result is that we often accept bureaucratic criticisms of politics such as the following.

Bureaucrats

Playing on modern human beings' search for stability and security, bureaucrats tend to attack politics.

A federal bureaucrat:

We draw up good legislation in the national interest with all the parts fitting into the whole properly, and what happens to it when it hits the [Capitol] Hill is like a Christian among the heathen. . . . So we spend lots of time figuring out how we can do something we want to do and think we should do, without taking a new piece of legislation over to Congress. . . .[21]

Apart from the use of engineering models in which all the parts neatly fit the whole, bureaucrats also tend to treat political issues as technical issues: matters for scientific research that will uncover the "facts" just waiting out there to be discovered.

Another federal bureaucrat:

The bureaucrat has a program to carry out that he believes in. The question of whether or not Congress has authorized it is not so important to him. He figures that if Congress really had the facts and knew what was right, it would agree with him.

There is a tendency among bureaucrats to denigrate the official political process. Yet in it politicians get a sense for the needs and wants of their constituents by discussing such often barely formed needs and wants in public and shaping them into a problem. Used to dealing with the administration of preformed policies and programs, bureaucrats themselves become easy victims to those who are aware that the party who defines a problem also wins the power to shape the range and the quality of solutions. At other times, bureaucrats believe they can play this political game of shaping problems without reference to the public at all—a kind of nonpublic or apolitical politics.

Lawmakers themselves are seduced into accepting the bureaucratic approach viewing politics as technical issues to be decided according to technical (problem-solving) rather than political (problem-shaping) standards. For example, one political scientist studying the increased use of staff and reliance on experts by members of Congress observed:

Overburdened and somewhat intimidated by the material the "experts" throw at them, they [Congressmen] are delighted when issues can be resolved in apparently noncontroversial, technocratic terms.[22]

In trying to compete with the organizational superiority of public and private bureaucracies, some state legislatures have tried to rationalize their politics by bringing in the foremost tool of bureaucratic rationality: the computer. However, early studies have shown that an increase in legislative technology simply centralizes the power of decision making at the top and center. Legislative leaders or the governors gain. But there is no evidence of any improvement in the *political* process of shaping reality-based problems founded on a sensitivity to the experiences of citizens.

As one political scientist, and former staff member of the Massachusetts legislature, observed:

A legislature can be entirely functional without being either efficient or productive.[23]

Finally we get to citizens' experience of bureaucratized politics. Not surprisingly their experience is as split as the two sets of values on which they operate: political values and bureaucratic ones.

Citizens

Citizens at large agreed by a majority of 65 percent with the statement offered by a congressional survey in 1973 that "The trouble with government is that elected officials have lost control over the bureaucrats, who really run the country." Agreement among elected officials registered at 57 percent.[24]

When the question was put slightly differently, 73 percent of citizens and 80 percent of elected officials agreed with the statement that "Federal Government has become too bureaucratic."[25]

At the same time, citizens were carried along in a continuing decline of participation in official politics. In contrast to the era of the *political* "machine"—in which voter participation in presidential elections, for whatever reasons, reached nearly 80 percent (1880–1896)—in the era of the *bureaucratic* machine such participation has hovered barely over the 50 percent mark (1952–1984).[26]

The correlation between the rise of perceptions of domination by bureaucratic power and the decrease in participation in official politics can hardly be overlooked. Learning how to work the bureaucracies pays; politics doesn't.

In summary, just about everyone—presidents, aides, legislators, political scientists, and citizens—faces up to the growing experience that:

1. Bureaucracies are increasingly *politically active.*
2. Bureaucracies are more than simple conduits for the flow of authority originating in the political sphere and serving to implement legal policies and programs; they *generate their own power.*

Something paradoxical, unintended, and dangerous happens when bureaucracies use this self-generated power politically: The tool of politics tends to become the master of politics in the polity at large. Internal politization ultimately would seem to threaten to undermine even bureaucracy's own power base if bureaucrats lose faith in their bureaucratic values and adopt political ones. We next turn to this second danger and what it means to the institution and society at large.

The Politization of Bureaucracy

One of the worst-kept secrets is the politization of bureaucracy internally. Unlike constituency-based political power, the control power of bureaucracy is entirely self-generated. This means that, unlike political power, control power does not arise from the consent of external constituencies allowing themselves to be led, but from internal structures of the organization. When Max Weber concluded from his comparative study of traditional and modern organizations that modern bureaucracy is a control instrument without compare, he pointed to specific sources of power within: hierarchy and division of labor.

DIVIDED LABOR AS A SOURCE OF CONTROL

Assume you go to work for a modern organization. You are given a job description and you are assigned to a desk or a production line position. Next to you are other employees with their own duty assignment. You don't do what the person next to you does, and he or she doesn't do what you do. This is division of labor or rule of jurisdiction. The overall work is a task broken down into individual tasks. But these somehow must be reassembled. The problem arises of how your work and everyone else's work is to be fitted together. In premodern organizations, you would simply turn to your neighbor and talk about it. In "working things out," you would not only share your knowledge and product but the two of you would, by working together, "gain the power" to get something accomplished. This is exactly what bureaucracy, by dividing labor, seeks to avoid. Control *over* any individual's task performance can only be exercised to the extent that that individual's tasks are radically distinguishable from the neighboring individual's. In short, organizational designers and managers can be in control over the exact task to be performed by defining it as purely as it can be defined and then manipulating the conditions that affect accomplishment of that individual task. Frederick Taylor, the father of scientific management, experimented with varying the length of shovel handles of coal shovelers; the experiment would have been disrupted if, unbeknownst to him, several shovelers had collaborated and helped each other shovel the coal.

In short, division of labor makes possible the *technical* definition of work, its *technical* (that is, scientific/experimental) manipulation to find ways of accomplishing it that take less input and produce more output, and therefore its *technical* control from above. The result is hierarchy. Hierarchy responds to the need of subordinates at one level to turn to someone immediately above them who has an overview (supervision) over their divided work. Supervisors must be able to oversee a large enough segment of the work process to be able to judge whether a change in the efficiency of one worker's work actually leads to a fitting of that worker's work into another worker's work.

HIERARCHY AS A SOURCE OF POWER

Hierarchy in the *technical* sense originates from *the* one great, single invention of the modern organization of work: the rationalized division of labor. Once tasks are scientifically divided, two kinds of knowledge are possessed only by management:

1. Precise knowledge of the *standards* according to which tasks are divided and jobs designed.
2. Precise knowledge of how each divided task *fits* with every other divided task.

It is no longer either the responsibility of workers to work together nor is it possible. The knowledge for working together has been scientifically, almost surgically, removed from them. It has been placed into the next higher level of supervision. The division of labor is therefore the source of *control* power for hierarchy. While the division of labor runs contrary to human instincts (I naturally turn my head to see what the person working next to me is doing), it *is* the basis for modern organization of work. In fact, to the extent that I am not divided from what the co-worker next to me is doing, to that extent I am also not required, in a technical sense, to lift my head upward with the spoken or unspoken query: "Boss, what do I do now?"

But that turning of the head upward also makes me dependent not only on the superior knowledge of technical task division and coordination possessed by my superior—*it also makes me dependent on that superior in a personal political way.* If that superior chooses to tell me to do things that express his or her personal self-interest rather than the requirements for scientific task design or technical task coordination, *I am no longer in a position to know or judge whether such demands are technical or political.*

The breaking apart of technical working together on a job also means the breaking apart of politically working together. Technically divided labor also surrenders political judgment. At the most basic level—two people working in a situation of divided labor—you and I are no longer able to judge whether what we are told to do by our superiors accords with the self-interest of the two of us—to say nothing of the public interest!

The potential for political misuse of technical control power is unlimited. This may explain why, next to bureaucratic structures and overlaying them (encapsulating their potential political power), we find civil service systems to control the narrowly political, self-serving misuse of technical power for personal political purposes of managers.

We are all acquainted with typical examples of the political misuse of technical control power by managers.* As bureaucrats we are subject not only to the bureaucratic experience but to the political experience within bureaucracy.

POLITICAL MANAGERS

In personality, the politician is an individual who displaces his or her private motives upon public objects. So Harold Lasswell, the late dean of American political science, told us.[27] Often childhood scripts of family passions are acted out again and again in adulthood as Erik H. Erikson has pointed out in regard to Martin Luther and Mohandas Gandhi.[28] On the more narrow stage of bureaucracy, balancing precariously on a platform provided by hierarchy and division of labor and hemmed in by civil service regulations, political managers often act out their psychological predispositions—their traumas, agonies, and pleasures—in more narrow ways. Their office politics gains in pettiness, intensity, and viciousness what it lacks in the broad, creative stroke. Nevertheless, with the bureau-

---

*Technical control aims to get work done; political power in the American mold aims to satisfy individuals' personal interests and passions.

cratization of the world, the impact of the office politician can be world-wide and the sword just as cutting. We all recognize the type of political manager. Whether the politicized manager's impact is personal or national or worldwide in scope, the political attack is always experienced with considerable surprise by those who trust in the ideology that bureaucracy is nonpolitical. To the victim the political manager's actions are never trivial. History has shown us:

1. The manager with a dislike for sweaty or moist palms—whose employees are driven to seek medical or psychiatric advice before facing an occasion on which they were expected to shake hands with him.
2. The manager who transfers an employee to Butte, Montana, on discovering the employee has uttered a critical comment.
3. The manager who forbids coffee drinking on the job, checks up on unmarried employees' sex life, and dismisses anyone knowing of illicit relations but failing to report them.
4. The manager who distrusts anyone who hasn't gone to the type of school he has gone to, especially those from higher status schools, and gets others to ghostwrite academic articles for him.
5. The manager who, coming in on a cold winter's day that is blowing snow, will comment on the nice weather we're having—expecting and getting employees to agree with him.
6. The manager who projects a childhood need to protect the mother into an adulthood obsession to protect the country—and uses his office to engage in national witchhunts that reenact the childhood script against contamination from without.

All of the above were attributed to late FBI Director J. Edgar Hoover.[29] More recent revelations support Lasswell's doctrine that the political project private motives onto public objects.

Manager–Employee Relationships

Why do bureaucratic employees put up with politicized managers?

A disturbing possibility is raised by the research of public administration theorist and planner Howell Baum about the institutionally created gap in knowledge between superior and subordinate in hierarchy. It is possible that this gap, so essential to generating the technical control power of the superior, also sets the superior up so that political manipulation is expected of her or him. When this manipulation, however, is actually applied to a subordinate, the subordinate goes into a syndrome of shame and doubt about his or her own autonomy. There is a shift from an emphasis on getting work done to pleasing the boss. The Baumian paradox is this: Apolitical bureaucracy itself creates superior/subordinate relationships that are technically necessary but which the human beings engaged in them translate into dominance/submission relationships. Bureaucracy creates both itself and its antithesis—politics.

Baum presents what he calls a "puzzling relationship":

The superordinate is significant, as an authority, and yet this person reveals virtually nothing personal about him- or herself. In order to make sense out of this relationship, in the absence of clues from the person in authority, a subordinate is compelled to turn to imagination to fill in personal characteristics of the authority and to define the relationship with the authority. Subordinates are likely to reflect on earlier experiences with authority figures. . . . One is likely to transfer much of the childhood feeling [for such a figure]. Because bureaucratic power is elusively difficult to understand, members find it hard to identify the ways in which the feelings may be inappropriate to the actual bureaucratic [technical] situation and to develop a realistic perception of the authority relationship.[30]

While this explanation of how politics arises in the technical work structure draws on psychoanalysis, it is not itself psychoanalytic. Rather, Baum, in his study of planners, recognizes the *knowledge gap* that division of labor and hierarchy structurally produce on behalf of the control imperative. The Baumian paradox is an explanation of political power in bureaucracy based on a structural epistemology. It is a theory of how knowledge is distributed through structure.

Managers, of course, are quick to pick up on the potential for power presented them by the knowledge gap. Managers may not care whether they are exercising legitimate technical control based on the rational division of labor or illegitimate political power based on a psychological deficit in mutual understanding (also produced by the division of labor and hierarchy). Confronted with the task of control, the individual manager may carelessly seize on any tool that comes to hand. If this tool happens to be based on a subordinate's transfer of feelings onto the superordinate and if manipulating such feelings "works" for the manager, all the better. Now the manager finds he or she has both technical control power and psychological political power. Add to that the fact that the manager may also have his or her psychological needs unsatisfied by a pure rational relationship and you have a recipe of a living hell in which the subordinate is trapped by acceptance of rational bureaucratic rules that produce psychological dependency.

As psychoanalytic organization theorist Michael Diamond has pointed out, this type of situation is an opportunity without parallel for the self-absorbed, narcissistic manager.

SUSTAINING THE KNOWLEDGE GAP

How can employees, especially professionals, live with themselves once they recognize they have surrendered not only professional but personal power to their managers?

The answer is that they don't. Employees develop a broad shield of unconsciousness to protect themselves against having to recognize that their integrity, their work, their professional values are undermined by submission to the political power of their manager.

Objectively, also, two cultures are promoted and reinforced through disciplinary action, one for managers and a different one for employees. Employees are structurally encouraged to accept the existence of these cultures as "normal"—one set of values for their manager, another for themselves.

In the first type of response (the psychological response), knowledge of wanting (professionally) to do one thing but having to (politically) do another is repressed. It is pushed into the unconscious. When this fails, pathologies result.

In the second type of response (the structural/cultural response), knowledge of wanting to do one thing and being forced to do another is externalized. That is, it is explained in terms of an external reality that, though contradictory in demands, must be obeyed.

In personal practice, this may mean that an individual employee simply alternates between two stances toward the world. In a truncated political stance he or she attempts to adjust himself or herself to political demands. In a second, professional stance he or she attempts to act out professional and social reality-oriented obligations. Michael Diamond has distinguished between the roles of a "false self" and a "true self" (see Table 6.1); clearly the first role is narrowly political and refers to constellations of self-interest; the second is professional and authentic and even open to recognition of public interest.[31]

Objectively, modern management systems simply enforce a dual system of discipline. For example, a study of arbitrators' awards in private management showed that, while a general bureaucratic culture was upheld in terms of values expected to be adhered to by both management and labor, arbitrators expected different types of behavior from managers and rank and file.[32]

In general, arbitration awards from 1953 through 1972 tended to reward managers for being just and fair, generous, *dominant,* decisive and firm, intelligent, careful and self-controlled, obedient to rules; trustworthy, reliable, truthful; and friendly and cooperative toward workers. At the same time workers were commended in arbitration awards if they were *at work* and *working well, obedient;* trustworthy, reliable and truthful; careful and self-controlled, intelligent; friendly and cooperative with management, and tolerant.*

In short, employees, reminded in disciplinary actions that theirs is to work and the managers' is to command, may simply accept illegitimate dominance/submission relationships as part of legitimate hierarchical separation in the broader context of a rule-bound organization. That is

*Here the *differing* categories for proper management and worker behavior are italicized.

Table 6.1
NARROWLY POLITICAL AND AUTHENTIC STANCES IN BUREAUCRACY

False self	True self
Cannot take personal responsibility	Can take personal responsibility
Lacks intentionality, 'I can't' attitude	Intentionality, 'I can' attitude
Disconnectedness from actions	Connectedness to actions
Maximum defensiveness	Minimum defensiveness
Engages in projections and distortions	Counterprojective remarks
Security oriented	Competence oriented
Compulsion to repeat mistakes	Reflective, learns by experience
Passive and submissive	Collaborative and consensually validating
Adaptive to bureaucratic demands	Nonadaptive to bureaucratic demands
Narrow-minded	Open-minded
Closed to criticism	Open to criticism
Blind loyalty and conformity	Questions authority
Dependency oriented	Relatively independent
Responds to external authority	Responds to internal authority
Form oriented, stresses formal organizational attributes	Substance oriented, stresses informal and interpersonal attributes

Source: Michael A. Diamond, "Psychological Dimensions of Personal Responsibility for Public Management: An Object Relations Approach," *Journal of Management Studies*, vol. 22, no. 6 (November 1985), pp. 649–67; chart from p. 654.

when they choose to face up to the political implications of work in organizations at all. Most of the time, one study found,[33] employees, especially those with claimed professional status, simply prefer to know nothing and admit nothing about the political realities of their organization—at great psychic cost to themselves.

Most important, the dynamic model here pursued—that bureaucracy both creates stability and predictability of behavior (through the division of labor) and opportunities for arbitrary political evaluation (through the personal psychological contract with superordinates that division of labor makes possible)—should get us away from simple assertions that bureaucratic structures either make people happy or unhappy. The model suggests that the rules of bureaucracy are appreciated by workers when they protect *work* autonomy as against the arbitrary evaluation by superiors.[34] Rules and the other characteristics of bureaucracy are likely to be appreciated when, and to the extent that, they are congruent with the worker's hands-on experience of reality (see Chapter 2). However, bureaucratic job definition itself is likely to run up against the worker's experience of what he or she needs to do to get work done. The cutting apart of work into jobs is generally undertaken from the top down and by individuals with scientific, engineering, or management background. In such cases, those designing the division of labor fail to appreciate what the quantitative division of labor according to mathematical principles does to actual work experience.

In summary, two dangers emanate when bureaucracy confronts politics:

1. Bureaucracy creates the illusion that all problems, including political ones, can be translated into administrative and technical ones.
2. Even when bureaucracy becomes sensitive to politics or generates its own politics, it produces a truncated politics that itself rests on bureaucratic assumptions, thereby obscuring the possibility of a full, human politics.

Against the first possibility, there are and have been recurrent "political" revolutions in America, including the cultural revolution of the 1960s and the cutback revolution of the 1980s. Can the world be rescued from the bureaucratization of politics? Can it be rescued from the narrowness of office politics? Can a fully human politics emerge out of and against bureaucracy, yet without a loss of the benefits of bureaucracy? The thinking of two experts orients our thinking on these questions.

WHAT THE EXPERTS SAY

Two futures arise out of the confrontation between bureaucracy and politics. One future sees more rationalization, more bureaucratization of politics. This view is represented here by the analysis of sociologist and philosopher Jürgen Habermas. The other future is both more hopeful and more difficult and calls our attention to the seeds of a fully human politics inherent even in bureaucracy. This second future is represented here by the thinking of the philosopher Martin Heidegger and by the doings of a number of analysts, consultants, and citizens.

Jürgen Habermas: Technical Power and the Decline of Politics

Jürgen Habermas distinguishes between the nature of power in society and in bureaucracy. These are contrasting life worlds: a world of "symbolic interaction" and "work." In the world of symbolic interaction, we orient all our activities, including our work, toward approval by other human beings. In the world of work, including bureaucracy, we orient all our activities toward work, making human relations secondary. In the first, work is a means; in the second, work becomes an end. How does this transition come about? How does work change power?

In the world of work, violation of a rule, that is, opposition to the exercise of power, has a totally different consequence from such violation in society; it is punished differently. *"Incompetent* behavior," Habermas states, "which violates valid technical rules or strategies, is condemned per se to failure through lack of success. . . . The punishment is built, so to speak, into its rebuff by reality."[35] It is this rule of nature on which the power of managers and technocrats is built. Science has created a world in which human beings manipulate nature (technology) and, in order to do so, manipulate other human beings (bureaucracy). In contrast to the worlds of community and society, what matters in the new world is whether such manipulation *works*, not whether it is approved by others. In such a world, managers have power as long as they succeed in manipulating functionaries.

In short, what is right and wrong in a technically work-oriented world is evident in the success or failure of any given piece of work as technically conceived.

In contrast, what is incompetent behavior in bureaucracy was deviant behavior in society. Not that work done in society did not have its own internal indicators of success or failure, of competence. But there also was a higher standard than competence in a given task. That standard was whether the task itself was considered by society at large as a desirable task, as a means toward an overall end that helped society to survive or achieve whatever cultural goals it might set for itself. In Habermas's words: "*Deviant* behavior, which violates consensual norms, provokes sanctions that are connected with the rules only externally, that is, by convention."[36]

In the world of society, we develop social competence, which resides in our personality. In the modern world of work, bureaucracy, we develop technical competence, skills: "Learned rules of purposive-rational action supply us with *skills*, internalized norms with *personality* structures. Skills put us in a position to solve problems; motivations allow us to follow norms."[37] Habermas offers an explanation not only for the differential perception of the nature of power in bureaucracy and society.

The difference between the world of work and the world of social (symbolic) interaction is explained by Habermas as follows:

By "work" or *purposive-rational action* I understand either instrumental action or rational choice or their conjunction. Instrumental action is governed by *technical rules* based on empirical knowledge. In every case they imply conditional predictions about observable events, physical or social. These predictions can prove correct or incorrect. The conduct of rational choice is governed by *strategies* based on analytic knowledge. They imply deductions from preference rules (value systems) and decision procedures: these propositions are either correctly or incorrectly deduced. Purposive-rational action realizes defined goals under given conditions. But while instrumental action organizes means that are appropriate or inappropriate according to criteria of an effective control of reality, strategic action depends only on the correct evaluation of possible alternative choices, which results from calculation supplemented by values and maxims.[38]

In contrast, the world of society was characterized by communication among people about what they, as a society, wanted to accomplish and what means might properly be used. This kind of interaction Habermas calls "communicative action" or "symbolic interaction" because it is defined by shared symbols commonly arrived at in a social context. This view of society—as a world of communications set in a context of mutually perceived problems leading to a shared meaning of symbols—is entirely compatible with John Searle's concept of social language. It is, of course, totally incompatible with the machine language of modern bureaucracy and computers, which relates not to people's norms but to getting a piece of work done. (See Chapter 4.) Symbolic interaction, Habermas writes,

is governed by binding *consensual norms*, which define reciprocal expectations about behavior and which must be understood and recognized by at least two acting subjects. Social norms are enforced through sanctions. Their meaning is objectified in ordinary language communication.[39]

Society dies when science, technology, and bureaucracy demonstrate the superiority of technical work over social action in achieving the goal with which modern humans are preoccupied—the conquest of matter. But not only society dies; its ways of applying sanctions and its ways of power also die.

The rationality of language games, associated with communicative action, is confronted at the threshold of the modern period with the rationality of means-ends relations, associated with instrumental and strategic action. As soon as this confrontation can arise, the end of traditional society is in sight: the traditional form of legitimation breaks down.[40]

It is at this point that we experience the transmutation of traditional political power into technical power.

As long as people the world over are concerned with the quick and general delivery of the means for purely material survival that science, technology, and bureaucracy promise, we are tempted by the irresistible appeal of power based on control over material work and over people to do the work. This power, organized into vast institutions, is, because it controls both humans and matter as material tools, superior to political power related to organizing people through symbolic interaction toward cultural goals.

Here we find not only a description of the transmutation of power from political into technical and administrative, but an explanation for the death of public politics. When power can be properly exercised only by experts, because these demonstrate their ability to exert control over people and machines, then the claim of the old participants in politics, citizens and politicians, to have a part in controlling such power is rejected.

In fact, both the citizen and the politician are disqualified from the new apolitics. They are replaced by functionaries, managers, and professionals. Habermas comments on this:

Old-style politics was forced, merely through its traditional form of legitimation, to define itself in relation to practical goals: the "good life" was interpreted in a context defined by interaction relations.[41]

The new substitute system is one of a "politics"* by experts and administrators. These now make decisions not only for their proper sphere, technology and bureaucracy, but for all spheres of life. Their ascendancy over politicians is assured as long as people bow to the superiority of expertise:

The solution of technical problems is not dependent on public discussion. Rather, public discussions could render problematic the framework within which the tasks of government action present themselves as technical ones.[42]

For this reason the new secret decision making of bureaucratic politics is also forced to enter into an attempt to wipe out the realm of the old-style public politics. Following this bureaucratic takeover, it may be correct, as Habermas says, that "the new politics of state interventionism requires a depoliticization of the mass of the population."[43] Further, to the extent that practical questions are eliminated, the public realm also loses its political function.[44] When politics becomes removed from designing means to reach ultimate social goals and instead concerns itself only with short-term maintenance of the internal standards of efficiency, reliability, and control that accompany the advent of bureaucratic decision making, then it can no longer be called politics.

Thus Habermas presents, through an exposition of the changed meaning of power, an explanation for the replacement of polity by bureaucracy. Bureaucracy contains a different kind of power from that existing in society. This kind of power is incompatible with traditional politics as a way of reaching social goals but is, at least initially, superior to it in promising or reaching material goals. By the time that superiority could appear to lead to doubtful results, the personal investment of bureaucrats, and their inability to evade the psychological power grip exercised over them, make a rethinking of the preference for bureaucratic over political systems impossible. Therefore bureaucratic power triumphs over political power. Bureaucracy replaces polity.

The possibility of a different future is opened up when we see how a philosopher can challenge the limited vision of politics put forward by today's political science.

*Put into quotation marks here for the same reason that "language" had to be put into quotations in Chapter 4: No one from the old system of politics would recognize technical and administrative decision making today as politics in the old public sense.

Lasswell versus Heidegger: The Struggle for Politics[45]

Some years ago, when I was teaching at Brooklyn College, a student came to tell me he was running for the student government.

"And what will your party do if you win?" I asked.

"We'll take all the money and give it to our friends," he said, not blinking an eyelash.

"No, no," I said. "What is your party's platform? What do you stand for?"

"Nothing in particular," he said. "The thing is to get control over the money."

"But, but . . . ," I stuttered. "Isn't there something like a set of ideas, an ideology, a philosophy that makes you different from the other party?"

My student relented. "I know what you are trying to get at," he said. "But it's really just about the money."[46]

* * *

The modern idea is precisely that politics is all about getting the goods. And how are goods to be gotten? The answer is: power. Modern Man* has even created a science of this. Harold Lasswell, the father of behavioral political science, captured the spirit of both modern politics and political science in the title of a memorable book: *Politics: Who Gets, What, When, How.*

Politics now is all about influence and the influential or, more strongly, power and the powerful.[47] "Political science, then, is the study of influence and the influential."[48] The attention of political science is focused on how elites manipulate the environment by the use of violence, goods, symbols, practices.[49] Influence itself is determined on the basis of shares in the values that are chosen for purposes of the analysis.[50] Where these values come from, however, is no longer a concern for the scientific study of politics.

Today, the parallel, or confusion, of politics with administration can hardly be overlooked. But Lasswell was not concerned with defending politics against decline into administration. He was concerned with drawing a boundary against political philosophy. Philosophy is engaged in endless disputations about the definition of politics. These seemed arbitrary and absurd from the viewpoint of science, which relied for the measure of truth on what the five senses could confirm. In the face of

*In the tradition of philosophical discussion, "Man" is used in the following wherever the reference is to *homo sapiens;* this is the more necessary in dealing with German philosophers in whose language "Man" is the generic *"Mensch,"* referring to both genders. The current gender reference of "he or she" is used when the reference is to individuals of the species.

indecision on the purposes or ends of politics, Lasswell issued his famous dictum excluding political philosophy from political science: "The science of politics states conditions; the philosophy of politics justifies preferences."[51]

THE EMPTYING OF POLITICS

Do citizens ever get together in the political arena and argue about preferences? What about disputing ultimate preferences between a values system that was intended and the one that unintentionally developed?[52] Today we might consider the conflict between democracy and bureaucracy. Yet, such public argument might yet be studied scientifically.[53]

But what about the quiet evocation of new political ideas? What of the systematic but silent searching by the political-minded for better ideas of living together? What about the testing of such ideas both against public acceptability (empirically establishable) *and* human potential (establishable only in the exercise of thinking)?[54]

Lasswell had abandoned any investigation into the sources of political ideas. Once a political idea was announced its impact could be studied scientifically: distribution of acceptance, intensity of support, effect of utilization, etc. But the sources of political ideas were beyond scientific study. Reenter the philosopher.

Martin Heidegger offers this suggestion: What is most political about politics turns around the selection of preferences about how we are to conduct our lives: philosophical issues. In truly political times, people again ask themselves the fundamental questions:

Who am I?

How can I find out what kind of life is worth living?

What are my obligations to a life that is worth living?[55]

For Heidegger only a people that philosophizes, in public, about such questions is truly political.[56]

What justifies Heidegger in this assertion?

THE RECOVERY OF POLITICS

For Martin Heidegger, the authentic life is that lived in the recognition that what I am I become out of my own potential-to-be. Modern political activists are not unaware of this potential. They seize their own potential and rush to make something of it: The model of the modern human being is the Self-Made Man. The Self-Made Man, in war or civil contracts or political elections, rips away or subtly seizes the potential of others and manipulates it to his own advantage in deadly serious games of power.

Heidegger warns that our way to the potential-to-be can be mistaken. Our relations to our potential must therefore be protected and safeguarded.[57] Whatever else a political order does, it must take care not to harm the human being's potential-to-be; for it is out of this potential that the human being is at all able to exist. This calls for a politics of care.

Not only do we know the world only through approaching things and other humans with the attitude of care[58]—no matter how deficient (as in the case of using political power)—but we must also *take care* of our potential, without which we cannot exist.

From the recognition of care as the foundation of human social and political being, it follows that a politics of care is prior to and fuller than a politics of control.

For example, take the strong-arm command, "Go take care of him!" While ironic in its opposite meaning of "Go kill him!," the command cannot be uttered or carried out unless all participants first take care to know a number of things. Who is to be done in? What are his or her strengths and weaknesses? Can I trust the hired killers? What are all the circumstances that must be taken care of to "make sure things go right"? What is the nature of things that must be arranged so that the perpetrators are safe from prosecution? All these are questions of attuning oneself to the victim, who cannot be treated merely as a thing, but must be carefully treated as a being him- or herself.

The same for political constituents. To keep other players on the political fields, even and especially the most sophisticated wielders of power must wield it with the utmost of care. They tread a fine line. Beyond that line, the exercise of power awakens others' sense that they are not being taken care of. Their counteraction can redound to the disadvantage of the powerful. The powerless can leave the field.

The ultimate irony of modern politics is that its politicians conduct it as technique, which Heidegger's teacher Edmund Husserl already defined as action without due care for its consequences.[59] Politicians especially become forgetful of their own dependence in the exercise of power on the mutual orientation of human beings toward each other and the world in an attitude of care. In the long term, politicians use up that reservoir. The electorate's faith fades. Doubt greets assurances issued that the system is interested in their care. When citizens discover they are being manipulated as mere things, they lose their faith in political relations as constituting relations that are human in a fundamental sense.[60]

So far removed from a politics of care are we today that, when care is given, we usually do not think of it as politics. Consider this instance at a sports event:

[There was] that time with eight seconds left in the 1982 NCAA basketball championship game between Georgetown and North Carolina, when big John Thompson, the Georgetown coach, saw his sophomore guard—what was his name? Fred Brown?—mistake an opposing player for a teammate and throw him the ball. That lost the final for Georgetown, and Thompson walked out on the court . . . put his arms around Fred Brown and *held him*.[61]

The modern mind interprets this gesture as signifying, "It was only a game." Yet, in terms of the politics of care, there is more politics in this sports event than in what we normally call politics. When a "mere" sports event shows more of human potential than the tool we use to safeguard our human potential—so-called modern politics—we sense there is something wrong with modern politics.

Modern civilization has redefined the potential for being, first in material and then in technical terms. What was modern society's original purpose? First, it was designed to protect individuals from untimely death at the hand of warring others[62] and later to provide property as the means to ensure civil life.[63] These protections result in a politics that has enframed Man in a way of thinking of himself that is narrow and forgetful of his own self-creative potential.

In Harold Lasswell's view, citizens are political when they are immersed in rearranging the way things are: the distribution of values, of influence over values, of power over values. They fight the battles of the day over scarce goods necessary to sustain biological life. In Martin Heidegger's vision, citizens do not remain stuck with merely rearranging things as they are; they contrast them against what can yet be.[64] In doing so, they make their own freedom-to-be the measure of all things.[65]

Man makes himself out of his potential; but he is not ungrateful or forgetful of that potential. The fully political Man lives in the tension between actuality and potentiality. A fully political society sits in judgment over the gap between what it has achieved and how this achievement opens or constricts human potential.[66]

Two things are clear: Politics can be seen as a response to the call of human potential; politics can be saved from being viewed as mere decision making over the administration of things. It is more than a distributive science; it can be an evocative art. In its fullest sense, politics is the art of the possible.

POSTBUREAUCRATIC POLITICS

Traditional American politics is a politics of self-interest. So the Founding Fathers conceived it and so it has stayed. The standards for self-interest politics are the personal passions and ends of individuals. In America, an individual can be expected to ward off fear and untimely death at the hands of other individuals by acquiring property and hiring guards.[67] Bureaucratized politics also is a fight for turf and survival, but using bureaucracy's own values.[68]

The thinking of both kinds of politics stops far short of ensuring the presence of conditions that safeguard human beings' most essential capacity: the continued potential for being. Both Habermas and Heidegger bring us to this insight. A bureaucratized politics can legitimate itself only if the values of bureaucracy—from efficiency to stability—are themselves adopted by whatever is left that calls itself politics. Are there no indications that anything beyond bureaucratic politics offers itself?

A Third Political Arena

Observe what happens when an individual well versed in the personal passions of interest politics and the impersonality and task-orientation of bureaucratized politics enters a situation in which neither self-interest nor purely instrumental values are appropriate. A third political arena is formed. On occasion this happens on a large scale. When Congress, under the prodding of budget director David Stockman, largely set aside particular interests to pursue the public interest of budget reduction in 1981, the political process was temporarily transformed. In trying to discover the nature of a third type of politics emerging, we are here asking: What happens when a "facilitator" used to overcoming bureaucracy's structures (like division of labor and hierarchy) and used to overcoming petty personal politics enters a public political arena in which participants recognize the *public interest* as the appropriate goal? A "process politics" emerges.

Listen to Michael H. Halperin, an organizational consultant and trainer, speak of his experience as head of a local school board in Massachusetts:

I wasn't really interested in the finagling behind the scenes because it was a small committee; I didn't see the need for it. I would be more interested in setting up, say, goal-setting sessions and through developing a collaborative atmosphere get everybody to talk about what they thought the issues and priorities were.[69]

Here politics as the *shaping* of problems precedes, and perhaps even replaces, politics as the decision making over which separate interests are satisfied. A leading consultant of our era, Donald Schön, reminds us that:

Underlying every public debate and every formal conflict over policy there is a barely visible process through which issues come to awareness and ideas about them become powerful. . . . These antecedent processes are as crucial to the formation of policy as the processes of discovery in science are crucial to the formation of plausible hypotheses. But our bias in favor of the rational, the "scientific," the well formed and the retrospective causes us to disregard the less visible process and to accept the ideas underlying public conflict over policy as mysteriously given.[70]

Halperin continues:

The commitment came not from individuals digging in their heels on positions they had staked out beforehand, but rather a willingness to engage in the process and to accept as a reasonable outcome whatever the group produced.

In short, the political facilitator says in effect to the members of the board: We may disagree on what the school system is about. But none of us disagrees that we have to have some goals. And none of you wants to be left out of the process of goal setting. Never mind the substantive issues that we all carried to the table, let's just all join in the process of determining what the goals might be. This gets participants into a problem-shaping mode and away from a mode assuming that choices are already brought ready-made to the table before discussion begins on what the problem is.

To the facilitator experienced in the politics of bureaucracy, "This is [as Halperin says] classic substance/process stuff." The political facilitator borrows from bureaucracy's experience that political fights over substances (different self-interest goals and human passions) can be sublimated under a process that commits participants to rational discussion of what a problem might be. Each participant contributes knowledge and perspective to the definition of the problem. However—and this is the crucial difference from bureaucratic politics—something new happens when the political facilitator carries such process facilitation over into a public interest situation. If everyone can be got to agree that what is at stake is not upholding instrumental values but the discovery of ends values in the public interest, a third political process is called for that is appropriate to the public interest goal. The process politics of public interest situations avoids a bureaucratic trap of allowing rationality to become an end in itself. Everyone now accepts that rationality is simply one means by which to arrive at a public good: a good school system for children. Process politics also admits self-interest expression; but self-interest now is no longer legitimate as an end in itself, it must be legitimated as a means—a motivation—to serve and define the public interest.

Process Politics: Examples and Objections

The objection might be raised that such a facilitated politics would have a tendency to become bureaucratic if the only standards for success were themselves rationalistic standards. Halperin says, for example: "It was not that decisions were not made; it was just that they were *better framed*." What is meant by "better"? The careless facilitator might be tempted, because of the rational bias of the process, to admit only standards that can stand rational calculation. On the other hand, it is entirely conceivable that the setting aside* of personal emotions and personal agendas might admit into the group observations and evaluations of knowledge that would not otherwise enter. Some such knowledge might derive from

---

*This does not mean suppressing such motives; it means admitting to them in order to overcome them.

greater group willingness to speak of what constituents were actually saying, what had been expressed perhaps in similar process sessions with constituents. In such an environment, individuals might actually bring into the group knowledge that either a merely self-interested approach or a set of bureaucratic standards would prevent them from bringing in.

The temptation of bringing in bureaucratic values into problem shaping according to "process methods" was certainly yielded to in Congress in 1985. Congress struggled with producing across-the-board cutbacks in the federal budget in the public interest of reducing the cost of indebtedness on behalf of all citizens. In fact, through the Gramm-Rudman law, a bureaucratic process was invoked allowing cuts to be made according to bureaucratic values: for example, formal equality of suffering across agencies. However, in the 1982 budget-cutting effort, directed by budget director David Stockman, members of Congress had showed themselves capable of setting aside the pressures of constituency interests *and* the merely instrumental values of bureaucratic reasoning to produce a result in the public interest—once the general process of goal setting in the public interest had been agreed to. That constituency interests could not be totally set aside should not obscure that a number of constituency-oriented budget amendments lost, leading Stockman to comment, "It was the kind of amendment that should have passed. The fact that it didn't tells me that the political logic has changed."[71] While interest politics has rebounded and while bureaucratic values are used to legitimate goals that cannot be justified in terms of constituency interests, the realization has dawned on many policy scientists that different policies are able to change the political process. These tend to be policies in which *everyone's* ox is in danger of being gored. They are policies in which reality—economic, social, or physical—can be shown to confront all Americans, not just those organized into interest groups. The postbureaucratic politics tends to deal with the growing recognition that interest politics and bureaucratized politics disable the polity from dealing with those issues that challenge its survival. It must be pointed out, however, that the postbureaucratic politics of survival is in its infancy, whether it takes place in the T-groups of modern organizations or in the polity itself. On one side lurk personal passions and interests and on the other the embedded faith that continued rationalization is the only alternative to the irrational basis of "dirty" politics. Against such probabilities for reversion and regression, the efforts of those advocating and processing a postbureaucratic politics are nothing less than heroic.

But are they adequate? Now that we have a fundamental vision of politics as the art of the possible—focused on human potential*—all innovations can be criticized according to a most severe standard.

*From Heidegger, see above.

We cannot give process politics a clean bill of health unless there is some evidence that its activities tend at least toward thinking whether policies free or encage citizens' potential for being. Merely talking openly with each other will not do it.* Behind that talk may lurk the model-dependency of modern rationalism† or self-interest hidden and disguised even from oneself. And merely focusing on the public interest will not do it. Such focus in the past has been interpreted within the American political culture as the mere aggregate of individual and group interests. It would be a hopeful sign to see the public interest once again defined in terms of a national community progressing onward and upward toward greater social justice and equality under the leadership of great presidents—the mythical part of the American political culture.‡ But such a hope is heavily counterbalanced by a set of operative ideals: These exalt a kind of politics severely limiting the possibilities of others when those of a single individual are taxed. Nowhere in the modern era do we see public thinking of the kind that served the Greeks. We are not as they were—in touch with our own potential for being. A process politics expects the process itself to produce ideas. It glosses over the cost of serious thought on the part of individuals. Thus, it does not come anywhere near a reconciliation between human beings' potential for being all they can be and the weight of a constraining world.

SUMMARY

Bureaucracy replaces politics. Bureaucracy does this in two ways. First, bureaucracy, trading on people's faith in its rationalistic values, moves into the public arena and competes successfully there with traditional political institutions. This is true both of corporate (private) and government (public) bureaucracy. Second, bureaucracy, by producing a knowledge gap between subordinates and managers, allows a truncated kind of interest politics to creep into bureaucracy itself. Within bureaucracy, this bureaucratized kind of politics, however, has lost *any* basis among *any* constituency: that is, its perpetrators are not forced as is any ordinary politician to touch base with a citizen constituency. Through division of labor, which reduces individuals' knowledge of the entire work process, and hierarchy, which allows bureaucratic politicians to exploit subordinates' dependency on superordinates for direction and coordination, bureaucracy generates a truncated internal politics that gives managers all the power they need without having to face up to any public responsibilities. There simply is no one in a position to judge whether a manager has exerted his or her powers legitimately in terms of the technical superi-

*See Chapter 4 on group process in speech.
†See Chapter 5.
‡See Chapter 2 on American political culture.

ority of knowledge given him or her by hierarchy or whether he or she is pursuing personal passions or interests. Suffering of subordinates as such power increases is likely to increase also: They are forced to adhere to a rational culture of bureaucracy imposed on them while blindly tapping their way along dark corridors of power. Finally, a postbureaucratic politics may be emerging as a third-force or process politics in those cases in which organizations, public or private, are confronted with the fact that their own values and knowledge structure, separated from political guidance, are inadequate to even defining what are continuing problems of survival. Early examples arose from markets that were not completely rationalized and from citizens not yet completely pacified.[72]

The revolutions in Eastern Europe and in the former Soviet Union may be interpreted as a rising against undue constraint of human possibility. A third-force politics has begun to enter the political mainstream, but not necessarily in the form of the exaltation of human possibility over technical rationality, raw self-interest, reversion to religious tradition, or the temptation of charismatic regression in the development of the human soul. In the prophetic words of Max Weber, reminding us of our rationalism's iron cage: "No one knows who will live in this cage in the future, or whether at the end of this tremendous development entirely new prophets will arise, or there will be a great rebirth of old ideas and ideals, or, if neither, mechanized petrification, embellished with a convulsive self-importance."[73]

New prophets we have had, some false, some true; and a rebirth of old ideas, often religious ones; mechanized petrification we live in; convulsive self-importance we embrace. Yet, with all these struggles and conceits, our politics does not go very far in satisfying social values nor can it make our soul feel at home in the world.

NOTES

1. Max Weber, "Parliament and Government in a Reconstructed Germany," Appendix II to *Economy and Society* (New York: Bedminster Press, 1968), p. 1393.

2. John F. Kennedy quoted in Louis Harris, *The Anguish of Change* (New York: Norton, 1973), p. 15.

3. Marriner S. Eccles, *Beckoning Frontiers*, Sidney Hyman, ed. (New York: Knopf, 1951), p. 336; cited in Peter Woll, *American Bureaucracy*, 2nd ed. (New York: Norton, 1977), p. 207.

4. Loc. cit.

5. Woodrow Wilson, "The Study of Administration," *Political Science Quarterly*, 2 (June 1887), pp. 209–210; reprinted in Jay M. Shafritz and Albert C. Hyde, eds., *Classics of Public Administration* (Oak Park, Ill.: Moore Publishing Company, 1978), pp. 3–17; combined citation from p. 10.

6. B. Guy Peters, *The Politics of Bureaucracy: A Comparative Perspective* (New York: Longman, 1978), p. 32.

7. Woll, *American Bureaucracy*, p. 6.

8. James David Barber, *The Presidential Character: Predicting Performance in the White House* (Englewood Cliffs, N.J.: Prentice-Hall, 1972), p. 328.

9. Steven A. Holmes, "U.S. Names New Coordinator for Aid to Ex-Soviet Lands," *The New York Times*, Feb. 23, 1993, p. A3.

10. Weber, *Economy and Society*, p. 224.

11. Ben W. Heineman, Jr., and Curtis A. Hessler quoted in Harold M. Barger, *The Impossible Presidency* (Glenview, Ill.: Scott, Foresman, 1984), p. 193. It may be argued that the White House staff is a political staff that does not meet the requirements of a true bureaucracy; nevertheless the description of political infighting also applies to the federal administrative apparatus in general.

12. Weber, *Economy and Society*, p. 223.

13. Presidential scholar James David Barber has suggested that, given the recent merger of the technical values of campaign management with the older self-interested values of large corporations, Ronald Reagan was selected by his original millionaire supporters exactly for his actor's ability to follow a script provided by his "directors." Whether such directors are heads of corporations or heads of bureaucracies ultimately makes no difference; the management culture of today may simply select manageable politicians who fit the dominant pattern of values and practices.

14. Thomas P. O'Neill, Jr., "Congress: The First 200 Years," *National Forum*, vol. 54, no. 4 (Fall 1984), p. 19.

15. Quoted in Mark Green, with Michael Waldman, *Who Runs Congress?* 4th ed. (New York: Dell, 1984), p. 29.

16. Percentage change measured in constant dollars. Source for data: Gary C. Jacobson, "Money in the 1980 and 1982 Congressional Elections," in Michael J. Malbin, ed., *Money and Politics in the United States—Financing Elections in the 1980s* (Chatham, N.J.: Chatham House, 1984), pp. 38–69; citation from p. 40.

17. Quoted in Green, *Who Runs Congress?*, p. 35.

18. Jeb Stuart Magruder in "Reflections on a Course in Ethics," conversation between Studs Terkel, Jeb Stuart Magruder, and William Sloan Coffin, Jr., *Harper's*, October 1973, p. 72.

19. Charles E. Lindblom, *Politics and Markets* (New York: Basic Books, 1977), p. 356.

20. Peter Woll, *American Bureaucracy*, 2nd ed. (New York: Norton, 1977), pp. 177–78.

21. This and the following quotation from a survey of opinion of high-level (GS 16–18) federal bureaucrats, in fact those who run the federal government, in Green, *Who Runs Congress?*, p. 185.

22. Michael Malbin, *Unelected Representatives: Congressional Staff and the Future of Representative Government* (New York: Basic Books, 1980), pp. 243–44.

23. Professor Raymond Cox III, then of Northern Arizona University, personal communication with the author, 1985. See also Raymond W. Cox III, "American Political Theory and the Bureaucracy," paper delivered at the annual meeting of the Midwest Political Science Association, Chicago, April 17–20, 1985.

24. U.S. Congress, Committee on Government Operations, Subcommittee on Intergovernmental Relations, *Confidence and Concern: Citizens View American Government* (Washington, D.C.: U.S. Government Printing Office, 1973), Part II, p. 115, and Part III, p. 61. The sample of elected officials was drawn from state and local incumbents in fifteen states.

25. Ibid., p. 60.

26. See Ralph P. Hummel and Robert A. Isaak, *The Real American Politics* (Englewood Cliffs, N.J.: Prentice-Hall, 1986), p. 83.

27. Harold D. Lasswell, *Politics: Who Gets What, When, How* (Cleveland: World Publishing, Meridian, 1958), p. 133.

28. Erik H. Erikson, *Young Man Luther: A Study in Psychoanalysis and History* (New York: Norton, 1958) and *Gandhi's Truth: On the Origins of Militant Nonviolence* (New York: Norton, 1969).

29. See Sanford J. Ungar, *FBI: An Uncensored Look Behind the Walls* (Boston: Little, Brown, 1976).

30. Howell Baum, "Psychodynamics of Powerlessness Among Planners," in R. P. Hummel, *The Bureaucratic Experience*, 2nd ed. (New York: St. Martin's Press, 1982), pp. 137–41; citation from p. 138.

31. Michael A. Diamond, "Psychological Dimensions of Personal Responsibility for Pub-

lic Management: An Object Relations Approach," *Journal of Management Studies*, vol. 22, no. 6 (November 1985), pp. 649–67; chart from p. 654.

32. Ivar Berg, Marcia Freedman, and Michael Freedman, *Managers and Work Reform: A Limited Engagement* (New York: Free Press, 1978), p. 180.

33. Howell Baum, *Planners and Public Expectations* (Cambridge, Mass.: Schenkman Publishing, 1983) and Baum, "Sensitizing Planners to Organization," in Pierre Clavel, John Forester, and William W. Goldsmith, eds., *Urban and Regional Planning in an Age of Austerity* (New York: Pergamon Press, 1980), pp. 279–307, especially p. 302.

34. This may be the type of theoretical basis necessary for the interpretation of studies on affective responses to bureaucratic role structure as, for example, Gerald Zeitz, "Bureaucratic Role Characteristics and Member Affective Responses in Organizations," *The Sociological Quarterly*, vol. 25 (Summer 1984), pp. 301–18.

35. Jürgen Habermas, "Technology and Science as 'Ideology'," in Habermas, *Toward a Rational Society: Student Protest, Science and Politics* (Boston: Beacon Press, 1971), pp. 81–122, citation from p. 92.

36. Ibid.

37. Ibid.

38. Ibid., pp. 91–92.

39. Ibid., p. 92.

40. Ibid., p. 96.

41. Ibid., p. 103. The argument that only citizens, because they are amateurs, are qualified to set societal goals and that experts and specialists are specifically disqualified from such activity is also made by Alfred Schutz in a classic article attempting to justify a return to the old-style politics: "The Well-Informed Citizen: An Essay on the Distribution of Knowledge," in Schutz, *Collected Papers* (The Hague: Martinus Nijhoff, 1964), pp. 120–34.

42. Habermas, op. cit., p. 103.

43. Ibid., p. 103.

44. Ibid., p. 104.

45. This section is based partly on a preparatory essay, "A Once and Future Politics: Heidegger's Recovery of the Political in *Parmenides*," forthcoming.

46. I could not help thinking what a wonderful training ground we were for New York State politics. At the time, one of our more successful students, Stanley Fink, was speaker of the State Assembly.

47. Lasswell, *Politics: Who Gets What, When, How*, p. 23.

48. Ibid., p. 26.

49. Ibid., p. 27.

50. Ibid., p. 26.

51. Ibid., p. 13.

52. To Heidegger, whose redefinition of politics in a philosophical direction is discussed below, this is the ultimate political struggle: the struggle—originally in Greek: *polemos*, from which we derive polemic—over the whole of what is, which is, already in the word of Heraclitus, thrown in its Being from one contradiction to another. Martin Heidegger, *Einfuehrung in die Metaphysik* (Introduction into Metaphysics) (Tübingen: Max Niemeyer Verlag, 1966), pp. 47 and 102 on *polemos* and p. 102 on Heraclitus.

53. Though political science's attitude toward such conflicts has been to wipe out one of the contenders. Having found little empirical evidence for the existence of democracy, behavioral political science simply sidestepped it as one of those preferences that Lasswell spoke about and concentrated on establishing the system that does exist: e.g., Robert Dahl's plurality of elites, polyarchy. For recent scientific evaluations of the democracy/bureaucracy entanglement: Larry B. Hill, ed., *The State of Public Bureaucracy* (Armonk, N.Y.: M. E. Sharpe, Inc., 1992).

54. Heidegger uses the term "thinking" instead of reason because of what he considers to be the degeneration of reason (*ratio*) in mere technical calculation in modern times.

55. The philosophically inclined will recognize the traditional questions of philosophy: Who is Man? What can he know? What must he do?

56. Martin Heidegger, *Parmenides* (Frankfurt am Main: Vittorio Klostermann, 1982).

57. Instead of a finished human nature and its "essential" characteristics, Heidegger

argues for a set of "existential" conditions that make possible the always unfinished human being's way of carrying its potential into the world. These, in his early work, include care, anxiety in the face of our own finitude, and resoluteness. See Martin Heidegger, *Being and Time*, trs. John Macquarrie and Edward Robinson (New York: Harper & Row—HarperSanFrancisco, 1962).

58. In *Being and Time*, Heidegger shows care to be a fundamental condition through which we orient ourselves and know the world. See Heidegger, *Being and Time*, paragraphs 39–44.

59. Edmund Husserl, *The Crisis of the European Sciences and Transcendental Phenomenology: An Introduction to Phenomenological Philosophy*, tr. David Carr (Evanston, Ill.: Northwestern University Press, 1970 [German original 1937]), p. 46: ". . . technique . . . is the art of achieving . . . results the genuine sense of whose truth can be attained only by concretely intuitive thinking actually directed at the subject matter itself."

60. Traditional political theorists and sociologists like Jürgen Habermas have spoken of this as a crisis of legitimation. Heidegger's approach shows the crisis to be more fundamental: When people are treated as things, and they discover this, they experience a crisis of meaning. There is more here than the loss of a system of its legitimation in people's faith in it; what is lost is people's faith in each other as the basis for the faith of each in him- or herself.

61. Told by the late tennis champion Arthur Ashe in Kenny Moore, "Sportsman of the Year: The Eternal Example," *Sports Illustrated*, vol. 77, no. 26 (December 21, 1992), pp. 16–27; quotation from pp. 23–24. Italics reflect Arthur Ashe's emphasis.

62. The purpose for civil society as seen by Thomas Hobbes as a founder of modern politics.

63. For example, John Locke's defense of politics.

64. This political attitude comes, for Heidegger, out of Man's foundational attitude toward himself: As human beings we are oriented toward the future, what we can still make of ourselves; we are not stuck with what we have become. A society that prevents human beings from access to what they might yet become is for Heidegger a profoundly unhuman society. "Man never is, but always is to be," William Barrett paraphrases a line from Alexander Pope. In the constitutive politics of Heidegger, the question is always asked: Does what is prevent us from being what we are yet to be? For Barrett: *Irrational Man: A Study in Existential Philosophy* (Garden City, N.Y.: Doubleday & Company, Inc.—Doubleday Anchor Books, 1962), p. 228.

65. Cf., Heidegger, *Being and Time*, paragraph 40.

66. Heidegger, *Parmenides*, paragraph 6b, pp. 141–42 ff. In his later language, Heidegger speaks of the need to ground what is (*Seiendes*) with its source, Being (*Sein*), but in his early *Being and Time*, he also uses the terms "potential-to-be" and "freedom-to-be" as an approach to Being.

67. This is a combined interpretation of American politics based on the work of Thomas Hobbes and John Locke as applied to the United States by H. Mark Roelofs. See his *Ideology and Myth in American Politics: Portrait of a Political Mind* (Boston: Little, Brown, 1976).

68. For some of these values, see Chapter 2.

69. From a conversation with Michael H. Halperin, Feb. 19, 1986.

70. Donald Schön, *Beyond the Stable State* (New York: Norton, 1971), p. 123.

71. Quoted in William Greider, "The Education of David Stockman," *Atlantic Monthly* (December 1981), pp. 27–54.

72. I owe the concept of politics as the pacification of citizens to Theodore Lowi. Since the revolutions in Eastern Europe and the former Soviet Union, this has taken on an entirely new meaning.

73. Max Weber, *The Protestant Ethic and the Spirit of Capitalism*, tr. Talcott Parsons (New York: Charles Scribner's Sons, 1958), p. 182. It is at this point that Weber adds his famous prophecy and curse: "For at the last stage of this cultural development, it might well be truly said: 'Specialists without spirit, sensualists without heart; this nullity imagines that it has attained a level of civilization never before achieved.'"

7

Conclusions:
A Terminal Critique
for a Terminal Society

Some years ago I walked into my bank at the corner of Fourteenth Street and Eighth Avenue in Manhattan to hand a check to a teller.

"Sorry," she said, "we have a new rule. I can't cash anything over five-hundred dollars. You have to get this initialed by one of the officers."

I knew just the officer I wanted. Mrs. Nicholas always took care of my problems. She was a vice-president. My wife always called her Loretta. But, as a person raised to respect authority, I called her Mrs. Nicholas.

There she was now, coming toward me under the great dome of the bank.

"Mrs. Nicholas," I said angrily. "What the hell is this about some damned new rule about getting a signature on this?" I was waving my arms and the check.

"Ralph," she said, apparently ignoring the question, "didn't you write a book about bureaucracy some time ago?"

"Yes," I said, flattered, but still steaming. "What's that got to do with this?"

"And didn't you give me a copy of that book?"

"Yes, but . . ."

"Well," she said with a great deal of satisfaction in her voice, "I read that book. You know all about this." And she walked away.

* * *

The story tells us something. But what? You now have read this book; or, if you read the way I read detective stories, you are looking here to find what it was all about. It was intended to be a critique of the bureau-

257

cratic experience. But, now comes the question which I can describe only as quintessentially American: So what? What can we *do* with it?

A critique can be expected to help us do three things:

- Understand a situation.
- Imagine alternatives to a situation.
- Change a situation.

The story tells us understanding alone may be insufficient to deal with even the simplest of bureaucratic encounters. In the words of my friend Sally Merchant, "You can understand the hell out of a problem and still not be able to do anything about it." Imagining an alternative does not seem to have helped much in this situation either: The bank officer didn't wait around to ask an alternative. Or what if I had managed to get the bank to change its policy? In the words of my friend Don Merchant, "Even if you talk a bureaucracy into changing, it may change in a way you didn't intend it to."[1]

If anything, the conclusion of this critique is not that there is anything wrong with particular bureaucracies but that there is something wrong with the world in which bureaucracies have come to dominate our lives. If the problem is that big:

- How much can understanding help?
- How much can imaginative alternatives help?
- How much can acting to change things help?

In these conclusions I would like to say something about the expectations in these questions.

What can we rightly expect from pure critique, what are its real consequences, how does it affect the life of the critic, why is it ultimately inadequate?

What can we expect from action, why is action in modern times never enough?

And, what about imagination? Does the author of this critique go too far to imagine a standpoint from which to critique—or does he, contrary to the hand-wringing of his critics about his "extreme" position, not go far enough?

THE INADEQUACY OF UNDERSTANDING

When somebody appeals to your understanding, it is not because they want your help. Such help might require them to change. No, they want *you* to change, beginning with your attitude toward them.

A bank officer appealing to your understanding of how banks work expects acceptance of rules good for the bank, not necessarily for you. I can imagine the reasons behind these rules: There may be people who steal our checks and it is good to have another security control built into the system.

But I thought I had written a critical book. Should not a critical insight give me the knowledge to *do* something about a situation that was not working in my perceived interests? After all, delay at the bank means time wasted for the customer. Lowering their discretion makes for grumpy tellers. The extra step reflects a whole maze of bureaucratic convolutions that add costs to the business of doing banking and these are passed on to me.

Several editions later I see myself still standing there with the uninitialed check in my hand. Knowing all about bureaucracy does not seem to help very much. I ended up, of course, going over to the bank officer and getting the check initialed. Understanding, at best, seems to change the person who understands, not the world.

In fact, understanding may contribute to a kind of moral disarmament. Professionally, I am so well trained now to be receptive to what a situation is all about that I am easily put upon by people who have no moral qualms about needing to understand me before they try to change me. The fully understanding person is in danger of his or her life and livelihood, especially in a time of the righteous who make a claim to a monopoly of moral correctness. As a friend of mine, a Vietnam grunt, likes to say: "Understanding is always a form of surrender."

This especially applies to the academician who, because he or she is obliged to present all sides of a story, is forbidden to speak on behalf of his or her own self-interest. (Academic freedom, contrary to the misunderstanding of many who aspire to be academics, is the freedom to take positions that are merely academic; it is never the freedom to misuse academe to take positions of personal self-interest. In short, it does not protect the life interests of the academic at all.)

To illustrate this danger of becoming a totally understanding person, I have taken an inventory of my own attitudes toward the world, which have changed as my understanding of modern organizations has increased. You may care to take an inventory of your own changes since beginning this book.[2]

Socially, I now know to develop good personal relations with people I work with or with bureaucrats whose help I will need. Failure to do this limits me to my assigned role and gives additional power to those who manage me or who are assigned to deal with my case. But doing so also adjusts me to the bureaucratic social structure as I face and understand it. Normal folks would say I am a better-adjusted person.

Culturally, I do not expect bureaucracy to satisfy my human needs. At best, I expect these will be translated into bureaucratic goals that will give me a technical version of what I really want. I am especially suspicious of claims that *total* management can put quality back into my working or personal life; the totalitarian implications of bureaucracy are bad enough without pursuing them explicitly to control all aspects of the inmates' lives. My attitude is, of course, one that is morally deprived: If I expect the bureaucratic experience to be devoid of ethical imperatives, I myself am and act a-ethically. For where is ethics to come from if not from people who expect and enact it?

Psychologically, I try hard *not* to surrender to my superiors my sense of what work it is good to do (an issue of conscience) and how work is to be done (an issue of both conscience and mastery). There are, of course, always compromises to be made: Otherwise one does not survive. Does an experienced academic colleague suggest that one should write more articles to balance a record of books? Why, it would be foolish to throw away such advice. But there *are* limits. Does a sadistic dean try to demean me during a job interview? Knowing that a hierarchy attracts narcissists who grovel to their own superiors but desperately need me to grovel before them, I keep myself from getting involved in situations like that if I recognize them in time. I give my superiors what they need: the power to make decisions about things I say I want. But I never submit to them needs I really care about—to do so would give them the power to damage or destroy me. I no longer expect an *organization* to care about me, but the psychological cost of accepting this reality is, of course, a deficit in solicitude on my own part.

I try to learn the language. But I expect no bureaucrat to stand behind his or her words; their word is not their bond, it is mine. And if language and action happen to coincide in a modern organization, it is because the connection works to the organization's advantage. The trick is to read the subtext behind the pretext.

Politically, I am not fooled by organizations' claim to political neutrality. Despite being bound to procedural and technical values, bureaucrats have learned to manipulate these values so they become goods in power games of office politics internally and tools of political domination externally. At the same time I no longer expect very much from public politics because I recognize it has been reduced to a version of office politics and technical domination. Politicians struggle for influence over the distribution and redistribution of available social values not much different from ones available in bureaucracy: for example, deference, income, safety. Politics as the art of the possible, evoking ever new formulations of where we are in the satisfaction of human potential, seems to have been killed with my last president: John F. Kennedy. Yet, I am well aware of the ostracism that Pericles pronounces on the apolitical man who claims politics is none of his business: We say he has no business here at all.

In short, understanding our world can lead to a kind of quietism against which an occasional outburst is an exception. Something more seems to be required: the will to engage the battle along with a certain street-smartness or practical know-how that enables us to make sense of what is going on and empowers us with the ability to reach into a tool chest for alternative tools to fix it. Constantly honing his sensibilities, the understanding observer may neglect to develop the hard core that will enable him to defend himself when attacked by the politically astute, the righteous, the disturbed, the merely vicious[3]—quite apart from pushing upward the rock of modernity that daily slides down again.

Inward sensibility, vision, and outward resoluteness are seldom combined in equal parts in one personality. The most penetrating of critics of our modern age has been singularly lacking in street-smartness: Martin Heidegger. A rare critic has had the predisposition for all three—for political battle, prophetic vision, and inner sensibility: Max Weber, though at great personal cost to himself. For most of us, engagement in the daily skirmishes of modern life leaves very little time for reflection. As a college president once told a panel of administrative theorists: I'm too busy to think. Or, as a secretary once told me, more penetratingly, about her experiences with embattled managers: They think in their actions.

To do all three—see through things, envision alternatives, and make the critique stick—do we need unusual personalities ascetic in self-denial, cut from prophetic cloth, and assuming heroic proportions? The existentialist philosopher Jean-Paul Sarte in his old age put his body on the line at factory gates in Paris, handing out radical literature, daring the police to knock him down as they had his fellow citizens. Is action the solution to the problem of modern life?

THE INADEQUACY OF ACTION

Action extends our range from inwardly changing ourselves in order to understand toward grasping power to change the world. Today our world is dominated by the modern system. That system rests on the kind of knowledge that is easily converted into power. The target is clear. Power itself is the enemy. Yet to oppose it means to put the knowledge behind it in its proper place. But what if this cannot be done? What if the system resists being fixed? And what, which is worse, if the only available tools to try to fix what Max Weber called a power instrument without compare are the tools of power itself? Then action also fails, for it surrenders itself to the enemy; by using power, activists surrender to power.

This failure has recently been the fate of reformers in academe, government, and business.

Academe

Say a critique of a key element of modernity is launched. Say modern organizations suddenly come under attack not only from scholars and consultants but from clients and customers. The response of the dominant world view is, of course, no less than expected. The knowledge enterprise that legitimates organizational power closes ranks.[4]

Citizens simply are depicted as not knowing what they are talking about. Surveys are taken, and these show that citizens "harbor anti-governmental, antibureaucratic attitudes in the abstract" but say their local bureaucrat is doing relatively well in delivering services. The analysts' judgment: "Our attitudes toward government and bureaucracy really are varied, contradictory, ambiguous, as well as ephemeral"; the "key" toward understanding how public opinion might actually constitute a position that is internally consistent—either pro or con—will always remain "elusive."[5] And this from a representative of the American political science tradition, which is suspicious of the danger that an authoritarian institution such as a bureaucracy poses for democracy. The possibility that modern organization's fragmentation of the individual is itself the cause of wildly uprooted opinion is not considered.

Empirical research, reduced to serving as a ploy in admitted polemics, is also directed at critics from the side of public administration scholars. Critics, it is suggested, have nothing to say unless they first engage in empirical research to see whether "deduced theories . . . are correct, just as we would in any honest social research."[6] The issue, of course, is not whether the research is honest—everyone after all does "honest" research—but whether the conceptual point of departure can claim the honor of being true to the interests of citizens and human beings or—bureaucrats.

In the extreme, the Big Guns are brought to bear. The director of the self-appointed National Commission on the Public Service tells a public meeting of scholars and practitioners that less criticism would be helpful in attracting more students to become future managers in the nation's capital. The spirit of the Enlightenment, seeing itself about to be boarded by ruffians perceived to be flying the skull and crossbones,[7] suddenly darkens ship.

When things go wrong in modernity, when a contrary perspective outlines the dark side of modern organization, the defenders and advocates of progress through human thinking and action suddenly become keepers of the flame. Huddling around their darkened light, they accuse critics of going to pathological extremes[8] and take to the ultimate refuge of moderns with an axe to grind: frequency distributions.[9] We are urged to see if the facts fit the case as they define it—proceeding bureaucratically in our investigation of bureaucracy, with entirely predictable outcomes.[10]

Think of modernity as a ship that has run aground. Its passengers seesaw between patient research and frantic action: They put their faith in the ship's clerk captaining a frightened crew at the ship's pumps. This guarantees that no thought is given to developing a standpoint and a leverage from outside the vessel.

The result is predictable: at best, repeated and vain attempts to use modernity against critique of modernity; at worst, career assassination[11] accompanied by uncritical, and therefore in the most profound sense unscientific, acceptance of the way things are: surrender to an ineluctable and inevitable present. This may work to reproduce the previous condition of relative unconsciousness. If not, reforms can be haltingly tried. But the reluctant reformers caution, through pursed lips, that experiments must, of course, be carefully controlled—while the modern mind silently dreams of subversion or, more genteel, of cooptation.[12]

Government

In the United States government, a twelve-year regime of two presidents attempted open resistance to continuing bureaucratization.[13] In the U.S. economy, during the same period, leaders of corporations attempted escape. Dragged from sullen obstinacy into recognizing the quantitative limits of modern organization, they sought to win competitive battles by reorganizing for quality. Neither attempt proved decisive.

Social values and qualitative product and service values were briefly recognized as satisfying a different set of human needs than could be met by the quantitative transmutation of such needs. Politics and management were poised to leap from producing goods and services that were merely technically correct to goods and services that were humanly appropriate.

But politics itself had been perverted by bureaucratic values.* Any political revolution would naturally end up using bureaucratic values in its fight against bureaucracy—a logical and practical absurdity.[14]

In using political force to push traditional social values through the bureaucracy, the political administrations missed an opportunity to evoke and crystallize a new sense of human beings' coming to terms with their new powers. Instead, the tactic divided the country and focused politics on a renewed struggle between parties. Shoved aside in this contest of mutual intolerance and puritanical ideology of the left and right was the opportunity for a politics as the art of the possible. This would have meant pursuing the possibility of struggling thoughtfully for a new communal sense of Man's relations with his own potential in confrontation with his technical and organizational powers.

Business

Similarly, both the modern economy and management science, despite a public trumpeting of conversion to quality, remained preoccupied with

*See Chapter 6.

quantity and the power interests associated with it. Even when the last bit of quality had dropped out of products such as American automobiles or air-conditioners, the long-delayed response was to leap over the quality problem and redefine it into a measurement problem. In the words of one popular advocate of so-called quality management: "What gets measured gets done."[15] Increased measurement by tightening tolerances would soon improve "quality."[16]

What was leapt over was quality itself: the what (*quale*)[17] that made up the thing that was to be measured. But knowledge of this "what" is first located in the experience of a worker with a thing; only after this experience tells us what to look at can management science step in and begin to measure. A bad judgment as to what is important in doing a piece of work on the part of the worker equals a bad basis for any measurement that may follow. A threat was soon perceived by the managers of private industry: If experience falls to the worker as first and ultimate judge of what is going on, then workers are the highest court of judgment in an organization—*not managers.*

Judgments of quality were increasingly being made by reference to human dimensions—the material and tool in the hands of the worker and the product in the hands of the user. Abstract dimensions did not satisfy. But management authority hinged on respect for knowledge of abstract dimensions. A successful challenge to abstract dimensioning also was a threat to management authority. An organization true to quality would also need to be true to politically recognizing the source of the knowledge of quality. One thing was clear: The source was not management. Unwilling to surrender status, income, and privilege to nonhierarchical knowledge networks integrating both computer and hands-on knowledge, management feared programmers, workers, and end-users could make legitimate knowledge claims to controlling the top of existing hierarchies.* It cannot be said much better than this: "The elite do either no work or a kind of police work that will reinforce hierarchy."[18]

Resistance and escape both trapped themselves in a paradox: using modernity to change modernity. Their practitioners used modern methods and standards to reform or revolutionize that form of organization which itself is the cutting edge of modernity.

In the private sector, reliance on the control powers of information technology, instead of freeing that technology's networking potential, soon obscured the briefly acknowledged and cynically misused source of the true innovation in quality production: working experience at the site of production.[19]

Quite aside from culture-induced sabotage, bureaucrats—the man-

---

*Compare sections in Chapter 2 entitled "A Theory of Organizational Culture" and "Possibility Two: Increased Bureaucratization as the Basis for Quality."

agers of both the public and private sector—resisted change, recognizing the danger to their position. Values essential to hierarchy were threatened, including the deference, income, and safety accorded to elites.[20] In the public sector, the direct threat to bureaucrats had come from cutbacks and the imposition of political appointees who pursued social values over technical ones.[21] Contrary to expectations that a Democratic administration would be more favorably disposed toward federal bureaucrats, cutbacks were renewed in the administration of President Bill Clinton. The remedy to bureaucratization in the private sector had been more brutal: one million managers and their staff fired or laid off in the 1980s.

By the 1990s, modern organization had begun to return with a vengeance. Public bureaucrats breathed a sigh of relief at the return of a presidential administration subscribing to positive government.[22] Government intervention in many aspects of human life, to a subscriber to bureaucratic doctrine, could mean nothing else except more and bigger top-down structures for administration—despite counterdoctrine advocating organization design grounded in bottom-up knowledge of the work. Private managers similarly took refuge in elaborate mathematical and computerized information processes.[23] These, legitimated by market measurements indicating no difference in the performance of firms' stocks, encapsuled and controlled the threat to their power contained in the quality movement: the idea that knowledge rested at the point of production with workers.[24] Similarly the awareness of consumers that they had the capability to judge products and services was retracked into an emphasis on speed of response to demand, timeliness of delivery, customization, and variety—all of which were thought to fall under the exclusive domain of quantitative information technology.

Despite the promises of the Reagan Revolution in the public sector and the quality revolution in the private sector, there was no real revolution.

What went wrong?

Just as understanding, by itself, is not enough, neither is action enough to overcome the modern spirit that pervades not only the institutional frameworks we have created for our lives but our own thinking. The limits of that thinking were captured by Max Weber when he told us that fate in modern times is the consequence of Man's action contrary to his intention. Martin Heidegger, the great critic of modernity, puts our failure to a lack of imagination. Trapped in a 2,500-year history of thought beginning with Plato's idealism and ending in our preoccupation with the ultimate pure ideas: the mathematica of technique, we are unable to think ourselves, much less fight ourselves, out of a paper bag. For, literally, to escape means to fight what we have become; but what we have become determines that the only way we can fight to escape is to use the tools of modernity itself.

Not better understanding is called for (meaning, in modern times, squeezing ourselves to fit the organizational realities of the day) nor more action. What then? Here I have the final opportunity to suggest something that runs not only against the American disposition to "do something" but against the modern grain altogether. Modernity has given us the power to "understand" ourselves and it has given us the power to "change" reality. Perhaps we should be suspicious of such gifts the way the Trojans should have suspected the wooden horse of Odysseus. For both understanding and changing involve the gift that modernity gives us as no civilization has ever given that gift: power. But if our aim is to change modernity or escape from it, then what we do must avoid the gift most suspiciously given by modernity. We must avoid power like the plague.

But what other tool is there beyond power? Is escape to be "beyond our power"? What, especially in modern times in which we have power over everything, can possibly be beyond our power? And how can it help us?

* * *

IMAGINATION: TOWARD A PHILOSOPHY
OF ADMINISTRATION[25]

To borrow a turn of phrase from the dean of contemporary public administration Dwight Waldo, a theory of organizations in our day means a philosophy of modernity also. From a general critical philosophy of modernity we can derive a critical philosophy of administration that gives us an understanding of the limits within which our life and work are organized. But a critical philosophy of administration must not be suicidal—it must not merely change the philosophers—and it must not play itself out on modernity's own playing field: in a game of power. A philosophy of administration must overcome the practice of dominating people; it must again turn to ministering to them or, better, allow them to minister to themselves. This requires thinking beyond modernity.

Martin Heidegger suggests we proceed not by changing individuals nor by using the power of modernity to change modernity but by changing mankind's entire picture of mankind.

This is an exercise in political imagination in the most profound sense. What he seeks is nothing less than a picture that will contain what Man has achieved so far, including the power of science and technology and modern organization, but giving these a place in a broader dimension of human potential. What if he succeeds? We can make a tentative list of the results:

1. Science would again be in the service of humanity rather than humanity being a guinea pig for science.

2. Technology would again be a mere tool for human aims, not a framework whose technical rules override human needs.
3. Organization—including political organization—would be a way of discovering and rediscovering again and again a society's place in history and the world rather than an iron cage where order is more important than awareness of who we are, where we are, and what we are about.

In such a world, the human being would not be a stranger but would again feel at home. Man would have a home.

In this short space, it is possible only to make a beginning by following an example of the kind of rethinking that is required. This means retracing the initial route Martin Heidegger took to remind us of who we are. We follow here Heidegger's attempt to re-answer an old philosophical question: Who is Man?

Why does Heidegger's way of proceeding to answer this question intuitively appeal to us? It is because he announces that he will proceed in a unique way that in itself breaks out of what we are used to thinking. Since thinking about power is not the way out, Heidegger asks us to think about that which rules without requiring power.[26]

Let us follow the pointing finger of his reasoning for a short while.

* * *

In the face of science's and technology's threat to what is human in the human being, Heidegger tries to establish how the human being is different from other beings and things. A whole range of experiences, especially the meaning of experiences, he observed, is not captured by the modern mind, including the modern political mind. What assumptions about the nature of Man must be made to capture Man's experiences in their totality? Here the old question is reopened: Who or what is Man? Heidegger answers in his own way.

Recovering the Concept of Man

Modern Man clearly is the being that is in control of its own identity, its own life, its own being itself. If so, why does the problem arise that we feel homeless in the world, considering all the knowledge and power that science and pure reason have created?

Imagine Heidegger is viewing this problem the way you would view two opponents at a chessboard.[27] Imagine that the aim of the chess game is not victory but knowledge of the game itself. We know who the players are in the modern game that seeks knowledge: on the one side, Man himself, equipped with science and reason; on the other side, the world that presents itself as requiring discovery.[28] The two need each other: without Man, no reason; without the world, no material to reason about.[29] But, again, imagine that the human player is not simply looking for knowledge of the world out there but is also asking himself, "What am I doing here?"

The way science sees this scene is as encounter between the two aims at knowledge of things—until the last object of Man's science and reason is taken apart and understood. But that ultimately means that Man himself becomes the object of his own scrutiny; now he is playing both sides of the board. And, it follows logically, when he has totally exhausted himself in explaining himself, not only he but the world and the game will disappear—perhaps in a technological equivalent of the apocalypse, a twilight of human subjectivity.[30]

Heidegger looks at this game differently: Not only knowledge of things is the aim but knowledge of the game itself. He deals with this problem of the game, human beings, and the world in three thinking moves.

THE FIRST MOVE

In a single thinking move, Heidegger redefines what is at play here. He removes the inevitability of the threat that science poses to the existence of Man.

Contrary to what science tells us, he points out, the human being does not initially experience itself as a subject nor can it ultimately exhaust itself in explaining itself and reshaping itself as an object.[31] The human being does not even experience itself as an entity limited to its body. Instead the human being experiences itself as a field that already includes relevant objects and other human beings. The chess game, if it is played as an end game for final knowledge of the human investigator and the world, is not only unnecessary but absurd. There will always be moves not encompassed by the rules of such a game.

As one piece of evidence of the way we experience ourselves, take the behavior of a young child, say Jean, who is asked, Where is Jean? At an early age, Jean, much to the disappointment of the parents, is as likely to point to Father or Mother as to the body that physically is Jean. The child identifies with the field encompassed by relevant others; Heidegger refers to this field as *Dasein*—literally "being here." Only later does the child learn to define where and how the child is as limited to the boundaries and location of the body.[32]

In adult experience, too, the whole experiential interplay between the being that is here and things is already involved before we can speak of anything like a self. But, without a self-subject, science cannot operate. Science therefore misses the fact that, before a scientific investigator approaches the objects of his or her study, experience has *already* operated to give the investigator an idea of what is to be studied:[33] The experiential interplay is already involved in anything like a separate thing.[34]

This is nowhere near Heidegger's entire argument for dissolving our modern view that the world consists of separate subjects and their objects and that there is a gap between them that can be bridged only through science. But avoiding the term "individual" and using the term "the being that is here" for Man may begin to convey a flavor of what he is trying to say.

With the inclusion not only of relevant others but relevant things in the field of the human being's being here, Heidegger does away with a nasty habit of philosophy widespread since Descartes: the radical separation of the human subject from the objects it observes and uses. Just as we are already involved with other human beings, we are also already involved with things even before we begin to define and analyze them.

Focusing on human experience has immediate implications for science's claim that the most truthful approach to things is to be detached and value-free. Obviously when we observe scientifically, we miss or set aside the original involved and value-laden relation with things. This in turn explains why it is so difficult to reintegrate scientific findings for use back into normal human experience.[35]

The implications for politics and a science of politics are clear; so are the implications for the running of organizations and a knowledge of organizations. A politics or organization that treats citizens as just a bunch of objects to be analyzed and manipulated like other objects misses something fundamental about Man: how he himself experiences himself. And this experience, to repeat, is that of a being involved with others and things rather than separate from them.

The most important implication for organizations is in the understanding of work: Administrators must recognize that the worker is already connected to his or her work[36] *before* scientific connections between "individual" and "object" are ever established. The problem for workers is that they must again return to this early state of naturally experienced connection in order to adequately deal with objects *after* the abstract calculations of scientific connections are handed down in orders and blueprints. Organizations whose administrators are unaware that the worker is already connected to his or her work before the manager begins even to have an inkling of "adding" calculations or motivations miss the entire point of the natural connection of workers and work.[37]

To put this point as clearly as possible: In a fundamental sense, Heidegger's phenomenology "challenges" the *entire* body of scientific findings regarding the organization of human beings for work without, however, declaring any of this body of research invalid in that approach's own terms. (After all, such science "works.") Those who insist on drawing the consequences from such research must simply confess that "it works" only if accompanied by a healthy dose of power, if not fear and terror. The scientific attempt at mastery over the organization of work is always an attempt at the domination of Man just as the science of work dominates nature. A scientist who does not admit to this aspect of his or her work is in a profound sense not amoral (because "neutral") but sustains the morality of the domination of Man by Man.[38]

Similarly, politics so conducted becomes a secondary reality, abstract and distant from the experience of citizens though such politics be ever so technically powerful.* A political science that advises politicians that they can so treat citizens as objects may get power over that part of Man that yields itself to power: ultimately, as the founders† anticipated, biological life itself. Such a politics misses the fundamental truth about Man that Man seeks in his political experience: a sense of where he and his political community stand in the encounter between what is and what can yet be.[39] A technically successful politics, precisely in inverse proportion to its might, is always and will always be judged at best irrelevant, at worst a danger, to the fundamental questions raised by the human experience.‡

An organizational science that advises managers to treat workers as objects will always be an *unbridgeable* step behind the knowledge that workers already have as soon as they lay their hands on the work.§ A political science that advises politicians to treat citizens as objects is able to force the moves of a scientifically controlled electorate but can only accidentally produce policies that have ultimate human legitimacy and reality.

THE SECOND MOVE

Brilliant though Heidegger's initial checkmating move is against science, we would be left with another problem had Heidegger stopped with the human being and its own self-experience: This is the tendency of modern Man to see himself as the center of the world. The danger here is a humanism that finds itself without any grounds to stand on.[40] For, with the "death of God"[41] and the powers of science, Man finds he no longer has a human nature in which he can feel at home and from which he can guide his life.

The fact now is that even if, through science, he finds the much-talked-about essential building blocks of his physical or chemical being, he can rearrange these to make himself into anything he imagines. He now can not only imagine himself to be anything at all, through genetic and behavioral engineering, but he can make himself into anything at all.

*See Karl Everett's discussion of authenticity in the section on the redefinition of work, Chapter 6.
†Initially Thomas Hobbes but, through his concern with property, also John Locke.
‡See the section on Lasswell v. Heidegger in Chapter 6.
§See Chapter 5.

This raises a classic problem for modern Man: the meaninglessness of choice. If anything is possible, nothing may be worthwhile. The Man who faces the possibility that he can be anything also faces the sense that he is nothing. Without an essential and inviolable human nature, Man not only feels homeless in the world, but he loses a sense of who or what he is.

Heidegger's solution interestingly is not to go back and dig up an essential and inviolable human nature. Such a project would, in any case, be bound to fail in the face of the denaturing effect of science. Instead, his advice is to have us face up to our fate. We cannot escape this advice. Our experience, when science and pure reason are set on one side, tells us this: It is the fate of Man to be thrown naked into the world and to be able to make himself. But this is so not in the narrow sense of science and human technology but in the full sense of being the being that makes itself as it lives its life. Here Heidegger speaks of Man's "thrownness." We have the ability to become our own "project." We hurl ourselves toward our own uncertain future in life.

Other philosophers have drawn from this the lesson of existentialism. Jean-Paul Sartre, for example, says Man is free to be what he wishes himself to be.[42] This raises the question of limits. Sartre himself finds limits in freedom. The very fact that I am totally free to be or do anything I like leaves me, and no one else, responsible for what I am or do. For Heidegger, this places Man too much at the center of the world—just as science does. Heidegger, while he admits Man makes himself, does not want to abandon the search for Man's foundation just at the point when he has become a homeless Man who is his own god.[43]

THE THIRD MOVE

Here Heidegger makes another profound move on his philosophical chessboard.

He introduces a third player.

Up to now, philosophy has focused either on the nature of Man or on the nature of things. Heidegger is modern enough not only to admit that Man makes himself but to push this insight to a radical extreme, asserting: Man becomes Man only as and when he makes himself by engaging in practical activity in the world. "Essentially the person exists only in the performance of intentional acts, and is therefore essentially *not* an object."[44] In later Heideggerian language: The human being becomes itself only in the encounter with the world in which human being's Being emerges. In his actions, Man reveals not only himself and the world but the underlying way of Being that makes him at all possible.

Being is the third player at the chessboard in which Man encounters the world; Being emerges only as the game is played, but it also *is* the game itself.[45] It can never be forced to emerge, nor does it "determine" the human being: It simply pervades the human being and all that is around it. It is that which reigns without power.

Heidegger has already established that Man is not like other things. Now he saves Man from the arrogance of power.

The third player that Heidegger introduces, and who joins the game of life along with the human being and things that exist, is named Being. We cannot point to it through any of our five senses but it pervades all we do in our doing of it, all we are in our being of it. It thus includes what we do as human beings in general and what we do in our more narrow incarnation as scientists or technical specialists, even as modern administrators, managers, and functionaries. Being therefore gives us a ground for the wider concept of Man that Heidegger seeks and a context for the more narrow concept of Man that modernity has developed.

We may not have a human nature to ground us but we exist in the world in a certain way: That way is the way of our Being.

At first this name seems to emerge from a mere wordplay, deriving from the word "is." One of the ways we are thrown into the world is to be unable to say anything about the relations between ourselves and the world without mentioning or averring to the word "is." I am here. This man is from the South. This book is yours. The enemy is in retreat. Red is playing defense. God is. In China there is a flood. The beaker is silver. The Earth is. The farmer is in the meadow. In the fields is the potato bug. The lecture is in Classroom 5. The dog is in the garden. This man is the devil. Above all treetops is silence.

In all these sentences there is a subject and there is an object. But both are linked by the same word, "is," which on closer examination seems to have an infinite variety of meanings. There is an "is-ing" involved in each relation between subject and object. In correct English, we say, instead of "is-ing"—being. There is here involved something that simply is, without being a thing that can be touched, heard, seen, tasted, or smelled. The third party that has come to play in everything we do and everything that relates a subject to an object is—let's recognize it by capitalizing it—something we can call Being. (That the Being of the human being is the result of more than a wordplay Heidegger argues throughout all of his dozens of books but perhaps nowhere as directly as in an essay from which the above examples are taken, "Being as an Emptiness and a Richness.")[46]

Being as the Home of Human Being

As soon as Being is recognized as a force that rules without power in the way we as human beings are in the world, it begins to provide a ground for us and a third pole to which to orient ourselves. Man's place now is that of the human being that is placed between Being and the world. Being promises to again provide a home for Man.

This is reflected in the way that the human being engages with its Being. "[The] human being," Heidegger tells us, "is an entity which does not just occur among other entities. Rather it is ontically* distinguished by the fact that, in its very Being, that Being is an *issue* for it."[47]

We worry about ourselves, we are anxious for ourselves. Care, in the sense of anxiety,[48] is the fundamental mode of our being in the world.[49] "The Being of the human being unveils itself as care."[50]

The question "Who am I?" can never be finally answered. I am always who and what I have just made myself in my engagement with the world; but I am also the being that *can* make itself. But what does it mean *to be able* to make myself? What does it mean *to be the way* I am? Putting the modern problematic into these questions locates our search for meaning not in ourselves nor in things but in a third place: the *way* we are.[51]

The question is no longer in general, What is the nature of things (Man included)? It is, What is the *way* I am able to be? What is the Being of what is, but especially of Man?

Being, itself, is *not* what I have just made out of myself. Nor is it how I have related myself to things and other human beings in the world. It is always that out of which my making and my relating becomes at all possible.[52] What is most important to us is the potential to be.[53] It is this potential that enables us to make ourselves at any given moment into what we are. Science would have us believe we play the chess game of life according to a script, which it can discover: the script of human nature; we know through experience that, inasmuch as we are players, we improvise.[54] Who or what is Man? In the interplay between Man and things lies our Being.

A Final Word on a New Politics

To repeat: A theory of organizations in our day requires philosophy. Two philosophies to be exact. The first is a critical philosophy; it criticizes modernity's configuration as science–technology–power that shapes and constrains modern life and the organization of life. The second is a new founding philosophy that takes us beyond modernity and its commitment to power; undergirding a theory or doctrine of administration this is a philosophy of care.

The way in which the philosophy of care is brought to life is through a politics that addresses itself to the ultimate question of human life: In any given historical society, what is the relation between what has already

*Ontically = the way it presents itself.

been achieved and the ever-replenished potential of the achiever—between world, Being, and Man?

Politics can be a way through which we inquire what communal life is all about: what it is and what it can yet be. If a political lesson is to be drawn from the play of Being,* it is that what must be protected is not merely life itself but the freedom-to-be.[55] Everything that already is, every actuality in which we find ourselves, always falls short of the potential of what we are free to yet do with it and ourselves. A political community's primary and never-ending task therefore is to judge actuality against potentiality. This means comparing the conditions for conducting a meaningful life that society has already established against the impact of that established way of life on its members' continuing ability to create and recreate themselves.[56] Unless we do this, Man will continue to be lost to himself.

If there is to be a politics in the narrow Lasswellian, Hobbesian, or Lockean sense of working together to protect something, what must be protected first of all is not property or even life itself but Man's Being, his freedom and potential to be, even unto death.† The political task is something larger: the constant reexamination and judgment over whether the actuality created by an entire historical society—and especially its institutions—forecloses or opens up its members' potential to be. A society, as much as an individual, must take care of its own Being. Out of this concern evolves the politics of care.

In summary, Heidegger tries to point to that which rules without power. What is that? It is that which makes all our being possible to begin with: our freedom-to-be, our potential for being; it is what he calls Being.

In the critique of modernity also, including the critique of the way moderns organize themselves, that which rules without power does not issue a call to action; it issues a call to thinking. If we heed this call we stand beyond petty concerns of the personal dangers of mere understanding and the short-term inadequacy of action. We have much to think about.

More profoundly than the tendency ascribed to bureaucrats in the first few pages of this book, we have become beings who, in dealing with our own real lives, have become headless and soulless. As sensualists without heart we believe too narrowly in science's immersion in those isolated facts, extracted from human life, whose parameters science's own hypotheses predefine. Of such beings it has been said: "Merely fact-minded sciences make merely fact-minded people."[57] As specialists with-

---

*Compare the section on Heidegger's "Recovery of Politics" in Chapter 6.
†Heidegger speaks of Man's freedom unto death; even and especially his death belongs to him, for no one can relieve him of this fate; if we are to take care of the dying we must leave them the freedom to face their own death (*Being and Time,* paragraph 53, p. 311 [German seventh edition, p. 266].)

out spirit we have too great a faith in technique, taking refuge from its real-time effects in the maze of its abstract and ever more inward and timeless reason. The angels have again begun to dance on the head of a pin.[58]

From our pure reason's love affair with decision making over paths ever more abstracted from real life, we are called back to consider the fate of the human being that is yet to be decided: "The highest decision that can fall and that always becomes the ground of all history is the one between the preponderant might of what is and the dominion of Being."[59]

On the relatively very small stage that is bureaucracy, this struggle is echoed as the decision between rules and freedom; but the larger battleground is worldwide, and in the fog of that ongoing battle the combatants are barely discerned. We are in the position of the college professors about whom one campus groundskeeper says to the other: "Now those professors, they say we don't know anything; but some of them, they don't even suspect anything." All of us need to ponder the meaning of might and dominion and try to make out the shape of the struggle between the way things are and the way we can always yet be.

In the end that which reigns without power is able to win out—but only if we bring it into our lives.

Are we ready to even suspect the problematic of our times—much less foresee the answers? Where to begin?[60]

NOTES

1. Conversation with Sally and Don Merchant about this chapter, February 1993, Spruce Head Island, Maine.

2. If the utility of this procedure needs to be justified, I refer the reader to an admonishment on the part of Thomas Hobbes. Himself referring to an old Latin saying, *nosce teipsum*, read thyself, Hobbes reminds us that "whosoever looketh into himself, and considereth what he doth, when he does *think, opine, reason, hope, fear,* &c. and upon what grounds; he shall thereby read and know, what are the thoughts and passions of all other men upon the like occasions." Thomas Hobbes, *Leviathan—or the Matter, Forme and Power of a Commonwealth Ecclesiasticall and Civil,* ed. Michael Oakeshott (Oxford: Basil Blackwell, undated [original 1651]), p. 6. Hobbes's italics.

3. Such attacks are, of course, in themselves quite justified: It is the scholar's obligation to show up the folly of a merely technical sophisticated politics, to point to the righteous as having clay feet, to disturb the undisturbed, and to expose the vicious to their own venomous bite.

4. Jean-Paul Sartre issues a harsher condemnation of defenders of the status quo in his own country: "A certain number of technicians of practical knowledge do eventually appoint themselves watchdogs of the culture. . . ."—Sartre, "Justice and the State" in Jean-Paul Sartre, *Life/Situations: Essays Written and Spoken* (New York: Random House—Pantheon Books, 1977), pp. 172–97; citation from p. 184.

5. All conclusions from my colleague Larry Hill's examination of Louis Harris and Survey Research Center polls on American public opinion of bureaucracy and bureaucrats. Larry Hill, "Taking Bureaucracy Seriously," in Hill, ed., *The State of Public Bureaucracy* (Armonk, N.Y.: M. E. Sharpe, Inc., 1992), pp. 15–57; reference to p. 23.

6. Charles T. Goodsell, "The Case Against Deduced Pathology," *The Bureaucrat*, vol. 17, no. 2 (Summer 1988), pp. 24–25; citation from p. 25. Goodsell's essay is a side-by-side commentary on Ralph P. Hummel, "The Case for Public Servants," *The Bureaucrat*, vol. 17, no. 2 (Summer 1988), pp. 24–28.

7. These ruffians would include Max Weber, Sigmund Freud, Ludwig Wittgenstein, Edmund Husserl, and Martin Heidegger, among others.

8. Goodsell, op. cit., p. 25.

9. Loc. cit.: "My view is that we must look at concrete bureaucratic institutions on an empirical, systematic basis before determining whether deduced theories about them are correct, just as we would in any honest social research. Also we should find out when they do *not* occur, and, indeed, when bureaucracies work quite well." We are left to wonder whether a mode of inquiry can investigate itself using its own tools.

10. There *are* outstanding exceptions, among whom is Dwight Waldo. Always the sage of public administration even in his early years, Waldo defined administration this way: "Administration is a type of cooperative human effort that has a high degree of rationality." He then goes on to develop the idea of rationality. But toward the end of his defining effort, he says this under the heading "The Importance of Nonrational Action": "The point is this: perhaps the model, by stressing rational action, creates a false impression of the amount of rationality (as defined) existing or possible in human affairs." And, having developed this thought, there follows his concluding sentence: "Some [students of administration] . . . are heard to say that complete rationality in human affairs is not the proper goal; that a world in which *all* is orderly and predictable, with no room for spontaneity, surprise, and emotional play, is an undesirable world." Dwight Waldo, *The Study of Public Administration* (New York: Random House, 1961 [originally 1955], pp. 6, 12, 13.

11. For some tactics and strategies still effective today: C. Wright Mills, *The Sociological Imagination* (New York: Oxford University Press, 1959), especially Chapter 5, "The Bureaucratic Ethos," pp. 107–13.

12. Thus do all reality systems defend themselves against challenge. See Peter Berger and Thomas Luckmann, *The Social Construction of Reality* (Garden City, N.Y.: Doubleday—Anchor Books, 1968).

13. The regime of Presidents Ronald Reagan and to a lesser extent George Bush, between 1981 and 1993. For an earlier evaluation: Ralph P. Hummel, *The Bureaucratic Experience*, 3rd ed. (New York: St. Martin's Press, 1987), Chapter 6. It may be argued that the presidency of Jimmy Carter already presaged an antibureaucratic politics and that the presidency of Bill Clinton, despite its activist commitment to positive government, holds little brief for traditional bureaucratic doctrine and practices. On the relation between political ideology and administrative doctrine and practices, see my "Toward a New Administrative Doctrine: Government and Management for the 1990s," *The American Review of Public Administration*, vol. 19, no. 3 (September 1989), pp. 175–96.

14. Ironically, conservative ideologists' use of "jigsaw-puzzle management" corresponded precisely to traditional bureaucrats' use of division of labor to produce the power of hierarchy. While the use of a bureaucratic tool to fight the power of bureaucracy may have worked in the short run, that use also further entrenched the culture of bureaucracy. Practically also, there is no guarantee that free-floating units of a bureaucracy will necessarily look to the legitimate political leadership for guidance; a likely alternative is a turning to established bureaucratic leaders for informal—and, when politically unsanctioned, nonlegitimate—guidance. For jigsaw-puzzle management: Michael Sanera, "Implementing the Mandate," in Stuart M. Butler, Michael Sanera, and W. Bruce Weinrod, eds., *Mandate for Leadership II: Continuing the Conservative Revolution* (Washington, D.C.: Heritage Foundation, 1984), pp. 514–15. For an argument against rising use of political appointees: James P. Pfiffner, "Political Appointees and Career Executives: The Democracy-Bureaucracy Nexus," in Patricia W. Ingraham and Donald F. Kettl, eds., *Agenda for Excellence: Public Service in America* (Chatham, N.J.: Chatham House Publishers, 1992), pp. 48–65.

15. Tom Peters, "Firms' Quantitative Measurements Reap Qualitative Benefits," *Columbia* [Missouri] *Daily Tribune*, April 28, 1986, p. 8.

16. This claim is what separates those who study life—and work—as measurement from those who study life as experience. One of Edmund Husserl's translators, David Carr,

comments, for example: "Having forgotten the abstractive and idealizing role of scientific thought, the philosophical interpretation comes up with an ontological claim: *to be is to be measurable* in ideal terms as a geometrically determined configuration. Thus it happens, says Husserl, 'that we take for *true being* what is actually a *method.*'"—David Carr, "Husserl's Problematic Concept of the Life-World," in Frederick A. Elliston and Peter McCormick, eds., *Husserl—Expositions and Appraisals* (South Bend, Ind.: University of Notre Dame Press, 1977), pp. 202–12; citation from p. 205.

17. Martin Heidegger, *What Is a Thing?*, trs. W. B. Barton, Jr. and Vera Deutsch (South Bend, Ind.: Regnery/Gateway Inc., 1967), p. 213, in his argument that something is *what* it is before it takes on the dimensions of actuality: "To which group does *reality* belong? What is its most general sense? It is *quality—quale—*a so and so, a that and that, a *what.*"

18. Sartre, "Justice and the State," op. cit., p. 177.

19. Compare Mike Parker, *Inside the Circle: A Union Guide to QWL* (Boston: South End Press—A Labor Notes Book, 1985) and Mike Parker and Jane Slaughter, *Choosing Sides: Unions and the Team Concept* (Boston: South End Press—A Labor Notes Book, 1988)—sources significantly omitted in the essentially one-sided literature on quality management, either public or private. So much for "honest" research.

20. To use the values Harold D. Lasswell ascribes to the power struggles of modern politics.

21. The Reagan administration's political distrust of bureaucrats is reflected in its early attempt to impose political appointees on government agencies. See Edie N. Goldberg, "The Permanent Government in an Era of Retrenchment and Redirection," in Lester M. Salomon and Michael S. Lund, eds., *The Reagan Presidency and the Governing of America* (Washington, D.C.: Urban Institute, 1984), p. 369. On counterproductive results: Peter M. Benda and Charles H. Levine, "Reagan and the Bureaucracy: The Bequest, the Promise, and the Legacy," in Charles O. Jones, ed., *The Reagan Legacy: Promise and Performance* (Chatham, N.J.: Chatham House Publishers, 1988), pp. 102–42.

22. For an original conception of positive government, see T. H. Green, *The Political Theory of T. H. Green*, ed. John R. Rodman (New York: Appleton-Century-Crofts, 1964).

23. The uncovering of the control aspect of mathematics in its origins in the Greek *mathesis* is one of Martin Heidegger's achievements. For the critique of the organization of production-line work as a questioning and challenging of reality that sets the parameters of any answer or response ahead of time (*mathesis*), see Ralph P. Hummel, "Behind Quality Management: What Workers and a Few Philosophers Have Always Known and How It Adds Up to Quality in Production," *Organizational Dynamics*, vol. 16, no. 1 (Summer 1987), pp. 71–78.

24. David Carnevale and Ralph Hummel, "The Soul in the Machine: Quality, Work and the Future of Power," forthcoming. See the critique of quality management in Chapter 2.

25. This theme is more fully developed in my "Call for a Philosophy of Administration," *Administrative Theory & Praxis*, vol. 15, no. 1, pp. 52–54.

26. Martin Heidegger, "III: Der Wille zur Macht als Erkenntnis" (The Will to Power as Knowledge), in *Nietzsche*, vol. I (Pfullingen: Verlag Guenther Neske, 1961), p. 475.

27. Choice of this metaphor means we are still speaking in the terminology of modern reason and science. Peter Vaill suggests a better metaphor is the dance: Then the human being and things are partners in a dance and the dance itself is what constitutes and sustains the being of both.

28. Immanuel Kant, *Critique of Pure Reason*, tr. Norman Kemp Smith (New York: St. Martin's Press, 1965), B xiii: "Reason, holding in the one hand its principles, according to which alone concordant appearances can be admitted as equivalent to laws, and in the other hand the experiment which it has devised in conformity with these principles, must approach nature to be taught by it. It most not, however, do so in the character of a pupil who listens to everything that the teacher chooses to say, but of an appointed judge who compels the witnesses to answer questions which he has himself formulated."

29. Ibid., B 75: "Thoughts without content are empty, intuitions without concepts are blind."

30. The phrase is taken from Fred Dallmayr, *The Twilight of Subjectivity: Contributions to a Post-Individualist Theory of Politics* (Amherst: The University of Massachusetts Press, 1981).

Such an apocalypse would only secondarily be physical; it would be triggered by something resembling two numerical values, technically representing all mankind and the world, canceling each other out in a computer.

31. The argument here is based on Martin Heidegger, *Being and Time*, trs. John Macquarrie and Edward Robinson (New York: Harper & Row—HarperSanFrancisco, 1962), especially the introduction. For a scathing critique of similar approaches from the viewpoint of analytic philosophy: Ernest Nagel, *Sovereign Reason—And Other Studies in the Philosophy of Science* (Glencoe, Ill.: The Free Press, 1954), especially Chapter 1: "Malicious Philosophies of Science," pp. 19–20 ff. In Heidegger's case, however, Nagel may miss the point. Heidegger does not attack the achievements of science; he merely tries to show it its proper place in the general context of human experience. This, of course, does threaten the scientist by removing him or her from a select place at the center of the knowable world.

32. This paragraph is based on William Barrett, *Irrational Man—A Study in Existential Philosophy* (Garden City, N.Y.: Doubleday—Anchor Books, 1962), pp. 218–19. The style of my presentation in this section owes much, I think, to the style of William Barrett.

33. It is a constant embarrassment to writers of books on scientific methodology to have to account for where the scientist gets his or her ideas on what to study. This process cannot itself be scientifically explained since it is synthetic, putting Man and things together, while science is analytic, taking things apart. The textbook "solution" is usually to accord a paragraph or two to scientific "insight" or "experience." For a typical example: Elizabeth O'Sullivan and Gary R. Rassel, *Research Methods for Public Administrators* (New York: Longman, 1989), p. 6.

34. Eugene Gendlin, "Analysis" to Martin Heidegger, *What Is a Thing?*, pp. 247–96; reference to p. 275.

35. Compare the argument of Heidegger's teacher, Edmund Husserl, in Husserl, *The Crisis of the European Sciences and Transcendental Phenomenology: An Introduction to Phenomenological Philosophy*, tr. David Carr (Evanston, Ill.: Northwestern University Press, 1970), especially Parts I and II.

36. Kant calls this connection "synthesis." In his terms external givens affix themselves on our senses (intuition) and are woven into an object by our concepts (reason). Eugene Gendlin describes the experience of fit between reason and the sensed, mind and sensing body, as "felt sense." Most of all, workers with their minds and hands both engaged in the belaboring of an object can guide their judgments as to whether to operate in this way or that by this felt sense. Felt sense is difficult to put into words in a world dominated by analytic rather than synthesizing terminology; that is why the best that can usually be said by a worker engaged in felt sense is: "It felt right." Such a statement, it is entirely true, admits of no further analysis; but this is because it is a statement of synthesis, not analysis. For felt sense: Eugene Gendlin, *Focusing* (New York: Bantam Books, Inc., 1981), pp. 17, 19, 165–66 ff. and *Experiencing and the Creation of Meaning* (New York: Macmillan—The Free Press, 1962).

37. No, the answer is not for managers to rush out and start studying, for the purpose of control, the "experience of workers." Remember: No matter how much of it you study from the outside in, there is always more where that came from: from the inside out.

38. I am reminded of an interview with a young woman in a *Time* magazine issue commemorating the anniversary of the hydrogen bomb. The young woman was making triggers for the bombs. Did she have any concerns over what she was doing? she was asked. She replied in words to this effect: As a young girl I always wanted to be a scientist; now I am one. Here one is forced to agree with Sartre that the morality promulgated by the political superstructure of society "is a joke, since it is necessarily built upon exploitation." Jean-Paul Sarte, "The Maoists in France," in Sartre, *Life/Situations: Essays Written and Spoken*, cited, pp. 162–71; reference to p. 169.

39. The immediate implications of modern representative politics have been developed by Jean-Paul Sartre, "Elections: A Trap for Fools," in Sartre, *Life/Situations: Essays Written and Spoken*, cited, pp. 189–210. This is a good place to note the inadequacy of Sartre's critique of politics, based in this essay on a development of Heidegger's discussion of the anonymous "One" into Sartre's concept of being just a number among many: "serialization." Because Sartre does not carry over Heidegger's concern with Being as the basis of human being, he stops short with the immediate political consequences of modernity's turning Man into an

inauthentic being. The issue of what is ultimately at stake in politics, namely the Being of the human being, is thus not developed by Sartre.

40. See Martin Heidegger, *Ueber den Humanismus* (On Humanism) (Frankfurt am Main: Vittorio Klostermann, 1968).

41. Declared by Friedrich Nietzsche in *The Gay Science*, tr. Walter Kaufmann (New York: Random House, 1974), Section 125.

42. Sartre, however, does not accept the infinitude, and ultimate irresponsibility, of the human being who finds it can make itself over through science. For Sartre this is true: In accepting his freedom, Man also accepts that he is responsible for what he does with it.

43. This would leave us with the dilemma of Nietzsche: Since, for modern Man, God is dead, all that is worthwhile is equally valuable. Man creates his own values, becomes his own god, finds himself in a world in which all values he creates have no foundation and are thus equally worthless. In the words of one commentator: "Nietzsche's famous slogan that 'God is dead' means, first and foremost, that there are no objective values."—L. Nathan Oaklander, *Existential Philosophy—An Introduction* (Englewood Cliffs, N.J.: Prentice-Hall, 1992), p. 93.

44. Heidegger, *Being and Time*, paragraph 10, p. 73.

45. Dallmayr, op. cit., p. 66 says this in more mundane terms: "Man and equipment are both ingredients of a larger life-context which molds user and utensils alike."

46. Martin Heidegger, "Das Sein als die Leere und der Reichtum," in *Nietzsche*, vol. 2 (Pfullingen: Verlag Guenther Neske, 1961), pp. 246–56; examples from p. 247.

47. Heidegger, *Being and Time*, paragraph 4, p. 32 [p. 12 in the German original of the seventh edition]. I translate *Dasein*, the being that is here, as human being.

48. Heidegger, *Being and Time*, paragraphs 40 and 68b. Two existentialists, Jean-Paul Sartre and Albert Camus, acutely describe this feeling of anxiety in *Nausea* and *The Myth of Sisyphus*, respectively. Unlike Heidegger, however, the existentialists are not concerned with Being but with the self-making of the individual. This may perhaps be explained out of the experience of oppression that Sartre, for example, suffered during the Second World War. Understandably Sartre might be more concerned with exploring Being as freedom-to-be rather than in its philosophical aspect as that against which Man must always judge his enactments. Correspondingly, Heidegger's "failure" to be similarly concerned with the freedom of the individual would have to be explained by a friendly critic in terms of his philosophical immersion and immunity, if not naivete, toward the politics of his day.

49. This is not to say that care is "in" Man as part of his human nature, only that the only way he can understand himself is in terms of care. Care is a condition of his existence; Heidegger calls care an "existentiell."

50. Heidegger, *Being and Time*, paragraph 39, p. 227. Retranslation by the present author of "Dasein's Being reveals itself as care." The standard translators have chosen not to translate the German *Dasein* as the mode in which the human being finds itself here in the world. However, while playing with words is considered by Heidegger to be of distinct advantage to pry German readers loose from such Cartesian terms as "individual," the English language provides a perfectly understandable term, human being, for what Heidegger is talking about: namely, the being of ourselves in the world. See Macquarrie and Robinson's footnote on their nontranslation of *Dasein* (literally being here [not being *there*]) in fn. 1, p. 27.

51. Perhaps it is here that the author who agonizes in the section on "The Inadequacy of Understanding" finds refuge, a not altogether unhuman an individual fate.

52. This includes the relating of Man to things established in science and the making of things established through technology.

53. Potential to be: "The kind of Being which Dasein [human being] has is not something present-at-hand which possesses its competence for something by way of an extra; it is primarily Being-possible. Dasein [human being] is in every case what it can be, and in the way in which it is its possibility." Heidegger, *Being and Time*, paragraph 31, p. 183 [German 7th ed., p. 143].

54. I owe this term to R. G. Collingwood's treatment of living one's life according to rules, which he says "always involves a certain misfit between yourself and the situation." Collingwood, *An Autobiography* (Oxford: Oxford University Press, 1967), pp. 104, 105.

55. On freedom-to-be: Heidegger, *Being and Time*, paragraphs 40, 41, 53, 58; for example, paragraph 40, p. 232 [German 7th ed., p. 188].

56. Martin Heidegger, *Parmenides*, paragraph 6, pp. 137–38 and 141–42 ff. Heidegger's position in this later work is already anticipated in *Time and Being*, paragraphs 7 B and 44 in his treatment of the Greek word for truth. *Aletheia*, as the understanding that brings what exists into the open, also points to its origins and ground in what is concealed in Being. In *Parmenides* he declares the Greek *polis* to be the quintessential place in which the inhabitants of that historical community tried to come to terms with the tension between what was opened up for them (in the world that they lived in) and what was still hidden in Being.

57. Husserl, *The Crisis of the European Sciences*, p. 6.

58. Classical medieval question: How many angels can dance on the head of a pin?

59. Heidegger, "Der Wille zur Macht als Erkenntnis," in *Nietzsche*, cited, p. 476.

60. The author wishes to thank an anonymous reviewer who said this about an early version of this chapter: "After first reading Chapter 7, I was tempted to say that the chapter was not relevant for the students I normally teach at the MPA [Master of Public Administration] level. I first reasoned that it was much too theoretical to be of use to them. . . ." The reviewer then went on to say: "Upon reading the chapter a second time, however, I realized how wrong my first impressions had been and how nearly I had disaffirmed Hummel's whole thesis. This chapter is exactly what MPA students need! . . . We need to get them to think critically and that is exactly what Chapter 7 is about." If we are to ask where to begin, this reviewer has shown us the place where beginnings are made.

Index

About the Author

Ralph P. Hummel (Ph.D., New York University) is known for his applications of phenomenology to the study of bureaucracy, American government, and politics in general. Aside from this fourth edition of his critique of bureaucracy, his books include the first phenomenological texts in the fields of politics and American government: *Politics for Human Beings* (Duxbury Press and Brooks/Cole, 1975 and 1980) and *The Real American Politics* (Prentice-Hall, 1986), both with Robert A. Isaak. Dr. Hummel is associate professor of political science and public administration at The University of Oklahoma, as well as executive director of the Institute for Applied Phenomenology, Spruce Head Island, Maine.